(MCTS): Microsoft BizTalk Server 2010 (70-595) Certification Guide

A compact certification guide to help you prepare for and pass exam 70-595: TS: Developing Business Process and Integration Solutions by using Microsoft BizTalk Server 2010

Johan Hedberg

Kent Weare

Morten la Cour

PACKT PUBLISHING enterprise
professional expertise distilled

BIRMINGHAM - MUMBAI

(MCTS): Microsoft BizTalk Server 2010 (70-595) Certification Guide Book

First published: June 2012

Production Reference: 1250512

Published by Packt Publishing Ltd.
Livery Place
35 Livery Street
Birmingham B3 2PB, UK.

ISBN 978-1-84968-492-7

www.packtpub.com

Cover Image by Karl Moore (karl@karlmoore.co.uk)

Credits

Authors
Johan Hedberg

Kent Weare

Morten la Cour

Reviewers
Jan Eliasen

Mikael Håkansson

Steef-Jan Wiggers

Todd Uhl

Sandeep Kesiraju

Basil Cheng

Acquisition Editor
Kerry George

Lead Technical Editor
Shreerang Deshpande

Technical Editors
Ameya Sawant

Mehreen Shaikh

Project Coordinator
Alka Nayak

Proofreaders
Mario Cecere

Joanna McMahon

Copy Editor
Brandt D'Mello

Indexer
Monica Ajmera Mehta

Graphics
Manu Joseph

Production Coordinator
Shantanu Zagade

Cover Work
Shantanu Zagade

About the Authors

Johan Hedberg is based in Stockholm where he works as a consultant, solutions architect, and certified trainer. His employer, Enfo Zystems, is one of the largest consultancy firms in Sweden and the Nordic region that's solely dedicated to integration. Johan has over 10 years of experience in architecting and developing enterprise-grade solutions based on Microsoft technologies. He works closely with Microsoft through the Business Platform Technology Advisory and Virtual Technology Solution Professional programs, and with the community as a Microsoft Most Valuable Professional and one of the founders of the BizTalk User Group Sweden. He blogs at `http://blogical.se/blogs/johan`. You can follow Johan on Twitter: @JoHed

I would like to say thanks to the people at Packt Publishing for the opportunity, and to my fellow authors, Kent and Morten, for sharing the work.

An extra mention of Mikael Håkansson; partner in crime in much I do professionally.

A special thanks to my family, Maria and the boys, for their patience as work takes up weeknights and weekends, and for keeping me balanced. To Max, for the struggle still ahead.

Kent Weare was born in Regina, Saskatchewan, Canada. He developed a love for ice hockey, football, and technology. He attended the University of Regina, where he obtained a degree in Computer Science. After completing his undergraduate degree, he spent time in India, completing a post-graduate diploma in Object Oriented Technology. He currently lives in Calgary, Alberta, Canada but remains a die-hard Saskatchewan Roughrider football fan.

Kent began his career at a small Internet startup before taking on a junior role with the Saskatchewan Government. Since then, he has worked on projects for the Canadian Federal Government, a multi-national bank in the United States, healthcare projects in Eastern and Western Canada, and has spent the last five years employed by a large electricity distribution company in Calgary. Kent's current responsibilities involve managing a Middleware team and architecting integrated solutions for the energy sector.

During Kent's time at the Federal Government, he had an opportunity to participate in his first BizTalk project. Seven years later, he is still "hooked" on BizTalk, having worked with every BizTalk version released since then. In 2008, Kent was awarded his first Microsoft MVP award for BizTalk Server. He continues to be active in the BizTalk community and recently received his fourth consecutive MVP award. Kent maintains active blogs at `http://kentweare.blogspot.com` and `http://www.MiddlewareInTheCloud.com`. He may also be seen presenting BizTalk-related material at local and international user groups.

Previous Publications by Packt Publishing:
Book name: *Microsoft BizTalk 2010: Line of Business Systems Integration*
ISBN: *1849681902*
Role: *Lead Author*

Being involved in two BizTalk book projects in less than 18 months takes a tremendous amount of commitment, determination, and perseverance. I would not have been able to participate, let alone fulfill my commitment, on these projects without the support of others.

I would like to thank my colleagues for their interest and support in this and the other projects that I get involved in. I would also like to thank the Directors that I report to; Rob Tisdale and Brian Dempsey for giving me the opportunity to get involved in such interesting projects, and then providing me the support to be successful.

The group of current and former BizTalk MVPs is second to none. I have learned so much through this group and am continually blown away every time we have a chance to sit down at events such as the MVP summit or the Swedish BizTalk User group. It is people like you who make these types of side projects fun and rewarding.

Finally, I would like to thank my family for their support with this initiative, especially my wife, Melissa, daughter, Brooke, and newborn daughter, Paige. Without your loving support, there is no way I would have been able to contribute to this initiative.

Morten la Cour has worked with the MS BizTalk Server platform for seven years. Besides designing and developing Integration solution for customers, he has also worked on deployment and maintenance of BizTalk applications and BizTalk Server environments.

He has taught several BizTalk server courses in development, deployment, and management.

Besides working with MS BizTalk Server, Morten has 13 years of experience on the Microsoft development platform, including the .NET Framework and SQL Server. Other experience includes XML, XSLT, XPATH, and Oracle databases.

I would like to thank my daughter and girlfriend for their patience during all the writing weekends leading up to this book.

About the Reviewers

Jan Eliasen is a Master of Science in Computer Science and has nine years of experience using BizTalk Server, starting from BizTalk Server 2002. Jan is a five-time and current Microsoft MVP in BizTalk Server and he has passed all five existing exams in BizTalk.

Jan is a co-author of "*Microsoft BizTalk Server 2010 Unleashed*", *Sams Technical Publishing* book.

Mikael Håkansson is employed by Enfo Zystems, and is currently engaged in the Integration Delivery Center to provide customers with a scalable and elastic offering of Microsoft BizTalk Servers and related technologies.

He has a long-standing commitment to the community through contribution of free software and components, such as BizTalk SFTP Adapter and BizTalk Benchmark Wizard.

Mikael works closely with Microsoft through BizTalk User Group Sweden, successfully organizing and presenting at events. His commitment to the community has earned him the Microsoft Most Valuable Professional (MVP) Award, and he is also part of the Microsoft Technical Advisor program working closely with the BizTalk and CSD product teams for future releases of BizTalk and related products.

Mikael maintains his blog at http://blogical.se/blogs/mikael. You can also follow Mikael on Twitter: @wmmihaa

Steef-Jan Wiggers is an IT architect with over 12 years of experience as a consultant, Technical Lead Developer, and Application Architect, specializing in custom applications, enterprise application integration (BizTalk), web services, and Windows Azure. He has experience in architecting, designing, developing, and supporting sophisticated and innovative software using many different Microsoft technologies and products. Steef-Jan is very active in the BizTalk community as blogger, Wiki author or editor on MSDN forums, writer, and public speaker. He has been awarded the Microsoft Most Valuable Professional (MVP) award (2010) for his contributions to the world-wide BizTalk Server community, and has been re-awarded in July 2011.

Steef-Jan lives in the Netherlands, is married to Lian, and has three lovely children, Stan, Ellis, and Cato. Last but not least, they are accompanied by their English Cocker Spaniel, Barry. Steef-Jan is a certified MCDBA, MCSD, MCSD.NET, MCSA, MCAD, MCTS: BizTalk Server BizTalk Server 2006, BizTalk Server 2006 R2 and BizTalk Server 2010.

He is the author of the forthcoming *"BizTalk Server 2010 Cookbook"*, *Packt Publishing* and technical reviewer of *"BizTalk Server 2010 Patterns"*, *Packt Publishing* book.

I like to thank Ordina for providing me the time to review this book and Bert van den Belt for his continuing support in my efforts. I like to thanks the authors, Kent, Johan, and Morten, for the opportunity to review this great book. In my view, this book provides excellent material to prepare for the 70-595 exam and be able to pass it.

Todd Uhl is an IT consultant with over 15 years of experience in Microsoft developer technologies. He has been working with all facets of BizTalk Server since its original launch. He currently works for a large software company supporting customers in all their endeavors with BizTalk.

I would like to thank my beautiful wife Mechelle for always putting up with me, and my two boys Owen and Sebastian for bringing a smile to my face every day.

Sandeep Kesiraju is a Senior Premier Field Engineer from Microsoft. He has worked with BizTalk Server since its early stages and has also been involved in the development of ESB Guidance Package (v1) for BizTalk Server, with the Microsoft Patterns and Practices Team. In his current role as a PFE, Sandeep is involved in supporting and advising customers for BizTalk server. He has been also involved with developing, architecting, designing, and supporting BizTalk server solutions.

Basil Cheng is currently in a consulting role and has helped many companies with using Microsoft Technologies, including BizTalk Server, IIS, and .NET.

www.PacktPub.com

Support files, eBooks, discount offers and more

You might want to visit www.PacktPub.com for support files and downloads related to your book.

Did you know that Packt offers eBook versions of every book published, with PDF and ePub files available? You can upgrade to the eBook version at www.PacktPub.com and as a print book customer, you are entitled to a discount on the eBook copy. Get in touch with us at service@packtpub.com for more details.

At www.PacktPub.com, you can also read a collection of free technical articles, sign up for a range of free newsletters and receive exclusive discounts and offers on Packt books and eBooks.

http://PacktLib.PacktPub.com

Do you need instant solutions to your IT questions? PacktLib is Packt's online digital book library. Here, you can access, read and search across Packt's entire library of books.

Why Subscribe?
- Fully searchable across every book published by Packt
- Copy and paste, print and bookmark content
- On demand and accessible via web browser

Free Access for Packt account holders

If you have an account with Packt at www.PacktPub.com, you can use this to access PacktLib today and view nine entirely free books. Simply use your login credentials for immediate access.

Instant Updates on New Packt Books

Get notified! Find out when new books are published by following @PacktEnterprise on Twitter, or the *Packt Enterprise* Facebook page.

Table of Contents

Preface   **1**

Chapter 1: Configuring a Messaging Architecture   **7**

Publish/subscribe   **7**
  Receiving the message   8
    Adapter   8
    Pipeline   9
    Maps   10
  MessageBox   10
  Subscriptions   10
    Message Context properties   11
  Orchestrations   11
  Sending the message   11
    Maps   11
    Pipeline   12
    Adapter   12
BizTalk platform settings and Applications   **12**
  BizTalk Administration Console   12
    The Group Hub   12
  Hosts and Host Instances   13
    Creating a Host   14
    Creating a Host Instance   17
  Managing Adapter Handlers   19
  Applications   20
    Referencing another Application   21
Setting up and managing Ports   **22**
  Receive Ports   22
    Port Authentication   23
    Receive Locations   24
    Receive Port Maps   28

Send Ports   30
  Transport Advanced Options   31
  Backup transport   33
  Send Port Maps   33
  Configuring Filters (Subscriptions)   34
  Port states   34
  Dynamic Send Ports   35
Send Port Groups   36
Failed message routing   37
Ordered delivery   37
  Receive Locations   38
  Send Ports   38
Configuring core Adapters   **40**
  HTTP   40
    Sending HTTP   40
    Receiving HTTP   41
  POP3   43
  SMTP   44
  FTP   46
    Receiving FTP   47
    Sending FTP   48
  File   49
    Receiving files   49
    Sending files   50
    Credentials   52
Configuring content-based routing   **52**
  Creating folders and Application   53
  Creating Receive Ports and Receive Locations   54
  Testing the Receive Locations   57
  Debugging the messages   58
  Setting up a Send Port   61
  Setting up Send Port for System II and a Send Port Group   62
Implementing messaging patterns   **64**
  Working with canonical messages   64
  De-batching   65
  Using the correct flow   66
  Adapter independence   66
Test your knowledge   **67**
Summary   **69**

Chapter 2: Developing BizTalk Artifacts—Creating Schemas and Pipelines   71

Creating Schemas   72
Type of Schemas   72
XML Schemas   72
Flat File Schemas   73
Property Schemas   73
Schema Identity   73
XML Identity   74
.NET Identity   74
Promoted property and distinguished fields   75
Promoting nodes as property fields   75
Promoting a node as distinguished field   78
Creating the structure of a Schema   79
Creating reoccurring parts of a Schema   81
Creating Envelope Schemas   83
Datatypes and formatting   85
Specifying custom formatting restrictions   85
Creating reusable types   88
Creating Schema hierarchies   90
Import   90
Include   90
Redefine   91
Creating Pipelines   91
Pipeline Stages   92
Receive Pipelines   92
Decode   93
Disassemble   93
Validate   94
Resolve Party   94
Send Pipelines   94
Pre-Assemble   94
Assemble   94
Encode   95
Default Pipelines   95
PassThruReceive   95
XMLReceive   95
PassThruTransmit   95
XMLTransmit   96
Custom Pipelines   96
Configuring Pipelines and Pipeline components   99
Working with XML messages   101
Working with envelopes   105

Working with secure data	107
Encryption and signing	108
Decryption and signature verification	112
Test your knowledge	**113**
Summary	**114**
Chapter 3: Developing BizTalk Artifacts—Creating Maps	**115**
Creating Maps	**115**
Why XSLT matters	117
Using Functoids	**118**
Conversion Functoids	119
Cumulative Functoids	119
Database Functoids	119
Table Query Functoids	120
Cross Referencing Data Functoids	120
Date/Time Functoids	124
Logical Functoids	124
Mathematical Functoids	125
Scientific Functoids	126
String Functoids	127
Using Advanced Functoids	**127**
Looping	128
Index	128
Iterator	129
Nil	129
Record Count	129
Looping	130
Table Looping	131
Conditional Mapping	134
Copy-based Mapping	136
Troubleshooting	136
Scripting	137
Using external assemblies	137
Using Inline Code	139
Using Inline XSLT	141
Maps and Orchestrations	142
Test your knowledge	**145**
Summary	**146**
Chapter 4: Developing BizTalk Artifacts—Creating Orchestrations	**147**
Developing Orchestrations	**147**
Basic shapes and configuration	148
Message and Data Handling	148
Containers	150

Flow control 150
Orchestration Nesting 151
Other 152
Orchestration activation 152
Activating Receive 153
Call and Start 153
Persistence 153
Dehydration and rehydration 154
Transactions 155
Transaction types 155
Scopes 156
Long Running 156
Atomic 157
Nesting 158
Transaction reach 158
Storing configuration information 159
Orchestration variables 159
Configuration placed in BTSNTSvc.exe.config 159
Configuration placed in web.config for isolated Hosts 160
Configuration placed in machine.config 160
Some configuration can be placed on the Adapter handlers 160
Through the message 160
Through the message context 161
Business Rules 161
SSO 161
Using a .NET helper component 161
Integrating with .NET assemblies 162
Configuring Orchestration bindings **164**
Ports versus Port Types 164
Logical ports versus physical ports 164
Port binding options 165
Specify Now 166
Specify Later 168
Direct 170
Dynamic 178
Configuring correlation **180**
Working with Correlation Types and Sets 180
Convoys 183
Sequential Convoys 184
Parallel Convoys 184
Test your knowledge **185**
Summary **186**

Chapter 5: Debugging and Exception Handling   187

Handling exceptions in Orchestrations   188
Scopes   188
Throwing exceptions   189·
Catching exceptions   190
Compensation   191
Sample exception handling scenario   193
Delivery notification   203

Debug Orchestrations   208
Handling messaging errors   213
Subscription errors   213
Transmission errors   215

Routing errors   217
Recoverable Interchange Processing   222

Validating and testing artifacts   227
Validating Schemas and Message Instances   227
Validate Schema   228
Validate Instance   228
Generate Instance   228
Validating, testing, and debugging Maps   229
Unit testing   230
Unit testing Schemas   230
Unit testing Maps   232

Test your knowledge   233
Summary   236

Chapter 6: Deploying, Tracking, and Administrating a BizTalk Server 2010 Solution   237

Installing and configuring a multiserver BizTalk environment   238
High Availability   238
Installation setup   239
Installation   240
Configuration   240
Active Directory Groups and Users   244

Deploying BizTalk applications   245
Sample deployment through Visual Studio   245
Preparing the solution   246
Binding Files   248
Sample deployment through MSI package   257
Binding File dependencies   261

BizTalk Application states   261
Runtime Application states   262

Tracking events in BizTalk Server   **264**
  Tracking Receive Ports   265
  Tracking Orchestrations   266
  Tracking Send Ports   269
Managing BizTalk applications using BizTalk
Administration Console   **270**
  Configuration Overview   271
  Work in Progress   271
  Suspended Items   272
  Group Suspended Service Instances   273
  Tracked Service Instances   274
  Tracked Message Events   274
BizTalk Settings Dashboard   **274**
  Viewing and modifying performance tuning settings   275
  Exporting and importing performance tuning settings   279
Test your knowledge   **283**
Summary   **286**

Chapter 7: Integrating Web Services and Windows
Communication Foundation (WCF) Services   **287**
Out of the box WCF Adapters   **288**
Configuring a WCF Adapter   **289**
  Using out of the box WCF-BasicHttp Send Adapter   289
  Using out of the box WCF-BasicHttp Receive Adapter   298
Custom behaviors   **303**
Exposing Schemas and Orchestrations as WCF Services   **306**
  Testing our WCF Service   314
Consuming WCF Services from BizTalk Server 2010   **315**
  Sample WCF Service   316
  Consuming our WCF Service from BizTalk   319
  Configuring generated WCF Service artifacts   324
  Testing our Custom WCF Service   330
Handling web exceptions   **331**
Test your knowledge   **340**
Summary   **342**

Chapter 8: Implementing Extended Capabilities   **343**
Business Rules Engine (BRE)   **343**
  Key Concepts   344
  Creating a BizTalk Solution with rules   345
    Create a Schema   345
    Creating a Policy   346
    Importing a Schema into Rule Composer   347

Adding an Action	348
Testing the policy	348
Creating an Orchestration	349
Deploying the policy and testing	350
Deploying a new version of the Policy	350
Adding Vocabulary	351
Electronic Data Interchange (EDI)	**352**
Finding and deploying the EDIFACT Schema	353
Adding a reference to BizTalk EDI application	354
Setting up a Receive Port, Location, and a Send Port	354
Setting up the Parties	355
Radio Frequency Identification (RFID)	**364**
Communication between RFID and BizTalk using SQL Server	364
Business Activity Monitoring (BAM)	**365**
Creating Activities	366
Setting up the BAM add-in inside Microsoft Excel	367
Creating an activity inside Excel	368
Deploy the Activity and view	373
Creating a Tracking Profile	374
Creating Continuations	378
BAM Portal	379
Searching for an order	381
Populating the aggregation	382
Creating view permissions	382
Roles and permissions	383
Test your knowledge	**383**
Summary	**385**
Chapter 9: Certification Test-taking—Tips and Tricks	**387**
Exam preparation	**387**
Preparation sources	388
Literature	388
Classes	388
Webcasts	389
Labs	390
Training kits	390
Sample code	391
Practice tests	392
Colleagues and peers	392
Forums, blogs and other online sources	393
Getting familiar with the certification objectives	393
Study time	393
Incentives	394
Knowledge	395
Money	395
Opportunities	395
Vouchers and offers	395

Learn more 396
At the test center 396
Exam structure 396
Before the exam 397
Questions 397
After the exam 398
Time management 399
Answering questions 400

Chapter 10: Sample Certification Test Questions 405

Configuring a Messaging Architecture 405
Developing BizTalk Artifacts 407
Debugging and exception handling 409
Deploying, tracking, and supporting a BizTalk solution 412
Integrating Web Services and Windows Communication Foundation (WCF) Services 414
Implementing extended capabilities 416

Appendix A: Test Your Knowledge—Answers 419

Chapter 1, Configuring a Messaging Architecture 419
Chapter 2, Developing BizTalk Artifacts—Creating Schemas and Pipelines 420
Chapter 3, Developing BizTalk Artifacts—Creating Maps 421
Chapter 4, Developing BizTalk Artifacts—Creating Orchestrations 421
Chapter 5, Debugging and Exception Handling 422
Chapter 6, Deploying, Tracking, and Administrating a BizTalk Server 2010 Solution 423
Chapter 7, Integrating Web Services and Windows Communication Foundation (WCF) Services 424
Chapter 8, Implementing Extended Capabilities 425

Appendix B: Sample Certification Test Questions—Answers 427

Configuring a messaging architecture 427
Developing BizTalk Artifacts 428
Debugging and exception handling 429
Deploying, tracking, and supporting a BizTalk solution 430
Integrating Web Services and Windows Communication Foundation (WCF) Services 431
Implementing extended capabilities 432

Index 433

Preface

(MCTS): Microsoft BizTalk Server 2010 (70-595) Certification Guide will give you all the information you need to pass the 70-595 TS: Developing Business Process and Integration Solutions exam with Microsoft BizTalk Server 2010.

The book's intent has been to be as focused as possible on providing content for just what you need to know, while still providing context to allow you to understand rather than just remember. Coverage of additional topics not included in the exam have been filtered out to reduce the noise.

Also included are over 50 sample questions that help to re-inforce what you need to know as well as to provide practice at the type and style of questions given in the exam itself.

At the same time that the book is tailored to fit the exam, you will not find the actual words or questions of the exam in this book. This book was made to help you, to strengthen your knowledge of the product and to allow you to focus your learning towards a goal. It is not a cheat sheet. But, if you understand the content of this book, you will pass the exam.

The book follows the same outline as the exam to provide mapping towards certification objectives. This helps you practice, as well as better understand, the certification objectives you are strong in and those which may need development. The certification objectives are supplied at `http://www.microsoft.com/learning/en/us/exam.aspx?ID=70-595`.

What this book covers

Chapter 1, Configuring a Messaging Architecture, covers the core architecture of BizTalk, including publish/subscribe, context and content-based routing, Receive and Send Ports, and other administrative artifacts.

Chapter 2, Developing BizTalk Artifacts — Creating Schemas and Pipelines, covers creating rich and useful Schemas with restrictions and reusable types.

Chapter 3, Developing BizTalk Artifacts — Creating Maps, covers creating Maps and applying logic, such as conditional mapping, looping, scripting, and external assemblies, and other map and functoid logic.

Chapter 4, Developing BizTalk Artifacts — Creating Orchestrations, covers creating Orchestrations and working with messages, scopes, transactions, binding, correlation, and other shapes, and processing logic.

Chapter 5, Debugging and Exception Handling, covers handling exceptions in messaging and Orchestration scenarios, and recovering from them using catch, compensation, and failed message routing.

Chapter 6, Deploying, Tracking, and Administrating a BizTalk Server 2010 Solution, covers performing administrative tasks, such as installing, configuring, tuning, deploying, maintaining, and troubleshooting BizTalk Server 2010 groups and solutions.

Chapter 7, Integrating Web Services and Windows Communication Foundation (WCF) Services, covers working with web services and WCF, exposing and consuming services, and applying custom configurations and behaviors.

Chapter 8, Implementing Extended Capabilities, covers using the additional features in BizTalk, such as Business Rules Engine (BRE), EDI, RFID, and Business Activity Monitoring (BAM).

Chapter 9, Certification Test Taking Tips and Tricks, covers additional resources for learning and tips, tricks, and strategies for preparing for and taking the certification.

Chapter 10, Sample Certification Test Questions, contains additional sample certification questions to reinforce what you learned and provides training on the certification format.

Appendix A, Test Your Knowledge — Answers, contains the answers and short explanations to the Test Your Knowledge question contained in each chapter.

Appendix B, Sample Certification Test Questions — Answers, contains the answers and short explanations to the sample certification questions in *Chapter 10, Sample Certification Test Questions*.

What you need for this book

This book comes with sample code to provide hands-on and practical implementation of the theory provided in the book. In some cases, the code is meant to be viewed in Visual Studio, and at other times, to be deployed to show the aspects of deployment, configuration, or runtime. To view, deploy, and run the code, you need the following:

- Windows Server 2008 R2 or Windows Server 2008 SP2 or Windows 7 or Windows Vista SP2
- IIS 7.0 or IIS 7.5
- .NET Framework 4 and .NET Framework 3.5 SP1
- SQL Server 2008 R2 Developer edition or SQL Server 2008 SP1 Developer edition
- Visual Studio 2010 with Visual C#.NET and Visual Web Developer
- BizTalk Server 2010 Developer edition
- Excel 2010 or Excel 2007 (for Business Activity Monitoring)
- MSMQ (for RFID)

Who this book is for

This book is for anyone wanting to achieve the certification of Microsoft Certified Technology Specialist (MCTS): Microsoft BizTalk Server 2010, by passing the exam 70-595: TS: Developing Business Process and Integration Solutions by Using Microsoft BizTalk Server 2010 exam.

The target audience for this book is similar as for the exam. The typical reader is someone who works as a BizTalk developer today. You are familiar with the product, and the technology in and around it, having had at least a year or so of exposure to primarily developing BizTalk Server integration solutions, but perhaps not using all parts of the product.

Even senior BizTalk developers aiming to get certified will benefit from this book.

This book is not for someone who wants to use it to learn the basics of BizTalk server, as it will start from a level and continue at a pace that assumes you are accustomed to those basics already.

The description of the typical exam candidate, as listed on the certification web page, suggests a little more than this:

> *Candidates should have at least two years of experience developing, deploying, testing, troubleshooting and debugging BizTalk Server 2006 or later across multiple projects and have experience using the Microsoft .NET Framework, XML, Microsoft Visual Studio, Microsoft SQL Server, Web services, and WCF while developing BizTalk integration solutions.*

Conventions

In this book, you will find a number of styles of text that distinguish between different kinds of information. Here are some examples of these styles, and an explanation of their meaning.

Code words in text are shown as follows: "It either takes a date or a datetime string."

A block of code is set as follows:

```
public interface IThirdPartyFinanceService
    {
        [OperationContract]
        FinanceResponse ThirdPartyFinanceApproval
            (FinanceRequest fRequest);
    } (in Code packt style)
```

New terms and **important words** are shown in bold. Words that you see on the screen, in menus or dialog boxes for example, appear in the text like this: "Clicking on the **Next** button moves you to the next screen."

Warnings or important notes appear in a box like this.

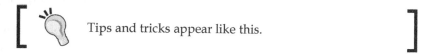

Tips and tricks appear like this.

Reader feedback

Feedback from our readers is always welcome. Let us know what you think about this book—what you liked or may have disliked. Reader feedback is important for us to develop titles that you really get the most out of.

To send us general feedback, simply send an e-mail to feedback@packtpub.com, and mention the book title via the subject of your message.

If there is a book that you need and would like to see us publish, please send us a note in the **SUGGESTATITLE** form on www.packtpub.com or e-mail suggest@packtpub.com.

If there is a topic that you have expertise in and you are interested in either writing or contributing to a book, see our author guide on www.packtpub.com/authors.

Customer support

Now that you are the proud owner of a Packt book, we have a number of things to help you to get the most from your purchase.

Downloading the example code

You can download the example code files for all Packt books you have purchased from your account at http://www.packtpub.com. If you purchased this book elsewhere, you can visit http://www.packtpub.com/support and register to have the files e-mailed directly to you.

Errata

Although we have taken every care to ensure the accuracy of our content, mistakes do happen. If you find a mistake in one of our books—maybe a mistake in the text or the code—we would be grateful if you would report this to us. By doing so, you can save other readers from frustration and help us improve subsequent versions of this book. If you find any errata, please report them by visiting http://www.packtpub.com/support, selecting your book, clicking on the **erratasubmissionform** link, and entering the details of your errata. Once your errata are verified, your submission will be accepted and the errata will be uploaded on our website, or added to any list of existing errata, under the Errata section of that title. Any existing errata can be viewed by selecting your title from http://www.packtpub.com/support.

Piracy

Piracy of copyright material on the Internet is an ongoing problem across all media. At Packt, we take the protection of our copyright and licenses very seriously. If you come across any illegal copies of our works, in any form, on the Internet, please provide us with the location address or website name immediately so that we can pursue a remedy.

Please contact us at copyright@packtpub.com with a link to the suspected pirated material.

We appreciate your help in protecting our authors, and our ability to bring you valuable content.

Questions

You can contact us at questions@packtpub.com if you are having a problem with any aspect of the book, and we will do our best to address it.

1
Configuring a Messaging Architecture

This chapter covers the *Configuring a Messaging Architecture* part of the exam. It will introduce some of the basic concepts of the messaging architecture in BizTalk, and also give the reader an insight into configuring some of the core Adapters in BizTalk. Other areas in this chapter will be: the publish/subscribe engine, Port Authentication, and some discussions about implementing messaging patterns.

The following topics will be covered:

- Publish/subscribe mechanism
- BizTalk platform settings
- Ports
- Core Adapters
- Messaging patterns
- Test your knowledge

Publish/subscribe

At its core, BizTalk is a publish/subscribe engine, nothing more nothing less. Whenever a message is received, BizTalk will look through all subscriptions and pass on a copy of the message to all the subscribers, if any. There are three kinds of artifacts inside BizTalk that can subscribe to messages:

- Send Ports
- Orchestrations
- Request-response Receive Ports (these will also subscribe for the response it awaits, but this is out of the scope for this chapter).

If messages, for some reason, cannot be sent to one or more of the subscribers, BizTalk will store the message for resuming, or later analysis as to why the message could not be delivered. When all subscribers have received their message, BizTalk will no longer need to hold on to the message, and the message will be removed from BizTalk. A new subscriber will not be able to subscribe to messages that have already been processed and delivered inside BizTalk.

The following model shows how the BizTalk publish/subscribe mechanism works:

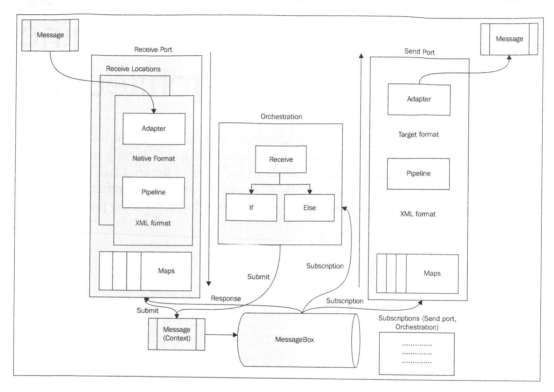

Receiving the message

First BizTalk will receive a message through the Receive Port. A message is received in a Receive Port through one of the Receive Locations associated with the port.

Adapter

The Adapter, responsible for communicating with the various Applications/ protocols needed, picks up messages or a batch of messages, writes metadata to the Context of the message, and sends the message to the Pipeline.

Examples of Adapters are:

- File
- FTP
- SQL
- HTTP

Pipeline

The main purpose of the Pipeline on the receive side is to recognize the Message Type and disassemble the native format of the message to XML. Out of the box, a Receive Location can choose between either a **PassThruReceive** or **XMLReceive** Pipeline, where only **XMLReceive** will recognize the Message Type, whereas the **PassThruReceive** will slip the message onwards to the MessageBox as an anonymous message.

Some examples of native formats are:

- XML
- FlatFiles (comma separated values, positional, and so on)
- EDI (X12, EDIFACT, and so on)
- Excel *
- PDF *

 * Not included in BizTalk, needs to be custom written or purchased from third party vendor.

The receive Pipeline will do parts or all of the following:

- Decrypt the message if encrypted
- Convert the native format into XML
- De-batch the message if batched
- Promote properties (write metadata to the Context of the message)
- Validate the message
- Resolve the sender of the message if signed (see more about this in *Chapter 2, Developing BizTalk Artifacts – Create Schemas and Pipelines*)

Maps

Now the message is evaluated with the Maps applied on the Receive Port (if any), and if the message matches the source Message Type on a Map, the Map will be applied.

MessageBox

The `MessageBox` is an SQL Server database, where all messages received by BizTalk are stored.

The three main purposes of the `MessageBox` are:

- Stores all messages and Context received
- Stores all subscriptions
- Stores all Host Queues

Whenever a message is received by BizTalk, the receiving message agent will store the message in the `MessageBox`. During the publishing of the message, the agent will check all the subscriptions inside the `MessageBox` with the Context of the message and all matching subscribers will get a reference to the actual message in their respective Host Queues. When all subscribers have successfully processed their message, the message is no longer required in the `MessageBox`, and will be removed or moved to the `Tracking` database. The `MessageBox` also consists of all the subscriptions inside the BizTalk Group. Subscriptions are primarily made by Send Ports and Orchestrations and will be discussed in the following section.

Subscriptions

A subscription in BizTalk means that if certain parameters concerning the message are met, the subscriber will get a copy of that message.

A subscription could look something similar to the following pseudo code:

```
((Message Type = Order) and (Customer = HP)) or (Message Type =
Invoice)
```

This would result in the subscriber getting all invoices entering BizTalk and also all orders from HP.

Subscriptions are typically made by Send Ports and Orchestrations. If a Send Port subscription is met, the message will be sent through the Send Port to the target system/location. If an orchestration activation subscription is met, a new instance of that Orchestration type will be initialized (read more about orchestrations in *Chapter 4, Developing BizTalk Artifacts – Create Orchestrations*). We will look further into Send Port subscriptions in the *Setting up and managing Ports* section later in this chapter.

Message Context properties

When subscribing, we cannot subscribe to any content of the actual messages entering BizTalk, but only to what information is on the Context of the message. The message metadata is called **Context Properties** and on receiving the message, both the Adapter and the Pipeline will add information to the Context.

Context properties can either be **Promoted** or **Not promoted** (also known as **Written**). Properties that are promoted can be used for subscribing to the message. However, written properties cannot be used for subscribing to the message.

Orchestrations

An Orchestration can receive messages from the `MessageBox`, based on its subscriptions. The subscriptions can be either activating (which will start a new Orchestration) or instance (which will deliver the message to an existing Orchestration). If the Orchestration needs to send/receive the messages during the execution, it will happens through the `MessageBox`, with the Orchestration submitting messages just like the Receive Port does.

Sending the message

When a message is sent to a Send Port, the process is almost the reverse of what happens in the Receive Port.

Maps

First, if Maps are applied to the port, BizTalk will try and match the message type with the source message type of the Map(s) on the port, and if a valid Map is found, it will be applied to the message.

Pipeline

Next, the Pipeline will typically do some or all of the following activities:

- Validate the message
- Convert the message from XML to the desired target format
- Encrypt and sign the message if needed

Adapter

Finally, the adapter will transmit the message to its destination location.

BizTalk platform settings and Applications

This section talks about how the various BizTalk platform settings and Applications work and are configured.

BizTalk Administration Console

In this section, we will look at the **BizTalk Administration Console**, which is used to manage and configure the BizTalk Server and to deploy, manage, monitor, and troubleshoot Applications.

The Group Hub

The **Group Hub** gives the user an overview of what is currently going on inside BizTalk.

In order to view the **Group Hub**, open the BizTalk Administration Console and click on the **BizTalk Group**.

A large dashboard will appear where we get an overview of which Applications are currently running, how many running messages are currently in the MessageBox, and how many suspended messages there are.

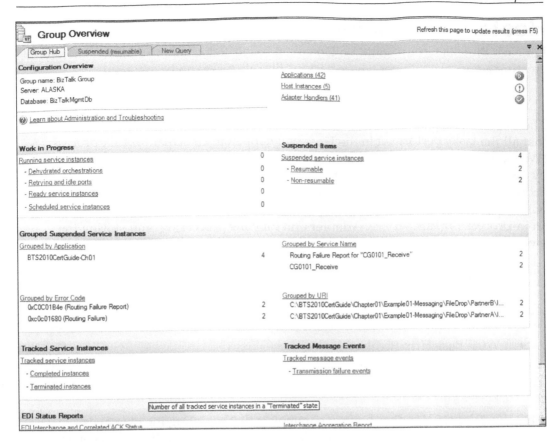

Work in Progress should not be of any concern to us unless the amount of messages are large and keeps rising, in that case we might have a bottleneck in one of our solutions that needs to be addressed.

Suspended Items, on the other hand, requires our attention, as they are messages that for some reason cannot be further processed until manual actions have been taken. **Suspended Items** fall into two categories:

- **Resumable**: Messages which can be manually resumed.
- **Non-resumable**: Messages, which typically hold metadata and cannot be resumed. They will either disappear when the corresponding resumable instance is resumed, or in other cases they might need manual termination.

Hosts and Host Instances

For each BizTalk Group, multiple **Hosts** can be created. Creating a Host is merely creating a logical container where various BizTalk tasks can be assigned.

A Host can be either of type **In-Process** or **Isolated**.

The In-process type is used for most BizTalk tasks and what *in-process* means is that all the tasks performed in the Host will happen in an actual BizTalk process (Windows Service). The Isolated Host, on the other hand, will have its work done by "someone other than BizTalk", for example an IIS receiving service calls and processing the message on its own. By using various BizTalk Modules, the IIS Host will run the received message through the same steps that would occur when using an in-process BizTalk service, Adapter and Pipeline processing, and storing the message in the MessageBox.

Out of the box, the use of Isolated Hosts is limited to:

- HTTP Receive
- SOAP Receive
- WCF-BasicHttp Receive
- WCF-CustomIsolated Receive
- WCF-WSHttp

What the Adapter Handlers have in common is that receiving the messages will happen through the IIS and not a Windows Service (when BizTalk receives HTTP messages, the submitter will actually call a URL on an IIS residing on the BizTalk Server).

Each Host should have at least one corresponding Host Instance running. An In-Process Host Instance is nothing more than a Windows service running on one or more BizTalk Servers and performs the tasks assigned to the Host.

Creating a Host

Creating a Host can be done through the BizTalk Service Administration Console, by choosing **Platform settings | Hosts | New | Host**:

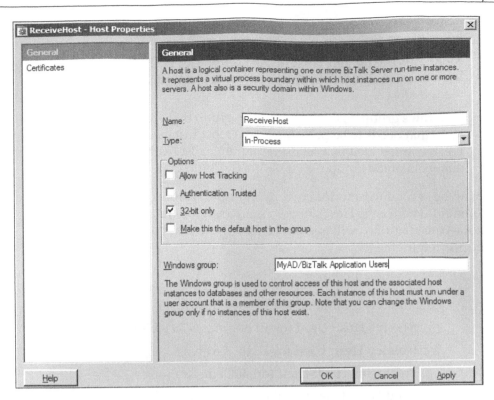

Creating a new Host will result in a new entry in the Host table inside the Management database, and also create a new Host Queue inside the MessageBox.

There are a few parameters that should be taken into consideration when creating Hosts:

- **Name**: The name of the Host is very important when moving a BizTalk solution from one environment to another. If we use binding files to replicate one environment to another, the naming of Hosts must be the same on each environment.

- **Type**: Either In-Process or Isolated.

- **Allow Host Tracking**: If enabled, the **Host Instances** created for the Host, will perform **Tracking** tasks such as moving data from the MessageBox to the Tracking database.

- **Authentication Trusted**: This is used to mark that the current Host is trusted. If a Host is trusted, other Hosts will trust the given Host and will be able to trust that the messages received from the Host have correct Sender ID and Party ID and will not overwrite these. This is mainly used if credentials from the original caller to BizTalk are needed to travel through BizTalk in order to make **Single-Sign On** credential control on the send side.

- **32-bit only**: This flag is enabled by default. If it is removed, then the process will run as a 64-bit process, otherwise as a 32-bit.

- **Make this the default Host in the group**: Any BizTalk Group will always have one default Host. If this checkbox is disabled, the Host is already a default Host.

- **Windows group**: Specify a Windows group that will be given access to all tasks that needs to be performed by a Host Instance running under the Host. It is recommended that all users running Host Instances under this Host are members of the group.

There can be several reasons for creating multiple Hosts inside a BizTalk environment. There is no Host setup recommendation that will fit all environments, and some considerations will need to be made based on the actual environment and the specific requirements.

Here are a few general guidelines:

- As a default it is recommended to have five Hosts:
    - **Receive Host**: Used for all in-process receiving
    - **Isolated Host**: Used for all IIS Receive
    - **Processing Host**: Used for all Orchestrations
    - **Send Host**: Used for all sending of messages
    - **Tracking Host**: A dedicated Host for moving data from the MessageBox to the Tracking and BAM databases, as this task can have a performance impact, the other Hosts should not be set to allow Host Tracking

- When using adapters that must run in a 32 bit process, 32 bit Hosts might need to be created on receive and/or send side to Host the 32 bit only adapters. Another approach could be to have the Receive and Send Hosts running in 32 bit mode. If 64 bit processing is required (typically when receiving large messages) a 64 bit Host can be created for handling the tasks where 64 bit is desired.

- Some Receive Adapters should not run in a multi-server environment (such as FTP, POP3, and MSMQ). So, in that case a special Host for hosting these Receive Locations might be created and only run on one server. If high availability is required, this Host should be clustered.

- Don't just make thousands of Hosts. The advantages of multiple Host Instances (Windows services) on each BizTalk Server are that they will use their own threads, have their own queues, and so on. However, each service will also consume resources (such as memory) and therefore creating too many Host Instances can have a negative impact. Therefore we need to find a balance. If we have a small BizTalk solution with only a few messages running through the BizTalk environment, chances are that performance will be fine by just using one in-process Host for everything.

Creating a Host Instance

Unlike creating a Host, creating a Host Instance will happen on both the BizTalk Server and also in the BizTalk databases. A new Host Instance will result in a new Windows service running on a BizTalk Server. Only one instance of a certain Host type can be created on each BizTalk Server in the BizTalk Group. When creating a new Host Instance, we are presented with the following screen:

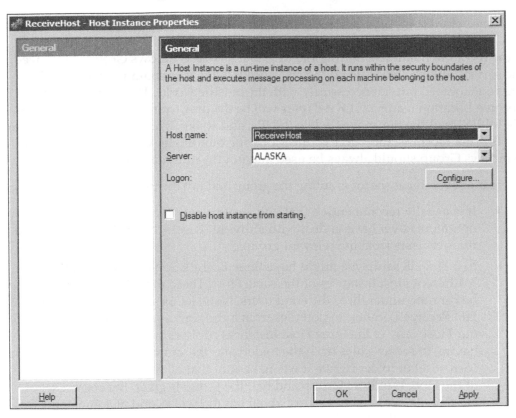

In the preceding example, we have created a new Host Instance of the Host **NewHost** on server **ALASKA**.

After selecting the correct Host and server, click on **Configure** to specify which user the service should run as. This user will need access to the Host queues/tables in the `MessageBox` and the easiest way to grant the user these privileges is to add the user to the Windows group that we associated with the Host when creating it.

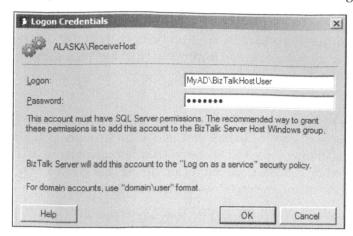

If the recommendation of adding the user to the Host Windows Group is followed, the service will be able to do all the tasks needed towards communication with the `MessageBox`, but not necessarily with the outside world. The user running a Receive Location using a **FILE Adapter** will be the user trying to access the source file folder, read the file, move/delete the file, and so on. When dealing with granting the BizTalk Host Instances access to various surrounding environments, the Host Windows Group should always be used and not the individual user.

There are several reasons for granting the group and not the users the required access:

- It is usually recommended that only groups get permissions so that IT operators never have to deal with individual users, but rather just add and remove users from the relevant groups.

- In a BizTalk setup, we might have three BizTalk Servers and therefore 3 different Host Instances of the same Host. These three Host Instances could be running under three different users. Now, let us say that we configure a File Receive Location to poll files from a certain folder and have it run under our Host. Any of the three Host Instances could now be getting the task of having to retrieve files from the folder, and therefore all three users need the correct set of folder rights. If we make sure that all three users are members of the Host Windows Group and that the group is given the correct set of credentials, we need not worry about anything else, and at some point we might even add an additional BizTalk Server with a new Host Instance and a new user, who, as long as they are added as a member of the Host Group, will be able to access the folder immediately.

Managing Adapter Handlers

Each adapter installed in the BizTalk Group has corresponding Receive and/or Send Handlers that are used to link the adapter to a certain Host.

Managing the Adapter Handler is done through the BizTalk Administration Console, as shown in the following screenshot:

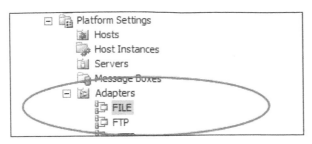

From here we can install new adapters and add Receive or Send Handlers to adapters.

In order to add a new handler to an adapter, click on the **Adapter** and right-click somewhere in the blank space underneath the existing handlers:

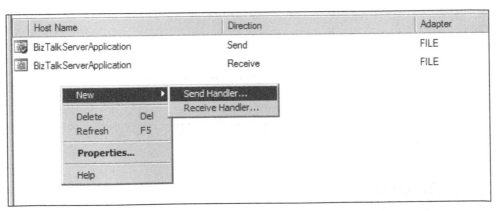

Each handler will be the link between an adapter and a Host. Only one handler per adapter and Host can be created, and only Hosts for which a handler of the correct type exists can be chosen when configuring the transport adapter and its handler in Receive Locations and Send Ports.

Some handlers have the ability to have some basic configuration that will be applied to all adapter settings using that Host as default.

The SMTP Adapter is an example, where we often set up some basic configuration on the Handler level, because these properties will often be the same for all Send Ports using the SMTP Adapter. To change these standard properties, open the relevant SMTP Handler and choose **Properties**:

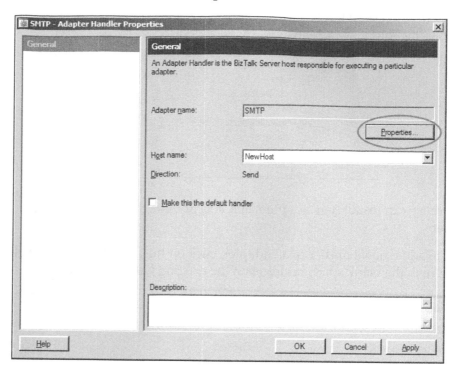

In the preceding screenshot, we can configure some general properties for all SMTP Adapter usage under the Host **NewHost**. (See the *Configuring core Adapters* section later in this chapter for more information.)

Applications

Applications are logical containers inside the BizTalk Administration Console, which allows us to group certain items together. The purpose of Applications is mainly to make planning, deployment, administration, and the general overview easier when working with BizTalk.

In order to create a new Application, carry out the following steps:

1. Open the BizTalk Administration Console.
2. Right-click on **Applications** and choose **New | Application**.
3. Give the Application an appropriate name and click on **OK**.

When working inside an Application, we are only able to work directly with the other artifacts in that Application. For example, if we need to use a Pipeline in a Send Port, that Pipeline needs to be deployed in the same Application, or we need to make a reference to the Application which contains the pipeline.

Referencing another Application

When making a reference to another Application, right-click on the Application that needs a reference to another Application, and carry out the following steps:

1. Click on **Reference**, and then click on **Add**:

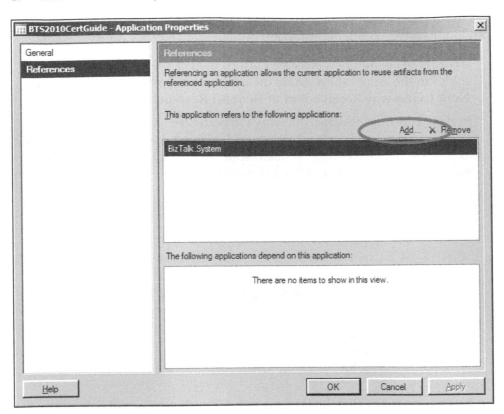

We now get a list of all available Applications other than the Application we are working with. Choose one or more Applications you want to reference.

Notice that **BizTalk.System** is already referenced in all new Applications. As a result of this, we can work with several Pipelines as soon as a new Application is created, even though these Pipelines are deployed in the **BizTalk.System** Application.

Setting up and managing Ports

Inside BizTalk, we have both Receive and Send Ports. Ports are entry points and exit points in and out of BizTalk. All messages entering BizTalk will be received through a Receive Port and almost all messages exiting BizTalk will be through a Send Port. (Even if it is possible to send out messages directly through code inside an Orchestration, this will not very often be the correct approach.)

Receive Ports

Receive Ports are the entry points for messages that enter BizTalk. Each Receive Port contains from one to many different Receive Locations (we can create Receive Ports without any Receive Locations, but that would not make much sense).

1. In order to create a new Receive Port, right-click on the **Receive Ports** folder in the Application where the Port should be created, and choose **New | One-way Receive Port** or **Request Response Receive Port**.

    In most routing scenarios, one-way Ports are used, and the use of Request-Response Receive Ports should be limited to flows where BizTalk exposes services, where an actual response message is required. (Read more about best practices later in this chapter in the *Implementing messaging patterns* section.

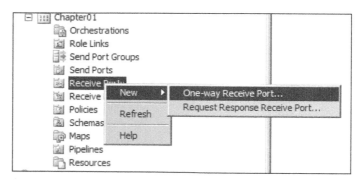

2. Next, we need to give the Port a name. (Note that names of the various Ports inside a BizTalk Group must be unique not just inside an Application but for the whole BizTalk Group.)

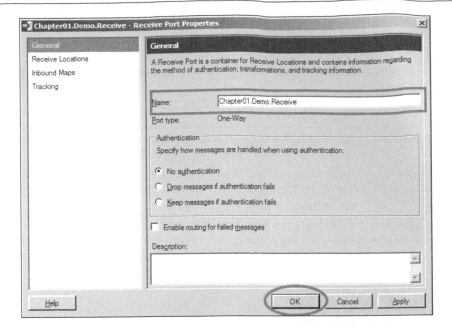

3.   Next, click on **OK** to create the Receive Port.

Port Authentication

One way of making sure that only messages from known partners enters BizTalk, is by using the **Port Authentication** feature available on Receive Ports, as seen in the following screenshot:

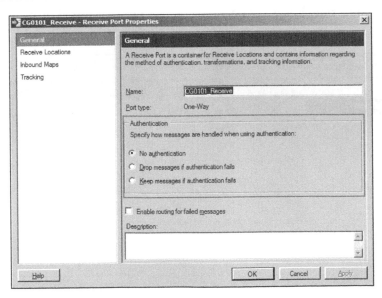

When using Receive Ports, we can set up filters so that only messages from known parties are allowed through to the `MessageBox`. This will only work if messages are signed and we have all the certificates of our parties in store, or if the Windows User who submitted the message can be located. There are three properties on each Receive Port:

Type	Description
No authentication (Default)	All messages will be let through to the `MessageBox` whether or not the party resolution inside the Pipeline finds a valid sender or not
Drop messages if authentication fails	If the party resolver does not match a valid sender from the message signature, the message will be thrown away and not submitted to the `MessageBox`
Keep messages if authentication fails	If the party resolver does not match a valid sender from the message signature, the message will be suspended inside the `MessageBox` and an error will be raised in the EventLog

Receive Locations

As mentioned earlier, a Receive Port with no Receive Location does not make any sense. No messages will ever be received through that Port. So for each Receive Port, at least one Receive Location should be created and configured.

The reason for having multiple Receive Locations inside one Receive Port is to have the ability to receive different messages from different locations and having BizTalk treat them as if they were received from the same place and/or had the same message type.

In order to create a new Receive Location, create a new Receive Location from within the Receive Port:

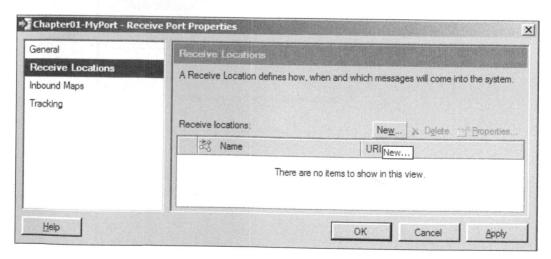

Alternatively, right-click on the **Receive Locations** folder in the Application and choose **New | One-way Receive Location** or **Request Response Receive Location**. As for Receive Location types, only one-way Receive Locations can be added to a one-way Receive Port, and only Request-Response locations to a Request-Response Port.

If a Receive Location is created directly, we will be prompted for a parent Receive Port before we can configure the location, since all locations must be part of one specific Port. In the following screenshot, we are presented with the available Receive Ports:

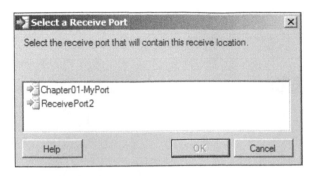

Choose the appropriate Receive Port, click on **OK**, and the Receive Location configuration will appear:

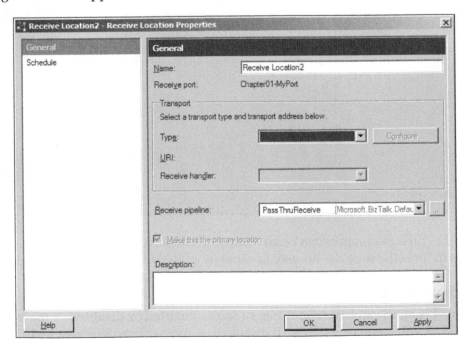

Like Receive Ports, Receive Locations need to be supplied with a **Name**. Also, a **Type** (Adapter) needs to be selected and configured, a Receive Handler (Host type) also needs to be selected (note that the default Host for the chosen handler will always be automatically selected), and finally a Pipeline needs to be selected. Read more about Pipelines in *Chapter 2, Developing BizTalk Artifacts – Create Schemas and Pipelines*.

Service Windows

Each Receive Location can be scheduled to only operate at certain times.

On the **Schedule** page inside the Receive Location, a **Start date**, **Stop date**, and a **Service Window** can be applied, as shown in the following screenshot:

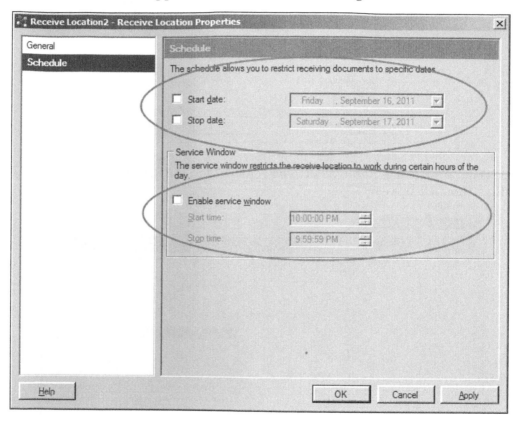

Each of the three parameters can be enabled or disabled, and each enabled time period will limit the time the Receive Location is enabled for receiving messages.

Location states

A Receive Location can have two different states: **enabled** or **disabled**. If the location is enabled, it will receive messages, if disabled, no messages will be received.

Enabling a Receive Location can be done by right-clicking on it inside the BizTalk Administration Console and choosing **enable**. It can also be done through code script.

Error threshold

The state of a Receive Location is merely a flag inside the `Receive Location` table in the `Management` database. It has nothing to do with whether or not the Host Instances (Windows services) are running. Therefore a Receive Location will only pick up messages if it is enabled, and at least one instance of the Host type it is using is running.

If errors occur in a Receive Location when trying to pick up messages (access denied in a file folder, or on a database, and so on), the Host Instance will start to write error/warning entries in the EventLog. At some point, the **error threshold** (this differs from adapter to adapter) might be reached, and the Receive Location will become disabled. If a Receive Location becomes disabled, it will not start itself again automatically, but instead it will write an error message in the EventLog of the BizTalk Server that did the shut down, and therefore monitoring these events is critical, as a disabled Receive Locations results in no messages being received by BizTalk.

In the following example, we are polling mails from a mail server by using the POP3 Receive Adapter, and want to examine the error threshold:

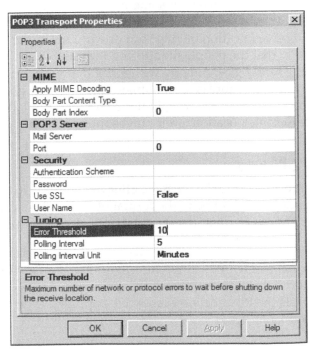

When setting up the adapter, we are asked for the polling interval and the error threshold. If set to 5 and 10, as shown in the preceding screenshot, the following is what would happen if Receive Location started failing:

- BizTalk will poll mails every five minutes. At some point, the mail server becomes unavailable and the process of logging on and retrieving mails starts failing.

- The first time BizTalk unsuccessfully tries to access the Mail Server, it will write a warning in the EventLog saying that it wasn't able to connect to the Mail Server, and that it will try again later.

- The second try will be five minutes later and unless the Mail Server suddenly becomes available again, this will go on for another nine times.

- When the 10th try occurs, BizTalk will no longer retry and will therefore put a stop to the retrying by disabling the Receive Location, writing an error to the EventLog saying that the number of retries were reached, and now it is up to the administrators to fix the problem and enable the Receive Location again.

When configuring the various Receive Locations, we need to find a balance between how many retries (the threshold) we configure. If we have an unstable environment, such as an FTP Server residing somewhere outside our control, with multiple unscheduled service windows and general unavailability, it might be tempting to increase the error threshold to 9,000 or something similar, so that we have long periods of unavailability, and when the FTP Server eventually comes back online, we do not risk the Receive Location having shut down. This might not be the best approach, as it is likely that the people monitoring BizTalk will only look at errors and not warnings in EventLog, so nobody will notice that we are not polling data from the source if something more critical happens (such as our password expires or something similar to it). In that case, we will not be notified until all 9,000 tries have been failing and the Receive Location, after maybe months, eventually shuts down.

Receive Port Maps

Receive Port Maps are applied to the message after the message leaves the Pipeline, in which case all messages should be in the format of XML. This is important since Maps can only take XML as input and also a Map will always output XML.

Maps can only be applied if the Pipeline has discovered the message type of the incoming message (this will happen automatically unless the **PassThruReceive** Pipeline is used, refer to the next chapter). If the message type is not known by the time the message exists the Pipeline, no Map will be applied, even if a Map matching the message is present on the port.

The matching of a Map works as follows:

If the message type was discovered and promoted by the receiving Pipeline, BizTalk will look for a Map with a source type matching the message type. If such a Map is found, it will be executed and the source message will be mapped using that Map.

It is also worth mentioning that after a Map has been executed on a Receive Port, an XML Disassemble Pipeline Component is executed against the output XML. This is why we can promote properties on the destination Schema of a Map executed on the Receive Port and still have the properties promoted before the message is submitted to the MessageBox. The following example will explain this.

On a Receive Port (PortA), we have applied three different Maps:

- MessageA_to_MessageU
- MessageB_to_MessageU
- MessageU_to_MessageI

If we receive message A (and the message type is applied in the Pipeline), the message will be transformed to Message U, but after that the message exits the Port, and no additional Map discovery will be done, so even though we might want message A to be transformed first into message U and then into message I, this will not happen. The same goes for message B, and only if we submit a message U will the Map (MessageU_to_MessageI) be applied.

Maps are applied to Receive Ports by selecting **Properties** on the Port and then selecting **Inbound Maps**, as shown in the following screenshot:

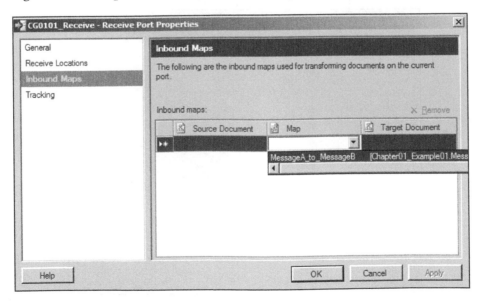

Under the **Map** section, use the drop-down list, then all Maps deployed in the Application (or Applications that are being referenced) should appear. Choose the Map that should be used in the Receive Port, remember that multiple Maps can be selected.

Send Ports

Unlike a Receive Port, Send Ports do not operate with more than one location. Each Send Port will point to a specific location, database, Application, service, and so on, somewhere outside of BizTalk. Like a Receive Location, a Send Port uses one Pipeline and one Adapter, so that the desired message(s) and the desired protocol are used for transporting the message to the target destination. In order to create a new Send Port do the following:

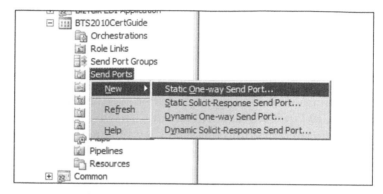

After choosing **New | Static One-way Send Port...** the following screen will appear:

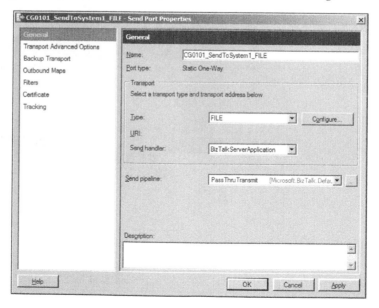

When creating a new Send Port, at least three properties should be selected, and in some cases, configured.

First, we need to supply the Send Port with a name. A type (Adapter) also needs to be selected and configured. Next we can choose a Send Handler (Host), if we do not want to use the default Host. Finally, if the default Pipeline is not adequate, another Pipeline must be chosen and configured.

Transport Advanced Options

In **Transport Advanced Options**, several common parameters can be configured in the Send Port:

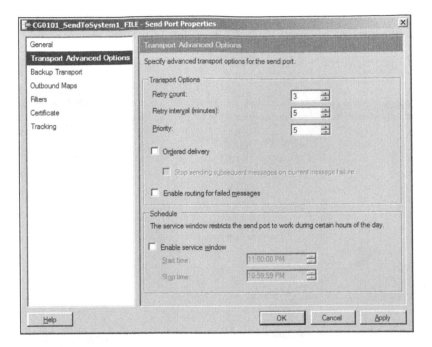

The transport options consist of three parameters:

Retry count	The number of tries the Send Port should try to resend the message on failure before giving up and suspending the message in the `MessageBox`
Retry interval	The number of minutes to wait between the retries in case of failure
Priority	The priority given to the Send Port subscription (**1** being the highest and **10** the lowest), the higher the priority, the faster the Send Port will get messages it has subscribed for

Retry on a Send Port is a bit different from Receive Locations. First of all, the behavior is per message and the port will never stop itself after any number of retries has been exhausted.

What the Send Port does is try to send each message it receives the number of times specified in the **Retry count** parameter, and with an interval specified in **Retry interval**. When the number of retries has been exhausted, the message will be suspended and an error will be written to the EventLog. (Like the Receive Location, the first failure(s) results in warnings being written to the EventLog, only the final try, with the following suspension of the message, will result in an error.)

Scheduling and Service Window

Each Send Port created can have a scheduled service window in which messages will be sent through the Port. The set up is done under **Transport Advanced Options**:

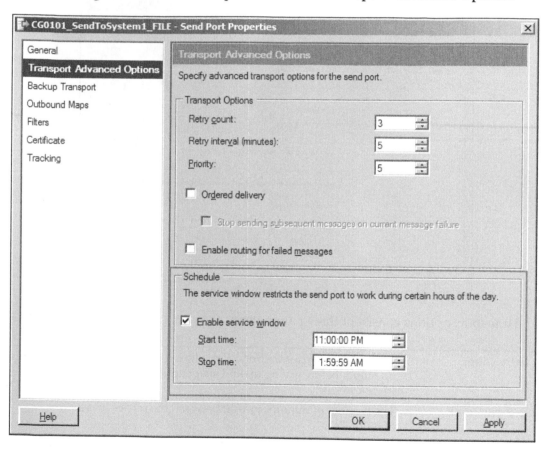

Like Receive Locations, certain operation periods can be set up on a Send Port. We can specify a period within the day, where messages should be sent through the Port. At all other times, all messages going to the Port will be queued up inside BizTalk, and when the **Operation Window** opens, all the queued up messages will be sent.

The term service window might be a bit confusing, normally a service window is a time period where maintenance is going on, and therefore a period where no messages should be sent to the system, but in this case the service window is the time where messages are actually sent through the Send Port.

Backup transport

Each Send Port can have a backup transport configured, where an alternative Adapter and/or address can be selected, so that if the primary target is unavailable the Send Port will try to send the message to an alternative location instead.

Send Port Maps

Just like Receive Ports, multiple Maps can be applied to the Send Ports in order to transform the messages being sent from the MessageBox to the target format requested by the target system. Just like the Receive Port, multiple Maps may be applied to the Send Port, but only one of them will be used, and only if the message type is known by BizTalk at the time the message is sent from the MessageBox to the Send Port.

In order to apply Maps to Send Ports, open the **Send Port properties** and select the **Outbound Maps**:

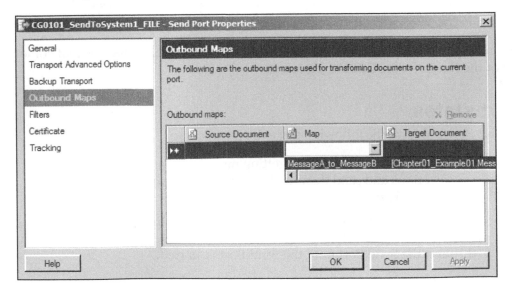

Configuring Filters (Subscriptions)

Inside the **Filters** page, it is possible to set up subscriptions for the Send Port. The filters can be a combination of several boolean expressions and include a combination of and/or with promoted properties deployed to the BizTalk Group (in Property Schemas). The following is an example of setting up a subscription on a Send Port:

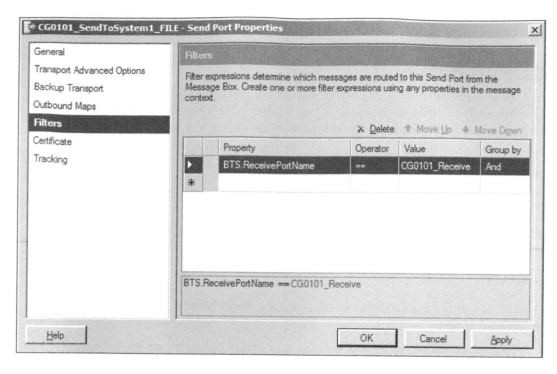

The example in the preceding screenshot will subscribe to all messages that comes out of the Receive Port **CG0101_Receive**.

Port states

A Send Port can have the following three different states:

- **Started**: The Send Port will be getting messages that matches its subscriptions and send them to the target system, if not outside the service window.

- **Stopped**: The Send Port will be getting messages that match its subscriptions but the messages will lie in a queue inside the MessageBox and not be sent through the Send Port until the Send Port is started.

- **Unenlisted**: The Send Port does not subscribe to any messages and no messages will be sent through the port. The port will not be able to get messages later on, which are already received in the MessageBox.

Port states can be changed by right-clicking on the port inside the Administration Console:

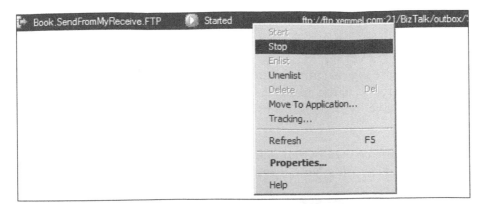

 Note that if we right-click on an **Unenlisted** Port, the state will be named **Enlist** in the menu and not **Stop**.

The **Stopped** state will queue up all messages for the Send Port, and when the Port is started again all messages will be sent immediately through the Send Port (if no service window is configured). This might not always be what is desired, especially if the Port was stopped due to some configuration error in BizTalk or the target system, resulting in messages failing upon arrival at the target. In that case, sending 100 messages all at once when we think the problem has been resolved might not be the best approach. If we just want to send one of the 100 messages currently lying in the MessageBox waiting for the Port to be started, we can go to the **Group Hub**, find the 100 suspended messages, and resume just one of them. This will force the one message to be sent through the Send Port even though the state is still set to stopped, and on acceptance that the problem has been fixed, we can then start the port and the last 99 messages (or more if more messages have arrived in the MessageBox) will automatically be sent through the Port.

Dynamic Send Ports

Dynamic Send Ports differ from Static Ports as their adapter and/or address are not configured and hardcoded. Both protocol (adapter) and address can be coded from inside BizTalk and therefore the port could send messages to different locations using different protocols (SMTP, FTP, and so on).

They are often used for SMTP, because an SMTP Send Port often requires sending mails to different addresses that might be located somewhere in the message. This is not possible with a static Send Port, which will always point to the same address (as will all other adapters). Hence, to solve that problem Dynamic Ports can be used.

Dynamic Ports are usually combined with Orchestrations and will be discussed further in *Chapter 5, Debugging and Exception Handling*.

Send Port Groups

Send Port Groups are logical subscription containers where one or more Send Ports can join the subscription of the group. A Send Port can be part of multiple Send Port Groups, and also have its own local subscription, and can therefore have multiple subscriptions.

Send Port Groups are created by right-clicking on the Send Port Group folder inside an Application, and choosing **New | Send Port Group.**

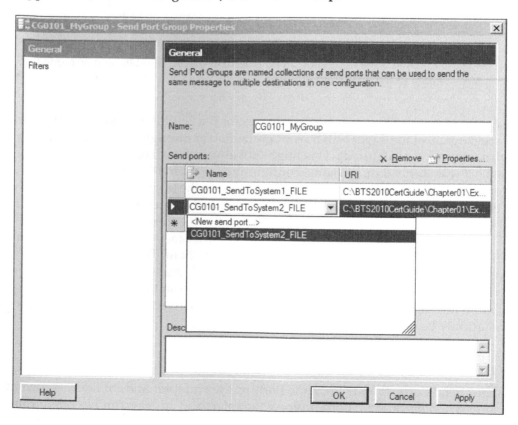

Failed message routing

On both Receive and Send Ports, it is possible to enable routing for failed messages. What this will do is, in case of an error occurring in the port (could be either the Pipeline throwing an error, mapping failing, or a Send Port that is not able to send to the target system, and so on), the message will have all the regular Context Properties unpromoted (written) and instead have some error-specific Context Properties promoted (all in the ErrorReport namespace).

Examples of Error Context Properties are: ErrorReport.ErrorType and ErrorReport.ReceivePortName.

A Send Port or Orchestration can then subscribe to these error properties and deal with the errors in some way.

In order to set up failed message routing on a Receive Port, go to the properties of the Port, on the **General** tab and enable the **Enable routing for failed messages** checkbox.

In order to set up failed message routing on a Send Port, go to the **Properties** of the port, on the **Transport Advanced Options**, enable the **Enable routing for failed messages** checkbox.

See more about failed message routing in *Chapter 5, Debugging and Exception Handling*.

Ordered delivery

Ordered delivery might not come as easy as one might think in BizTalk. Out of the box, only few Receive Adapters are able to provide true ordered delivery.

An example: We receive files during the day from a file drop location. Our ERP system has requested that it receives all files in the same order as they were submitted to the file folder, because receiving data in the wrong order could potentially cause inconsistent data. Let us think of BizTalk as a post office. If some customer has asked the mailman to deliver today's letters, the exact same way he received the letters in the mailbox on the street, the mailman immediately faces a problem. He can give the customer the letters in the same order that he got the letters out of the mailbox, but that is not necessarily the same order that they were put into the mailbox. The same is true for BizTalk: we are able to send messages through a Send Port or to an Orchestration in the same order they were submitted to the MessageBox, but that order might not be the same order the original submitter intended.

Again, back to the file drop example: The FILE adapter, like many other adapters, might not submit the messages received in the same order as one might intend/ expect. The FILE adapter does not look at timestamps, file sizes, or even filenames when choosing which file to process first. There could also be more than one Host Instance receiving batches of files at the same time from the same folder, and submitting them in the same `MessageBox`. In other words, if BizTalk is started and two files are present at a certain file location, we have no way of knowing whether the oldest file is taken first or second, and therefore have no certain way of making a total FIFO (first in first out) scenario using the File Receive Adapter. In fact this is true for most of the BizTalk Receive Adapters, and out of the box, only the message queue adapters (MSMQ and MQSeries) support true ordered delivery. (Some database adapters and WCF Service Adapters can be set up to implement ordered delivery, but only with certain limitations such as only one Host Instance, and so on.)

Receive Locations

On the receive side, it is based on the different protocols (Adapters) if ordered delivery is supported or not. For the very few Adapters that do support it (mainly MQ), it can usually be enabled on the Receive Adapter.

Send Ports

Each Send Port can be set up to use ordered delivery. Setting a Send Port to ordered delivery means that all messages will be sent through that Port in the same order as they were received in the `MessageBox`. If messages are not received in the `MessageBox` in the order intended, as discussed earlier, using ordered delivery on a Send Port might not have the desired result.

Using ordered delivery on a Send Port has some serious performance impacts, because only one thread can submit messages through the Port, and each message has to wait for the message ahead to complete before it can be processed. This can be both an advantage and a disadvantage. The disadvantage is obvious. BizTalk will perform more slowly when using ordered delivery. In some cases, however, this might turn into an advantage. If, for instance, a Send Port calls a service that cannot handle multiple calls, we might experience a lot of messages going into a retry or even fail state, because the amount of messages being sent to the service is exceeding the amount of messages the service can handle. In this case, it could make sense to introduce ordered delivery to the Send Port, not because we necessarily need the messages to be sent in a certain order, but merely because this will result in BizTalk only sending one message at a time:

1. In order to set up ordered delivery on a Send Port, go to the properties of a Send Port (either by double-clicking on the **Send Port** or right-clicking and choosing **Properties.**

2. Go to the **Transport Advanced Options** page, and enable **Ordered delivery**:

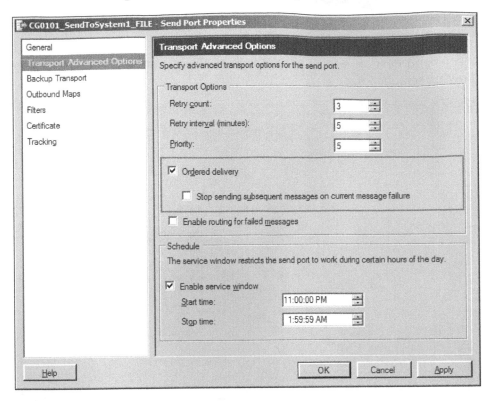

When enabling ordered delivery, an additional sub setting will become active: **Stop sending subsequent messages on current message failure**. This means that if 10 messages are currently queued up to be sent through the sent port (message 1 to 10) and message 3 fails, the rest of the messages (4 to 10) will get suspended together with message 3. If true ordered delivery is required, this option should be enabled, simply because if it is not, the solution is not 100% ordered delivery. On the other hand, if ordered delivery is nice to have, not 100% vital for the solution, or we are simply using ordered delivery to slow down the Send Port, then the option should be disabled.

 Note that ordered delivery does not work on the backup transport, if used.

Configuring core Adapters

When choosing an Adapter on both Receive Locations and Send Ports, the Adapters need to be configured.

On either a Send Port or Receive Location, choose the **Configure** button as shown in the following screenshot:

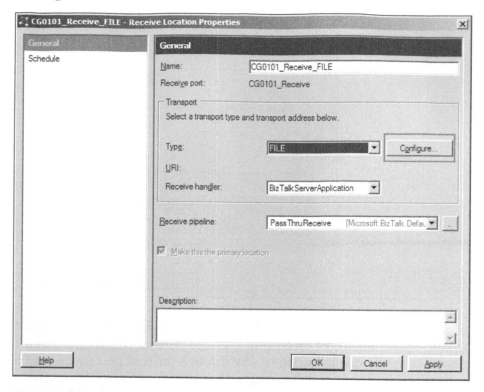

What will appear next depends on which type of adapter was chosen. In this chapter, we will look at some of the core adapters and how they are configured.

HTTP

This section will discuss the use of the HTTP Adapter in both receive and send scenarios.

Sending HTTP

When configuring the HTTP Send Adapter, the URL of the target HTTP site needs to be configured. The following screenshot shows the basic configuration, and the **Destination URL** being configured:

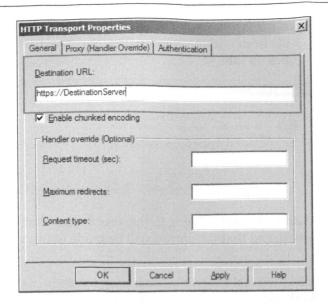

Receiving HTTP

Setting up BizTalk to receive HTTP requires more work than sending HTTP. In order to be able to receive HTTP, we need to use the local IIS (Internet Information Services) and have it receive the actual message for us using an Isolated Host.

First, we need to add `BTSHttpReceive.dll`. This file is found in the `%Program Files%\Microsoft BizTalk Server 2010\HttpReceive64` folder (`HttpReceive` folder if not using a 64-bit IIS). This DLL needs to be added as an extension inside the IIS. Open the IIS Manager (**Start | Administrative Tools | Internet Information Services(IIS) Manager**), click on the computer name and double-click on **Handler Mappings**. In the action pane on the right, choose **Add Script Map**:

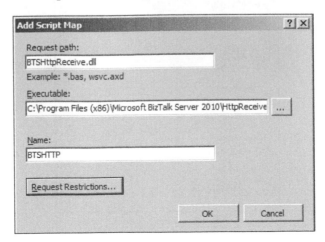

In the Request path type `BTSHttpReceive.dll`. In executable, choose the `BTSHttpReceive.dll` file from within program files, and give the mapping a proper name. Now, click on **OK**:

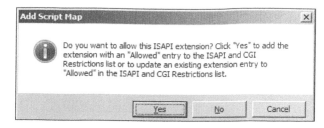

Click on **Yes** in the **Add Script Map** dialog to the information that an ISAPI extension will be created, and that the entries will be made in other configuration stores inside the IIS.

Now, we need to make a Virtual Directory containing the `BTSHttpReceive.dll` mentioned earlier. Right-click on the **Default Web Site** folder and select **Add Virtual Directory**. Set the **Alias** property to the name that we want the callers of our HTTP service to use in the URL (`http://servername/Alias/BTSHTTPReceive.dll`). Under **Physical Path**, choose the folder where the `BTSHTTPReceive.dll` is located (under `Program Files`) and click on **OK**.

Next, we need to set up a HTTP Receive Location. The HTTP flow that we are receiving in BizTalk can be both one-way or request-response (refer to the *Implementing messaging patterns* section).

When configuring the HTTP Receive Adapter, we need to specify the Virtual Directory and the DLL extension, as shown in the following screenshot:

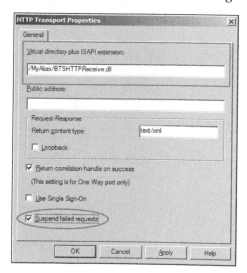

In some cases it also makes sense to enable **Suspend failed requests**. What this option does is to give BizTalk the responsibility of processing the message as soon as it has been submitted. If this option is not enabled, the caller will get an error back if the message could not be processed correctly (the Pipeline fails or no subscribers were found, and so on). This could be a valid set up, but in some situations it would make more sense to have the HTTP receive Adapter handle errors the same way as a FILE adapter, by taking responsibility of the message as soon as it was submitted and not bother the caller with any problems inside BizTalk, but rather suspend the message and deal with the problems internally and let the caller believe that everything processed as expected.

POP3

The **POP3 Adapter** is used to receive e-mails. The Adapter is a receive-only Adapter, because sending something through POP3 does not make any sense. The send equivalent of POP3 is usually SMTP, which we will look at in the following section.

 Under certain conditions, the POP3 Adapter will not run under a multi-server set up, and in these cases the use of clustering Hosts might be needed. Read more about this at http://msdn.microsoft.com/en-us/library/cc296808(v=bts.10).aspx.

Here are the possible parameters used for configuring the POP3 Adapter, with the most common parameters highlighted:

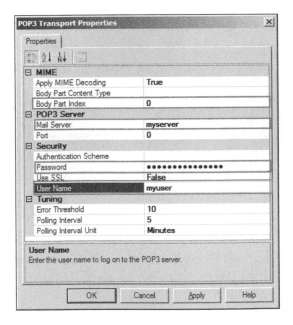

As a minimum, the **Mail Server, User Name, Password**, and **Body Part Index** need to be configured.

The body part index is used to choose what part of the mail will be considered the actual message inside BizTalk. **0** is the message body, **1** is the first attachment, **2** is the second attachment, and so on.

 Note that if **Body Part Content Type** is set to a specific content type, the algorithm for choosing which part of the mail to use is a bit more complex. For further information see http://msdn.microsoft.com/en-us/library/aa560251(v=bts.70).aspx).

SMTP

The **SMTP Adapter** is used for sending e-mails. In order to set up the SMTP Adapter, it is often a good idea to configure the **General Server Credentials** inside the SMTP Send Handler (refer to the *Managing Adapter Handlers* section).

The following screenshot shows the configuration screen of the SMTP Adapter:

On the Send Handler, the **SMTP server name** and the **From (e-mail address)** can be configured as they will likely be the same for all SMTP Send Ports. These parameters can be overwritten on a single Send Port if required.

When configuring the actual SMTP Adapter on a Send Port, carry out the following steps:

1. In the **General** tab, choose the e-mail address to send to in the **To:** textbox. Also give the email a subject and, if needed, specify a CC address.

2. In the **Compose** tab, choose either the **BizTalk message body part** as the e-mail body or choose **Text** for standard text.

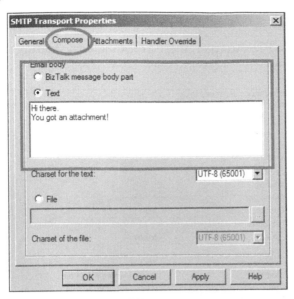

3. If a standard text is chosen, move to the **Attachments** tab:

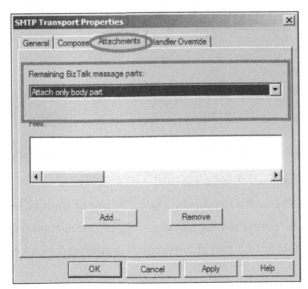

4. Choose **Attach only body part** to have the actual message as an attachment.

5. Use the **Handler Override** options if the SMTP server setup in the Adapter Handler should be overwritten.

FTP

The FTP Adapter can be used on both the receive and send side of BizTalk. On the receive side only single server setup is allowed.

When configuring the FTP Adapter, there are some basic features that apply to both sending and receiving:

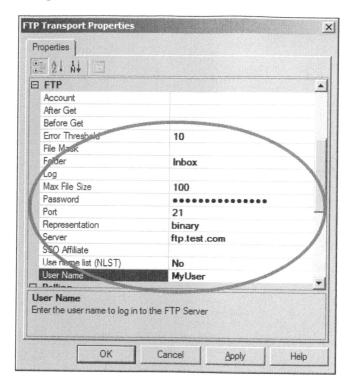

For all FTP configurations, at least the following four parameters should be configured:

- **Server**: The name or IP address of the FTP Server
- **User Name**: The username of the user logging onto the FTP Server
- **Password**: The password for the user logging onto the server
- **Folder**: The folder to either download files from (receive) or upload files to (send)

Receiving FTP

When using basic configuration, the FTP Server will delete the files from the FTP Server when they are processed, so that the same files are not fetched more than once.

However, this might not always be the desired functionality, as we might not be allowed to delete the files, the server could be holding files that are not just for us, but published for many subscribers.

In order to overcome this issue, new polling features have been introduced in BizTalk Server 2010, which are shown in the following screenshot:

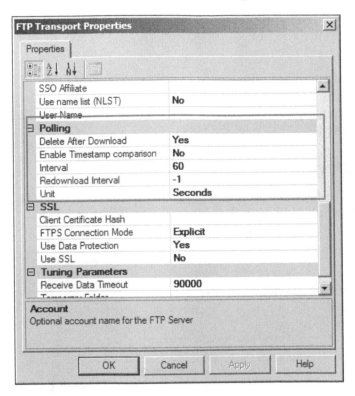

It is now possible to change the **Delete After Download** attribute on the FTP receive Adapter from **Yes** to **No**. By doing this, BizTalk will keep a track of which files have already been downloaded, and the same files will not be downloaded again even though they are still on the FTP Server. If existing files are edited and overwritten on the FTP Server and we want a new copy if changes happen to the files, we should also set the **Enable Timestamp comparison** to **Yes**. By doing this we will both get new files once, but also a fresh copy of any files that have changed on the FTP Server.

The interval (in the previous example is 60 seconds) should also be taken into consideration when setting up the receive FTP. This is an indication of how often BizTalk will look in the FTP folder for new messages. If set too often, we might experience too much network traffic and problems with the FTP Server. If it is set to only poll rarely, we might experience that messages submitted for BizTalk take a long time to process, because they are not polled by BizTalk often enough.

The FTP protocol does not have any proper lock mechanism, so if a large file is being written to the folder where BizTalk is polling from, BizTalk will start downloading the file as soon as the file is visible, and not necessarily when the file is complete. This problem needs to be addressed by the systems uploading the files to BizTalk in the FTP folders, either by creating the files with a temporary extension (`filename.xml.tmp`), and then removing the `.tmp` after the file is completed. In that case, we also need to set up the **File Mask** property on the FTP receive to look for files with the XML extension (`*.xml`).

Another way of dealing with the problem of files being downloaded by BizTalk before the file is fully written, is having the uploader upload the file to a temporary folder and then moving it to the correct folder where BizTalk is polling from, when the file is completed.

Sending FTP

When sending FTP, it is basically the core configuration that is needed (server, username, and so on). However, there are two other properties that are often relevant to take into consideration:

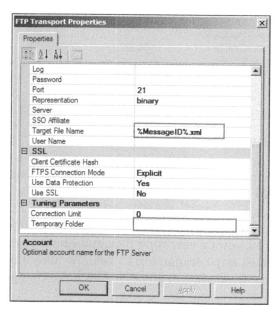

First, we will look at **Target File Name**. This is used to specify the name that BizTalk will give to the file written to the FTP Server. The default is %MessageID%.xml where %MessageID% will be replaced with an internal GUID unique for each message, so that no two files uploaded to an FTP Server from BizTalk will ever have the same name. The use of hardcoded names (such as Order.xml) is not recommended, as this will cause a failure on the send side if BizTalk tries to upload a file with the same name twice, and the first file has not been processed by the destination party yet.

It is also possible to use %SourceFileName% as a file mask in **Target File Name**. This will give the file the same name as it had when submitted to BizTalk by either a file or FTP. Again, we need to take into consideration whether or not two files could end up with the same name and therefore cause the FTP Send Adapter to fail, also this will only work if all files sent through the FTP Adapter were in fact received into BizTalk by either the File or FTP Adapter (See *Implementing messaging patterns* section).

Another property that might be useful when sending FTP is the **Temporary Folder**. This enables the adapter to upload the file to another, than the one specified in the **Temporary Folder** property, and move the file to the correct folder when upload has completed. As we discussed with the receive FTP Adapter, this might be useful because FTP does not have any proper locking mechanism.

File

The FILE adapter is one of the most used adapters, both for testing/demo but also for communicating with several legacy systems where the only protocol supported is exporting and importing files.

Receiving files

Configuring the **Receive File Adapter** requires a path to the folder where BizTalk should pick up files (**Receive folder**), as well as a **File mask** that specifies which type of files and/or filenames should be received. This folder can be either local or located on a file server somewhere on the network. Using local folders is not recommended when working with multi-server environments as that would cause BizTalk to have more than one file entry-point. It should be transparent to the surrounding environments how many BizTalk Servers a BizTalk Group contains.

If using a File Server, be aware that using mapped drive letters in the **Receive folder** might not work as intended (z:\Inbox), because it will use the mapped drives of the user running the Host Instance and not necessarily the mapped drives seen by the user configuring the port. Therefore, UNC paths are recommended (\\ServerName\Path\Inbox). The following screenshot shows the general configuration properties for a receive FILE Adapter:

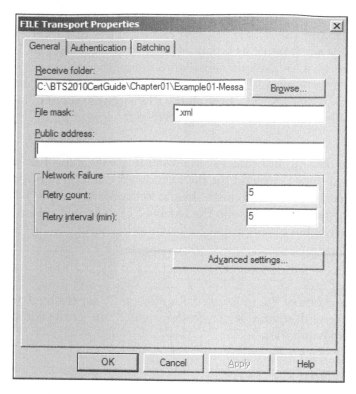

The **Receive folder** can only point to a single folder. It is not possible to have the same Receive Location probing in more than one folder. This limitation also includes subfolders.

If working on NTFS file systems, the FILE adapter will work using File System Events, so every time a file is submitted, BizTalk will be notified almost immediately and will start processing the file (except if Service Windows are implemented on the Receive Location).

Sending files

When using the FILE adapter on the send side, the configuration looks similar to the following screenshot:

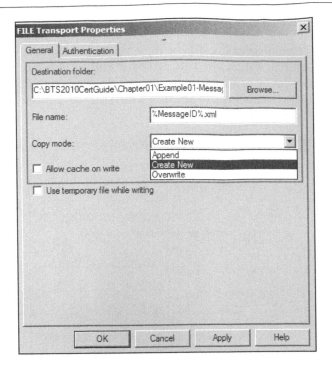

When sending files using the FILE adapter, we need to specify the **Destination folder** and the **File name**. The default file name is %MessageID%.xml, which will give the filename a unique GUID, to make sure no two files are given the same name.

Like the FTP Adapter, %SourceFileName% can also be used on the FILE adapter, but again we should use it with caution, as it will only work if the original message was received through either a FTP or FILE adapter.

It is also possible to set how the FILE adapter should write the file to folder using the **Copy** mode. There are three possible modes:

- **Append**: This will append the message to an existing file, if the file is already present. It requires a hardcoded filename, and it is usually used for FlatFiles (comma delimited, positional text files) and not for XML.

- **Create New** (default): This setting is the most commonly used setting. It will create, or try to create, a new file each time a message is sent to the port. Using this setting it is recommended that the filename is unique, which can be done by using %MessageID%.

- **Overwrite**: This also requires a hardcoded filename; it will overwrite an existing file with the file currently being written to a file folder. This is often used when dealing with daily inventory reports and so on where the old data is obsolete as soon as new data is present.

Credentials

If no credentials are specified in the FILE adapter configuration, it will be the user running the Host Instance which needs to have the correct amount of rights to the folder it is receiving from or sending to. If the user does not have the sufficient amount of credentials, we can supply another username and password for the FILE adapter to use, shown as follows:

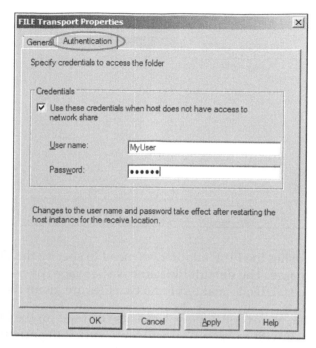

Click on the **Authentication** tab and specify a username and password, and that user will be used instead of the Host Instance user. This can be done for both receiving and sending files.

Configuring content-based routing

The following is a walk-through of a routing sample in BizTalk. The sample is done by using the FILE adapter only, and also no coding is done. The next chapter will introduce us to creating various BizTalk artifacts inside Visual Studio, but for now let us look at an example showing how BizTalk routes messages.

The setup is as follows:

- We receive files from both partner A and B in different file folders
- These files need to be routed to both System I and System II

Creating folders and Application

The first step is to create a Receive Port with two different Receive Locations.
We should to be able to pick up messages at two different file locations:

- `C:\BTS2010CertGuide\Chapter01\Example01-Messaging\FileDrop\`
  `PartnerA\Inbox`
- `C:\BTS2010CertGuide\Chapter01\Example01-Messaging\FileDrop\`
  `PartnerB\Inbox`

We should be able to send messages to two different systems (file locations):

- `C:\BTS2010CertGuide\Chapter01\Example01-Messaging\FileDrop\`
  `SystemI\Outbox`
- `C:\BTS2010CertGuide\Chapter01\Example01-Messaging\`
  `FileDropSystemII\Outbox`

Make sure that the BizTalk Host user has sufficient permissions for the folders. Give
the user **Full control** permissions on folder `C:\BTS2010CertGuide\Chapter01\`
`Example01-Messaging\FileDrop`, shown in the following screenshot:

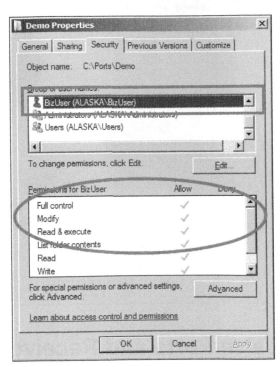

Next, we need to create an Application called **BTS2010CertGuide-Ch01**. In order to do this we need to carry out the following steps:

1. Open the BizTalk Administration Console.

2. Right-click on **Applications** and then click on **New** | **Application**:

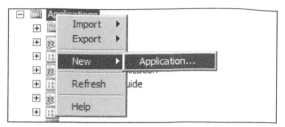

3. Name the new Application as **BTS2010CertGuide-Ch01** and click on **OK**.

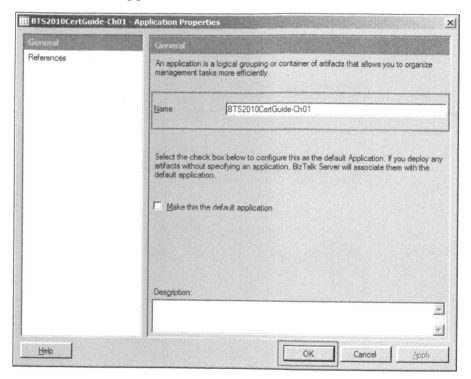

Creating Receive Ports and Receive Locations

Now we need to create a Receive Port inside our new Application and add two file Receive Locations, one for each partner (A and B). Carry out the following steps in order to do this:

1. In the **BTS2010CertGuide-Ch01** Application, right-click on **Receive Ports** and choose **New | One-way Receive Port**:

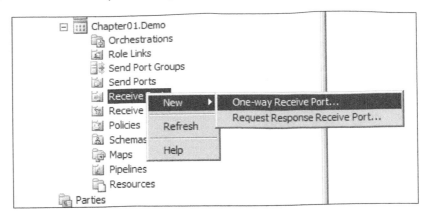

2. Name the Receive Port as **CG0101_Receive** and click on **OK**:

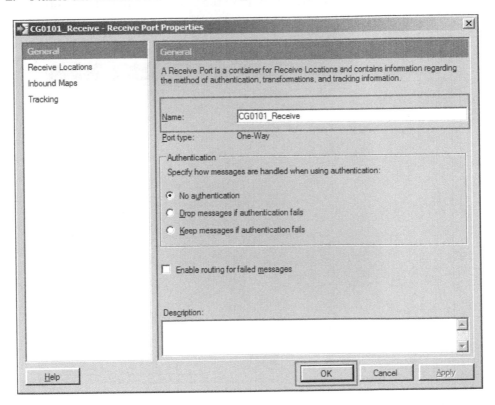

3. Right-click on **Receive Locations** and choose **New | One-way Receive Location**.

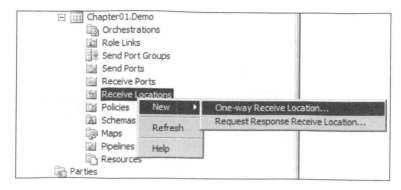

4. Select Receive Port **CG0101_Receive** and click on **OK**.

5. Name the location as **CG0101_ReceiveFromPartnerA_FILE**, choose **FILE** in **Transport Type** (adapter) and click on the **Configure** button, as shown in the following screenshot:

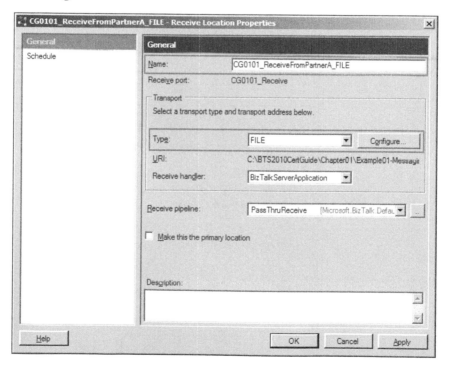

6. Configure the FILE adapter, as shown in the following screenshot and click on **OK**. (The **Receive folder** path is **C:\BTS2010CertGuide\Chapter01\ Example01-Messaging\FileDrop\PartnerA\Inbox**):

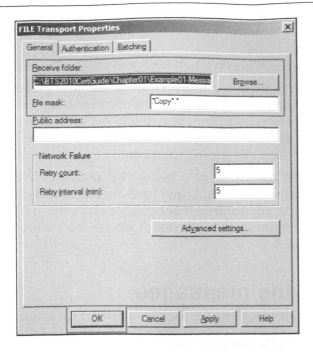

7. Click on **OK** again.

8. Make another Receive Location from steps 3 to 7, name it **PartnerB** instead of **PartnerA** and choosing the **PartnerB** file folder instead of **PartnerA**.

In the Administration Console our **Receive Locations** should now look similar to the following screenshot:

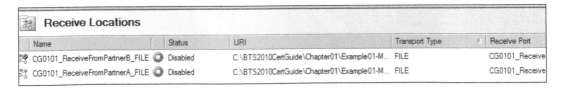

Testing the Receive Locations

Now we need to see that everything is running as intended, by testing the solution:

1. Create a small text file and fill it with a few characters and copy the file into each inbox folder (PartnerA, PartnerB). The files must consist of at least one character as the FILE adapter will throw away empty messages, as they do not make sense in a BizTalk perspective. Do not give the files a name containing the phrase "Copy".

2. Verify that the BizTalk Host Instance executing the Receive Locations is running.

3. Right-click on each **Receive Locations** and choose **Enable**.

4. Check the Event Viewer and verify that no BizTalk Server errors have been written to **Windows Logs/Application** when enabling the Receive Locations. If errors are present, examine them as they are most likely caused by the BizTalk Host user not having sufficient permission in the folders (refer to the *Creating Folders and Application* section).

5. Go to **C:\BTS2010CertGuide\Chapter01\Example01-Messaging\ FileDrop\PartnerA\Inbox**. Copy/paste the file into the same folder so that a copy is inserted, and confirm that BizTalk deletes the file. If the file is deleted by BizTalk, it means that our **PartnerA** locations are working. Do the same test for **PartnerB**.

Debugging the messages

Now let us examine what happened to the messages that we had submitted to BizTalk:

1. Open the Event Viewer again and we should find four errors (two for each message submitted).

2. Open the last error submitted in the Event Viewer, it should look something similar to the following screenshot:

General | Details |

A message received by adapter "FILE" on receive location "CG0101_ReceiveFromPartnerA_FILE" with URI "C:\BTS2010CertGuide\Chapter01\Example01-Messaging\FileDrop\PartnerA\Inbox *Copy*.*" is suspended.
Error details: The published message could not be routed because no subscribers were found. This error occurs if the subscribing orchestration or send port has not been enlisted, or if some of the message properties necessary for subscription evaluation have not been promoted. Please use the Biztalk Administration console to troubleshoot this failure.
MessageId: {851DBE7D-C24B-4F3A-8138-14CB4DBEE8F0}
InstanceID: {EA898458-DA2D-402B-A467-C240737F183E}

What BizTalk is telling us here is that even though received processing of the messages was successful, the messages could not be routed, because there were no subscribers. In other words, no Send Ports or Orchestrations were created with a subscription matching the Context of the messages.

Now we will examine the Context of one of the messages that failed to be routed:

1. Go to the **Group Hub**, by clicking on the **BizTalk Group** folder in the Administration Console, and then press *F5* to refresh the dashboard showing in the right pane.

2. We should now see four suspended items:

3. Click on the **Resumable** link. (The **Non-resumable** instances are not important right now. They are used internally by BizTalk, and will not make sense to look at until we start working with Pipelines). We should now see the following screen:

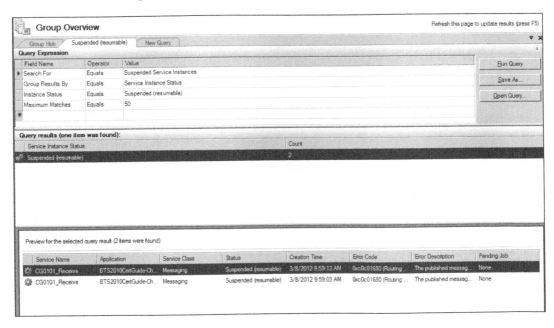

4. Double-click on one of the suspended items:

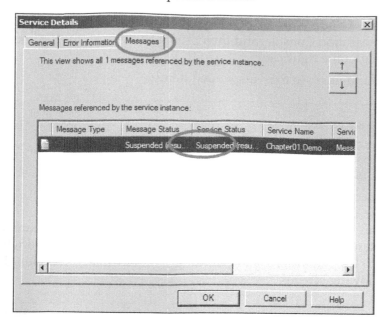

5. Choose the **Messages** tab, and double-click on the message:

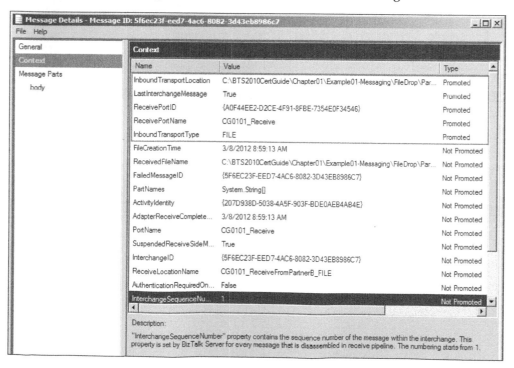

6. Choose **Context** and click on **Type** until the promoted properties are shown on top.

7. Examine the five promoted properties. These are the only properties we can use for subscription for now. The best candidate for subscription might be the **ReceivePortName** with the value of **CG0101_Receive**.

Setting up a Send Port

Now we will make a Send Port that subscribes to all messages with **ReceivePortName** with the value of **CG0101_Receive** in the **Context**:

1. Create a new Send Port by right-clicking on the **Send Port** folder and choosing **New | Static One-way Send Port**.

2. Fill in **Name** and **Type** as shown in the following screenshot and click on **Configure**.

3. The **FILE Transport Properties** window will pop up. Fill in the **Destination folder** path (**C:\BTS2010CertGuide\Chapter01\Example01-Messaging\ FileDrop\SystemI\Outbox**) and the **File name** as shown in the following screenshot. Click on **OK**:

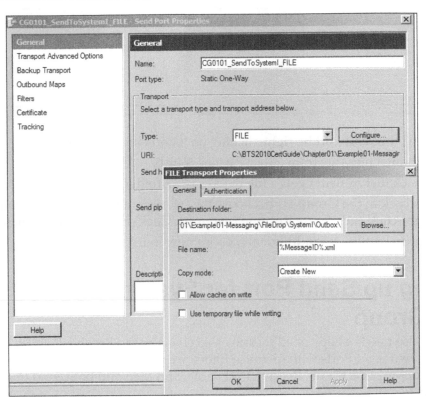

4. Choose the **Filters** page. Select **BTS.ReceivePortName** in the **Property** drop-down list. Leave the **Operator** as == and type the Receive Port name in the **Value** textbox. (Note that string values should not be placed inside quotation marks) and click on **OK**:

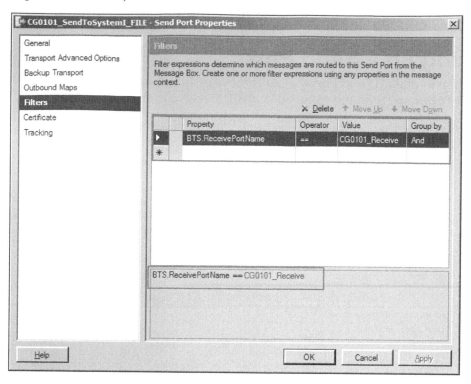

5. Start the Send Port by right-clicking on it and choosing **Start**.
6. Submit a message from either Partner A or B.
7. Check that System I gets a file in its Outbox folder.
8. Go back to the **Group Hub**, choose the two resumable suspended items, right-click and choose **Resume Instances**. Click on **Yes** and then click on **OK**.
9. Verify that the two additional files are now in the System I folder.

Setting up Send Port for System II and a Send Port Group

System II also needs a copy of all messages received by the Receive Port. So instead of making two Send Ports with identical filters, we will make a Send Port Group with the subscription for the Receive Port name, and then add both Send Ports to the group:

1. Create a new Send Port for System II, the same way we created the first Send Port, with *SystemII* in its name instead of *SystemI* and also use the `SystemII outbox` folder instead. Do not give the new Send Port any filter. Start the Send Port.

2. Create a new Send Port Group, by right-clicking on the **Send Port Groups** folder and choosing **New | Send Port Group…**:

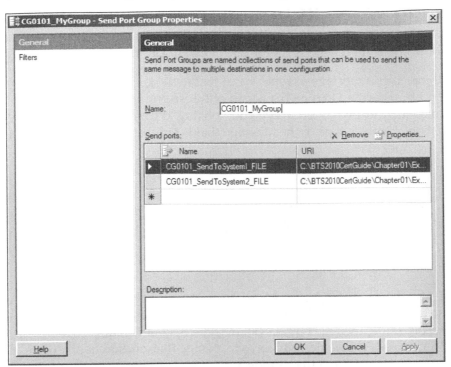

3. Give the group a name as shown in the preceding screenshot, and add the two Send Ports to the group.

4. Give the group a filter with the Receive Port name, just as we did with the first Send Port and click on **OK**

5. Right-click on the group and start it.

6. Submit a message from one of the partners.

7. Notice how System II got one message, but System I got two. This is because a Send Port inside a Send Port Group will have two subscriptions: its own as well as the group subscription. If both of them are met, the port will receive two messages.

8. Go to the System I Send Port, and remove the subscription inside the **Filter** page, by clicking on **Delete** and then on **OK**.

9. Test again; this time System I should only get one copy.

Implementing messaging patterns

When working with BizTalk, the design considerations are very important. A bad design might result in poor performance, difficulty in changing the solution if the surrounding environment changes, and redundant code.

Working with canonical messages

One of the design patterns that we should always try to meet (unless there is a good reason for doing something else) is the use of **canonical messages** inside BizTalk.

If BizTalk receives a message of type A and that message needs to be sent to another system and transformed to type B, instead of transforming directly from A to B, we should make up our own internal type not looking at the structure of either type A or B, but rather make a type of the message that is independent of both types (type I).

This will require two transformations, one from type A to type I, and another from type I to type B.

We should also make sure that only the canonical/internal messages hits the MessageBox, so the Map *A to I* should be applied on the Receive Port, and *I to B* on the Send Port.

This pattern has the following advantages:

- If we receive messages from various partners/systems (type Ai, Aii, Aiii, and so on) and we Map all of these different structures to a canonical type on the receive side, then the target system (type B) could change structure or format. In this case, we would only have to change the solution in one place, the transformation from the canonical type to B.

- If more subscribers are interested in the message, and we make transformations directly from message type A to all of the desired formats of the subscribers, and we start receiving the messages in other formats, we would again need to make transformations from the new format to each of the subscribers, instead of just transforming the new format to the internal format.

This is also the case when working with Orchestrations. Try not to use the Adapter-specific Schemas inside the Orchestrations. Instead use internal versions of the messages. Use these internal versions inside the Orchestrations and then Map from and to the internal Schemas in the Receive and Send Ports. By doing this, we do not have to recompile (let alone recode) an Orchestration if a message type on a Send or Receive Port was changed. The structure of the XML sent and received from the old and new messages would be different, but if we are only dealing with internal messages in our Orchestrations, only the Maps on the Send and Receive Ports would need to be changed.

De-batching

Another pattern we should try to implement, for most solutions, is the use of **singular messages** inside BizTalk. If we receive batches, such as several items inside the same message, we should de-batch them into individual items on the receive side of BizTalk (the Receive Pipeline).

The rule of thumb is that the solution should act in the same way if we receive one large file containing 10 orders, as it should, if we receive 10 orders in 10 files.

BizTalk cannot handle the items individually if they are kept as a batch through BizTalk. If we receive orders and some subscribers are only interested in orders containing a specific customer number, we would have no means (at least not with normal content-based routing) of subscribing to just those messages if all of them were kept inside a batch.

There are other cases where keeping multiple items inside a batch and not de-batching them makes sense. If a solution picks up a large batch of products, because full inventory is done once a day and all subscribers are interested in seeing these products as a whole inventory report, we should not try to de-batch them. Also note that as BizTalk comes with great de-batching functionality on the receive side there is no automatic way of batching these items again. If some subscribers need the inventory report as it was received and others need them individually, then we would need to keep the batch inside BizTalk, and then do some extra code (possibly using Orchestrations), to also make de-batched copies.

In other words, a de-batched message is not easily assembled again with the same items in the same order.

Using the correct flow

We often stand with a decision whether to use a one-way or request-response flow. The following table describes some of scenarios where it makes sense to use one over the other:

Direction	Type	Usage
Receive	Request-response	Used only if the caller submitting messages to BizTalk needs an answer back or if it is vital to the calling system to know that everything in the flow went well
Receive	One-way	Used for all other cases than the ones described in request-response
Send	Request-response	Used if BizTalk calls a system and needs an answer back from that system
Send	One-way	Used for all other cases

It is important not to use request-response when only one-way is needed. If calling a Web Service on a Send Port, it does not provide us with more reliability if we can use a request-response port, instead of a one-way port. The one-way port will, just like all other adapters, wait for the service to finish and the acknowledgement that everything went well until the message is removed from the MessageBox. Also, using request-response when not needed, will give us less performance and less flexibility, because a request-response message submitted to the MessageBox can only have one subscriber.

Adapter independence

When designing, whenever possible try not to make BizTalk solutions where code or logic is dependent on messages being received or sent using specific adapters.

It might seem like a good idea to send files to an FTP Server using the %SourceFileName% macro in the **Target File Name** property, because we want to give the target server the same filename as the file had when we received it either by file or FTP. If this is a requirement, then this is of course how the solution should be made. However, always try to focus on whether the solution will work if we change the adapter. If tomorrow we start receiving messages from both a file folder and also from an Oracle database, well then the %SourceFileName% logic on our Send Ports will fail to work for the messages received from Oracle, simply because no original filename exists.

On the send side, people also tend to hardcode specific adapter properties inside Orchestrations, which would result in a situation where changing the adapter type would require us to change and recompile Orchestrations.

Test your knowledge

1. HWLC Motors, is sending XML orders to our BizTalk server using FTP and BizTalk picks up the messages using a FILE adapter. All orders have been signed by the partner using certificates. We need to implement a secure solution where only orders from EAS Industry get through the processing inside BizTalk. If any orders with an unknown signature are received, we want to keep those messages as we would still assume they are valid. What certificate needs to be stored where for this to work in BizTalk?

    a. Install EAS's public key certificate in the Current User/Personal store

    b. Install EAS's public key certificate in the Local Machine/Other People store

    c. Install our own private key certificate in the Current User/Personal store

    d. Install our own private key certificate in the Local Machine/Other People store

2. We receive XML from several trading partners through Receive Port *RP1*. At times, the XML is not well formed, and the XMLReceive Pipelines throws errors and the messages are suspended. Our partner coordinator Brian has requested that invalid XML be sent to him in an e-mail, instead of being suspended in BizTalk. How would you achieve this? (Choose all that apply):

    a. Set up e-mail alerting on the server if errors occur in the Event Viewer with BizTalk Server as the source.

    b. Create a Send Port: *SP1*, using the SMTP Adapter and target it to Brian's e-mail address. Set up a filter on the Send Port with the following format: **BTS.ReceivePortName == RP1 and (ErrorReport.ErrorType Exists)**.

    c. Enable **routing for failed messages** on the Send Port *SP1*.

    d. Enable **routing for failed messages** on the Receive Port *RP1*.

    e. Create a Send Port: *SP1*, using the SMTP Adapter and target it to Brian's e-mail address. Set up a filter on the Send Port with the following format: **BTS.ReceivePortName == RP1 and (BTS.FaultName Exists)**.

3. HWLC has several Send Ports that point to different internal systems. One of the Send Ports targets the company's ERP system. The adapter used is an HTTP Adapter. The ERP administrator wants to take the system offline for the next 24 hours, and no messages should be sent to the system during that time. How should we accomplish this with the minimum amount of interference with the other systems?

    a. Disable all Receive Locations so that no messages are received in BizTalk for the next 24 hours

    b. Stop the ERP Send Port and start it again when the system comes back online

    c. Unenlist the ERP Send Port and start it again when the system comes back online

    d. Stop all in-process BizTalk Services

4. HWLC receives XML from an FTP site using a standard FTP Receive Adapter. The messages received are of type: `http://namespace#Root`. You set up a Send Port with the following filter: **BTS.MessageType == http://namespace#Root**. The schema for the message type is also deployed. You start your Application and the Receive Location starts receiving messages from the FTP site. However, no messages are sent through the Send Port, and when examining the Event Viewer, you realize that you get the following error: **The published messages could not be routed, because no subscribers were found**. You examine the **Context** of the messages suspended and realize that the message type is not **Promoted**. What should you do?

    a. Write a custom Pipeline component that promotes the message type.

    b. Enable **Failed Message Routing** on the Receive Port and change the filter on the Send Port to **ErrorReport.ReceivePortName == [Name of Receive Port]**.

    c. Change the Pipeline on the Receive Location from PassThruReceive to XMLReceive.

    d. Create an Orchestration that receives XMLDocument messages and bind it to the Receive Port. Finally, have the Orchestration send the message to the Send Port.

5. You are receiving messages from customers sending mails with attachments through an Exchange Server 2010. You want BizTalk to process the messages. How should you approach this?

   a. Use the FTP Adapter to receive messages from the exchange server

   b. Use the FILE adapter to receive messages from the exchange server

   c. Use the POP3 Adapter to receive messages from the exchange server, and set the **body part index** to 0

   d. Use the POP3 Adapter to receive messages from the exchange server, and set the **body part index** to 1

Summary

This chapter has dealt with some of the basics of BizTalk, looking at the subscription engine, Ports, and Adapters. You should now have a basic knowledge of how BizTalk works, and how to navigate through the Administration Console. Next, we will look at XML, Schemas, Pipelines, and start using Visual Studio.

2
Developing BizTalk Artifacts—Creating Schemas and Pipelines

This chapter maps to parts of the Developing BizTalk Artifacts section of the exam. It is not an introduction to developing BizTalk Artifacts, instead it will point out some of the most relevant areas where you should have a proven practice today in your BizTalk development; these in turn are areas that you need to know about when taking the exam.

This builds on and leverages the knowledge we acquired in the first chapter about how to compose messaging architectures by involving Schemas and Pipelines instead of just passing untyped messages. The Developing BizTalk Artifacts objective is split into three logically coherent chapters of manageable size, so that you can focus your effort on the area where you most need to improve. This is the first, and it covers these main areas:

- Creating Schemas
- Creating Pipelines
- Test your knowledge

The section in the certification skills measured called Construct Messages does not exist as a single self-contained section, but instead is covered in different parts of this book.

After this chapter, we will have learned how to create clear reusable schemas. We will send and receive cleartext as well as signed and encrypted messages. We will work with simple messages and enveloped messages in batches and use Pipelines to validate and split them.

Schemas and Pipelines explicitly targeting EDI and AS2 are excluded from this chapter. Information on EDI is included in *Chapter 8, Implementing Extended Capabilities*.

Creating Schemas

Creating schemas is core to handling messages in BizTalk Server. It's not uncommon to come across poorly created Schemas, without namespaces, with only string types, with mandatory fields not specified and not followed, or simply with everything optional. To create truly usable and explanatory schemas that promote re-use and coherence, we need to go further. This section helps with that.

Type of Schemas

There are essentially four types of Schemas that you can create in BizTalk Server:

- XML Schemas
    - Envelope Schemas
- Flat File Schemas
- Property Schemas

XML Schemas

A Schema, or **XML Schema**, describes the format of an XML file, using a standardized form. Most of the Schemas you will typically see in a BizTalk Server solution are XML Schemas. Even Flat File structures are described using XML Schemas, with added annotations, as are Envelope Schemas.

Envelope Schemas

An Envelope Schema is really a type of XML Schema, but is has a very special purpose: it serves as a container for one or more messages, and although it can be otherwise empty, it often contains header-like information. When you specify that a Schema is an Envelope Schema, you are saying that the body content is contained in a node within the Schema, at a set XPath location.

BizTalk is capable of both receiving and sending messages with envelopes.

 Envelope Schemas are covered in more depth later in the chapter.

Flat File Schemas

BizTalk Server uses the XSD standard of annotations to include information that helps to also explain what an instance of a Schema may look like if it were a Flat text file instead of a structured XML file.

Flat files may be delimited:

```
Car,ABC123,Audi,RS6,NurburgringBlue
Car,123ABC,Corvette,ZR1,DaytonaRed
```

Or positional:

```
Car     ABC123     Audi       RS6     NurburgringBlue
Car     123ABC     Corvette   ZR1     DaytonaRed
```

Or, they may be a combination (which in some sense is often the case with positional files, since rows of Flat files are commonly delimited by some combination of carriage return and linefeed characters).

Property Schemas

Property Schemas are a special type of Schema. These Schemas are not created to describe messages and instead describe context properties. They have multiple root nodes (in the form of elements) and no hierarchy. These root nodes represent so-called promoted properties, and you populate them by promoting values from non-repeating SimpleContent records, elements, or attributes, of Message Schemas. The act of promotion creates associations between the fields of the Message Schema and the fields of the Property Schema. At runtime, BizTalk Server will identify these associations and promote the fields into the message context, so that they can be used for routing.

Schema Identity

The identity of a schema, and subsequently that of a message, is crucial to all message handling in BizTalk Server. There are a couple of different properties that are important when handling the identity of a Schema. Since BizTalk lives and operates in both the .NETand XML worlds, those identities also identify the Schema in both those worlds.

XML Identity

The XML identity of a Schema determines the identity of the Schema file, and also the identity of a message instance based on the Schema as a separate entity. This is true regardless of whether the Schema is then made part of a .NET BizTalk component or not.

targetNamespace

Sometimes, there are entities that will occur multiple times within an integration solution. To make sure they are uniquely distinguished, you use the `targetNamespace` property. `targetNamespace` is to a Schema what a namespace is to a .NET object. Take for example the object Color in .NET. It exists in many different namespaces. The same thing might over time be true for objects in an integration solution. In Schemas, it is the root node that acts as the class name in this analogy. Perhaps a `PurchaseOrder` entity (root node) will be described in multiple Schemas, with small variations in their structure based on, say, the vendor they belong to. Their `targetNamespace` is then what separates them. You should never have a Schema without a `targetNamespace`, if you can avoid it. There are proven Pipeline component examples of adding a namespace to a message being sent to BizTalk Server, if it does not have one arriving to BizTalk.

MessageType

In BizTalk Server, every message that is recognized and parsed by a disassembler has MessageType. MessageType is a combination of `targetNamespace` and the root node. MessageType is heavily involved in routing and acts as the sole filter expression in many solutions, especially in service or enterprise bus architectures. This is one of the primary reasons why you should make sure that you have a good `targetNamespace` to match your root node, so that the MessageType, represented as `targetNamespace#Rootnode`, is unique within your system. If it is not unique, then it will be a poor candidate for routing, and you will not be able to disassemble a message with that MessageType unless you specifically point out the Schema to be used.

Messages that are not parsed by a disassembler do not have a MessageType. Such messages can travel through Ports and Orchestrations, but as they are untyped, they can never be used as input to a Map.

.NET Identity

As mentioned, a Schema also has a .NET class representation, and as any .NET class, it has a namespace and a typename.

Namespace

The default namespace in a BizTalk project is that of the name of the project, but it can be changed to anything you want.

Typename

The typename is by default the same as the filename of the Schema (and not the root node), but again, it can be changed to anything you want.

Promoted property and distinguished fields

Promoting a node to a property field (or promoting a property for short) means to make a node value available in the context of a message. You will typically promote properties from a Schema that you want to use as part of your routing logic. You can promote only parts of a Schema that are not reoccurring (that have their Max Occurs value set to 1, which is also the default if nothing is set). You may also feel tempted to promote properties, so that you can more easily access them in places such as Orchestrations or in Pipeline components. Don't. For easy access in Orchestrations, you use distinguished fields that allow you easy and familiar IntelliSense and dot notation in expressions. Other good reasons to promote a property is when there is information not contained in the body of the message, say header or envelope information that you want accessible later on. Also, when you set up correlation, which implicitly means setting up routing logic, the property that you wish to correlate on must be promoted.

Not all context properties are promoted, and not all context properties come from Schemas. Many parts of the BizTalk infrastructure, such as adapters and Pipeline components, write to the context. One example of this is ReceivedFileName (http://schemas.microsoft.com/BizTalk/2003/file-properties#ReceivedFileName or FILE.ReceivedFileName) that the FILE adapter writes to the context. Another example is MessageType (http://schemas.microsoft.com/BizTalk/2003/system-properties#MessageType or BTS.MessageType) that the XML Disassembler promotes.

Promoting nodes as property fields

To promote a node as a property field, perform the following steps in Visual Studio 2010:

1. Create or locate a Property Schema.
2. Create or identify the element in the Property Schema that you wish to promote a property to.

3. Open your Schema. In this case, we are using a `SimplifiedCar` Schema, as follows:

Downloading the example code

You can download the example code files for all Packt books you have purchased from your account at http://www.packtpub.com. If you purchased this book elsewhere, you can visit http://www.packtpub.com/support and register to have the files e-mailed directly to you.

```xml
<xs:schema xmlns="http://Chapter02_Example01.Schemas.
SimplifiedCar" xmlns:b="http://schemas.microsoft.com/BizTalk/2003"
targetNamespace="http://Chapter02_Example01.Schemas.SimplifiedCar"
xmlns:xs="http://www.w3.org/2001/XMLSchema">
  <xs:element name="Car">
    <xs:complexType>
      <xs:sequence>
        <xs:element name="RegistrationNo" type="xs:string" />
        <xs:element name="Make" type="xs:string" />
        <xs:element name="Model" type="xs:string" />
        <xs:element name="Color" type="xs:string" />
      </xs:sequence>
    </xs:complexType>
  </xs:element>
</xs:schema>
```

4. Bring up the context menu for the Schema and select **Promote | Show Promotions...**, to bring up the **Promote Properties** dialog shown in the following screenshot:

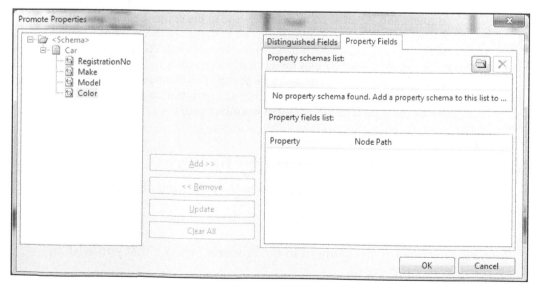

5. Select the **Property Fields** tab and press the button that looks like a folder, to bring up the **BizTalk Type Picker** shown in the following screenshot:

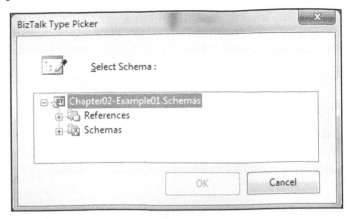

6. Locate your Property Schema. You need to have one already created, that holds a property that you wish to promote the field to.

7. In the Schema view, on the left-hand side, in the **Promote Properties** dialog, select the (non-repeating) node in the Schema that you wish to promote.

8. Click on the **Add >>** button to promote the node as a **Property field**.

9. Select the property in the Property Schema that you wish to promote the node to, in this case, the Property Schema has a property called **Color**, as shown in the following screenshot:

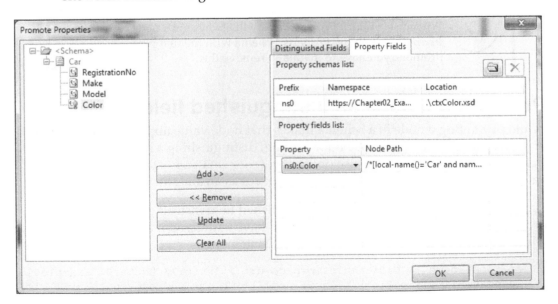

10. Complete the process by clicking on the **OK** button in the lower-right corner.

 All Schemas used in examples in this section can be found in the solution `C:\BTS2010CertGuide\Chapter02\Example01-SchemaConstructs\Chapter02-Example01\Chapter02-Example01.sln`.

Quick Promotion

The **Quick Promotion** option that is available, if we bring up the context menu for a selected node in the Schema Editor, is a faster way to promote properties, should you be ok with some default behavior. Choosing to **Quick Promote** a property will do the following:

1. Create a new Property Schema (if it does not already exist) in the `projects root` folder using the name specified on the Schema files properties in the `Default Property Schemas` property, which by default is `PropertySchema.xsd`.

2. Place a new property in that Property Schema, named the same as the node we are promoting (unless that property already exists in the Property Schema, in which case it will not create a new node, but instead assume that you meant to promote to the existing property).

3. Promote the field that you choose to quick promote to that property.

 When using Quick Promote, you will always get a node called `Property_1` in the Property Schema with the first property you promote; you have to manually remove this.

Promoting a node as distinguished field

While promoting a node in a Schema makes that node value appear as a promoted property and enables you to use it for routing, distinguishing a node does none of that. Instead, it enables you to use dot syntax (`root.subrecord.node`) to access the value of a node within an Orchestration. It serves as an alias for an XPath statement.

Had we made the `Color` property a distinguished field instead of a promoted property, it would have meant that we could have addressed it as `Car.Color`, which in turn would have aliased this XPath statement:

```
/*[local-name()='Car' and namespace-uri()='http://Chapter02_Example01.
Schemas.SimplifiedCar']/*[local-name()='Color' and namespace-uri()='']
```

Let's look at the process to do that. To promote a node to a distinguished field, you perform the following steps:

1. Open your Schema.

2. Bring up the context menu for the Schema and select **Promote** | **Show Promotions...**, to bring up the **Promote Properties** dialog.

3. Select the **Distinguished Fields** tab.

4. In the Schema view, on the left-hand side in the **Promote Properties** dialog, select the (non-repeating) node in the Schema that you wish to promote.

5. Click on the **Add >>** button to promote the node as a **Distinguished field**, as shown in the following screenshot:

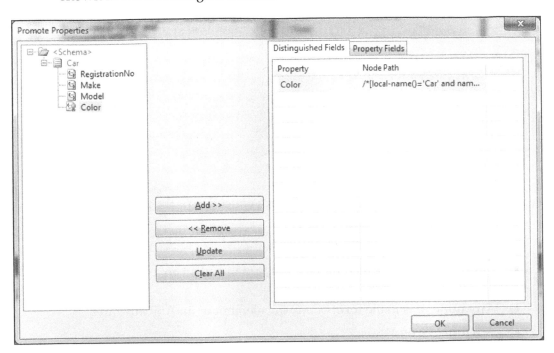

6. Complete the process by clicking on the **OK** button in the lower-right corner.

Creating the structure of a Schema

In BizTalk Server, Schemas are made up of **records**, **elements**, and **attributes**.

A sample structure may look something like:

```
RootNode
|
+-SubRecord1
|   @attribute1
|   element1
|
\-SubRecord2
    element2
```

As XML, it would be:

```
<RootNode>
  <SubRecord1 attribute1="">
    <element1 />
  </SubRecord1>
  <SubRecord2>
    <element2 />
  </SubRecord2>
</RootNode>
```

A **record** is a container node that can contain a collection of the following:

- **Complex types**: They include other records or groups (`Sequence`, `Choice`, or `All`)
- **Simple types**: They include `strings`, `ints`, and so on, contained in child elements or attributes.
- **Any node**: It is in the form of an Any element or an Any attribute.
- **Attribute Groups**

Elements and attributes are, in contrast, simple types, such as `string` or `int`. There are a few things to consider when choosing whether to use an element or an attribute, such as max occurrence, sequence, length, and size of values. Another difference between them is how they are visually represented in a Schema or an XML document instance.

Here is a sample Schema shown in the BizTalk Schema Editor that uses a mix of records, elements, and attributes:

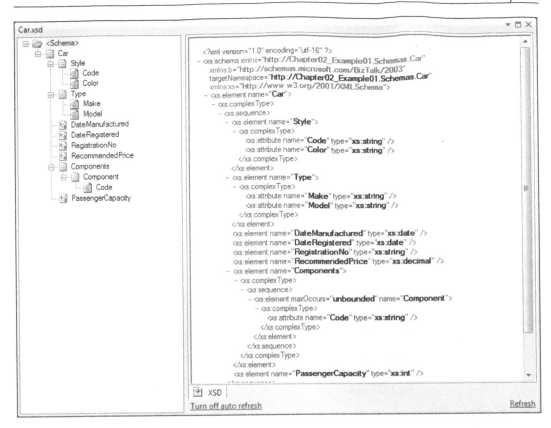

To best describe the format of a message, you will most likely combine records, elements and attributes. You should also set their namespaces as well as define types, multiplicity, restrictions, and other properties, according to how they are used. This produces clear and usable Schemas that represent the actual rules applied to the content, and not just the structure.

Creating reoccurring parts of a Schema

Often in Schemas, there are certain parts of it that need to occur more than once. Take for example Car, which is made up of multiple Component nodes, as follows:

```
<xs:schema xmlns="http://Chapter02_Example01.Schemas.
CarComponents" xmlns:b="http://schemas.microsoft.com/BizTalk/2003"
targetNamespace="http://Chapter02_Example01.Schemas.CarComponents"
xmlns:xs="http://www.w3.org/2001/XMLSchema">
  <xs:element name="Car">
    <xs:complexType>
      <xs:sequence>
        <xs:element name="Components">
```

```xml
        <xs:complexType>
          <xs:sequence>
            <xs:element maxOccurs="unbounded" name="Component">
              <xs:complexType>
                <xs:attribute name="Code" type="xs:string" />
              </xs:complexType>
            </xs:element>
          </xs:sequence>
        </xs:complexType>
      </xs:element>
    </xs:sequence>
  </xs:complexType>
</xs:element>
</xs:schema>
```

In this case, the Component element has its maxOccurs property set to Unbounded (which can also be written as * in BizTalk server's Visual Studio Schema Editors. The XML document matching this Schema may look like the following:

```xml
<ns0:Car xmlns:ns0="http://Chapter02_Example01.Schemas.CarComponents">
  <Components>
    <Component Code="01" />
    <Component Code="02" />
    <Component Code="03" />
  </Components>
</ns0:Car>
```

There are also occasions where you may prefer to describe that the group of nodes beneath a record may appear multiple times, even though the node itself does not. The preceding Car XML document may as well have been created and will validate equally well against the following Schema:

```xml
<xs:schema xmlns="http://Chapter02_Example01.Schemas.
CarComponents" xmlns:b="http://schemas.microsoft.com/BizTalk/2003"
targetNamespace="http://Chapter02_Example01.Schemas.CarComponents"
xmlns:xs="http://www.w3.org/2001/XMLSchema">
  <xs:element name="Car">
    <xs:complexType>
      <xs:sequence>
        <xs:element name="Components">
          <xs:complexType>
            <xs:sequence maxOccurs="unbounded">
              <xs:element name="Component">
                <xs:complexType>
                  <xs:attribute name="Code" type="xs:string" />
```

```
            </xs:complexType>
          </xs:element>
        </xs:sequence>
       </xs:complexType>
     </xs:element>
   </xs:sequence>
  </xs:complexType>
</xs:element>
</xs:schema>
```

It's hard to give a clear example of when one is more preferable to the other. In any case, as XML is inheritably hierarchical, creating Hierarchical Schemas is preferable to keeping the structure flat.

Creating Envelope Schemas

Creating envelopes is not so much a part of creating the structure of a single message as it is about creating the structure of a batch of messages. When we create an envelope, we are saying that this Schema (the envelope) will contain one or more messages that are based on other Schemas.

The following steps are required to create an Envelope Schema, once you have a BizTalk project that you want to create it in:

1. Select **Add ... | New Item** from the context menu of the project, and choose to add a new Schema. Name it CarEnvelope.

2. Select the root node, and rename it to ManufacturingReport.

3. Create an attribute below ManufacturingReport, call it BatchNo, and make it an int type.

4. Create a record below ManufacturingReport and call it Cars.

5. Create an Any element below Cars, and set **Max Occurs** to **Unbounded**, to allow for many cars to be sent inside the envelope.

6. Now select the **Schema** node, and in the **Properties** window, change the value of the **Envelope** property to **Yes**.

7. Select the root node ManufacturingReport, and in the **Property** window, change the value of the **Body XPath** property to point to the Cars node.

The finished Envelope Schema looks like the following screenshot:

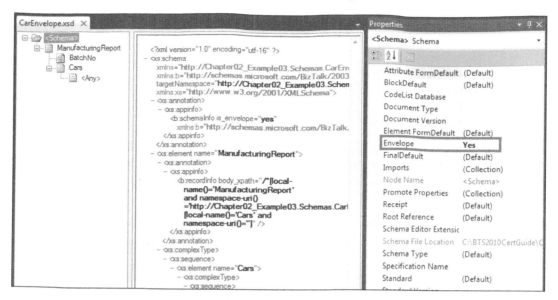

Now we have created an Envelope Schema with an Any node. We can use it to send in any number of documents within it.

The Envelope Schema we just created is available in the `Chapter02-Example03` sample. This sample is expanded in the Pipeline section of this chapter to show the Pipeline configuration used with envelopes when splitting messages and configuring recoverable interchange processing.

Flat File Envelopes

Messages based on Flat File Schemas can be received in batches as well. The concepts of envelopes applies just as equally to Flat files as it does to XML messages, however, it is configured slightly differently and instead includes configuring Header Schemas, Document Schemas, and Trailer Schemas. The preceding process applies to XML Schemas only.

Datatypes and formatting

To create a usable and descriptive Schema, it is important to not only create the correct structure, but also to describe the content of all nodes, as best as possible.

One of the basics of describing a Schema field is to set the field's datatype correctly. The default datatype is `string`, which arguably is the most commonly used, but there are many different types to choose from, of which other commonly used ones are `int`, `decimal`, `date`, and `Boolean`. One of the first things to do is to make sure to select appropriate datatypes, as follows:

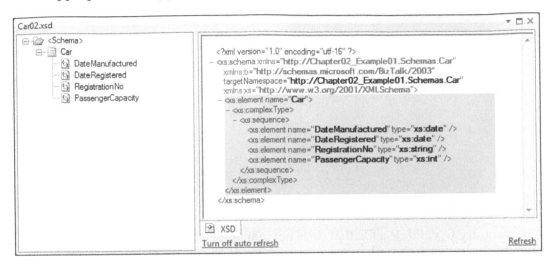

Specifying custom formatting restrictions

You may, and should, choose to apply additional restrictions or derivation of the basic datatype, so that the Schema becomes really descriptive of what the expected content could look like.

Restricting string values

Say for example that we wanted to create a restriction on a registration for a car so that it matches the format of a Swedish license plate — three uppercase letters (A-Z) followed by three integers (0-9). This is how we can accomplish it:

1. Set **Base Data Type** to **xs:string**.
2. Set (leave the default) **Derived By** property to `Restriction`.

3. Set the **Pattern** property by adding a regular expression in a suitable pattern to the list of allowed patterns. In this case, a regular expression of **^[A-Z]{3}\d{3}$** would do the trick. This will produce the following Schema:

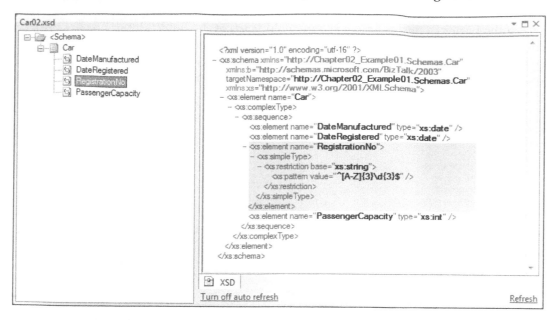

When you try to validate a file that does not match the criteria, you will get something similar to the following exception inside Visual Studio (paths and filenames omitted for brevity):

```
Invoking component...
```

```
error BEC2004: The 'RegistrationNo' element is invalid - The value
'RegistrationNo_0' is invalid according to its datatype 'String' - The
Pattern constraint failed.
```

```
error BEC2004: Validate Instance failed for schema Car02.xsd, file: <
Car02_output.xml>.
```

Controlling date formats

Say that we wanted to create a date format that matches the pattern **yyyyMMdd**, for example, 20110203 (February 3 2011). In this case, you do not have as much flexibility out of an XML file adhering to an XML Schema, and only the ISO 8601-derived format of CCYY-MM-DD is allowed. You can add a pattern to restrict what values you allow in these fields, but you cannot change the format. Should you use other date formats in XML, you must treat those fields as strings.

If you are accepting Flat files on the other hand, more flexibility is given. Due to the inherent legacy nature of flat Files, you can specify a **Custom Date/Time Format** when using a date or time datatype in a Flat File Schema. The steps to do this are as follows:

1. Create a Schema with **Flat File extensions**.
2. Create an element or attribute field under the root node.
3. Set the **Data Type** of the field to **xs:date**.
4. Choose one of the values for **Custom Date/Time Format** out of the drop-down box or enter your own, as follows:

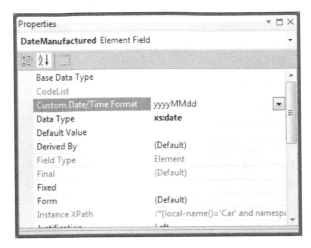

 If you cannot see the **Custom Date/Time Format** property, remember that it is only available for Flat File Schemas.

Restricting integer formats

Say that we have an integer, such as the maximum number of allowed passengers in a car and we want to illustrate, in the Schema, that (by an imaginary law) cars can have a minimum of zero passengers and a maximum of seven passengers, or else the vehicle is filed as a bus. One of the ways to do this would be to use the same procedure as described in the section about controlling date formats, and to use a pattern restriction. Another option would be to do the following:

1. Set **Base Data Type** to **xs:int**.
2. Set **MinFacet Value** to **0**, and accept the default value of **Inclusive** for **MinFacet Type**, meaning that the allowed values must be greater than or equal to this value.

3. Set **MaxFacet Value** to **7**, and accept the default value of **Inclusive** for **MaxFacet Type**, as shown in the following screenshot:

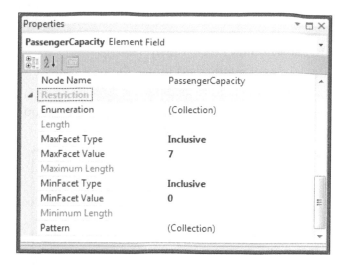

 The **MinFacet** and **MaxFacets** properties are only available for datatypes that are value-based, that is, they are not available for the `string` datatype, but they are also available to, for example, the `date` datatype.

Creating reusable types

Often when you apply a pattern restriction to a node, that node is not alone in having those restrictions. If you, for example, have a Schema with several dates, say `PurchaseDate` and `RegistrationDate`, that both need to conform to the same format, it makes sense to create that restriction once, instead of on each and every node. The same goes for if you have something that's more complex, say a customer and the customer's address; these are something that you want as reusable types, so that you can use them again in different constructs, in different Schemas.

Simple types

With `simpleType`, the way to create a reusable type is as follows:

1. Create an element (or attribute).
2. Select a **Base Data Type**.
3. Optionally apply meaningful restrictions to it.
4. Select the **Data Type** property, and enter a name for your new reusable type.

Doing this creates a new `simpleType` element at the bottom of the Schema; name it according to the naming convention you adopted, and set the current element to be of that type.

If you want to create a second element that has the same properties, all you have to do is create a new element and set its **Data Type** to be of the type you just created:

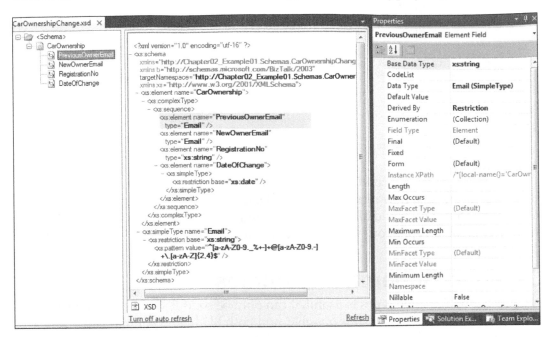

Alternatively, you could also select the second element's **Base Data Type**, and select the newly created type. You would do that if you are to apply further restrictions.

Complex types

With `complexType`, the procedure to create a reusable type is very similar, though not exactly the same as with `simpleType`:

1. Create a record.
2. Fill it with other records, elements, and attributes, so that it creates a reusable unit.
3. Select the **Data Structure Type** property, and enter a name for your new reusable type.

Doing this will create a new element named `complexType`, at the bottom of the Schema, and set the current record to be of that type. In the following example, I did this for the entire car definition:

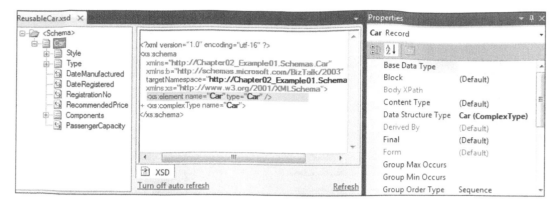

If you want to create a second record that has the same structure and content, all you have to do is create a new record and set its **Data Structure Type** to be of the type you just created. You could also select the second record's **Base Data Type** and select the newly created type. You would do that if you are to apply further restrictions.

Creating Schema hierarchies

While creating reusable types is useful, it can only be so, if it's limited to re-use within the same Schema file. It is possible, and both likely and common, that re-use of common types will be preferable Cross-schema files. For that reason, we have `import`, `include`, and `redefine`, that allow us to do just that.

Import

XSD Import is arguably the most commonly used import of a Schema. Import is often used when you want to build new Schemas that re-use already defined types:

- Allows use of types defined in another Schema
- Types must be in another `targetNamespace`
- Uses types as defined; cannot make additional restrictions on included types
- Can define new types based on imported types

Include

XSD Include is very similar to Import, the difference being the `targetNamespace` rules. Include is often used when you want to extend an existing Schema with new types.

- Allows use of types defined in another Schema
- Types must be in same `targetNamespace`, or have no `targetNamespace`
- Uses types as defined; cannot make additional restrictions on included types
- Can define new types based on imported types

Redefine

XSD redefine is very similar to Include, the difference being the ability to specify additional changes to the included types without having to create new derived types. Redefine is often used when you want to redefine existing types to suit your needs.

- Allows use of types defined in another Schema
- Types must be in the same `targetNamespace` or have no `targetNamespace`
- Uses types as defined, makes changes to them, or creates new types based on included types

Creating Pipelines

Pipelines are meant for pre- or post-processing of messages as they enter or leave BizTalk Server. In special cases, they may also be used from within BizTalk Server Orchestrations to perform specialized tasks, such as splitting or aggregating a message. Pipelines execute between the adapter and the Map, or vice versa for Send Ports, as follows:

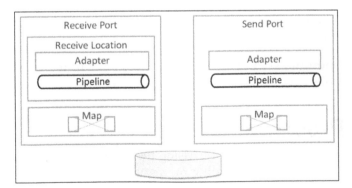

When receiving a message into BizTalk, the components displayed in the preceding diagram are triggered in the order Receive Port, Receive Location, Adapter, Pipeline, Map – `MessageBox` (- Subscription(s)) – Send Port, Map, Pipeline, Adapter.

There are two approaches to Pipelines in BizTalk Server development: use the out-of-the-box ones available when you install or create your own. Although the first approach will, and should, be your starting point, you will often end up creating your own. When you do, it's important that you know what Pipeline components are available. Knowledge of Pipeline components and what possibilities the built-in ones provide, as well as the possibilities with, and limitations of, creating custom Pipeline components, is key to creating a successful integration design and deciding what task is best performed where.

Pipeline Stages

A Pipeline is made up of a predetermined number of stages that differ between Receive and Send Pipelines. Stages put limitations on the type of Pipeline component that can be used there and on the execution of Pipeline components.

The Receive Pipeline has four stages: Decode, Disassemble, Validate, and Resolve Party. The Send Pipeline has three stages: Preassemble, Assemble, and Encode.

A stage has three notable properties besides its name: Execution mode, Maximum components, and Minimum components.

The execution mode can be either All or FirstMatch. All means that all Pipeline components are executed sequentially. FirstMatch means that they are executed sequentially until a component is found that accepts the processing of a message, in which case, the chain stops and that component gets handed the message, and the next component to execute is the first component of the next stage.

All stages except the Disassemble stage have execution mode All. The Disassemble stage is FirstMatch.

All stages take a minimum of zero components and a maximum of 255 components, except the Assemble stage that has a maximum of one.

Receive Pipelines

Receive Pipelines are meant for preprocessing the message, such as parsing a Flat file or XML file, decrypting or validating the signature or a message, validating full conformance to a Schema, and so on. They consist of four stages: Decode, Disassemble, Validate and Resolve Party, as follows:

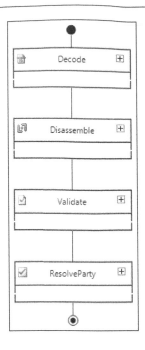

Decode

The Decode stage is meant for Pipeline components that perform decoding or decryption of the message. The MIME/SMIME decoder component fits this stage.

> The Decode stage can also be used by any custom component that needs to act on the message before it reaches the Disassemble stage. Examples of such processing could be adding an XML namespace or correcting known faulty data.

Disassemble

The Disassemble stage is meant for disassembling a message into XML. This stage can be resolved in more than one message being delivered to the next component. The components here can have a Probe method that looks at the message to determine whether the component is configured to parse the message or not. Only the first component that gives a true return to the Probe call will be executed. The components in this stage also handle property promotion, and optionally, message validation. The XML Disassembler or Flat File Disassembler components fit this stage. Only the XML Disassembler is capable of probing the message. The Flat File Disassembler will always try to disassemble using the configured Schema, and Pipeline processing will fail if it is not successful.

Validate

This stage is used to validate the XML contents of the message, for example, to verify Schema conformance. The XML Validator Pipeline component fits this stage.

Resolve Party

This stage is meant for the Party Resolution Pipeline component, but it can also be used for any component that needs to run after the Validate stage.

Send Pipelines

Send Pipelines are meant for post-processing, for processing the message before it gets sent out by the adapter. The common scenarios include transforming XML into Flat File format, adding a signature, or encrypting the message. They consist of three stages: Preassemble, Assemble, and Encode, as follows:

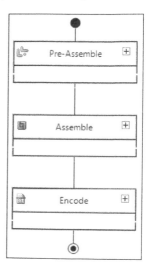

Pre-Assemble

This stage is meant for any component that needs to perform some form of processing on the message before it is assembled, such as inspecting or modifying the XML. This is the only step for which there are no out-of-the-box Pipeline components to place in. It is meant for custom Pipeline components.

Assemble

This stage is meant for components that assemble or format the message, say by converting it to a Flat file. The XML Assembler and the Flat File Assembler components fit this stage.

Encode

This stage is meant for components that encode or encrypt the message, or to add a signature or do any other form of processing needed on the message after it is assembled. The MIME/SMIME encoder component fits this stage.

 By default, the Pipeline templates used by Visual Studio are empty. You can change them by altering the template files that are located in the `<BizTalk Install Folder>\Developer Tools\BizTalkProjectItems` folder. Pipelines have a file extension of BTP.

Default Pipelines

When you install BizTalk Server, you will get access to four Pipelines to use, two Receive and two Send. They are `PassThruReceive` and `XMLReceive`, for Receive Pipelines, and `PassThruTransmit` and `XMLTransmit` for Send Pipelines. They are meant to get you started and to allow for simple scenarios to be built, without the need for any custom Pipeline development.

PassThruReceive

The `PassThruReceive` Pipeline has no components. It does no processing of the message and allows you to accept any message for transportation and/or later processing in BizTalk Server.

 Although BizTalk Server can accept any message in any format, it can only transform, or access data in, messages that have been disassembled into XML. That includes messages that consist of XML. They must be disassembled using the XML Disassembler as well, for them to be recognized as XML.

XMLReceive

The XMLReceive Pipeline contains the XML Disassembler and the Party Resolution component.

PassThruTransmit

As with the PassThruReceive Pipeline, it has no components and performs no message processing before the message is sent out by the adapter.

XMLTransmit

The XMLTransmit Pipeline contains the XML Assembler component.

You do not need to use the XMLTransmit Pipeline just because you are sending out XML. Using PassThuTransmit for that is perfectly reasonable and, in many cases, the best choice. Use XMLTransmit when you want further processing of the message, such as adding an envelope, influence encoding, demoting properties from the context into the message, or adding (InfoPath or other) processing instructions.

Custom Pipelines

Developing custom Pipelines is about adding Pipeline components to the Pipeline stages discussed earlier to form new Pipelines that conform to the capabilities you need out of your solution. You can use either the out of the box available components or custom Pipeline components.

You create custom Pipelines using the Pipeline Designer inside Visual Studio. We can derive, from looking at the Default Pipelines, that all the pipeline components installed with BizTalk are not included in the Default Pipelines.

The following is a list of the standard Pipeline components that you can use to create a custom Pipeline:

Name	Pipeline Type	Target Stage	Short Description
BizTalk Framework Disassembler	Receive	Disassembler	The **BizTalk Framework (BTF)** is an approach to doing exactly one guaranteed delivery using HTTP or SMTP, mainly using acknowledgements. The components parse the BTF envelope and context properties and act according to BTF rules.
BizTalk Framework Assembler	Send	Assemble	The component is responsible for assembling BTF messages, using envelope and context properties, and for resending messages, should an acknowledgement not have arrived before timeout.
Flat File Disassembler	Receive	Disassemble	The component handles flat text file parsing, using Schema annotations to disassemble the message into XML.
Flat File Assembler	Send	Assemble	The component serializes an XML message into its Flat File format.

Name	Pipeline Type	Target Stage	Short Description
XML Disassembler	Receive	Disassemble	The component parses inbound XML messages.
XML Assembler	Send	Assemble	The component serializes outbound XML messages.
MIME/SMIME Decoder	Receive	Decode	The component is used to decrypt and verify signatures on inbound messages. It can also be used with the POP3 adapter to handle attachments.
MIME/SMIME Encoder	Send	Encode	The component is used to encrypt or sign outbound messages. It can also be used to send multipart messages.
XML Validator	Receive or Send	All except Assemble or Disassemble	The component validates that the incoming message conforms to its Schema.
Party Resolution	Receive	Resolve Party	The component uses the sender's certificate or Security Identifier (SID) to resolve a BizTalk Party.

The XML Disassembler, the XML Assembler, the MIME/SMIME Decoder, and the MIME/SMIME Encoder will be covered in more depth, later in this chapter.

EDI and AS2 add additional Pipeline components, namely EDI Disassembler, BatchMarker, AS2 Decoder, AS2 Disassembler, EDI Assembler, and AS2 Encoder. EDI will be covered later in the book, in *Chapter 8, Implementing Extended Capabilities.*

Configuring Pipelines and Pipeline components

Pipelines have two places where you can edit their configuration: BizTalk Server Pipeline Designer in Visual Studio or BizTalk Server Administration Console. The values entered in the **Properties** dialogue of the Pipeline Designer act as your Pipeline's default settings, as follows:

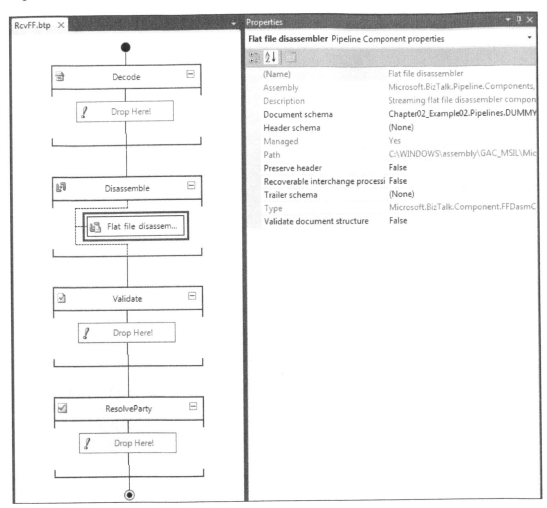

Once you deploy your Pipeline, you will be able to see it and select it among the available Pipelines, when configuring a Send Port or Receive Location in the Administration Console, as shown in the following screenshot:

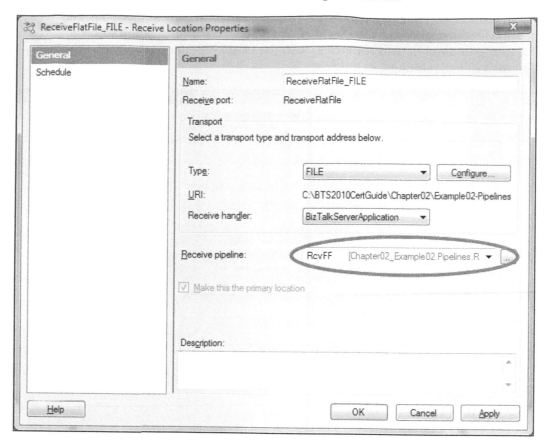

If you click on the ellipsis to the right of the drop-down box, this will bring up the **Configure Pipeline** dialog, where you have the option to override some or all of your default settings with new runtime settings. From a user interface perspective, those overridden runtime settings will then be shown in bold, as follows:

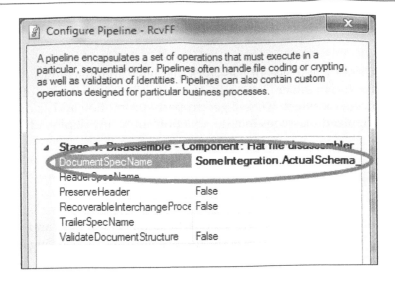

The alternative to overriding settings in runtime is creating additional Pipelines, which can result in many more Pipelines than actually needed.

The RcvFF Pipeline that uses a dummy Schema as a default setting for the Flat File Disassembler component is available in `Chapter02-Example02`.

Working with XML messages

Working with XML messages is not always as easy as using the `XMLReceive` Pipeline, with default settings to receive the message and `PassThruTransmit` to send it out, although it could be. It's useful to know the capabilities of the components that process XML messages, among which we can find: XML Disassembler, XML Assembler, and XML Validator.

Disassembling and parsing

Disassembling and parsing an XML message is done in the XML Disassembler to ensure that the message of the message is deployed to the BizTalk Server and that the message contains valid XML data, has the correct number of matching start and end tags, and so on. By default, the component does not validate that the message conforms to its Schema, although it can be configured to do so. The XML Disassembler component has the following properties:

Allow unrecognized messages

Default: `False`

This property allows you to accept messages that have an unrecognized format to pass through the disassembler. Setting this to `True` allows processing of messages that are recognized, for which we will get property promotion and so on, while still allowing unrecognized messages that do not conform to any deployed Schema to pass through.

Document Schemas

Default: `Empty`

`Empty` means that it is not limited to a specific Schema or Schemas, and will accept messages matching any deployed Schema (or any message, depending on the setting of Allow unrecognized messages).

This property allows you to specify what Schemas are expected, and therefore authorized, to pass through this Pipeline.

Envelope Schemas

Default: `Empty`

`Empty` means that it will inspect the message for any deployed Schema marked as being an Envelope Schema and will try to remove the envelope if found.

This property allows you to specify which Envelope Schemas are expected, and therefore authorized, to pass through this Pipeline.

Recoverable interchange processing

Default: `False`

This property is only interesting when the Disassemble stage forwards more than one message to the next stage, such as when an envelope is used and the message is split into several messages within the interchange. It allows you to indicate that the Pipeline is to use recoverable interchange processing.

If the value is set to `False`, the entire interchange is treated as a transactional unit against `MsgBox`. It will not recover (if that helps you remember) from an exception that occurs in the processing of any single message—if one of the split messages fail, the entire interchange fails.

If it is set to `True`, it means that each message within the interchange is treated in isolation and the interchange can recover and be processed completely even if any one or many messages get suspended.

Validate document structure

Default: False.

False means that there is no validation outside of well-formed XML and that any received message with a MessageType that matches a deployed Schema will be accepted, regardless whether the rest of the content matches the schema or not.

True means that validation for Document and Envelope Schema conformance will be performed as applicable. If you set this property to True, you must also supply the Document Schemas that validation should be performed against.

Assembling and serializing

The XML Assembler has the following properties:

Add processing instructions text, Add processing instructions, Processing instruction scope

These properties specify the processing instructions' text to Append (default), Create New (overwrite) or Ignore (clear) at the Envelope or Document (default) level.

Processing instructions are instructions directed at the application for processing of the XML document on how to interpret it, visualize it, authorize it, and so on. A closely related application that uses this is InfoPath.

Add XML declaration

Default: True.

Determines if an XML declaration, <?xml version='1.0' encoding='UTF-8'>, should be available in the outbound document.

Preserve Byte Order

Default: True.

This property determines whether a byte order mark should be prepended to the outbound message. A byte order mark is a Unicode character placed first in the stream to indicate which Unicode representation the text is encoded in.

Target charset

Default: Empty.

It allows you to specify a specific character set to encode outbound messages in.

Envelope Schemas

Default: Empty.

This property allows you to specify which Envelope Schemas are to be expected when assembling the document.

 Working with XML envelopes is covered in more depth, later in this chapter.

Document Schemas

Default: Empty.

This property allows you to specify what Schema the processed messages are expected to belong to. If left empty, it will accept any valid message that belongs to any deployed Schema.

Validating data

Sometimes, there are scenarios where you need to insert document validation without it being performed by the XML Disassembler, for example, the XML or Flat File Assemblers do not do Schema validation. If you want to enable outbound message Schema validation, a suitable option is to place an XML Validator component in the Preassemble stage of a Send Pipeline. It could also be placed in the Validate stage of a Receive Pipeline. This could be useful, say, when you want to validate the pieces of an interchange after it's been split into several messages.

The XML Validator only has two properties:

- **Document Schemas:** It indicates which Schemas are valid for messages. It also uses Schema information to validate messages against Schema for conformance. If left empty, messages matching any deployed Schema are valid to be processed through the Pipeline.

- **Recoverable Interchange Processing:** If the component is located in a Receive Pipeline and you set recoverable interchange processing to True on the XML Disassembler, you must also set recoverable interchange processing to True on this component, if you want them to follow the same pattern.

Working with envelopes

Working with envelopes is a common scenario that we are going to look at a bit more closely. We are going to use an Envelope Schema and, with the help of that Schema and a Pipeline, split an enveloped batch message into its part and send them through BizTalk. The Schema has the following structure:

```
<xs:schema xmlns="http://Chapter02_Example03.Schemas.CarEnvelope"
xmlns:b="http://schemas.microsoft.com/BizTalk/2003"
targetNamespace="http://Chapter02_Example03.Schemas.CarEnvelope"
xmlns:xs="http://www.w3.org/2001/XMLSchema">
  <xs:annotation>
    <xs:appinfo>
      <b:schemaInfo is_envelope="yes" />
    </xs:appinfo>
  </xs:annotation>
    <xs:element name="ManufacturingReport">
    <xs:annotation>
    <xs:appinfo>
        <b:recordInfo body_XPath="/*[local-
name()='ManufacturingReport' and namespace-uri()='http://Chapter02_
Example03.Schemas.CarEnvelope']/*[local-name()='Cars' and namespace-
uri()='']" />
      </xs:appinfo>
    </xs:annotation>
    <xs:complexType>
      <xs:sequence>
        <xs:element name="Cars">
          <xs:complexType>
            <xs:sequence>
              <xs:any maxOccurs="unbounded" />
            </xs:sequence>
          </xs:complexType>
        </xs:element>
      </xs:sequence>
      <xs:attribute name="BatchNo" type="xs:int" />
    </xs:complexType>
  </xs:element>
</xs:schema>
```

Note the `recordInfo` annotation with its `body_XPath` attribute that contains an XPath that points out the Schema node that contains the message body.

To make sure we have a Schema to represent a message that we can send inside the envelope, a copy of the `SimplifiedCar` Schema created earlier in the Schema section of this chapter has been placed in the solution.

Let's examine what we must do to split the incoming envelope message into its document parts.

The following is the instance message we are sending through BizTalk:

```
<ns0:ManufacturingReport BatchNo="10" xmlns:ns0="http://Chapter02_
Example03.Schemas.CarEnvelope">
  <Cars>
    <ns0:Car xmlns:ns0="http://Chapter02_Example03.Schemas.
SimplifiedCar">
      <RegistrationNo>ABC123</RegistrationNo>
      <Make>Audi</Make>
      <Model>RS6</Model>
      <Color>NurburgringBlue</Color>
    </ns0:Car>
    <ns0:Car xmlns:ns0="http://Chapter02_Example03.Schemas.
SimplifiedCar">
      <RegistrationNo>XYZ789</RegistrationNo>
      <Make>Corvette</Make>
      <Model>ZR1</Model>
      <Color>DaytonaRed</Color>
    </ns0:Car>
  </Cars>
</ns0:ManufacturingReport>
```

No custom Pipelines are needed to complete this exercise – the Default Pipelines will do the job. These are the steps needed to configure the Pipelines to receive and split the message:

1. Make sure the project has a key file and a string name, and deploy it to BizTalk Server.

2. Configure a **Receive Port** and **Receive Location**.

3. In the **Receive Location**, make sure you select **XMLReceive Pipeline**. No further configuration is needed.

4. Create a **Send Port** that has a **Filter** property that subscribes to messages from the **Receive Port**. No further configuration is needed on the Send Port.

5. Send the message.

The result is two messages sent from the Disassemble stage, on to the Send Port and out to the location we choose.

This sample is available in the `C:\BTS2010CertGuide\Chapter02\Example02-Envelope\Chapter02-Example03\Chapter02-Example03.sln` solution, and the bindings are available in the `C:\BTS2010CertGuide\Chapter02\Example03-Envelope\BTS2010CertGuide-Ch02-Envelope.XML` file

Flat File Envelopes

Flat files can be received in batches as well. The concept of envelopes applies just as equally to Flat files as it does to XML messages. However, a Flat file is configured slightly differently and instead includes configuring Header Schemas, Document Schemas, and Trailer Schemas in the Flat File Disassembler component. Flat File Envelopes are not covered in this book. The Envelope Processing BizTalk Server sample is found in the `<BizTalkInstall>\SDK\Samples\Pipelines\AssemblerDisassembler\EnvelopeProcessing` folder; the article at `http://msdn.microsoft.com/en-us/library/aa578216.aspx` discusses this further.

Working with secure data

Sometimes, there is a need to secure the conversation between BizTalk Server and the systems it uses to communicate. For those situations, you can use the MIME/SMIME Pipeline components in either Receive or Send Pipelines and take on the job of verifying digital signature and decrypting messages, and signing and encrypting messages.

In *Chapter 1, Configuring a Messaging Architecture*, we learned about certificates and how to install and configure them in the certificate store and in BizTalk Server; now, it's time to examine how to configure the MIME/SMIME Pipeline component to use them. Using the MIME/SMIME component is really the simple part of the equation—it's getting all the public key infrastructure and Host and Group configuration right that is the messy part. Once you have that, setting up a secure conversation using either encryption/decryption or signing/verification is easy.

Encryption and signing

To use the MIME/SMIME Pipeline component to encrypt a message, create a configuration along the following steps:

1. First, we need to create a custom Send Pipeline to contain the **MIME/SMIME Encoder** component. All component properties are left at their defaults at this point, as follows:

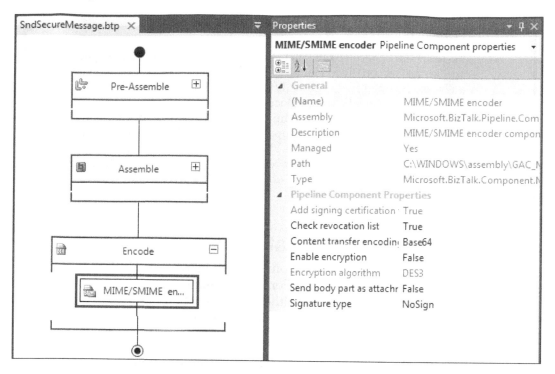

2. Next, we deploy the Pipeline to BizTalk Server.

3. Then, we need to create a Receive Port to receive a cleartext message, just so that we have something to encrypt.

4. Create a Send Port that subscribes to the Receive Port.

5. Configure the Port with an **Encryption certificate** (the partner public key of the encryption certificate needs to be installed in the Local Computer\Other People store), as follows:

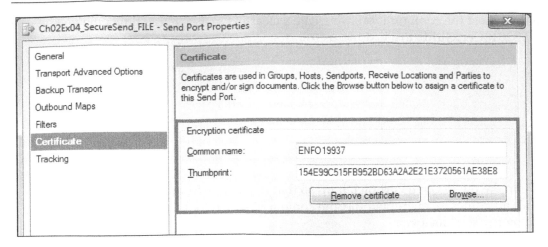

6. Configure the Send Port to use the **SndSecureMessage** Pipeline.

7. Configure the Pipeline and MIME/SMIME component by setting **EnableEncryption** to **True**. We could also choose one of DES3 (0), DES (1) or RC2 (2) as our encryption algorithm. DES3 is default:

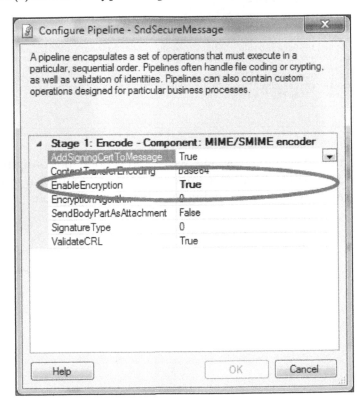

Now to test the configuration, we create a cleartext message that holds the text **BTS2010CertGuide** in a text file, as follows:

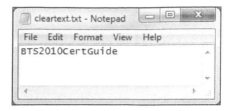

We make the Receive Port pick it up so that it gets routed to the Send Port, and out comes an encrypted file, the content of which looks similar to the following screenshot:

If instead we wanted to sign the message, we would change the configuration of the Send Pipeline and the MIME/SMIME component. The following is a screenshot of a possible configuration where we are using the **ClearSign (1)** option:

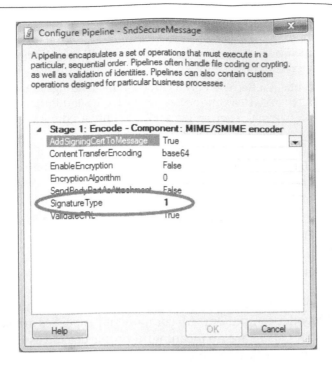

It's also possible to both encrypt and sign, in which case the signature would be made using the **BlobSign (2)** option.

Signing requires our private key certificate to be in the `Host Instance User\ Personal` store, and configured at the BizTalk Server Group level.

Now if we supply the same cleartext message, the output has a new look, as follows:

The sample `Chapter02\Example04-Security` contains a Send Pipeline configured with a MIME/SMIME Encoder named `SndSecureMessage`.

It also contains a Receive Port included in the bindings named `Ch02Ex04_ClearTextReceive`, as well as a Send Port named `Ch02Ex04_SecureSend_FILE`, configured to use the `SndSecureMessage` Pipeline.

Please note though, that you need to create and deploy a certificate and update the sample with your own certificate's thumbprint, where applicable.

Decryption and signature verification

Now that we have encrypted and signed messages in the previous section, let's look at how to go about decrypting the message to get back to the cleartext representation:

1. First, we need to create a custom Receive Pipeline to contain the **MIME/SMIME Decoder** component. All component properties are left at their defaults. In fact, there are no meaningful properties for us to change to affect either signature verification or decryption:

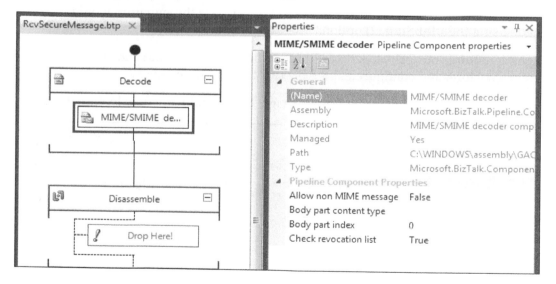

2. Next, we deploy the Pipeline to BizTalk Server.
3. Then, we need to create a Receive Port to receive secure messages.
4. We configure the Receive Port to use the **RcvSecureMessage** Pipeline.

5. Since we already established that the **MIME/SMIME Decoder** component had no properties we needed to alter to be able to receive encrypted or signed messages, we do not need to do any configuration.

6. We also create a Send Port that subscribes to the Receive Port, to be able to see the end result.

Now to test the configuration, we will send in the encrypted and signed messages we created in the previous section. It is sufficient to say that it will result in cleartext messages.

To decrypt encrypted messages, we need to configure our certificate to use at the Host level and have the private key installed in the Host Instance User\Personal store (same store as when signing messages). For verifying signatures, we need to have the partner's public key deployed to the Local Computer\Other People store (same store as when encrypting outbound messages). No additional BizTalk configuration is necessary.

The sample Chapter02\Example04-Security contains a Receive Pipeline configured with the MIME/SMIME Decoder named RcvSecureMessage.

It also contains a Receive Port included in the bindings named Ch02Ex04_SecureReceive, as well as a Send Port named Ch02Ex04_ClearTextSend_FILE using the PassThruTransmit Pipeline.

Test your knowledge

1. Rob, a developer at HWLC motors, is working with a Schema that is to hold Supplier contact details. Just the other week, the team finished work on a Customer Information Schema. Both have e-mail addresses. While working with the Customer Schema, they created an EmailAddress type with a restriction for e-mail addresses that he would like to reuse in the Supplier Schema. The Customer and Supplier Schemas are in different namespaces. What should he do?

   a. Import the Customer Schema to the Supplier Schema, and set the Data Type of all e-mail addresses in the Supplier Schema to the EmailAddress type defined in the Customer Schema.

   b. Include the Customer Schema in the Supplier Schema to be able to set the EmailAddress type as the Data Type of the e-mail addresses in the Supplier Schema.

    c.   Import the Supplier Schema to the Customer Schema, and set the `Data Type` property of all e-mail addresses in the Supplier Schema to the `EmailAddress` type defined in the Customer Schema.

    d.   Define a new Schema named `EmailAddress`, to hold the definition of the `EmailAddress` type.

2.   You are configuring a secure communication with signed messages with a partner to ensure that messages are not tampered with while in transmission. You need to make sure that you can receive the messages and that the signature used is valid. What do you do?

    a.   Create a Pipeline using the MIME/SMIME Encoder component. Install that partner's private key to the Certificate store of the computer, and configure the Host to use it.

    b.   Create a Pipeline using the MIME/SMIME Decoder component. Install that partner's private key to the Certificate store of the computer, and configure the Host to use it.

    c.   Create a Pipeline using the MIME/SMIME Encoder component. Install that partner's public key to the Certificate store of the computer.

    d.   Create a Pipeline using the MIME/SMIME Decoder component. Install that partner's public key to the Certificate store of the computer.

Summary

In this chapter, we learned about Schemas and Pipelines. We looked at how to create schemas. We created hierarchies in and between Schemas. We investigated how we can control the format for Schema nodes and how to reuse those formats as types. We looked at property promotion and discussed its use. We then continued to learn about creating Pipelines and how they can enable us to secure our interchanges and work with our messages in different ways. In the next chapter, we will look at the Developing BizTalk Artifacts — Creating Maps objective of the exam.

3
Developing BizTalk Artifacts—Creating Maps

This chapter will takes us one step further than passing typed XML messages and using Pipelines and teach us how to transform messages between Schema formats. We will cover **functoids**, and look closer at how to use them to incorporate conditional logic, to control looping behavior and external assemblies, and to use scripting of different sorts to advance our maps. We will also look at how Maps and Orchestrations work together to enable multi-part Schemas as the source in Maps. This chapter will cover the following main areas:

- Creating Maps
- Using Functoids
- Using Advanced Functoids
- Test your knowledge

Creating Maps

Mapping is one of the areas that have gotten the biggest attention in **BizTalk Server 2010** in terms of user interface. It is also one of those areas, where in many cases, simple integrations might not do anything more than transform messages, before sending them on to the subscribers. The point being that, almost all integrations out there will use one or more maps while processing the message. Being skilled at creating well-performing, change-friendly, and maintainable maps is therefore one of the most sought-after skills among BizTalk developers.

Maps range from simple to very complex, where the user interface changes have really improved the usability around complex maps.

Simple maps may only include connecting a few elements together using simple direct links, as shown in the following screenshot:

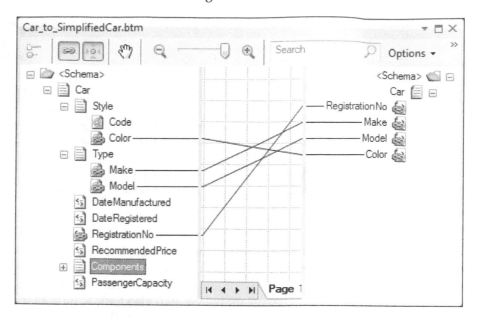

All samples and Map images throughout the map chapter can be found in the `C:\BTS2010CertGuide\Chapter03\Example01-Mapping\Chapter03-Example01\Chapter03-Example01.sln` solution.

Please note that the sample code in this chapter is not built to be deployed, but only to illustrate concepts, so there are no bindings.

More complex Maps may include a lot of functoids and complex logic. The following screenshot is an example of a rather more complex Map from a real-life project (though far more complex and mapping-intense transformations than these are not uncommon):

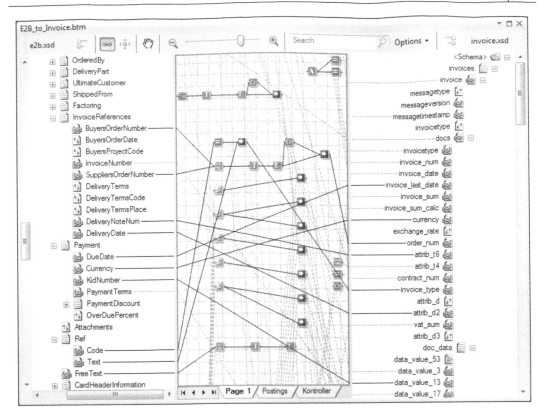

Making Maps maintainable is important, and the design and housekeeping of the mapping surface play into that.

Why XSLT matters

XSLT (Extensible Stylesheet Language Transformations) is a declarative, XML-based language to describe the transformation of an input format to a different, or the same, output format.

Although mapping in BizTalk Server and Visual Studio is overlaid with a nice designer to abstract you away from the fact, XSLT is something that forms the foundation of mapping in BizTalk. Maps are XSLT scripts, or at least get compiled into them. Advanced Maps can contain parts that contain pure XSLT (through the Scripting Functoid), or fully raw XSLT through the **Custom XSLT** property (where the mapping design surface is empty). Advanced troubleshooting will often mean looking at, and sometimes debugging, the generated XSLT of a Map. Getting used to and understanding what kind of XSLT the designer creates in different situations, can be really helpful in those situations, where experimenting with links and functoids to reach the desired result is not quite enough.

It is outside the scope of this book to cover details on XSLT. For a detailed walkthrough of XSLT, go to `http://www.w3.org/TR/XSLT`.

We will look at some sample XSLT when we review the Scripting Functoid.

Using Functoids

Once you get past the simplest of mapping constructs, where simply connecting source and target Schemas using direct links is not enough, you will start using **functoids**. Functoids are small reusable snippets of code that execute predefined logic based on parameters (inputs from source Schema or other functoids in the map). Functoids typically take zero to many inputs and deliver one output, with a few exceptions.

There are nine different categories of functoids, as follows:

- Conversion
- Cumulative
- Database
- Date and Time
- Logical
- Mathematical
- Scientific
- String
- Advanced

As someone preparing to take the certification, you should be well aware of the available functoids — they are important in overall BizTalk and Map development. Most functoids are however easy to use and quite self-explanatory, and an in-depth description of their use would be useless to the target audience of this book.

On top of the existing functoids, custom Functoids can be created by developers extending the functoid toolbox with custom functionality.

Conversion Functoids

The **Conversion Functoids** do what the name says, that is, they convert between different formats. The available out-of-the-box conversion functoids are as follows:

- **Character to ASCII**: It converts a character to an ASCII value
- **ASCII to Character**: It converts an ASCII value to a character
- **Hexadecimal**: It converts a decimal number to a hexadecimal value
- **Octal**: It converts a decimal number to an octal value

Cumulative Functoids

All **Cumulative Functoids** accept the same two input parameters as follows:

1. The source value to accumulate
2. The scope of accumulation as follows:
    - 0 means entire message
    - 1 means values that have the same parent
    - 2 means values that have the same parent's parent
    - 3 means values that have the same parent's parent's parent, and so on

Except for the Cumulative String Functoid, all Cumulative Functoids accept only numeric values and will ignore any non-numeric values received. The following type of accumulation can be made:

- **Average**: It returns the average value of all values
- **Concatenate**: It returns a string that is the concatenation of all values
- **Maximum**: It returns the maximum value of all values
- **Minimum**: It returns the minimum value of all values
- **Sum**: It returns the accumulated sum of all values

Database Functoids

The **Database Functoids** merit something of an explanation besides a list explaining their individual meaning. First, under the Database Functoids category, there are functoids that are divided into two areas: Table Query and Lookup Functoids, and Cross Reference ID or Cross Reference Value Lookup Functoids.

Table Query Functoids

These functoids enable us to query tables and supply lookup columns to look for an equally supplied value. The return is a single row from that table to extract values from. This is quite a limited database query functionality, and stored procedures cannot be called, as shown in the following table:

> If you are not careful using the Database Lookup Functoid, it can easily become a bottleneck in your process, especially if you handle large files that end up making tens of thousands of calls to the database.

Functoid	Input and output
Database Lookup	*Input*: 1. A lookup value 2. A connection string 3. Name of table 4. Name of column *Output*: The first row that matches the query (in an ADO Record Set). > It is not a good idea to hardcode a connection string inside a map.
Value Extractor	*Input*: 1. A link from the Database Lookup Functoid - an ADO Record Set containing a row. 2. The name of the column to extract the value from. *Output*: The value from the configured column.
Error Return	*Input*: A link from the Database Lookup Functoid. *Output*: A string of the error that occurred, if any.

Cross Referencing Data Functoids

The **Cross Reference Functoids** is one way by which you can fulfill the often-occurring requirement of cross-referencing data, the need to translate values from one system identifier or value, to another.

How it works is that you use either the **BizTalk Server Cross Reference Import Tool** (BTSXRefImport.exe) to import data defined in a series of XML files into your database, or you use SQL statements to manipulate the tables directly. The tooling in this case is quite crude, and if you are serious about using this built-in feature for data cross-referencing, you are often better off designing an alternative strategy. We are not going to cover the underlying database structures that data ends up in any depth. Let us just assume that the data is in there, and look at getting it out. To help in understanding the relationship between data, let us look at the relationship between the tables and entities in play, as shown in the following diagram:

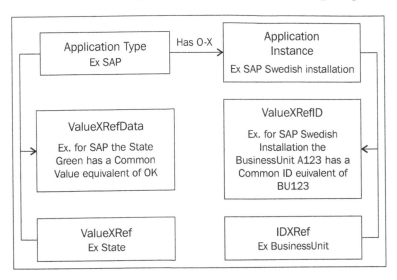

Working with application IDs

A part of Cross Referencing Functoids is about working with IDs that differ between application instances. They are unique identifiers in their respective application instances. These are often not the IDs of things like Order or Invoice but of something a bit more limited, say the ID of types, for example, BusinessUnit or CostCenter. Since they are IDs, they are suitable candidates for a one-to-one mapping relationship, that is, the ID of an application instance will always have (and map to) one and only one common ID. Similarly, one common ID will always map to one and only one application instance ID. Since it is moving data, new BusinessUnit may appear at any given time. There is also logic available to handle new or removed IDs.

In the middle of cross-referencing of data between two applications, there is a common ID, which is something that you map to and from, to map between application instance IDs, as shown in the following table:

Functoid	Input and output
◄◻ Get Common ID	*Input*: 1. Type of object 2. The application instance we are mapping from 3. The application instance's ID *Output*: The common ID equivalent of the applications' ID
◄◻ Get Application ID	*Input*: 1. Type of object 2. The application instance we are mapping to 3. The common ID *Output*: The application instance ID equivalent of the common ID

There are also ways for you to administer IDs in runtime when you find new IDs, or find a situation that suggests you remove application IDs, as follows:

Functoid	Input and output
◻↗ Set Common ID	*Input*: 1. Type of object 2. The application instance we are mapping from 3. The application instance ID 4. An optional common ID: If this is not supplied then a new unique identifier is generated. *Output*: The common ID that is same as parameter 4, or the generated ID

Functoid	Input and output
Remove Application ID	*Input*: 1. Type of object 2. The application instance we are mapping to 3. The common ID *Output*: The application instance ID equivalent of the common ID; the application instance ID that is being removed

Working with application values

Application values stand in relation to the application type, rather than the instance of an application. They are mostly used for values such as enumerations, or other static values such as states or types that are steadier in their nature. Therefore, there are no functoids available to add or remove values at runtime. It is a one-to-many mapping relationship, for example, one application can have the states as green, yellow, orange, and red, while another has only green, yellow, and red. In this case, both yellow and orange may result in a mapping to yellow as follows:

Functoid	Input and output
Set Common Value	*Input*: 1. Type of object 2. The application type we are mapping from 3. The application value *Output*: The common value
Get Application Value	*Input*: 1. Type of object 2. The application type we are mapping to 3. The common value *Output*: The application value equivalent of the common value

Date/Time Functoids

The **Date/Time Functoids** help in determining the current date and time as well as provide some simple date calculation. They are as follows:

- **Add Days**: It either takes a `date` or a `datetime` string and adds X number of days to it and returns the new date
- **Date**: It returns the current date
- **Date And Time**: It returns the current date and time
- **Time**: It returns the current time

> All dates are ISO 8601-compliant values, meaning that a date is represented as `YYYY-MM-DD`, time as a 24-hour `hh:mm:ss` format, and `datetime` as `YYYY-MM-DDThh:mm:ss`. Optionally, you can specify a timezone by suffixing either a Z for UTC or by adding a positive or negative time, like +hh:mm. For example: `2011-11-10T14:02:02+02:00`.

Logical Functoids

The **Logical Functoids** category is arguably the most used and useful functoid category. The functoids in this category can take a wide variety of datatypes as input, and even perform comparisons between parameters of different types in some cases. They all yield a Boolean output, representing whether or not the operation or comparison that the functoid performed resulted in a `true` or `false` value. Since it is Boolean, the output should be used as input to other functoids or nodes that can accept a Boolean. It should not be used as input to a functoid, or a destination node expecting to get a string such as `true`.

> While connecting the output of a logical functoid to a destination node, the result determines whether or not we can output that node, depending on the value's being `true` or `false`. It is a very useful and common operation.

The Equal, Not Equal, Greater Than, and Less Than Functoids all accept two inputs:

- Equal
- Not equal
- Greater than
- Greater than or equal to

- Less than
- Less than or equal to

The rest of the Functoids in the category are as follows:

- **Logical Existence**: The Logical Existence Functoid must be connected to a source node and checks to see whether or not the message contains that node.

- **IsNil**: The IsNil Functoid can be used to inspect whether a node that exists is nil. A node that does not exist is not evaluated as nil, since this functoid checks if the node has an xsi:nil attribute set to true.

- **Logical String**: The Logical String method evaluates whether or not a value can be interpreted as a string. This will return false if the value is null, for example, if the node does not exist, or if the value is an empty string. This in the case of an empty node, that is, <x></x>.

- **Logical Numeric** and **Logical Date**: The Logical Numeric and Logical Date Functoids basically work the same way. The only difference is that they test to see whether the value can be interpreted as numeric or date, respectively.

- **Logical AND**: The AND and OR Functoids accept two to 100 inputs that are evaluated as either true or false, and then combined to return a single Boolean value. An AND operation means that all values given must evaluate to true for a Boolean value of true to be returned. If only a single value is evaluated as false, then the value returned is false.

- **Logical OR**: The OR Functoid works the opposite. It evaluates all inputs, and if at least one evaluates to true, the functoid will return a Boolean value as true.

- **Logical NOT**: The NOT Functoid is used to negate the input within it, that is, if it is given a value that is evaluated as true, it will return false, and vice versa.

Mathematical Functoids

The **Mathematical Functoids** allow us to use some common mathematical operations on the data in our map. This ranges from what is extremely common, say addition or subtraction, to the lesser used ones such as square root. The full list of Mathematical Functoids supplied is as follows:

- **Addition**: It returns the result of adding between one and 100 inputs.

- **Subtraction**: It returns the result of subtracting one to 99 values from the first value. This works as P1- (P2-P3...-Pn).

- **Multiplication**: It returns the result of multiplying two to 100 values.
- **Division**: It returns the result of dividing two values.
- **Absolute Value**: It returns the absolute value of the input. An absolute value is a positive value, or a value with disregard for its sign, so for example, input 7 will return 7, and input -7 will also return 7.
- **Integer**: It returns the integer portion of a decimal value without doing any rounding, so for example, input 4.67 will return 4.
- **Modulo**: It returns the remainder of an integer division, a division that results in a non-decimal result, for example, inputs 5 and 2 will result in 1 (5 cannot be divided by 2 to produce an integer result, but 4 can, and so the remainder is 1).
- **Round**: It returns the rounded value as given by the first parameter, rounded to the number of decimals given in the second. The round to nearest, round to even (or banker rounding) is used, that is, if the second parameter is 0 or missing, 1.5 rounds to 2, while 4.5 rounds to 4.
- **Square Root**: It returns the square root of the supplied value.

Scientific Functoids

Using the **Scientific Functoids**, built on mathematical concepts, is basically the same as switching between the regular and scientific calculator in Windows. It adds a number of calculations that are considered outside the regular mathematical operations. They cover **trigonometric**, **logarithmic**, and **exponential** operations and are as follows:

- **10^n**: It returns 10, raised to the specified power
- **Arc Tangent Functoid**: It returns the arc tangent of a number
- **Base-specified Logarithm**: It returns the base-specified logarithm of a value
- **Common Logarithm**: It returns the base 10 logarithm of a value
- **Cosine**: It returns the cosine of an angle
- **Natural Exponential Function**: It returns e, raised to the specified power
- **Natural Logarithm**: It returns the base e logarithm of a value
- **Sine**: It returns the sine of an angle
- **Tangent**: It returns the tangent of an angle
- **X^Y**: It returns the specified value, raised to the power of a specified second value

All functoids take one argument, with the exception of the Base-specified Logarithm and the X^Y Functoids, which take two.

String Functoids

The **String Functoids** are relatively simple but extremely useful string manipulation or exploratory functoids. They are as follows:

- Lowercase
- Uppercase
- String Concatenate
- String Left
- String Right
- String Left Trim
- String Right Trim
- String Find
- String Extract
- Size

Most functoids in this category map to the corresponding .NET functions, such as ToLower, ToUpper, Substring, TrimStart, TrimEnd, IndexOf, and Length.

 String Functoids that refer to a position within the string will refer to the first character as position 1, and not 0.

Using Advanced Functoids

The **Advanced Functoids** help in five areas, as follows:

- Looping
- Conditional Mapping (which makes use of the logical functoids)
- Copy-based Mapping
- Troubleshooting and Testing
- Scripting is done using external assemblies, inline code or XSLT.

These are areas that are used in this book to allow a logical division that makes explaining these functoids easier. These are not areas that you will find in the toolbox or anywhere else in Visual Studio or BizTalk; it's all just Advanced Functoids.

Looping

Most of the Advanced Functoids deal with looping. In this subcategory, these functoids exist as follows:

- Index
- Iteration
- Nil Value
- Record Count
- Looping
- Table Looping
- Table Extractor

Index

The **Index Functoid** will return a specific node in a looping node structure, for example, the second Component node in the Components structure is always the engine. The following map gets the Code attribute of the Component record corresponding to Engine by supplying the Code attribute as the first parameter and 2 as the second parameter:

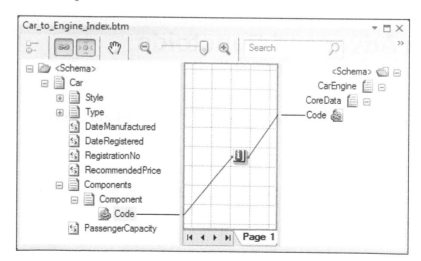

Iterator

The **Iteration Functoid** will tell you what the index of the current nodes is, in a looping node structure. The same sample as the one in the preceding screenshot can be used to show a sample use of the Iteration functoid, as follows:

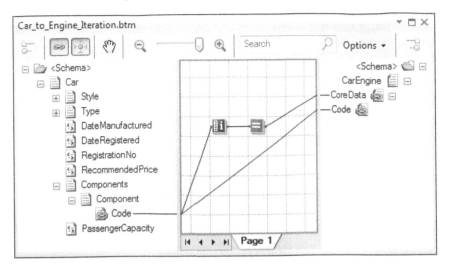

The sample gets the current iteration or index, uses a Logical Equals Functoid that compares the current index to the value 2, the index of the engine, and returns a Boolean value that controls the output of the CoreData node.

> All functoids that return a Boolean value can be used this way to control the output.

Nil

The **Nil Value Functoid** will give a record a null value, that is, it will give it a xsi:nil attribute set to true.

Record Count

The **Record Count Functoid** will tell you how many nodes of the input type are under the same parent node. In the preceding screenshot, it could tell you how many Component nodes are there.

Looping

The **Looping Functoid** will help the Mapper understand how you want looping to occur. The Mapper automatically understands that it needs to loop if you are mapping from one simple looping structure to another. It will automatically insert code, to do the looping and extract the values. However, in cases where several loops are involved, it needs guidance, for example, if you want to loop over and combine multiple source looping structures while you create the output, you need to convey that instruction to the Mapper by using a Looping Functoid, as shown in the following screenshot:

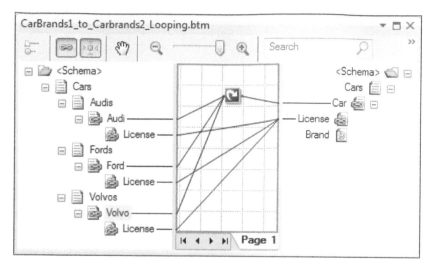

The previous example works only due to the use of the Looping Functoids. Had it not been for the Looping Functoids, only the Audi license would be outputted, and we would get a warning in our **Output** window in Visual Studio, as follows:

CarBrands1_to_Carbrands2_Looping.btm: warning btm1030: The destination node "Car" has multiple source loop paths.

CarBrands1_to_Carbrands2_Looping.btm: warning btm1004: The destination node "License" has multiple inputs. For a destination node to have multiple inputs, one of its ancestors should be connected to a looping functoid.

 You can create conditional looping logic by connecting a Logical Functoid to the same destination node as the Looping Functoid.

Table Looping

The **Table Looping Functoid** is another way of controlling looping structures. It lets us configure an internal table and the columns within it, and fills the rows of that table using data such as nodes from the input Schema, links from other functoids or constants, and so on.

It allows you to create multiple output rows from one input row.

Creating many outputs from one input node is trivial if it has two different node structures in the same destination, for example, if we turn the map CarBrands1_to_CarBrands2_looping.btm the other way and once again use Logical Functoids to control our output, as shown in the following screenshot:

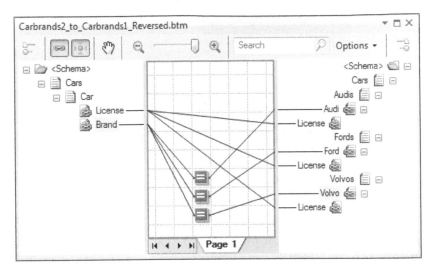

This will work fine. It is when you need to create two rows in the same destination structure based on only the single input that it gets difficult.

Let us look at a sample in which the use of Table Looping Functoid solves a mapping challenge. The car manufacturer HWLC Motors is selling directly to consumers as well as leasing firms and dealerships. As a part of the process for selling a car, HWLC needs to update the **Customer Relationship Management (CRM)** system. It keeps information on cars sold, who the current owner is, and who the actual person using the car is (which is important for leasing, but not so for consumers).

In the case of a consumer, the buyer of the car will be both the owner and the user. Let us go through the steps to complete this Map, as follows:

1. Create a new Map with appropriate Schemas, as shown in the following screenshot:

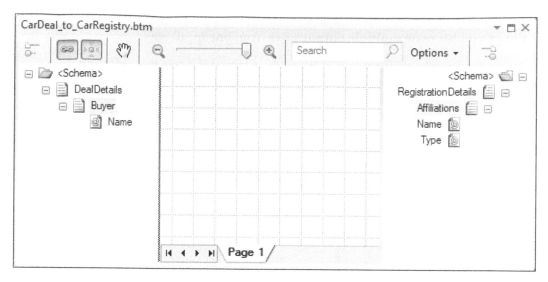

2. Drag-and-drop a **Table Looping** Functoid onto the mapping surface.

3. Link the **Buyer** node to the **Table Looping** Functoid to create a scoping link, and connect the **Table Looping** Functoid to the **Affiliations** destination node.

4. Right-click on the **Table Looping** Functoid, and select **Configure Functoid Inputs**.

5. Enter **2** as the second input, for two columns.

6. Enter the string **Owner** as the value for the third parameter.

7. Create a fourth parameter, and enter the string **User** as the value.

8. Click on **OK** to close the functoid configuration.

9. Link the **Name** column to the **Table Looping** Functoid.

10. Right-click on the **Table Looping** Functoid, and select **Configure Table Looping Grid**.

11. Create two rows, one with **Name** and **Owner**, and one with **Name** and **User**, as shown in the following screenshot:

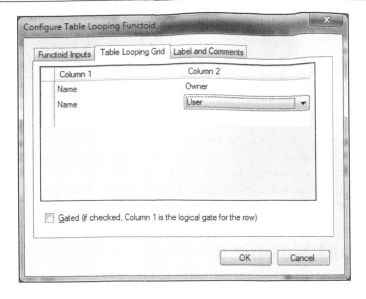

12. Click on **OK** to close the functoid configuration.

Next, to get anything out of the **Table Looping** Functoid, we need to use the **Table Extractor**. It takes two inputs: the Table Looping Functoid, and the number of the column to retrieve the value from. In this case, we need two functoids, one for each of our columns.

1. Drop two **Table Extractor** Functoids onto the Mapper, and connect both of them to the **Table Looping** Functoid.

2. Configure the first functoid to use **Column 1** and the second to use **Column 2**.

3. Connect them to **Name** and **Type**, in the destination, respectively.

4. The finished result should be similar to the following screenshot:

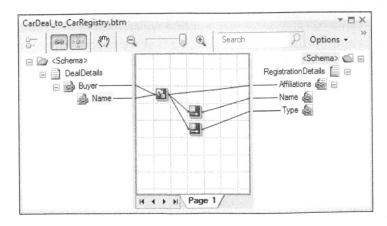

5. The input looks like the following code snippet:

```
<ns0:DealDetails XMLns:ns0="http://Chapter03_Example01_Schemas.
CarDeal">
  <Buyer Name="Felix" />
</ns0:DealDetails>
```

6. We will have an output that looks like the following code snippet:

```
<ns0:RegistrationDetails XMLns:ns0="http://Chapter03_Example01_
Schemas.CarRegistry">
  <Affiliations Name="Felix" Type="Owner"></Affiliations>
  <Affiliations Name="Felix" Type="User"></Affiliations>
</ns0:RegistrationDetails>
```

Conditional Mapping

We have already seen samples of conditional mapping, conditional looping, and controlling output. These samples were using a Logical Functoid, connected directly to the output. The functoids that fall under Conditional Mapping Functoids in the advanced category are **Value Mapping Functoid** and the **Value Mapping (Flattening) Functoid**.

 Value Mapping Functoid is often used in conjunction with Looping Functoid. Value Mapping (Flattening) Functoid, on the other hand, should not be used in conjunction with Looping Functoid.

The main difference between the two is that while Value Mapping Functoid will create one output for each input row, Value Mapping (Flattening) Functoid will flatten the input into only a single output row, as you will see in the following example:

We will use the same `CarRegistry` Schema that we created in the Table Looping sample for input and for output. Let us assume that we need to transform that to a more typed registry, where the `Owner` and `User` of the car exist as nodes.

The input is as follows:

```
<ns0:RegistrationDetails XMLns:ns0="http://Chapter03_Example01_
Schemas.CarRegistry">
  <Affiliations Name="Felix" Type="Owner"></Affiliations>
  <Affiliations Name="Felix" Type="User"></Affiliations>
</ns0:RegistrationDetails>
```

The Map used is shown in the following screenshot:

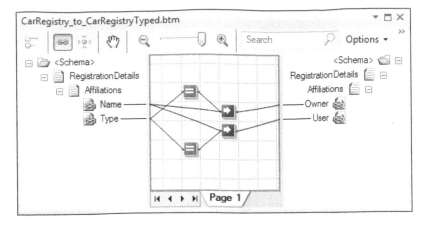

Using **Value Mapping** Functoid, we will get the following output:

```
<ns0:RegistrationDetails XMLns:ns0="http://Chapter03_Example01_
Schemas.CarRegistryTyped1">
  <Affiliations>
    <Owner>Felix</Owner>
  </Affiliations>
  <Affiliations>
    <User>Felix</User>
  </Affiliations>
</ns0:RegistrationDetails>
```

Now, on the other hand, if we create a new Map that looks exactly the same, with the only difference being that we replace the Value Mapping Functoid with Value Mapping (Flattening) Functoid, we will get a different result. The Map is shown in the following screenshot:

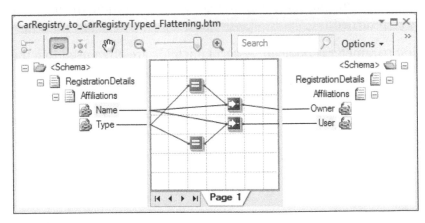

Our (flattened) output is as follows:

```
<ns0:RegistrationDetails XMLns:ns0="http://Chapter03_Example01_
Schemas.CarRegistryTyped1">
  <Affiliations>
    <Owner>Felix</Owner>
    <User>Felix</User>
  </Affiliations>
</ns0:RegistrationDetails>
```

As you can see, it no longer creates two rows for the output but instead compacts them both into one.

Copy-based Mapping

The Copy-based messaging subcategory, or the simple mapping category as the BizTalk Server documentation calls it, consists of one single functoid, that is, the **Mass Copy Functoid**. It does something very simple by recreating the linked input node and everything beneath it, at the specified location in the output. It can simplify Schema development, where only the parts of a large Schema structure that are used need to be defined. The rest can be hidden under an xs:any node, as unknown content. It is also useful while mapping between two Schemas with the same structure, or even the same Schema when you want to do some small calculation or similar small operation, yet do not want to relink all nodes.

Troubleshooting

This category holds the **Assert Functoid**. It takes three parameters. The first is a Boolean value that indicates Error or Success. The second is the string thrown in an exception if the first parameter is false. It will do so only when the project is built in debug configuration. The third is the value returned, if the first parameter evaluates to true. If the project is built in release configuration, the third parameter will always be returned.

Since the first parameter is Boolean, Assert Functoids are often used together with Logical Functoids.

The Assert Functoid must still, like any other functoid, be either directly or indirectly connected to an output node for it to trigger.

Scripting

The **Scripting Functoid** is the most advanced functoid available. It gives you a multitude of options on how to extend, and expand on the functionality of BizTalk Mapper. You have the following options:

- External Assembly (default)
- Inline C#
- Inline JScript
- Inline Visual Basic .NET
- Inline XSLT
- Inline XSLT Call Template

Most of the things, if not everything, that you can do with other functoids, can be done with the Scripting Functoids. Through the use of external assemblies, inline code, the ability to chain and make use of multiple Scripting Functoids that save values in internal .NET variables, for inter-functoid communication, and the access to the full array of .NET functionality coupled with the full power of going directly to XSLT, when you need it. The scripting functoid really does offer endless possibilities.

With great power comes great responsibility. Even though you can use scripting functoids to do just about everything, you should not. Designing and developing a good maintainable map is all about visibility and comprehension in your modeling. One of the unique selling points of BizTalk Mapper is the fact that it is a model. It is easy to change as it is all really visual. Over-using Scripting Functoids will seriously cripple that intention.

Using external assemblies

There are a lot of benefits of storing code outside your Map. The rule of thumb is that anything bigger than the editing window will benefit from being stored outside the Map. Placing code in a library makes it easier to unit test, easier to maintain and update, easier to debug, and enables code sharing. It also gives you an extra component to deploy and manage. The bigger-than-editor-window rule is a bit crude, but if you follow regular common sense, it will usually be ok.

These are the steps required to call an external assembly using the Scripting functoid:

1. Identify or create an external assembly that has a method that you would like to call. In this example, I am using a method that has the following signature:

```
public static string Reverse(string s)
{
   return new string(s.Reverse().ToArray());
}
```

2. Drop a **Scripting Functoid** onto the map.

3. Configure the **Scripting Functoid** to use an **External Assembly**, and set **Script assembly**, **Script class** and **Script method** according to your needs, for example, using a `HelperLibrary` assembly with a `CodeHelper` class and a `Reverse` method, as shown in the following screenshot:

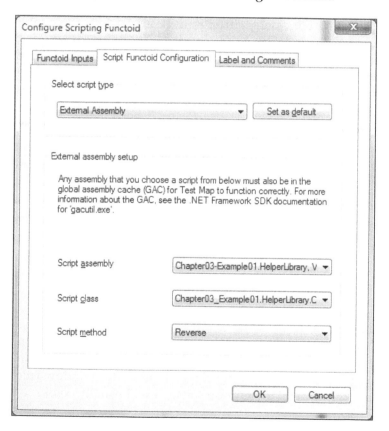

4. Click on **OK** and connect the **Scripting Functoid** according to the input parameters of the method, and to a destination node in the output, or a subsequent functoid, as shown in the following screenshot:

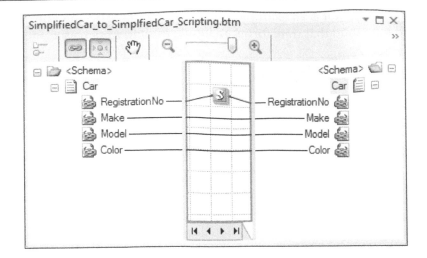

> Before we test the Map, we need to make sure that
> `HelperLibrary` is in the **Global Assembly Cache** (**GAC**).
> We can develop without it, but cannot run test map.

5. We test the Map using the following input:

    ```
    <ns0:Car XMLns:ns0="http://Chapter03_Example01.Schemas.
    SimplifiedCar">
      <RegistrationNo>RegistrationNo_0</RegistrationNo>
    </ns0:Car>
    ```

6. We get the following output, that is, my external component has been called
    and executed correctly:

    ```
    <ns0:Car XMLns:ns0="http://Chapter03_Example01.Schemas.
    SimplifiedCar">
      <RegistrationNo>0_oNnoitartsigeR</RegistrationNo>
    </ns0:Car>
    ```

Using Inline Code

The way the Scripting Functoid works while using **Inline C#**, **Inline JScript**,
or **Inline Visual Basic .NET**, is similar to using an external assembly. The main
difference is that the code is stored within the Map instead, and the configuration
looks different. You also don't have access to the full power of the .NET framework
in Inline Code, but are limited to only a few namespaces.

The following screenshot is an example of configuring the Scripting Functoid, using Inline C# and a method that transforms an input string to uppercase:

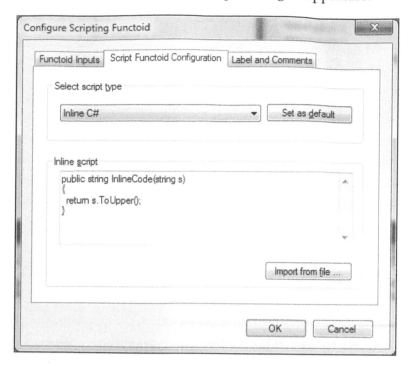

 Other than in an example, it is bad practice to implement something with the Scripting Functoid that already exists. In this case, I should have used the **Uppercase Functoid** of the **string** category instead.

Besides the code contained within the method signature, choosing inline code also allows us to declare global variables outside the method declaration. These are accessible throughout the map from within all Inline Code Scripting Functoids.

Just like when it is configured to use an external assembly, the Scripting Functoid used with inline code can take its input from several sources, such as input nodes or other functoids, and its output may be linked to output nodes or to other functoids, similarly.

Using Inline XSLT

Using Inline XSLT allows us to tap XSLT directly. This gives us more freedom in accessing the full document in a way that other functoids normally are not capable of doing.

Since we are running XSLT, the **Scripting Functoid** using any of the XSLT options, can only be connected to an output node as it explicitly creates an XML structure.

The difference between the two options, that is, **Inline XSLT** and **Inline XSLT Call Template**, is that while the former is not allowed to take inputs, the latter is.

In advanced scenarios, XSLT Scripts may access global variables created in inline code as well as call the inline code methods and external assemblies.

Let us look at a simple example of using XSLT inside a Map. In the following **Inline XSLT** sample, XSLT has the same effect as a direct link, but XSLT can do so much more. Even if the example itself is simple, it does show one of XSLT's many powerful features—the ability to access any part of the source document regardless of context. In this case, it finds the `RegistrationNo` node and outputs its value to the destination, as shown in the following screenshot:

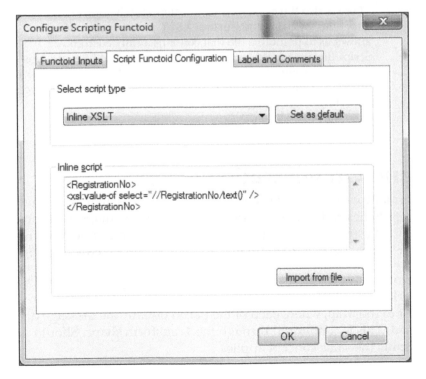

The Map looks similar to the following screenshot:

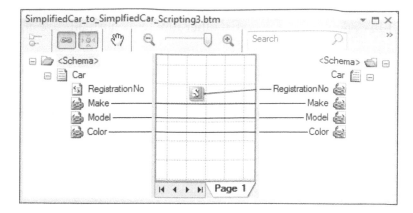

If we were to use an Inline XSLT Call Template instead, we would be able to take in a parameter, but other than that, it behaves exactly the same and has the same benefits and limitations.

 There is also the possibility of sidestepping the BizTalk Mapper altogether by using the **Custom XSLT** property on a Map. It allows us to point to a file that contains a fully custom XSLT Script that is then responsible for the full Map. While opinions differ, it is generally agreed that this option should not be taken unless performance optimization or specific requirements, such as sorting or grouping, make it a much better, and perhaps even the only, option.

Maps and Orchestrations

Maps are normally configured to run in one of three places, that is, Receive Ports, Send Ports, or Orchestrations. There are some things, some maps, that can only be made inside Orchestrations—specifically the Maps using multiple input messages to produce their output or, though more uncommon, Maps that create *multiple outputs*.

XSLT only works with one input message and one output. The way the Orchestration Designer works around this is by creating a temporary multipart message that is used as input to the Map, where each of the parts contains the message details of the messages used. This is configured through the **Transform** shape. Should you need multiple outputs the same concept applies.

You can also use the concept of multipart messages to pass parameters to a map by creating a Schema for the parameter, a message to hold it, and using it as one of the input messages to the map.

Orchestrations are covered in *Chapter 4, Developing BizTalk Artifacts – Creating Orchestrations*. So let us focus just on how to configure the **Transform** shape to perform a multimessage mapping, as follows:

1. Create an Orchestration.

2. Create the messages and Receive and Send Ports that you need, to gather the information.

3. Drop a **Transform** shape into **Orchestration Designer**.

4. Configure the **Construct** shape, and select the message that will be created by the map.

5. Open the **Transform** shape configuration, and select the messages that you need to use as input. Each message will become part of the multipart message, as shown in the following screenshot:

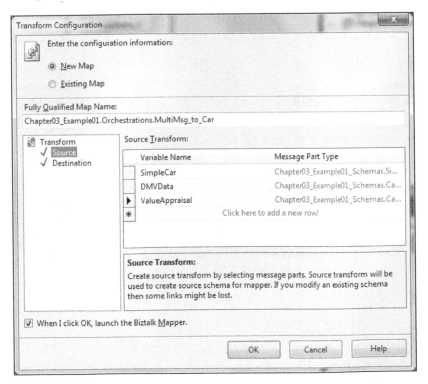

6. Click on **OK** to open the Mapper.

7. You can now see the multipart message; each selected message is contained within the parts, for example, messages such as Car, DMVData, and CarValue are shown in the following screenshot:

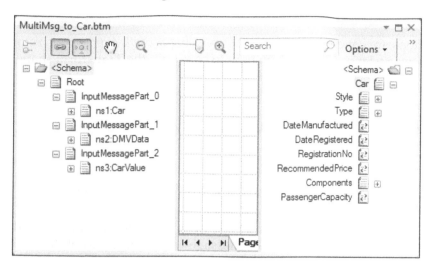

8. Complete the Map, as shown in the following screenshot:

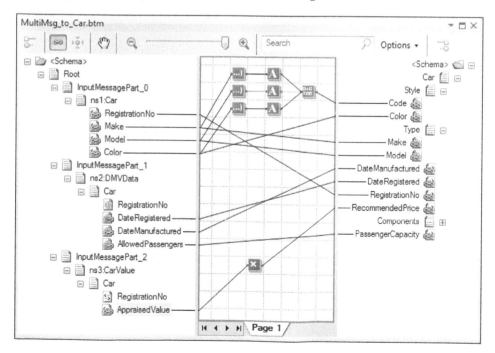

Test your knowledge

1. As part of a transformation, you need to reuse a piece of business logic, previously defined in an instance method in a .NET component. You need to do this without writing any additional lines of code. What do you need to do to call the method from the transformation?

    a. Use the Expression shape, and call the component using a XLANG statement.

    b. Use the Scripting Functoid, configure it to use Inline C#, and call the method using a C# statement.

    c. Use the Scripting Functoid, configure it to use an External Assembly, and call the method by pointing out the assembly, class and method.

    d. Drag-and-drop the activity created when you add a reference to the component to the mapping surface, and configure inputs and outputs.

2. HWLC Motors is starting a marketing campaign, and wants to target strong customers that bought high-end cars. You are developing a Map that is going to process an input Schema that contains a list of customer nodes containing CustomerID and CarValue as child nodes. The output document is the same as the input document. You want to only include those customers whose cars had a value above $70000 in the output. What do you need to do?

    a. Add an Equal Functoid. Link CarValue as the first input, and set the second input to 70000. Connect the output to the Customer node in the destination Schema.

    b. Add a Greater Than Functoid. Link the CarValue node as the first input, and set the second input to 70000. Connect the output to the Customer node in the destination Schema.

    c. Add a Less Than Functoid. Link the CarValue node as the first input, and set the second input to 70000. Connect the output to the Customer node in the destination Schema.

    d. Add a Value Mapping Functoid. Connect the CarValue node as the first input, and set the second input to 70000. Connect the output to the CarValue node in the destination Schema.

Summary

In this chapter, we learned about creating Maps and using functoids. We took a closer look at connecting to a database as well as controlling looping, doing conditional mapping, and other advanced functoids. The Scripting Functoid was examined closer, and the options it enabled for integrating with external assemblies and writing XSLT Scripts. We also looked at using Maps from within Orchestrations to enable multipart Schema maps. The next chapter is about the Developing BizTalk Artifacts — Creating Orchestrations part of the exam.

4

Developing BizTalk Artifacts—Creating Orchestrations

This chapter covers Orchestrations and Orchestration shapes and logic. It will provide an overview of all shapes and go into the details of a couple of them, such as using the Expression shapes to call additional logic in .NET components. It talks about how an Orchestration gets activated by subscribing to messages, getting called or started, as well as dives deep into the port bindings that are available, and how to use them. We will also take a closer look at persistence, transactions, and scopes, though using scopes for exception handling and compensation will be covered in the next chapter. This chapter will cover the following:

- Developing Orchestrations
- Configuring Orchestration bindings
- Configuring correlation
- Test your knowledge

Developing Orchestrations

Many integrations are based on pure messaging scenarios, that is, they do not need Orchestrations. They consist of receiving a message through an adapter, applying some form of transformations to the message, routing it to one or more subscribers, and sending them out again, using the same or another adapter. They might also require a response. In cases where that response is synchronous, and the ports are configured with the request-response message exchange pattern, this can be handled without an Orchestration. However, as soon as you have an integration that implies more than one logical step, you use an Orchestration.

It is usually stated that Orchestrations exist to coordinate business processes. I would drop the word "business" from that. In a nutshell, the Orchestration engine is the workflow engine employed by the BizTalk Server to allow you to handle various processes, whether they have their roots based in business or technology. Orchestrations are based on the C#-like language named **XLANG/s**. Though you sometimes resort to writing XLANG/s statements directly, you most often work with modeling your process using Orchestration shapes and setting properties.

Basic shapes and configuration

Orchestrations, and the executable processes they implement, are modeled using a sequence of shapes. Each shape has a distinct meaning and usage. The shapes can be divided into five areas, as follows:

- Message and Data Handling
- Containers
- Flow Control
- Orchestration Nesting
- Other

The available shapes are the ones you have to work with. Orchestration shape is not an area of extensibility. You do, however, like with the Scripting Functoid for Maps, have a way of writing code or calling external components to perform processing. In Orchestrations, this has the form of the Expression shape.

Message and Data Handling

Within this category, there are shapes that help to receive, send, construct, transform, or assign message variables as follows:

Shape	Description
Receive	Used to receive a message.
	A selection of its properties are as follows:
	• Activate
	• Initializing Correlation Sets
	• Following Correlation Sets

Shape	Description
Send	Used to send a message. A selection of its properties are as follows: • Initializing Correlation Sets • Following Correlation Sets
Construct Message	Used as a parent to any shape-constructing message. The possible nested shapes are as follows: • Message Assignment • Transform A selected property is as follows: • Messages Constructed
Message Assignment	Used to assign a value to a message, or to part of a message, for example, assignment to a node through the use of a distinguished field. It is also used to assign values to context available as promoted properties. A selected property is as follows: • Expression
Transform	Used to apply a transform or Map to a message to create a new message. A selection of its properties are as follows: • Input Messages • Output Messages • Map Name

Some shapes require nesting, such as the Assign and Transform shapes, which always need to be put into a Construct shape, as shown in the following diagram:

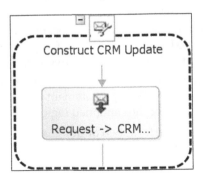

Containers

Containers are shapes that, either visually or technically, group other shapes, as follows:

Shape	Description
Group	Used to visually group shapes together and be able to expand and collapse that view in the Orchestration Designer.
	These are also not part of the code at all (similar to a region in C#).
Scope	Used to divide logic into units of work or transactions that may make use of exception handling or compensation.
	Scopes are diversified and have many interesting properties.
	Scopes are similar to the combination of `TransactionScope` and a try/catch block in C#.

Flow control

Since Orchestrations model processes, and processes are much about the flow of messages, there are many shapes used to handle that flow, as follows:

Shape	Description
Decide	Used to create different branches of logic, based on "if", "else if" (, else if, …), and "else" types of conditions.
	Each "if" branch takes an XLANG/s expression evaluating to `true` or `false`.
Delay	Used to create a `TimeSpan`-based delay in your Orchestration.
	A selected property is as follows:
	• Delay allows you to create a new `TimeSpan` object to configure the delay.
Listen	Used to create different branches of logic, based on messages received or a timeout value. Only one of the branches will execute. A Delay shape is used to configure the timeout.
Loop	Used to create a looping logic similar to a "while" statement, where an XLANG/s statement that must be `true` before each execution of the contained logic, is evaluated.
Parallel Actions	Used to perform two or more independent branches of logic where all branches execute.

Shape	Description
Suspend	Used to suspend an Orchestration instance to allow administrative action to be taken. An administrator can then either resume or terminate the Orchestration instance. If `Resume` is chosen, then execution will continue from the next shape. A selected property is as follows: • Error Message
Terminate	Used to end the execution of the Orchestration instance. It is often used after handling an exception and possibly (although less often) while ending up in a branch of logic where no more work is required by the Orchestration. A selected property is as follows: • Error Message
Throw Exception	Used to forcefully throw an exception, for example, after evaluating data or some logical condition. A selected property is as follows: • Exception Object, referring to a variable of base type `exception`, caught within an exception block, or created in an expression.
Compensate	Used to call the compensation block of nested scopes. One compensation shape is required per nested compensation block to be called.

Orchestration Nesting

Orchestrations can be nested and called from other Orchestrations, similar to methods in .NET. The shapes that control that are as follows:

Shape	Description
Call Orchestration	Allows for *synchronously* starting another Orchestration and holding additional execution until it has completed. A selection of its properties are as follows: • Called Orchestration • Parameters (in and out)

Shape	Description
Start Orchestration	Allow for *asynchronously* starting another Orchestration. Processing in the calling Orchestration will continue to the next shape, as soon as the Orchestration has been started, and will not await the outcome.
	A selection of its properties are as follows:
	• Called Orchestration
	• Parameters (in only)

Other

These shapes are dynamic and either allow for advanced message processing, decision making, or actions through calling Business Rules, or allow for making arbitrary XLANG/s statements through calling .NET helper components. The shapes are as follows:

Shape	Description
Call Rules	Allows calling Business Rules from within Orchestrations. Using Business Rules will be covered in a later chapter.
Expression	Allows for writing XLANG/s statements that provide C#-like inline coding capabilities.

More information about the limitations and structure of the XLANG/s language can be found at `http://msdn.microsoft.com/en-us/library/aa577463(v=BTS.70).aspx`.

Orchestration activation

Orchestrations can be activated in one of two ways: by message publication to the `MessageBox`, fulfilling the Orchestrations activation subscription, as specified by the activating Receive Port and its binding option, or through their being called from another Orchestration. This activation process is not arbitrary. Instead, you need to determine how an Orchestration should be activated when you design it.

Activating Receive

An activating Receive shape is used when the Orchestration is first constructed. It is fulfilled by a message publication matching the activation subscription. This port can be of any binding type. The two main differentiators from any other port in the Orchestration are as follows:

1. The port is triggered by an activation subscription, based on **design-time-determined** filter criteria.

2. The **Receive** shape connected to the port is marked with **Activate** set to **True**, as shown in the following screenshot:

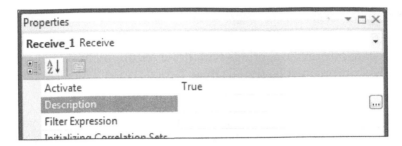

In this case, the **Filter** criteria for subscription has not been set explicitly. We will examine when it is needed and when it is not, later in this chapter, as we discuss port binding options.

Call and Start

Call or Start Orchestration is used when an Orchestration is used in the same way as a .NET method, that is, when it is called from another Orchestration directly using design-time coupling. Parameters are used to relay information. Such parameters might be variables, ports, messages, and so on.

Call is a direct **synchronous** instantiation that does not rely on message publication. It waits for the called Orchestration to complete and then returns the control back to the caller. **Start** is a fire-and-forget style **asynchronous** instantiation that uses message publication. A called Orchestration can return a response in the form of out or updated reference parameters, while a started Orchestration cannot return a result through parameters to its starter. However, it can use ports to receive a result.

Persistence

During the execution of an Orchestration, the state of the process is saved, or persisted. This enables the Orchestration to recover from failures and retry or restart from a previous point of execution.

Persistence may occur at the following occasions:

- After the execution of a Send Port
- After the execution of a Start Orchestration shape
- After the successful execution (commit) of a transactional scope
- When the Orchestration instance is suspended
- When the Orchestration instance is completed
- When the Orchestration engine shuts down gracefully
- When a debugging breakpoint is hit
- When dehydration is determined appropriate by the engine

Persistence and **serialization** of the entire Orchestration, including all messages, variables, and state information, brings with it the requirement that everything used within an Orchestration must be serializable.

 If a class used within an Orchestration is not serializable, you must use it within a transactional scope marked as atomic.

Dehydration and rehydration

Persistence also enables **dehydration** and **rehydration**, saving on precious processing resources by removing Orchestration from active memory and serializing it to the database awaiting its next step (dehydration), for example, the correlation of a response message.

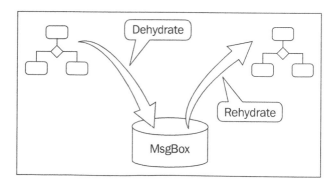

Once that event occurs, usually in the form of a message being published to the MessageBox, the Orchestration is rehydrated and processing is continued.

The scenarios in which dehydration is considered by the engine are as follows:

- When the Orchestration instance is waiting for a response message
- When the Orchestration is listening for a message using the Listen shape
- When the Orchestration engine determines that it has reached an idle delay threshold

The algorithm that the engine uses to determine dehydrations is based on the last 10 delays at that point in the Orchestration, and compared with a runtime calculated value, that differs depending on available resources and other factors, but is between a configurable minimum and maximum time (that, by default, is 0 and 1800 seconds respectively).

Transactions

Orchestrations employ the use of transactions to compose operations in units or work, isolated from others, and to recover from failures.

Transactions in BizTalk Server can be either Long Running or Atomic.

Transaction types

Long Running transactions are Long Running units of work for which you want to have the ability to define custom compensating logic and exception handling, or those that need to serve as an **umbrella** for nested transactions. Long Running transactions persist state, and send operations are committed to the MessageBox and seen by subscribers immediately.

Atomic transactions are transactional, and follow the **Atomicity, Consistency, Isolation**, and **Durability (ACID)** rules. Either everything within the transaction is correctly committed, or none of it is. The persisted state of the Orchestration is either the state before the transaction began or the state after all operations are committed. The changes performed by any operation during the transaction, such as a message being published to the MessageBox, is not visible to anyone during the transaction, but only after commit. Any changes, once committed, are persisted so that they are available, even if the system fails after the transaction is committed.

Read more on the ACID rules of transactions at the following URL:
http://en.wikipedia.org/wiki/ACID#Characteristics

Scopes

Scopes are the way to handle transactions within the Orchestrations.

All scopes have the following properties:

- Synchronized
- Transaction Type

Synchronized scopes ensure that the data being read is not simultaneously written to by other branches in a parallel shape. Scopes are, by default, not synchronized, though Atomic scopes are implicitly synchronized, regardless of the property value.

A scope can be marked as transactional by the **Transaction Type** property being set to either **Long Running** or **Atomic**. The third option for the **Transaction Type** property is **None**, as shown in the following screenshot:

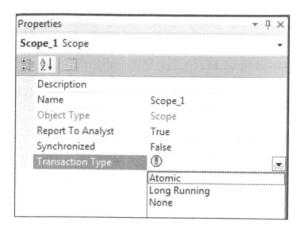

Long Running

When configuring the **Long Running** Transaction Type, the following additional properties (over a non-transactional scope) will become available:

- Compensation
- Timeout
- Transaction Identifier

Compensation can be **Default** or **Custom**. Setting it to **Custom** has the same effect as selecting to add a new Compensation Block to the scope.

The **Timeout** property specifies the amount of time spent in the scope before `TimeoutException` is raised.

Atomic

While configuring the Atomic Transaction Type, the following additional properties (over a non-transactional scope) will become available:

- Compensation
- Isolation Level
- Retry
- Timeout
- Transaction Identifier

For Atomic transaction, the `Timeout` value indicates the amount of time that passes before the transaction is marked as failed and is rolled back, but only if it was coordinated in a transaction, together with another resource, by the **Distributed Transaction Coordinator (DTC)**.

The `Retry` value indicates whether `PersistenceException` (caused by database connectivity issues) and `RetryTransactionException` (explicitly thrown in the Orchestration) should cause the transaction to be retried. Only these exceptions will be affected by the `Retry` flag. All other exceptions will cause the transaction to fail.

Isolation levels

Isolation levels control the locking levels used in the database by the engine while dealing with reads and writes for the actions performed by shapes in the scope. These transaction levels are available as follows:

- **Read Committed**: It reads only committed rows and prevents reading changes that are not yet committed by other transactions, but it does not prevent data it has read from being changed by other transactions before it has completed.

- **Repeatable Read**: It prevents updates to rows read by this scope until the transaction is completed.

- **Serializable**: It prevents data being committed by other transactions in such a way that queries used by this transaction would give a different result than when executed.

The default `Isolation Level` is `Serializable`.

Nesting

Long Running transactions can contain other transactions, either Long Running or Atomic. Atomic transactions can contain no other transactions.

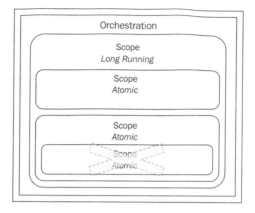

Conceptually, when it comes to transactions and nesting, you can look at the Orchestration level as a scope, that is, the Orchestration can be marked as a transaction in the same way as a scope. If you want to put an Atomic transactional scope directly inside the Orchestration, then the Orchestration needs to be configured as Long Running.

Transaction reach

Another important concept about transactions in BizTalk Server is their reach. Transactions initiated in Orchestrations end in the `MessageBox`. This means that marking a scope as Atomically transactional does not allow you to have a transactional conversation with the intended recipient of the message through the `MessageBox` from within the Orchestration. The reach of a transaction is depicted in the following diagram:

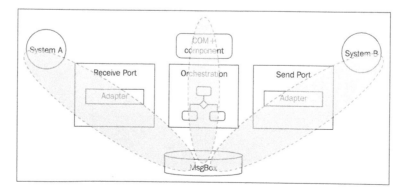

As the diagram shows, it is possible to extend the reach of a transaction from an Orchestration to a COM+ (Enterprise Services-managed) component.

Storing configuration information

Many Orchestrations may rely on configuration parameters. There are different ways of supplying configuration to an Orchestration. We will examine some of these and look for the pros and cons.

Orchestration variables

Orchestration variables are a very static place to have configuration values. If variables point to a class, the default constructor of that class can be called automatically to instantiate the variable. If anything other than the default constructor is called, this needs to be done in an Expression shape. Also, when Orchestrations are called or started, the caller can supply the initial values for parameters. However, they have to originate from somewhere.

Configuration placed in BTSNTSvc.exe.config

The BTSNTSvc.exe file is an executable file used by all BizTalk in-process Host Instances. As a .NET executable, it reads its configuration from the BTSNTSvc.exe.config file at startup. It is possible to place custom configuration into that file. The issue with this approach is that any addition or change to a configuration value requires the Host Instance to be restarted. Since the introduction of 64-bit processes, there is also a BTSNTSvc64.exe file with a corresponding configuration file. This requires configuration to be duplicated in two places (and on as many BizTalk Servers as there are in the group). Also, any configuration property supplied in this file is not available to the isolated Hosts, though that is not an issue with Orchestrations, since they only run in process. Accessing files under the Program Files folder might also be restricted in some organizations.

Configuration placed in web.config for isolated Hosts

For Isolated Hosts, it is possible to place configuration in `web.config`, in the directory of the web service being called. In the end, this is just a bad practice resulting in many configuration duplications and maintenance challenges, not to mention configuration being overwritten and removed if the service is republished.

Configuration placed in machine.config

Configuration in `machine.config` solves the issue of having different places for in-process or isolated Hosts. There is still the issue of whether to choose 32- or 64-bit, which will have their machine configs in `C:\Windows\Microsoft.NET\Framework\v4.0.30319\Config\machine.config` and `C:\Windows\Microsoft.NET\Framework64\v4.0.30319\Config\machine.config`, respectively. Also, as with `BTSNTSvc.exe.config`, if your BizTalk environment consists of more than one server, you will need to apply settings to all machines. `machine.config` settings are also only read when the process is initiated, so this placement also requires Host restart for updates or new additions. Accessing the `machine.config` file is also often restricted in many organizations.

Some configuration can be placed on the Adapter handlers

Specifically, WCF extension configuration can be placed in the Send and Receive Handlers for the WCF-Custom adapter. This is detailed in *Chapter 7, Integrating Web Services and Windows Communication Foundation (WCF) Services*.

Through the message

Configuration values can be sent in as part of the message. It is not uncommon to determine the outcome of a process, based on the content of the message. However, sending in pure configuration values through the message is uncommon.

Through the message context

Configuration values can be part of the message context. A common place to configure values to be placed in the context is through the use of a custom Pipeline component, whose job is to write (or promote) the appropriate values to the context. Configuration can then be done in the Pipeline on a per-instance runtime configuration. The downside of this is that Orchestrations that can get their messages from more than one Receive Location must have those properties configured in all the locations. Also, more than one value (that is, either two Pipeline components or an un-typed one) needs to be put into the context, where it is hard to keep track of the format for inputting configuration values.

[The ESB Toolkit uses a variation of this approach where the "itinerary" is included in the message context.]

Business Rules

For configuration values that change often or for those you would like an out of the box-versioned user interface for, Business Rules are a good choice. They are centrally stored in the database, and as such are available on all machines to all types of Hosts. Business Rules can be, in some cases, a cumbersome addition to the solution just for the sake of configuration properties from some perspectives, but they are definitely a good viable option. There are also Application Programming Interfaces (APIs) available in the form of the Call Rules Orchestration shape that allows you to call Business Rules easily.

SSO

Single Sign-on (SSO) can be used as a centralized data store for configuration values. Besides storing user account mappings, it also stores custom configuration for adapters and can be used for secure storage of custom configuration for custom logic, as well. Although there are no easy, out-of-the-box options for using SSO this way, there are samples in the documentation and tooling available from the BizTalk Community that makes this relatively easy.

Using a .NET helper component

If you decide to use a .NET helper component to store and retrieve your configuration, then you can get the configuration from anywhere, say a file or a database. File storage will have its drawbacks, but it is certainly possible. In many cases, using a custom component may seem easy, but you should strive to use built-in functionality and features wherever possible, if you want to minimize maintenance costs.

Integrating with .NET assemblies

Sometimes there are methods or logic contained within .NET helper components that you would like to use from within an Orchestration. Even though there is no option to call an external assembly, like with the Scripting Functoid, doing so is easy. It requires an assembly reference added to the project, a variable of that type, and an Expression shape. The following are the steps required to call a .NET assembly from an Orchestration:

1. Create a .NET assembly. In this sample, we will use a Helper component that uses directory services to find the full name of the sales representative that created a sales order for a car. The `ADHelper` class is contained in the `Chapter04-Example01.ClassLibary` project. The code looks as follows:

```
namespace Chapter04_Example01.ClassLibrary
{
  public class ADHelper
  {
    public static string GetFullname(string username)
    {
      // Lookup code goes here
      return ""Max Mooremountain"";
    }
  }
}
```

2. Create an Orchestration that will call the assembly. The Orchestration `SalesOrderProcess` is implemented in `Chapter04-Example01. Orchestrations` in `Chapter04-Example01.sln`, for this sample, look similar to the following screenshot:

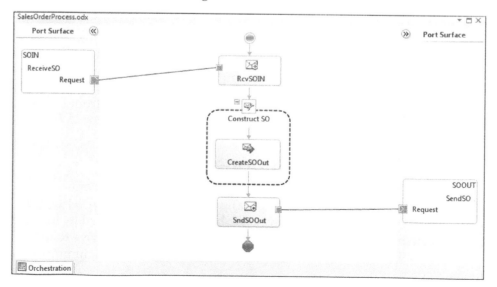

3. The expression in the `CreateSOOut` Message Assignment shape looks similar to that in the following screenshot:

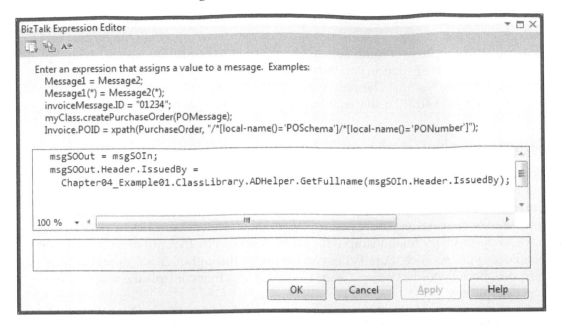

> Since the expression is using a static method, no variable of type `ADHelper` is required, and the method can be called outside an Atomic scope, even if the class is not marked as serializable.

4. Build the solution.
5. GAC the `Chapter04-Example01.ClassLibary` assembly, so that it can be located and used from the BizTalk Server.
6. Deploy the Orchestration.
7. Create ports. For simplicity, a Binding File is located at `C:\BTS2010CertGuide\Chapter04\Example01- Orchestrations\BTS2010CertGuide-Ch02- Orchestrations.xml`.
8. Configure the Orchestration.
9. Start and test the Orchestration.

Configuring Orchestration bindings

Orchestrations subscribe and publish messages to the `MessageBox`. Orchestrations can also be bound to Receive and Send Ports in different ways, which logically reflects as different kinds of subscriptions. As an extension to that, Orchestrations can also be configured to route messages between Orchestration instances, so that more than one Orchestration can participate in the execution chain, but they also go through the `MessageBox`. The only time the `MessageBox` is not involved is when you use the Call Orchestration shape to initiate execution of another Orchestration.

Ports versus Port Types

Ports in Orchestrations describe how the Orchestration will communicate with the `MessageBox` and the direction of that communication, that is, inbound or outbound. Ports are based on Port Types. The Port Type describes the communication pattern (one-way or request-response) and `MessageType` communicated. A Port Type can have a one-to-many relationship with ports. Ports can be thought of as an instance of a Port Type. As such, Port Types can be reused throughout a solution. For that purpose, Port Types has a `Type Modifier` property that controls the scope of the type, as follows:

- **Private**: Only ports in the same Orchestration may use it
- **Internal**: Only ports in Orchestrations in the same project may use it
- **Public**: Any port in an Orchestration project that references this project or assembly may use it

Logical ports versus physical ports

Ports in the Orchestration Designer are logical ports; they describe the logic of the operation and the direction of the communication to the `MessageBox`. Depending on the binding mode specified within the Orchestration (excluding Direct binding), the logical ports have to correlate to the physical ports (Receive and Send Ports). This process is also known as binding an Orchestration.

Using the Specify Now binding mode, you can also create the actual port configuration at the same time that you create the Orchestration, although that procedure is not recommended.

A selection of the properties of ports are as follows:

- Port Type
- Communication Direction
- Binding
- Ordered Delivery (on ports with Communication Direction Receive)
- Delivery Notification (on ports with Communication Direction Send)

There are more properties that become available depending on the binding option chosen.

Port binding options

There are several ways that logical ports can be bound to the MessageBox and physical ports. The most common are Specify Later or Direct (MessageBox).

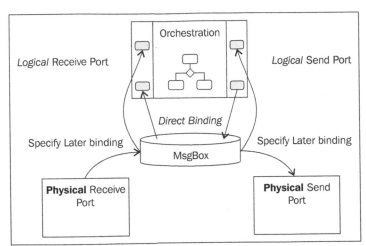

The complete list of available options is:

- Specify Now
- Specify Later
- Direct
    ◦ MessageBox
    ◦ Self Correlating
    ◦ Partner Orchestration
- Dynamic

While Specify Later and Direct `MessageBox` are both common, Self Correlating is not as widely used and understood, and Partner Orchestration is something that even experienced developers are often uncertain of how and when to use.

Specify Now

The **Specify Now** binding is utilized when the Receive or Send Port locations are defined at design time. This is typically not recommended.

The configuration interface has fewer options than the port configuration in the BizTalk Administration Console.

Using **Specify now** in the **Port Configuration Wizard** for a port with **Receive Communication Pattern** allows the usage of adapters, **HTTP**, **SOAP**, and **FILE** as **Transport** and requires the **URI** and **Receive pipeline** to be specified, as shown in the following screenshot:

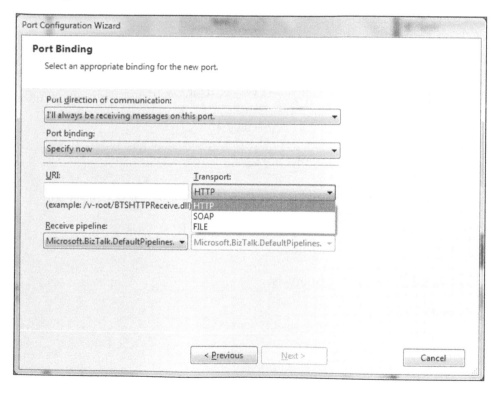

Using **Specify Now** in the **Port Configuration Wizard** for a port with a **Send Communication Pattern** allows the usage of **HTTP**, **FILE**, and **SMTP** as **Transport** and requires the **URI** and **Receive pipeline** to be specified as shown in the following screenshot:

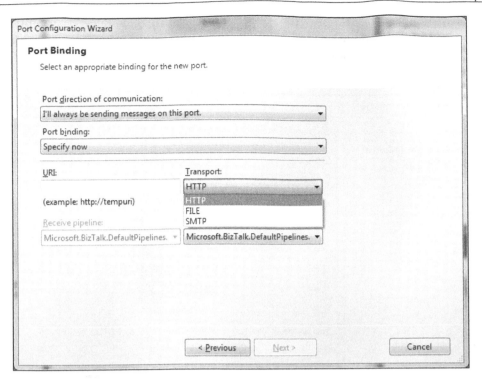

Regardless of what binding option you choose in the **Port Configuration Wizard**, the port can be reconfigured later during design time by going to **Port Properties**, as shown in the following screenshot:

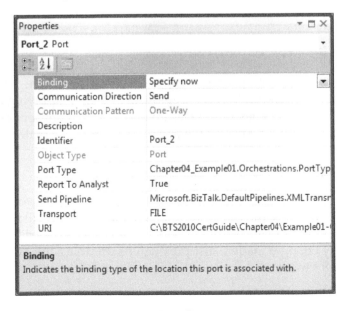

By deploying an Orchestration with Specify Now bindings, the Receive or/and Send Ports would be created with the properties specified within the Orchestration using automatically generated names. The logical to physical port association, known as binding, would be deployed as well, as shown in the following screenshot:

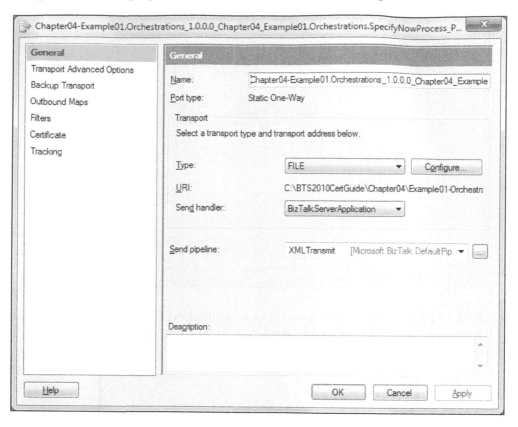

Be careful with using this option since changes made to ports, once deployed, will be overwritten when the Orchestration is redeployed, as with reapplying a Binding File. If you want to keep your Orchestration Design and Deployment separate from your Port Configuration, using the **Specify Later** binding option is a better choice.

Specify Later

The **Specify Later** binding allows you to make the connection between a logical port and physical port once the Orchestration is deployed. You will need to create the physical port on your own, as it will not be created for you during deployment. On the upside, any changes made to the port will be durable across Orchestration change and redeployment.

Using Specify Later makes no additional Port Configuration properties available in the Orchestration Designer, since all properties are configured on the physical port. Once deployed, the Orchestration's logical ports are bound to the physical ports.

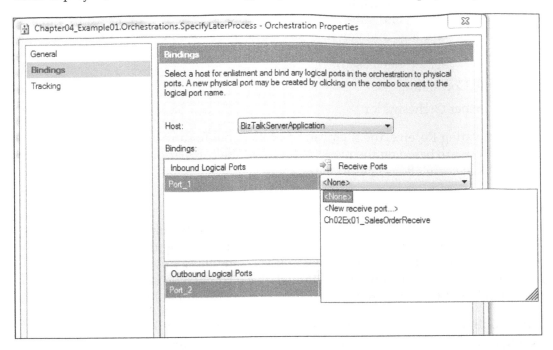

This still does not mean that messages bypass the MessageBox; it is just a shortcut to create very explicit subscriptions between Orchestration and its ports. Inspecting our Orchestration's subscription shows us that it is indeed activated by an explicitly identified Receive Port, as shown in the following screenshot:

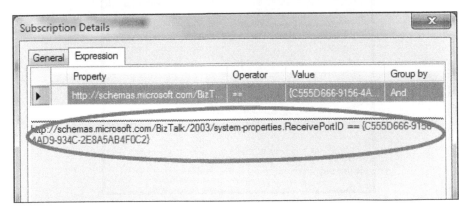

Direct

Direct Bound Ports are ports that are not bound directly to physical ports using the Administration Console GUI. Instead, they use the `MessageBox` and different kinds of pub or sub patterns and subscription filters to achieve their goal. There are three types of Direct bindings that you have to choose from, as follows:

- `MessageBox` (filter-based)
- Self Correlating
- Partner Orchestration

On an activating Receive, the filter can be explicit, but for any other Receive instance subscriptions are based on the message type and the correlation. We will take a closer look at correlations later in the chapter.

MessageBox (filter-based)

Direct Bound Ports are closest to the concept of pub or sub architecture. They allow you to deliver a message to the `MessageBox` without knowing the recipient and allow you to subscribe to messages without knowing the sender. There could be one recipient or many, something that, although it is also possible with Specify Later Ports, might not be as apparent, and is not the purpose of that binding.

When configuring a Receive Port to have **MessageBox Direct Binding**, the Port Configuration in the Orchestration Designer will set the **Binding** to **Direct** and the **Partner Orchestration Port** to **Message Box**, as shown in the following screenshot:

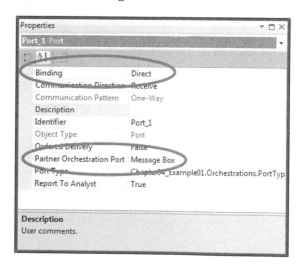

The configuration of a Send Port will differ slightly, as far as available properties go, but for these two properties they will look the same.

We should also specify a filter criterion on the Receive shape. If we do not, we will have created an Orchestration that subscribes to all messages that match the message type of the message that the Receive shape expects.

 Filters should be made as detailed as possible to avoid subscribing to unwanted messages.

Once a `Direct MessageBox Port` is deployed, there will be no configuration of ports needed or possible. As the following screenshot shows, the only thing left to configure (if all ports are Direct) is the **Host** under which the Orchestration should run:

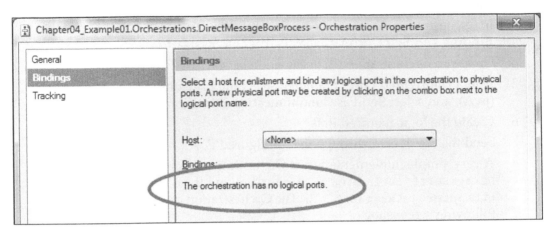

Self Correlating

By configuring a port with **Direct Self Correlating Direct** binding and passing it as a parameter to an Orchestration, you enable the Orchestration to send messages back to its caller without the use of a Correlation Set, through the use of the Start Orchestration shape.

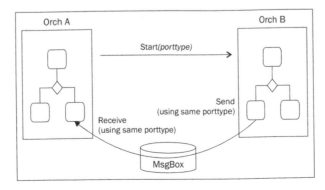

Instead, Self-correlated Ports generate an instance-specific (unique) correlation token, stored using the `PartnerService` promoted property. That property (among others) is then used to create a correlation.

 We will cover correlation later in this chapter. In short, a correlation token is required when you need to be able to get a response back to the correct Orchestration instance.

To use a Self-correlated Port, follow these steps:

1. Create and implement an Orchestration (A).
2. Identify the use case in the processing logic to start another Orchestration asynchronously, and requiring a response.
3. In Orchestration A, create a new **Port** and **Port Type** and select **Direct** as **Binding** and **Self Correlating** as **Partner Orchestration**.
4. Create an Orchestration (B) designed to be started.
5. Add a **Configured Port Parameter**, select the previously created Port Type (in A), and select **Send** as **Communication Direction**.
6. Create the logic required in B.
7. Send the result back through the Configured Port.
8. A very simple implementation of Orchestration B, named `DirectSelfCorrelatingChild.odx`, showing the concepts can be found in `Chapter04-Example01.sln`. The Orchestration can be seen in the following screenshot:

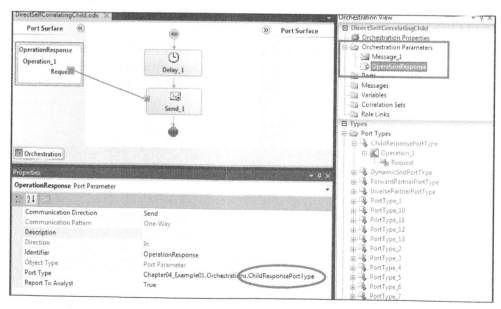

9. The preceding screenshot highlights the **OperationResponse Port Parameter**. Defining a Port Parameter places a port on the **Port Surface** of an Orchestration. In this case, the Orchestration also takes a Message Parameter, and all it does is send the same message back using the Port Parameter.

10. Use the **Start Orchestration** shape in A to call B, and supply the parameters needed, including the port (**Port Type**).

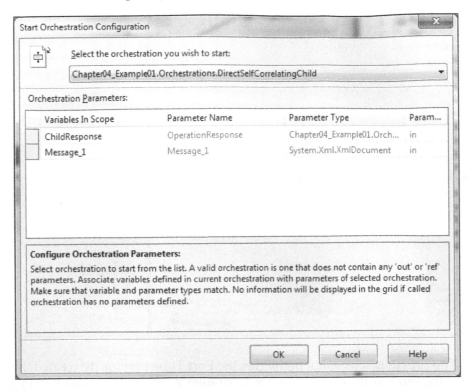

11. After starting the Orchestration, use a Receive shape to block the reception of the response from Orchestration B through the Configured Receive Port.

12. A very simple implementation of Orchestration A named
    `DirectSelfCorrelatingParent.odx` showing the concepts can be found
    in `Chapter01-Example04.sln`. The Orchestration can be seen in the
    following screenshot:

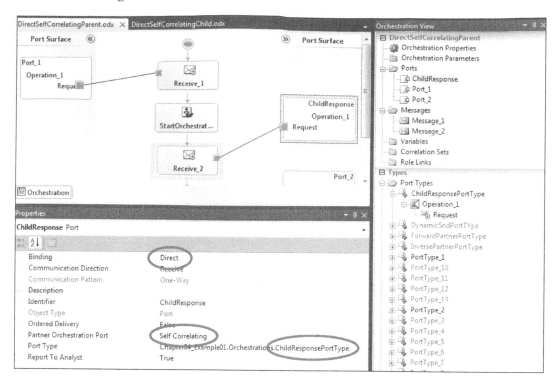

13. The previous screenshot highlights the Port Type previously created, how it
    is the same as the one used in Orchestration B—**ChildResponsePortType**,
    and that the port is **Direct** and **Self Correlating**.

If we run the sample, we can catch the instance subscription created by the parent
while it is waiting for the started child to publish a message to the `MessageBox`, using
the self-correlated port sent in as a parameter, as shown in the following screenshot:

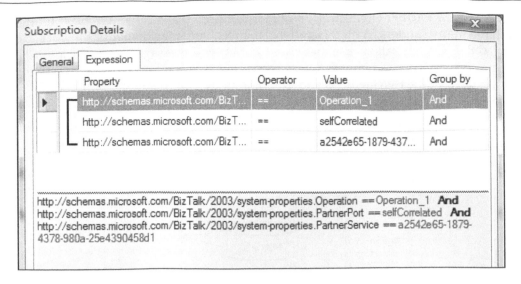

As you can see, it is based upon the unique `PartnerService` property, together with the `PartnerPort` property, which tell us `PartnerPort` is `selfCorrelated` and that the operation used is named as `Operation_1` (which is the default name given to the operation of the port by BizTalk).

Partner Orchestration

The **Partner Orchestration** option allows us to implement two patterns: **Forward Partner Orchestration Direct Binding** and **Inverse Partner Orchestration Direct Binding**. Basically, this means either receiving messages in one Orchestration from other Orchestrations, or sending messages from one Orchestration to other Orchestrations.

One of the differences between using `Direct MessageBox` binding and using Direct Partner Orchestration binding is that, like with Self-crrelated Ports, you use the Port Type to connect the Orchestrations together and, like the Self-correlated Port, one side sends the message and another side receives it. The main difference is that this is not solved through passing the port as a parameter in runtime; instead, it is a pure design-time configuration.

With **Forward Partner Orchestration Direct Binding**, the Receiver Orchestration can have many senders. With this pattern, the receiver is the owner of the Port Type. Other Orchestrations use that Port Type to send messages to the receiver. The receiver has no forehand knowledge of who is sending it. This is the most commonly used pattern of the two methods and is shown in the following diagram:

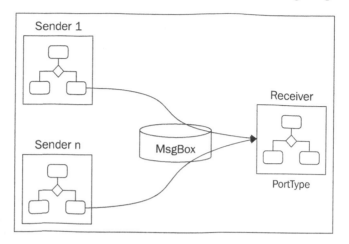

If we look at a sample subscription in a Receiver Orchestration, it looks similar to the following screenshot:

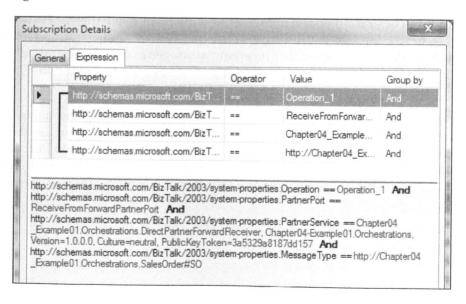

As you can see, the `PartnerService` property, as set by the sender(s), will have a direct binding with tight coupling to the receiver.

With **Inverse Partner Orchestration Direct Binding,** a single sender can have multiple receivers. With this pattern, the sender is the owner of the Port Type. Other Orchestrations connect to that Port Type to receive messages. The sender has no forehand knowledge of who the receivers are, as shown in the following diagram:

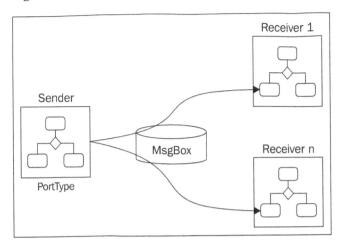

If we look again at a sample in one of the receivers connected to the sender, it looks similar to the following screenshot:

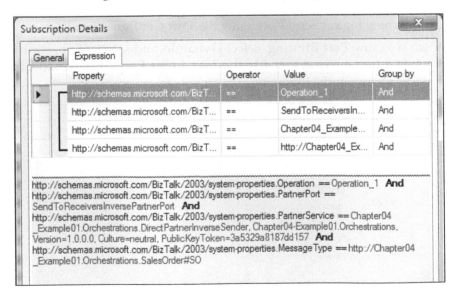

The big difference here is that the receiver is connected to the sender, and as such the sender owns the Port Type and the receiver is the one that has a direct binding with tight coupling to the sender.

Dynamic

A **Dynamic Send Port** is a port where you do not specify the address and transport type in the static configuration, as shown in the following screenshot:

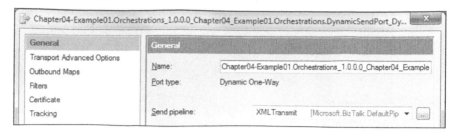

Instead, you are expected to supply it in runtime. This does not need to be through the use of an Orchestration, although it often is, when talking about the out-of-the-box capabilities.

 You could easily use a Dynamic Send Port by populating the same properties through the use of Pipeline components—something that the ESB Toolkit relies heavily on.

To use a Dynamic Send Port in an Orchestration, these are the steps we need to follow:

1. Create a new logical Send Port using the **Port Configuration Wizard**.

2. When selecting **Port Binding**, select **Dynamic**, and select an appropriate Pipeline (you can always change this later in the Properties window for the port), as shown in the following screenshot:

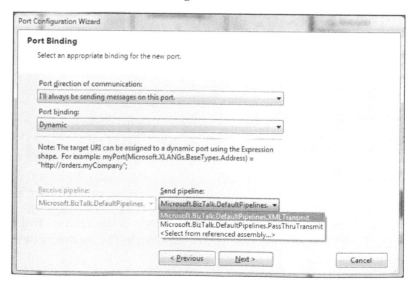

3. In an Expression shape, set the `Microsoft.XLANGs.BaseTypes.Address` property of the port. For a file transport, this may be `C:\BTS2010CertGuide\Chapter04\Example01-Orchestrations\FileDrop\%MessageID%.xml`, as shown in the following screenshot:

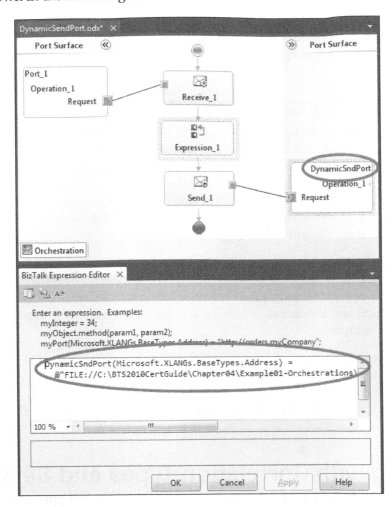

4. Use a **Send** shape, and connect it to the logical **Send Port** to send the message to `MessageBox` and the physical Dynamic Send Port.

The adapter BizTalk used in a Dynamic Send Port is chosen based on the first part of the address, that is, `C:\` which points to a file. For some addresses and transport types, you may have to set additional properties, for example, if you use an HTTP address, you will have to specify `Microsoft.XLANGs.BaseTypes.TransportType`, to ensure that BizTalk selects the adapter that you wanted, since the WCF-BasicHTTP, WCF-WsHTTP, WCF-Custom, and the HTTP adapter all handle HTTP addresses.

Also, some adapters may need additional configuration after that, such as for usernames, passwords, configuration, and binding information—everything that you would normally change from the defaults in the adapter configuration in the physical Send Port.

Once deployed, a Dynamic Port acts like a Specify Now Port, in that, a port is automatically created for you, but you can still use the bindings configuration to bind the logical port to another physical port.

Configuring correlation

Correlation is used throughout BizTalk Server Messaging and Orchestration engines. In many cases, it is automatic and there is little or nothing you need to do to take advantage of it. Such examples are when using a Request-Response or Solicit-Response port, when using a Self-correlated Binding, or Partner Orchestration Binding. In these cases, correlations are created for you, in the engine, without your explicitly having to define the properties and the values of those properties needed to make sure that the second message gets routed back.

Correlation subscriptions are instance subscriptions, that is, they do not exist in sync with the status of an Orchestration (when it is Stopped or Started), and the Orchestration does not activate a new instance when met; instead, it exists only until it is fulfilled and the message gets back to the Orchestration instance that created the subscription.

The typical case is asynchronous responses, where we need to instruct BizTalk on how to route (by a separate Receive Port or Orchestration) the reply message published to the `MessageBox`, back to the correct Orchestration instance. However, not all correlations are about receiving a response. Other common correlation uses are convoys.

Working with Correlation Types and Sets

Creating correlations in Orchestrations is based on **Correlation Types** that define the properties the correlation consists of. A Correlation Type is made up of one or more properties from Property Schemas, either out-of-the-box BizTalk Property Schemas or your own.

A Correlation Type is instantiated by creating a Correlation Set.

The following screenshot shows a simple Orchestration using correlation:

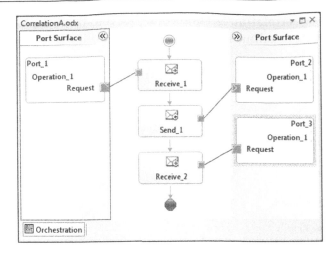

These instructions illustrate the relevant steps to enable correlation in an Orchestration:

1. Make sure that the message sent out, as well as the one received back in, have at least one promoted property that can be used for correlation. In this sample, we are using a `SalesOrder` Schema with an `OrderNo` node promoted to an `OrderNo` property in a Property Schema that we will use for correlation.

2. Choose to create a new Correlation Type and configure it by selecting the `OrderNo` property from our Property Schema and clicking on the **Add** button, as per the following screenshot:

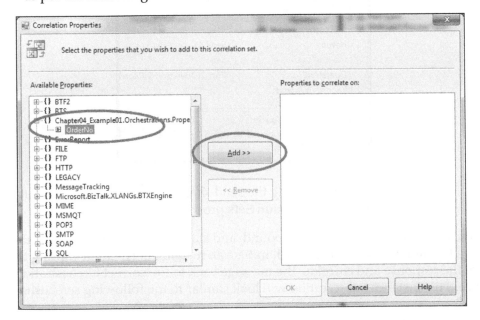

3. Create a new **Correlation Set** and configure it to be of the **Correlation Type** created in the preceding step, as shown in the following screenshot:

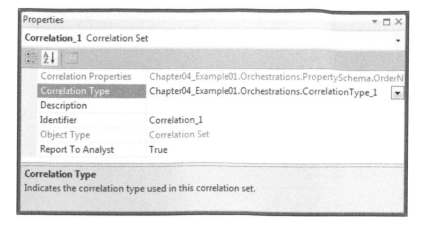

4. In the **Send** shape, select the Correlation Set created in the **Initializing Correlation Sets** property, as shown in the following screenshot:

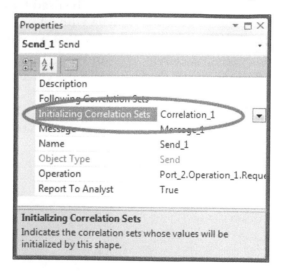

5. In the Receive shape following the Send shape, select the same Correlation Set as the **Following Correlation Sets** property, instead.

Once the Orchestration is deployed, bound, and started, whenever it sends out a message through the Send Port, it will initiate an instance correlation waiting to receive the response and correlate the message back to the correct Orchestration instance. This instance subscription will look similar to the following screenshot:

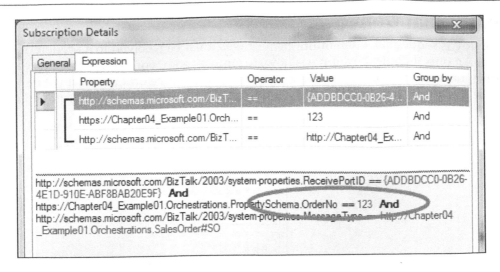

The `ReceivePortID` property is there only because the port binding used in this sample was Specify Later and the logical Orchestration Port is bound to a Receive Port. `MessageType` is always there when working with typed messages in Orchestrations. The circled part is what we get from using the Correlation Set, the part that specifies a specific value that the `OrderNo` property must have to relate to the subscription of this particular Orchestration instance, which is what the preceding screenshot shows.

Had the receiver of a message been another Orchestration that would receive the message through the `MessageBox`, do some work, and then return a response (much like what a Self-correlated Port accomplishes, except through the `MessageBox` and not by using Start Orchestration), then that Orchestration would have defined a Correlation Type and Set that would have been configured in the Initializing Correlation Set on the Receive shape and in the Following Correlation Set on the Send shape.

Convoys

Convoys are about receiving multiple messages in sequence or in parallel to achieve a goal. There are two types of convoy scenarios that you can implement using Orchestrations:

- Sequential Convoys
- Parallel Convoys

Sequential Convoys

A convoy is sequential when multiple messages must be received in a predetermined order. An out-of-context example is how, to enter a room, you must unlock three doors, one after another. A BizTalk example might be three orders that must be received in order, batched, and delivered to a backend store in a predetermined time.

The first Receive order is set to initialize the Correlation Set and the other Receive orders in the Convoy Set to follow that Correlation Set, as shown in the following diagram:

 For more information on Sequential Convoys, you can read further at the following URL:

```
http://msdn.microsoft.com/en-us/library/
aa561843(v=BTS.70).aspx
```

Parallel Convoys

A convoy is parallel when multiple messages must be received to achieve a goal but the order that they are received in is not important. An out-of-context example is how, to enter a room, you must unlock all three locks on its door, which you can do in any order. A BizTalk example might be that, when receiving scanned invoices, you will receive invoices both as scanned images as well as XML files describing the content. Both must be received before billing can be performed, as shown in the following diagram:

All the parallel Receive orders are set to initialize the Correlation Set.

For more information on Parallel Convoys, you can read further at the following URL:

`http://msdn.microsoft.com/en-us/library/`
`aa546782(v=BTS.70).aspx`

Test your knowledge

1. An Orchestration is currently configured with a Specify Later binding and is meant to be connected to a port that sends messages using the FILE Adapter. The requirements are that the folder and name of the file need to be specified at runtime, based on the data in the message. What should you do?:

   a. Configure the port binding to be Dynamic, and in a Message Assignment shape, set the `Microsoft.XLANGs.BaseTypes.Address` field for the message to point to the correct folder and name of the file.

   b. Configure the port binding to be Dynamic, and in an Expression shape, set the `Microsoft.XLANGs.BaseTypes.Address` field for the message to point to the correct folder and name of the file.

   c. Configure the port binding to be Dynamic and in an Expression shape, set the `Microsoft.XLANGs.BaseTypes.Address` field for the port to point to the correct folder and name of the file.

   d. In a Message Assignment shape, set the `BTS.ReceivedFileName` context property of the message to point to the correct folder and filename. Leave the port binding as it is.

2. A big Orchestration contains a smaller part of the logic that either needs to succeed fully, or if something fails, nothing is to be committed to the `MessageBox`. The Orchestration has neither any transaction type nor any scope. What do you need to do?:

   a. Configure the Orchestration as an Atomic transaction and set it to have a timeout of 90 seconds.

   b. Configure the Orchestration as a Long Running transaction. Use a scope configured as an Atomic transaction, and place the logic within the scope.

   c. Configure the Orchestration as a Long Running transaction. Use a scope configured as a Long Running transaction, and place the logic within the scope. Add a Compensation Block and an Exception Handler Block. If anything fails, call the code in the Compensation Block.

   d. Set the Synchronized property of all shapes included in the logic to `true`.

Summary

In this chapter, we learned about Orchestrations and focused on scopes, activating, nesting, and connecting Orchestrations, and using Call and Start shapes as well as bindings. We also learned core concepts, such as persistence and dehydration, and transaction support. We examined alternatives for storing configuration information, and saw how to integrate with .NET assemblies.

In the next chapter, we will examine how we can handle errors as they occur throughout our solutions, and messaging as well as Orchestration.

5
Debugging and Exception Handling

This chapter maps to the debugging and exception handling part of the exam.

In the previous chapters, we have seen how to configure BizTalk Server to create a basic routing architecture and extended that architecture with identifying, transforming, orchestrating, and correlating requests and responses in that architecture. So far we have not discussed the errors that you might encounter while doing that or how you debug and troubleshoot the solution when that happens.

This chapter will cover the important concepts and topics that you need to know about to be able to efficiently debug and handle exceptions in your integration solution, while focusing on the areas in which you need to succeed in the exam.

This chapter covers the following main areas:

- Handle exceptions in Orchestrations
- Debug Orchestrations
- Handle messaging errors
- Route Errors
- Validate and test artifacts
- Test your knowledge

After this chapter, we will have dived deeper into concepts introduced in the previous chapter, such as scopes, how to throw and handle exceptions, and how to do compensation. We will also handle exceptions outside of Orchestrations as they occur in our messaging architecture and look at which ones are common, and how we can handle them by routing them when they occur to enable programmatic handling instead of requiring administrative handling of suspended messages.

In order to examine why an exception occurred, we will also look at how we can do debugging, both of Orchestrations, and by way of Schemas and Maps by validation and testing in Visual Studio.

Handling exceptions in Orchestrations

Following on from the last chapter where we dealt with developing Orchestrations, let's look at how to handle exceptions as they occur in Orchestrations.

Scopes

In the previous chapter, we looked at how we could use scopes to configure and use transactions, whether Long Running or Atomic. The other two major uses for the Scope shape are to handle exceptions and to trigger compensating logic. These two uses are in a way intertwined with the use of transactions.

A Scope configured with a Transaction Type of None or Long Running can have **Exception Handling blocks** added, but Atomic scopes cannot. The rationale is that Atomic scopes either complete, or they do not. If they do not, all state is reset to how it looked before the scope was initiated, and it is the initiator of the Atomic scope, usually a Long Running scope that should decide what action is to be performed.

A Scope configured as Atomic or Long Running can have **Compensation blocks** added, but scopes that are configured with no transaction type cannot. The rationale is that only transactional scopes that consider the steps performed to be part of a unit of work will need to compensate that work should it be required.

The following screenshot shows how Exception Handling and Compensation blocks can be added to Scopes with different transaction types:

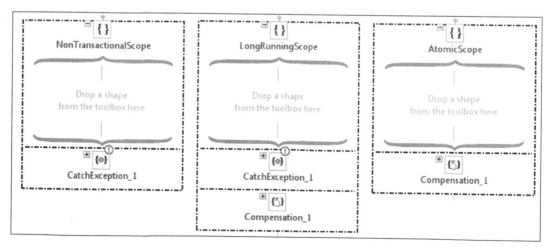

Throwing exceptions

Although the majority of all exception handling in BizTalk is about catching exceptions thrown by other parts in or outside BizTalk, sometimes you can also explicitly **throw exceptions**.

Throwing an exception may be a valid action for example in the following situations:

- When you reach a situation from which you cannot recover
- When a fatal error is relayed as part of a response rather than an exception
- When a Listen shape ends in a timeout
- When you discover an error situation in an atomic scope and want to make sure that the transaction is rolled back

In order to throw an exception, follow these basic steps:

1. Define a variable with the type set to the exception class you wish to throw (in this example the variable is called sysEx and is of type System.Exception).
2. Instantiate it and set any values according to the error conditions.
3. Use the **Throw Exception** shape and configure it with the **Exception Object** (in the following screenshot this is sysEx):

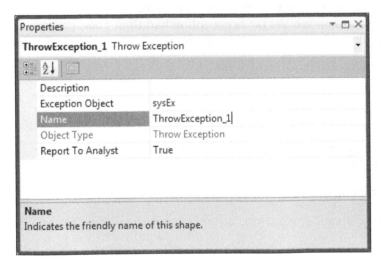

Catching exceptions

In order to catch an exception, you use an **exception handling block**. The exception block has two properties of interest, which are shown in the following screenshot:

- **Exception Object Name**
- **Exception Object Type**

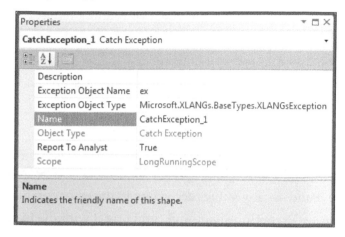

They allow you to define the type of exception to catch and a name by which you can access the caught exception. As far as exception handling goes, you can think of scopes and exception blocks in the same way that you would the .NET equivalent seen here:

```
try
{
  //code equivalent to shapes inside the scope goes here
}
catch (Microsoft.XLANGs.BaseTypes.XLANGsException ex)
{
  //code equivalent to shapes inside the
  //exception block goes here
}
catch (System.Exception exAll)
{
  //code to handle all .NET based exceptions goes here
}
```

When an exception is thrown, the engine will check for the closest exception handling block that can handle it. They are considered the way you would expect; inside out, sequentially. Like in .NET, exception handlers should be specified from the most detailed exception type to least detailed, with `System.Exception` as the least detailed catch-all base type. When determining which exception handler to trigger, it first checks at the scope that the exception occurred in, then the parent scopes in the hierarchy, then the scope that called the orchestration, and so on.

If an exception handler is found, processing will continue in that exception handling block. If no exception handler is found, the default exception handler is triggered. This means that the compensation block for any nested scopes will be triggered, after which the exception is re-thrown and the Orchestration will become suspended.

Also as in .NET, if an exception handling scope completes successfully, the Orchestration continues after the scope that held it if nothing else is specified, such as ending the Orchestration using a Terminate shape or re-throwing the exception using a Throw Exception shape.

Compensation

If a transaction has completed (execution has left the scope) and an exception occurs in the orchestration then the process might be in a state where, although technically coherent, it is logically incorrect. In such a situation, the actions performed in an already committed transactional scope might need to be compensated; un-done. This is done by adding a **compensation block**.

 Adding a compensation block is the same thing as setting the Compensation property of a transactional Scope to Custom.

The **Compensation** block has no meaningful properties. It only exists as a container for compensating logic:

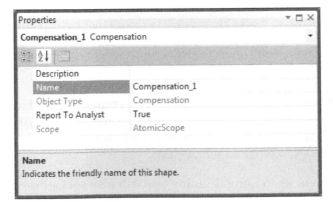

 The **Report To Analyst** property exists on many shapes. Regardless of the value it is given, it has no effect on the behavior of your Orchestration. It is a property used to integrate with the **Orchestration Designer for Business Analysts (ODBA) Visio** plugin. If set to `False`, then that shape is considered a low level detail that will not be visible in the Visio designer.

Although Atomic scopes do have the functionality of automatic rollback, if an exception occurs inside the scope, there is no such functionality once the scope has committed.

The **default exception handler**, if triggered, will initiate the compensation by calling the Compensation blocks for any nested scopes, but if you catch an exception in a custom exception handler then you must explicitly do the compensation. When you do explicit compensation, you need to use one or more Compensate shapes and configure them to compensate either the current scope or a selected nested scope.

The Compensate shape can only be used inside an exception handling or another compensation block. When choosing to compensate the current scope this will trigger the default compensation handler, and not the compensation code that may be defined by the scope (since the transaction will not have completed). Explicit use of the Compensate shape to compensate nested transactions allows us to specify the order in which to compensate transactions if the default order does not fit our logic. One Compensate shape is used to trigger one compensation block, and thus the way to specify the order is by the use of multiple sequentially ordered compensate shapes.

If you have not added a custom compensation block, **default compensation** will be performed. In the same way as the default exception handler this will call the compensation blocks of any nested scopes, starting with the most recently completed one and working its way back.

 Compensation blocks are possible in scopes that have their Transaction Type set to Long Running or Atomic. However, not for scopes which have their Transaction Type set to None. Such scopes cannot be compensated.

Although default compensation is triggered, if no compensation blocks are added anywhere, nothing will be performed. Compensation is explicit; you must add the logic that compensates the actions performed, and you can use any shape you want inside the Compensation block to achieve this.

If the Orchestration is set to Long Running you can also set Compensation to Custom on an orchestration level. This will give you a Compensation block tab accessible at the bottom of the orchestration window.

Regardless of whether you are handling Compensation at the scope or orchestration level, the Compensation block can contain any shape and perform any logic; the same as any other part of an Orchestration.

Sample exception handling scenario

We are going to look at a scenario that incorporates the concepts of exception handling and compensation and see how they work in practice.

The completed sample is available in the `Chapter05-Example01` solution.

Let's start with a simple process. We will receive a `SimplifiedCar` Schema, equipped with `FuelTankCapacity`, `FuelConsumption`, and `OperationalRange` fields. The message in will contain only the first two and we need to calculate the last one. Inside a Scope we will have a Send shape that sends the same message out again, for archival, and after that we will create a new message so that we can calculate and fill out the correct value for the `OperationalRange` of the car. This is done by calling a .NET helper component that returns that by dividing `FuelTankCapacity` by `FuelConsumption`. If the `FuelConsumption` is 0 a divide by zero exception will occur. When we start out no transactions are configured on the scope or on the Orchestration; the Transaction Type is None, which is the default.

 We are using a static method on the .NET component. Had we been using a instance method, the class would have to be instantiated and it would either have to be marked as serializable or used only from within an atomic scope (as no persistence is done while inside an atomic scope).

The Orchestration looks as follows:

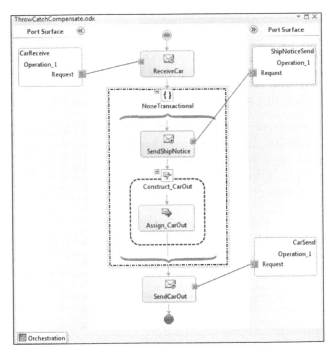

We could just as easily have done the simple division directly in the XLANG expression in the Message Assignment shape, but there is a lesson in doing it in a helper class — to show what we must do to handle exceptions thrown by a .NET component.

The **Assign_CarOut** shape contains the following code:

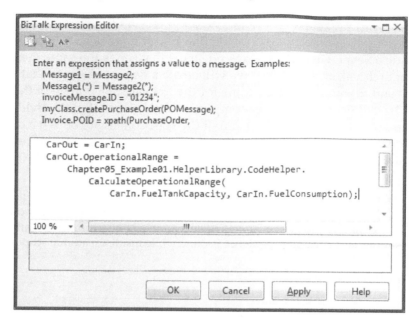

Let's run this sample. If you want to follow along this state of the orchestration is contained in the `ThrowCatchCompensate.odx` file. We will build upon this sample.

We will start by sending in a `SimplifiedCar` message that looks like this:

```xml
<ns0:Car xmlns:ns0="http://Chapter05_Example01.Schemas.SimplifiedCar">
  <RegistrationNo>ABC123</RegistrationNo>
  <FuelTankCapacity>60</FuelTankCapacity>
  <FuelConsumption>0.7</FuelConsumption>
  <OperationalRange></OperationalRange>
</ns0:Car>
```

This will not cause an exception and we will get an output for both the **SendShipNotice** and **SendCarOut** sends respectively. In the case of the **SendCarOut**, the output will contain a correctly calculated operational range:

CarOut_{F681DF7E-A9E0-4393-BF00-3EBE206DC44F}.xml

ShipNotice_{2D39ECF0-E464-4E0B-B3CF-A0CFFF46D76A}.xml

What if we update the value of the `FuelConsumption` to hold the number 0 instead? (Except for making that one cheap car to drive).

It will create a suspended Orchestration instance:

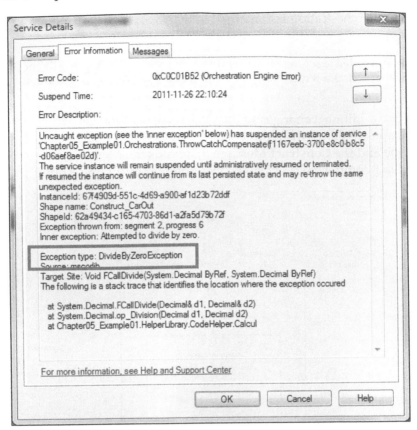

The Orchestration instance is resumable, but if we try to resume it will continue from its last persistence point, which in this case is after the **SendShipNotice** send shape, and all that will end up happening is that it will call the .NET helper component and get the same exception again. There is no fix to be made to the component to correct its behavior; it's the content of the messages that is creating the error. In another scenario, resuming the orchestration from the last persistence point to retry the operation might result in a successful result should the reason for the exception be fixed or removed.

In this scenario, the Orchestration will still have created the ship notice file.

> ShipNotice_{535F24DA-31E8-446C-8128-FC679A609A00}.xml

This happens because the scope that contains the archive send and the .NET helper component is not transactional. In order to make them succeed or fail as one, we need to set the Transaction Type of the scope to Atomic.

Once we do that no output will be created when the .NET helper component fails. This state of the orchestration is contained in the `ThrowCatchCompensate1.odx` file.

To be able to set the scopes Transaction Type to Atomic, the Orchestration that contains it must have its Transaction Type set to Long Running.

Let's make two additional changes to the Orchestration. One, let's move the Construct shape outside of the atomic scope, and two, let's add another scope around both the scope and the Construct Message that holds the Message Assignment calling the .NET component. Let's make that outer scope a Long Running scope:

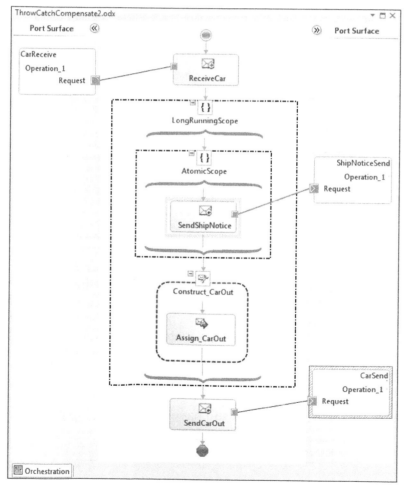

This state of the Orchestration is contained in the `ThrowCatchCompensate2.odx` file.

When we have done this, and run the sample, we will once again get the `SendShipNotice` outputted to disk, because it is contained in an Atomic Scope that has been committed before the exception happens.

ShipNotice_{62C5A62D-7661-40FC-A8E3-3BF33612CD26}.xml

In this situation, we could well imagine that some compensating logic would be required for the SendArchive operation when an exception happens later in the Orchestration. Let's look at how to implement that.

If we select the atomic scope, we can right-click it and select **New Compensation Block**, or we can set **Compensation** to **Custom** in its properties window. We can add any logic we need within the compensation block. In this case, to compensate for the **SendShipNotice** operation, we need to send a new message to retract the ship notice. The **RetractShipNotice** send operation represents that.

This state of the Orchestration is contained in the `ThrowCatchCompensate3.odx` file seen in the following screenshot:

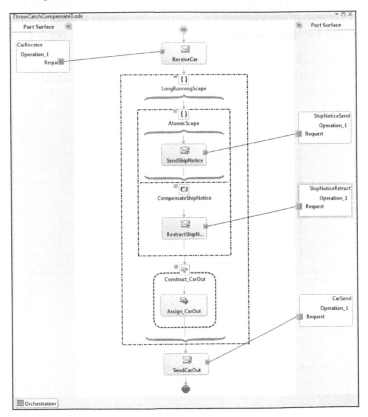

If we send the `SimplifiedCar.xml` message through, that does not contain an error, the messages outputted are a `CarOut` and a `ShipNotice` message.

What if we send the `CarSimplified_zero.xml` file that causes a `DivideByZero` exception?

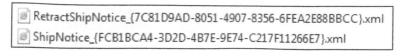

RetractShipNotice_{7C81D9AD-8051-4907-8356-6FEA2E88BBCC}.xml

ShipNotice_{FCB1BCA4-3D2D-4B7E-9E74-C217F11266E7}.xml

We get a `ShipNotice` and then a `RetractShipNotice` message. Why?

The Atomic scope completes, sending out the `ShipNotice` message. Then an exception occurs. Remember, when we have no explicit exception handler that can handle the exception, the default exception handler kicks in. It automatically calls the compensation blocks of any nested scopes that have completed, in this case the **CompensateShipNotice** block that makes the `RetractShipNotice` send. Then it re-throws the exception. In this case it means that the orchestration is suspended.

The next step to take is that when we get an exception we want to notify a car shipment clerk by sending him (or her) a message about the car that failed shipment processing. That means implementing a custom exception handler. We do that by right clicking on the **LongRunningScope** shape and selecting **New Exception Block**.

We could be very specific in the exceptions we catch, which in this case means that if we suspect that we could get a `DivideByZeroException`, or any other exception that requires special handling we could catch that specifically:

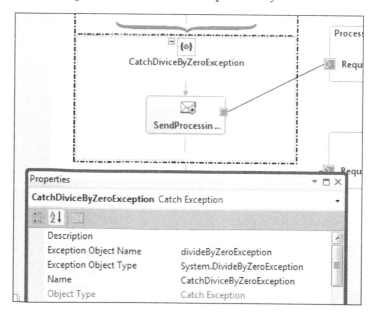

In this case, no exception requires special treatment, they should all result in a processing error notification being sent, so we'll create a catch all exception handler:

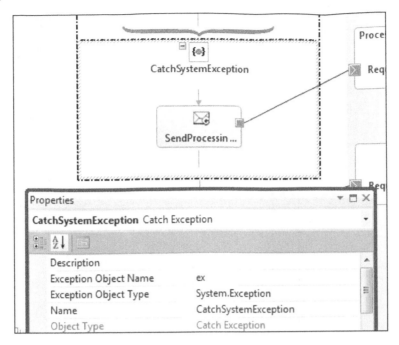

If we just leave it like that we will now get an exception: **"Use of unconstructed message 'CarOut'"**. This is due to the fact that as the logic stands an exception could (and in our test of the exception handling, will) occur before the construction of the CarOut message. As we are now handling that exception, execution will continue to the Send shape after the scope that is configured to send the CarOut message, which in this case can potentially be unconstructed. We will solve this by moving the SendCarOut shape inside the Long Running Scope.

This state of the Orchestration is contained in the `ThrowCatchCompensate4.odx` file seen in the following screenshot. As the orchestration is now beginning to grow, the Construct shape has been minimized to save space:

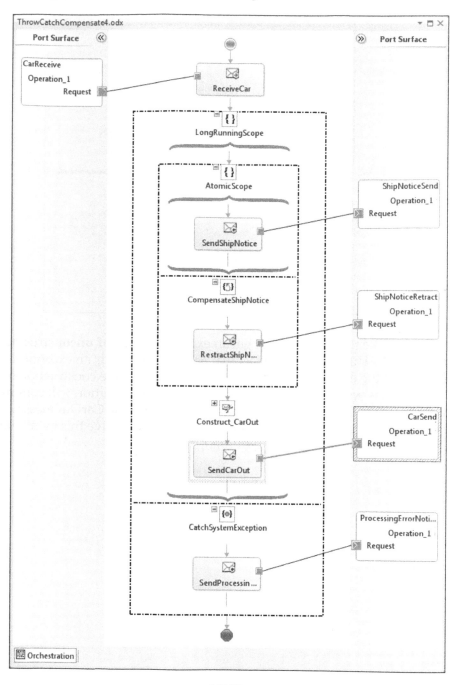

Now let's deploy and test this scenario. A correct message will create the same two outputs as a correct message always has; the ShipNotification and CarOut message. However, what about a message resulting in the DivideByZeroException in the Construct/Message Assignment shape?

We will get a ShipNotice, and an ErrorNotifcation message:

ErrorNotification_{866E7139-C2AE-4D2B-B1D7-F2123F502E15}.xml
ShipNotice_{49663C95-53C4-48EC-9F54-058DFE5434CF}.xml

The explanation for this is that the ShipNotice is sent in the atomic scope, which completes successfully and sends out the message. After that an exception occurs. However, as it is no longer the default exception handler that catches it, but instead our own custom exception handler, no automatic compensation will occur. Instead, the logic implemented by us in our custom handler will take place. In this case, the sending of the ErrorNotification message. Also, in this scenario, unlike when we have been notified of an error in previous scenarios, we will not have a suspended orchestration instance as we are handling the error. If we would have liked to handle the exception and suspend the Orchestration instance then we could have used the Throw Exception shape within our exception handler to re-throw the exception.

As a final step in this scenario, we will add back logic to allow the compensation to be explicitly triggered. In order to do that we need to use the Compensate shape.

When we configure the Compensate shape that we place inside the exception handler, we have a choice of either compensating the Atomic transaction or the Long Running Transaction (the following screenshot displays their identifiers):

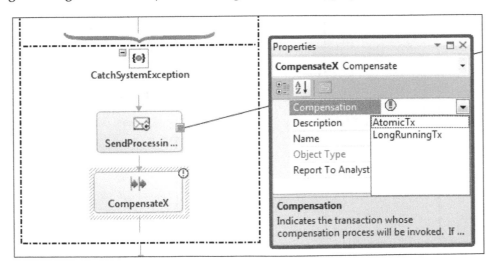

As we are in the long running transactions exception handler, choosing the LongRunningTx in this case means compensating the current scope, which has a special meaning. This will automatically compensate for all nested transactions, in a last completed first compensated manner. If we want to choose the transactions we compensate, or dictate the order, we need to use Compensate shapes. Each Compensate shape can be configured to compensate for one transaction. This means we will execute the Scopes Compensation block. However, in this case we will select to compensate the current transaction and trigger default compensation handling.

This state of the orchestration is contained in the `ThrowCatchCompensate5.odx` file seen in the following screenshot. As the Orchestration has gotten larger than can be comfortably visualized in one page, the AtomicScope and the Construct shape has been minimized to save space:

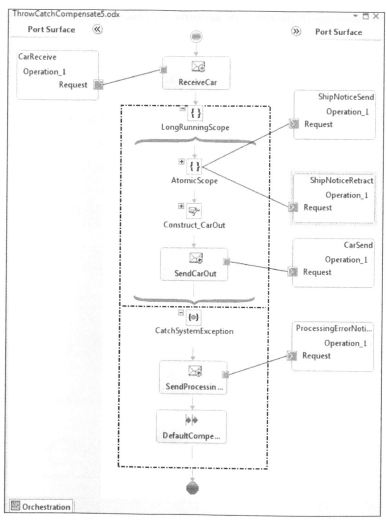

At this point the output in case of an exception in the Construct/Message Assignment shape is the ShipNotice, ErrorNotification, and RetractShipNotice, in that chronological order.

ErrorNotification_{AA9F52F6-2DBA-410C-B0AA-2F8F07AA960B}.xml

RetractShipNotice_{578DF607-118A-4ECE-9E9C-30F2DE3D0602}.xml

ShipNotice_{C79A2A60-7C61-45A7-A93E-C4CE413810A2}.xml

Delivery notification

BizTalk Server is built on a publish-subscribe architecture. Messages always go to the `MessageBox` before being delivered to a port. With a two-way port, a correlated response, or another response aware pattern, you will potentially be aware of an error occurring somewhere after you sent the message from the orchestration. With a one way Send Port you will likely not be aware when an exception occurs. This is true even for an Atomic scope that will happily complete even though the message may never reach its intended destination. This is because the transaction initiated by the atomic transaction scope commits to the `MessageBox`; successful delivery by the intended Send Port is not included in the transaction.

We will use the Simple Orchestration contained in the `DeliveryNotification.odx` Orchestration as a starting point; it has the components needed for this illustration:

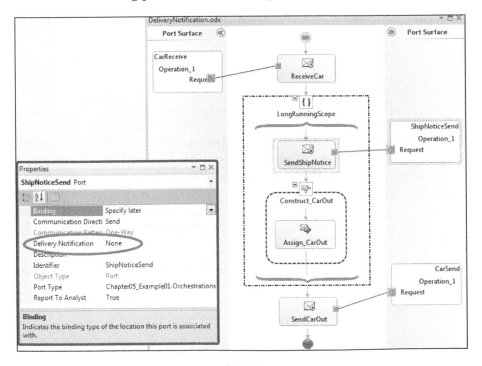

Without making any changes to the Orchestration, let's alter the SendShipNotification physical port so that it sends to an invalid location. In other words, it will fail:

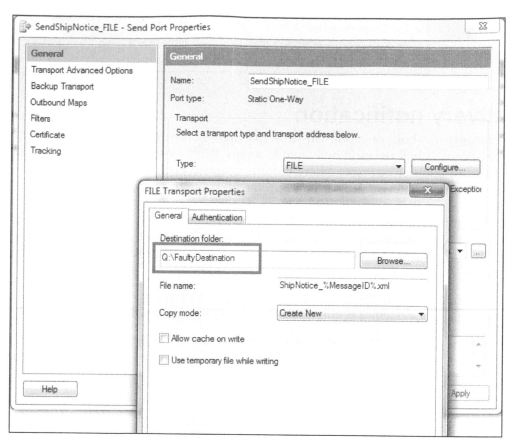

Now let's try the scenario. If you skipped the previous section, the correct behavior should result in two messages outputted—the ShipNotice and CarOut messages. In that chronological order (as you can see from the Orchestration screenshot). The output however is this:

CarOut_{CF6FCDBD-1AF8-4E7C-97C3-5DF820A4F937}.xml

At the same time, we will have a suspended message on the SendShipNotice Send Port. As expected, it could not send out our message:

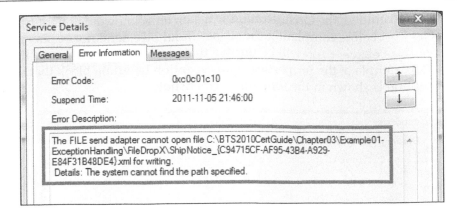

Still, the orchestration continues, the scope completes without exceptions and the orchestration sends the CarOut message and completes successfully.

If this was not intended behavior and you would like to be sure that the ShipNotification message has indeed been delivered, you can use Delivery Notification.

The **Delivery Notification** is a property available on Send Ports in the Orchestration designer:

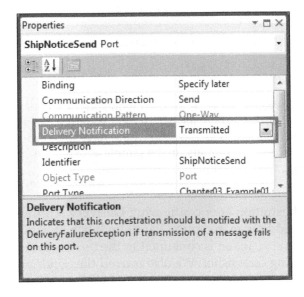

When set to Transmitted, the Orchestration waits on an acknowledgement from the physical Send Port before completing the scope. Should the send not be successful, a `DeliveryFailureException` will be thrown that can be caught to handle the exception. An example of the properties of an exception handling block that handles such an exception is shown in the following screenshot:

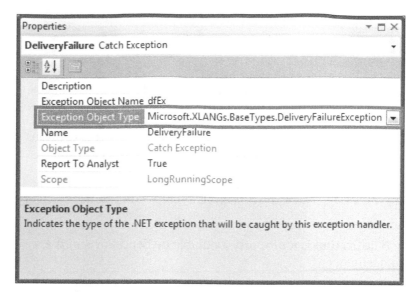

The `DeliveryFailureException` is thrown once all retries of a Send Port are exhausted.

> Delivery Notifications can be used with Atomic scopes as well, but as they cannot have Exception Handling blocks the `DeliveryFailureException` would have to be caught in a parent scope. In order to simplify, in the sample above we are using a Long Running scope directly.

This state of the Orchestration after configuring **Delivery Notification** to `Transmitted` and adding an exception handling block to handle the `DeliveryFailureNotification` is contained in the `DeliveryNotification1.odx` file seen in the following screenshot. We also moved the SendCarOut shape into the scope to avoid the *use of unconstructed message* build error as explained in the previous section on error handling:

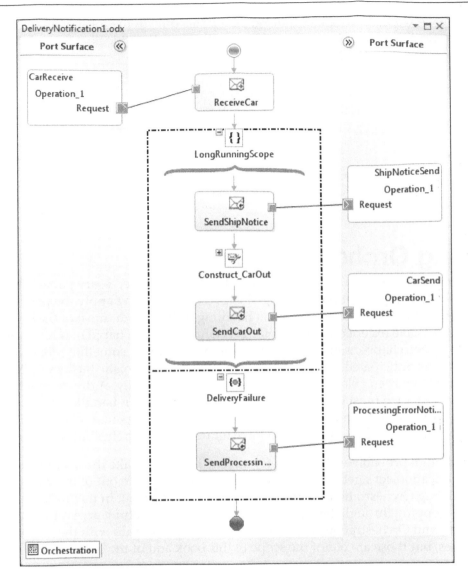

Now let's try out the scenario, still with the same faulty configuration on the physical Send Port that the ShipNoticeSend Port is bound to.

This time we will get a single output again, but this time in the form of an ErrorNotification message sent from the exception handling block:

ErrorNotification_{6BD58367-DB03-455A-A6E5-02BFB2E03836}.xml

Also, as the exception is handled, we will get no suspended Orchestration instances. You will however get a suspended message instance on the Send Port.

 In order to get rid of that you can use failed message routing, which we will discuss later in this chapter.

Debug Orchestrations

When exceptions happen it's a useful and often absolutely necessary pattern, to handle them using exception handling blocks. Often, we don't apply the pattern of more detailed to less detailed exception handling. When we do most of the time, we simply can't have exception handlers for everything that can happen. If for example, a divide by zero happens in our Orchestration process that's something that we couldn't have anticipated. It's a runtime error, not a deterministic business error that we should have been able to anticipate and handle specifically. A divide by zero exception will then most likely end up in a catch all exception handling block. The difficult part now is to find out exactly what and why it happened. We are going to take a look at some of the options you have for debugging Orchestration execution.

First, although probably well known for anyone looking to take the BizTalk Server 2010 certification, let's get the simple yet long time annoyance out of the way: You cannot debug Orchestrations using Visual Studio. At least, not in the traditional sense of stepping through the shapes of the designer and getting access to variables, messages, and Orchestration state. There are things you can do with the generated C# classes, but those are out of the scope of this book and of the certification.

You need to use the BizTalk Server Administration Console. First, let's use the **Group Overview** and create a **New Query** to get at some **Tracked Service Instances** with **Service Class** of type **Orchestration**:

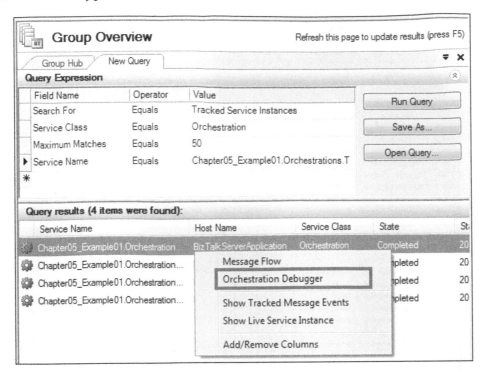

The Orchestration Debugger is available through the context menu of any of the tracked orchestration instances. Let's bring it up for the final state of the exception handling and compensation sample orchestration `ThrowCatchCompensate5.odx`, that we walked through in a previous section (if you have just read the section on Delivery Notification, for your information the SendShipNotice port has been set back to its correct path).

Using the Orchestration Debugger, we can step through the tracking that the Orchestration left behind, and see what happened. You can see exactly what shapes have triggered and in what order. The numbers on the Orchestration surface are an addition to aid the visualization in this book. They correlate to the numbers on the left-hand side. They are not there in the Orchestration Debugger:

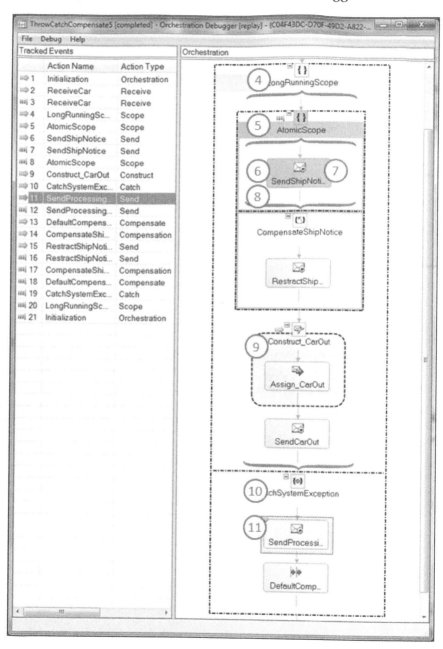

Using the Orchestration in this after the fact manner can be very useful. In the **Tracked Events** pane, should you expand it to the right, you will also see the date and time of each event. You can also get access to any exception that has occurred by going to the **Debug** menu and choosing **Show Tracked Exceptions**, which brings up the exception dialog.

 The level of information available is dependent on the level of tracking configured. By default, the Orchestration start and end, Message send and receive, and Shape start and end is configured, but nothing else.

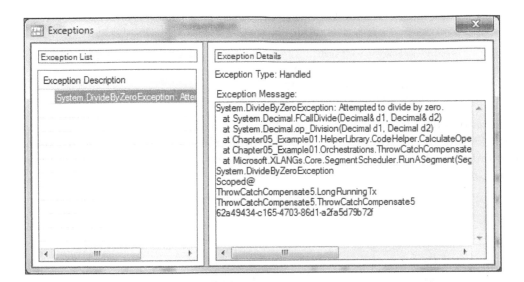

However, it does not give you access to the variables, messages, or state of the Orchestration as part of the tool experience. Hence, you can't really troubleshoot why it happened. Not even if you apply all the tracking possible (having done that the information will be available to you through other queries, but that's beside the point for this walkthrough).

What you can do in the orchestration debugger is to set a breakpoint. You do this by right clicking a shape and selecting **Set Breakpoint on Class**. After you have done this you can close the Orchestration Debugger window. The next time an instance of the Orchestration runs, it will break on the spot you placed the breakpoint and the orchestration will be in an In Breakpoint (Active) state:

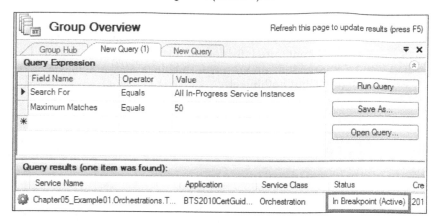

If you launch the Orchestration Debugger for this instance you will have the option, on the **Debug** menu, to attach to the Orchestration instance. This will bring you to the point of the breakpoint and you will have access to state, variables, and messages in the Orchestration:

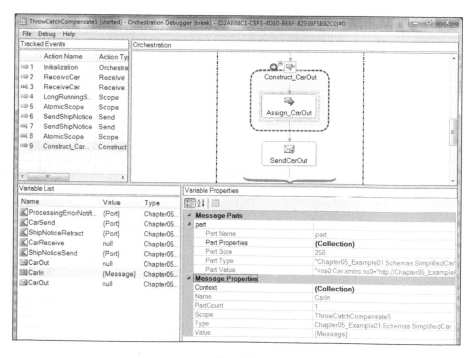

From here you can step through the Orchestration and observe the changes as they occur. You can't really step through as you would have expected from a Visual Studio experience, but you can set new breakpoints (which are applied to that instance only) and choose to continue, which is the equivalent of *F5* or Run when you debug in Visual Studio. Execution will then halt once it reaches the next breakpoint.

Orchestrations will keep ending up **In Breakpoint** until you remove the breakpoint on the class level. You can only add and remove breakpoints to the class level when you are viewing an orchestration while not attached.

Handling messaging errors

Now that we have looked at handling exceptions in Orchestrations, we are going to change focus to messaging solutions and examine some of the common exceptions that can occur and how we can eliminate or handle those exceptions through configuration.

Subscription errors

Failure in subscriptions usually comes from one of two main problem areas:

- Incorrectly configured subscribers, such as incorrect filters or an unenlisted state
- Faulty messages or message handling resulting in the required promoted message context properties not being available

Regardless of which, the exception that occurs when BizTalk Server cannot find a configured subscriber after evaluation of a message is "**The published message could not be routed because no subscribers were found**". This is shown in the following screenshot:

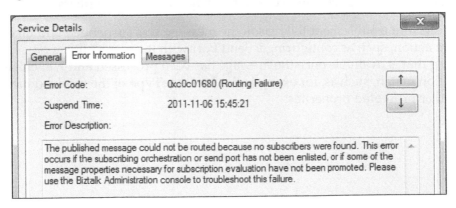

The message will (most of the time) be in a Suspended (resumable) state.

The problem with this suspended service instance is that when an error occurs, BizTalk will always abort the current transaction and the message will have the form that it had before the operation was attempted. This will mean that you could have big difficulties in determining why the error occurred; since all states including the message context will also be reset to before the operation was attempted. For example in a receive pipeline, much of the properties that will be used for routing, at least when that routing is based on any form of information that is the result of a disassembler component parsing the message, will not be available in that earlier form, because what creates them has not yet occurred at that point. For this reason BizTalk Server also creates another service instance in a Suspended (not resumable) state; a **Routing Failure Report**:

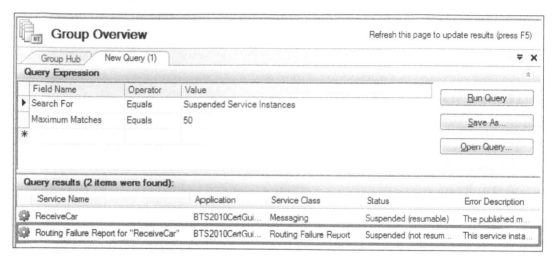

This service instance allows you to review the state of the message and its context as it was when the messaging engine evaluated it against any subscribers.

You can use it to troubleshoot the reason the message was suspended and take necessary action, such as configuring a Send Port with the correct filters on something that is available once the message has been processed and will create a subscription match, such as, for example the **MessageType** of the received message, or any other promoted properties:

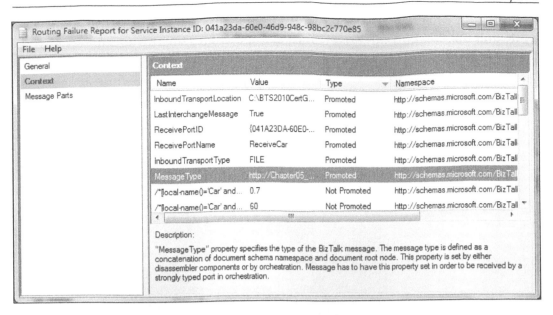

You could also use the Routing Failure Report to review the actual message, which could potentially be very different after the receive pipeline has triggered. Especially, if the original message was a FlatFile.

Transmission errors

In transmission errors, all errors are included that are the result of a send adapter call failing and resulting in a suspended service instance. Transmission errors can occur under many different conditions, all depending on the adapter being used and the system or transport you wish to connect with. Common examples might be:

- A file share is unavailable or the BizTalk Host Instance user is not authorized
- A WCF call results in a "Connection was actively refused" exception
- An application adapter gets a runtime exception from the system it connects to, for example a SAP system
- A connection to an FTP server cannot be made

Regardless of what the exception is, BizTalk Server has a built-in retry capability. By default this will be configured to retry the operation 3 times with 5 minutes in between:

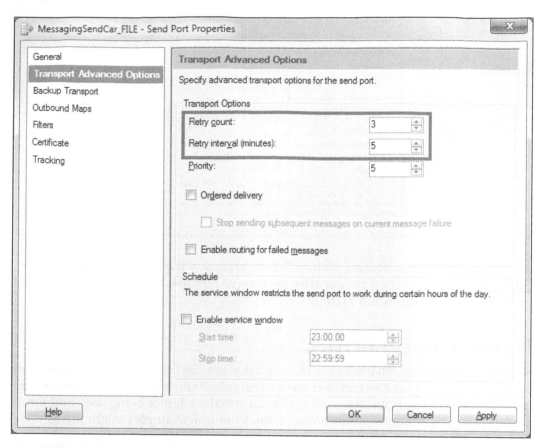

This configuration means that it will take up to 15 minutes before a message gets suspended.

 In a situation where the message needs to suspend or switch to the backup transport option (if configured) immediately you should configure the **Retry count** to **0**. This is also a suitable development setting.

Send Ports also have the possibility of configuring a **Backup Transport** that will trigger instead of the message being suspended, once the retry attempts are exhausted. The **Backup Transport** has some of the same configuration as the primary transport has:

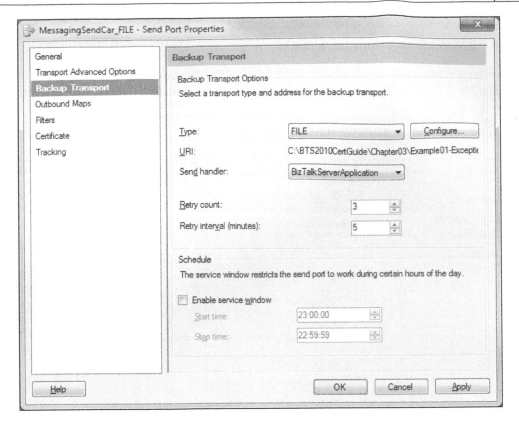

You can configure the backup transport with the same or another adapter, whichever suits your needs. You could even configure it against the same exact URI with different retry options if you wish to continue retrying, for example, once an hour for 12 hours if the initial retries fail.

Routing errors

Orchestrations allow for try, catch, and compensate patterns. For subscriptions, routing exceptions, failing adapters, handling exceptions that occur in interchanges with many parts, or in Maps or Schema validation, a feature known as **Failed Message Routing** is utilized.

When an exception occurs in a port, one of the following actions is performed by BizTalk Server Runtime:

- The port has retries left so it will wait to retry (only possible in Send Ports)
- The port has no retries configured but has a backup transport configured and will fall back to that (again, only possible in Send Ports)

- The service instance becomes suspended
- Failed Message Routing kicks in

A message ends up in a suspended state when all retries and backup transport options have been evaluated and no Failed Message Routing has been implemented.

The Failed Message Routing option is available on both Receive and Send Ports. On Receive Ports it is available on the **General** tab:

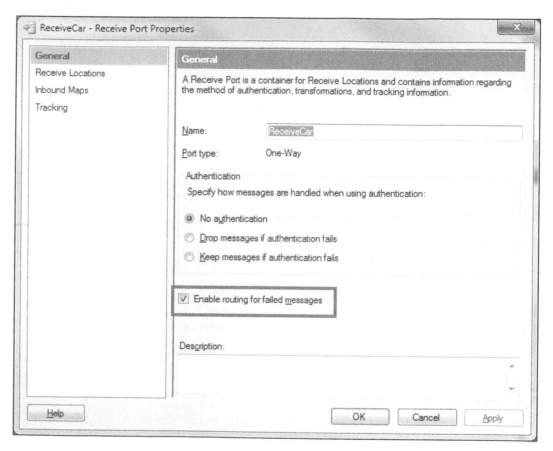

While on Send Ports it is available on the **Transport Advanced Options** tab:

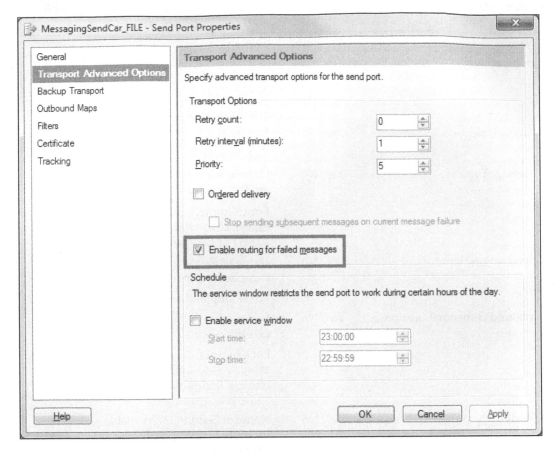

If **Enable routing for failed messages** is selected, the service instance will not become suspended in case of an exception. Instead, the following will happen:

- A clone of the message is created
- All current promoted message context properties are demoted
- Additional properties describing the error condition are promoted to allow for routing of the error

The properties promoted from the ErrorReport namespace (`http://schemas.microsoft.com/BizTalk/2006/error-report`) are shown in the following table:

Name	Promoted	Description
FailureCode	Yes	A hexadecimal value. The same value that is visible in the Admin console if the message is suspended.
		For example: 0xC0C01680
FailureCategory	Yes	Not used.
		Ex (always): 0
MessageType	Yes/No	Only available if known, for example when an XML message fails on a Send Port.
		For example: `http://Chapter05_Example01.Schemas.SimplifiedCar#Car`
ReceivePortName	Yes/No	Name of Receive Port. Promoted if exception occurred on a Receive Port.
		For example: ReceiveCar
InboundTransportLocation	Yes/No	URI of receive location. Promoted if exception occurred on a Receive Port.
		For example: `C:\BTS2010CertGuide\Chapter05\Example01-ExceptionHandling\FileDrop\*copy*`
SendPortName	Yes/No	Name of Send Port. Available and promoted if exception occurred on a Send Port.
		For example: MessagingSendCar_FILE
OutboundTransportLocation	Yes/No	URI of Send Port. Available and promoted if exception occurred on a Send Port.
		For example: `C:\BTS2010CertGuide\Chapter05\Example01-ExceptionHandling\FileDropX\MessagingCarOut_%MessageID%.xml`
ErrorType	Yes	The type of message that the error contains.
		For example (always): FailedMessage
ProcessingServer	Yes	Name of the server where the error occurred.
		For example: BTSSRV01

Additionally, the following properties are also available:

Name	Promoted	Description
Description	No	Error description. Also visible in the event log.
		For example: The published message could not be routed because no subscribers were found...
RoutingFailureReportID	No	Contains the ID of the routing failure report if the error occurred due to a routing failure.
		For example: Empty or a GUID.
FailureAdapter	No	Name of the adapter that failed.
		For example: FILE
FailureInstanceID	No	ID (GUID) of the service that failed.
FailureMessageID	No	ID (GUID) of the message that failed.
FailureTime	No	The time of failure.
		For example: 2010-06-08 10:00:00

Let's look at a scenario for using failed message routing. For this scenario we have a simple messaging integration. We will use a ReceiveCar port and a MessagingSendCar_FILE Send Port connected by a simple BTS.ReceivePortName filter and see what happens when we experience errors on those and how we can route the exception that occurs. Both ports are configured with failed message routing as per the previous screenshots.

We will begin looking at how we can handle an error on the Receive Port. When that error occurs it will be routed instead of becoming suspended so we need to set up a port (or Orchestration) to handle the failed message routing message (or we will get a routing failure for the failed message routing message).

In order to receive failed messages from the Receive Port, we will configure an additional port to receive those messages with the following filter:

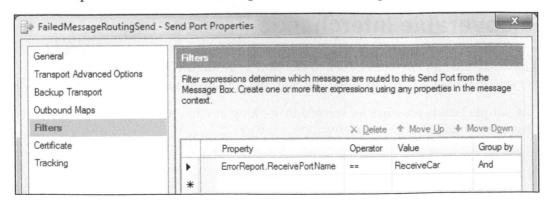

We can use only the properties under the ErrorReport Schema as those are the only properties promoted.

What if the error occurred on a Send Port instead? The configuration is very similar. We will add an additional filter to the same port using an Or statement:

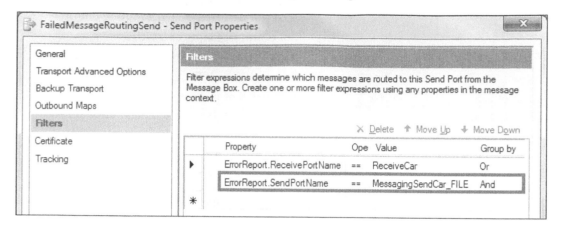

We could just as easily have used different ports for handling Receive and Send Port errors had we wished to.

Earlier in this chapter, we had an Orchestration that had Delivery Notification = Transmitted configured. In that case the orchestration handled the exception which resulted in no suspended orchestration instances. Yet, the suspended Send Port remained even though the exception was handled. The way to get rid of it is to use failed message routing as explained previously. You can select any of the promoted properties under the ErrorReport Schema to configure a filter on a Send Port you wish to send the failed messages to.

Recoverable Interchange Processing

In *Chapter 2, Developing BizTalk Artifacts – Create Schemas and Pipelines*, we looked at how to create an envelope Schema, and how to configure a pipeline to accept a message that contains an envelope and split the contained message into its parts.

This sample builds on what we learned by looking at what happens if one of the messages contained within the envelope is incorrect.

Let's start by setting the stage. The code for this sample is contained in the
Chapter05-Example01 solution within the Chapter05-Example01.Schemas project.

The project contains the following envelope Schema:

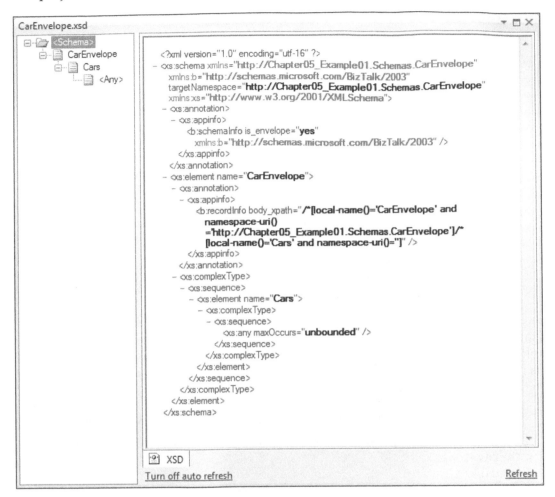

Where the **Envelope** property on the **<Schema>** node is set to Yes, and the **Body
XPath** property on the **CarEnvelope** node is set to the XPath of the **Cars** node,
/*[local-name()='CarEnvelope' and namespace-uri()='http://Chapter05_
Example01.Schemas.CarEnvelope']/*[local-name()='Cars' and namespace-
uri()=''].

It also contains the SimplifiedCar Schema that we have worked with in many previous samples:

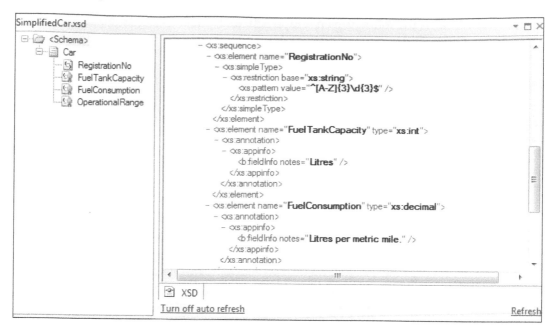

In *Chapter 2, Developing BizTalk Artifacts – Create Schemas and Pipelines,* we established that when sending in an envelope message using the XMLReceive pipeline, it was split into its containing parts automatically by the XML Disassembler, without us having to do any custom configuration. This time though we are sending in a message that is incorrect according to its Schema.

The following is the instance envelope message we are sending through BizTalk:

```
<ns0:CarEnvelope xmlns:ns0="http://Chapter05_Example01.Schemas.
CarEnvelope">
  <Cars>
    <ns0:Car xmlns:ns0="http://Chapter05_Example01.Schemas.
SimplifiedCar">
      <RegistrationNo>ABC123</RegistrationNo>
      <FuelTankCapacity>60</FuelTankCapacity>
      <FuelConsumption>0.7</FuelConsumption>
      <OperationalRange>86</OperationalRange>
    </ns0:Car>
    <ns0:Car xmlns:ns0="http://Chapter05_Example01.Schemas.
SimplifiedCar">
      <RegistrationNo>XYZ789</RegistrationNo>
      <FuelTankCapacity>70</FuelTankCapacity>
```

```
        <FuelConsumption>ERROR</FuelConsumption>
        <OperationalRange>88</OperationalRange>
      </ns0:Car>
    </Cars>
  </ns0:CarEnvelope>
```

What will happen if we send in this faulty message? What will be the output?

MessagingCarOut_{0B095E7F-77A4-4E9A-BDA5-2D08CFC11867}.xml
MessagingCarOut_{1CC0E47E-4691-4735-BA4A-A782853702EB}.xml

Two messages are outputted. Why? Remember, by default no Schema validation is performed, only that the message belongs to a valid Schema and is of well-formed XML.

In order to enable Schema validation, we must do two things:

Configure the **XMLReceive** pipeline and the **XML disassembler** component to validate documents against their Schemas by setting the **ValidateDocument** property to True.

Configure the **Document schema** to use for validation:

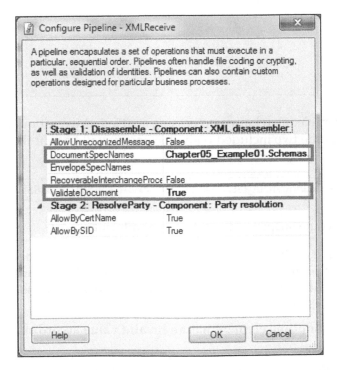

Now, if we send in the messages again, we will get no output! If we inspect our suspended messages, we will see that the entire interchange has failed with an error information that says "**The Messaging Engine encountered an error during the processing of one or more inbound messages.**"

In order to enable the successful delivery of the correct message we need to enable **RecoverableInterchangeProcessing**:

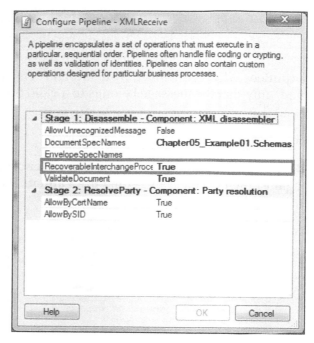

Now with recoverable interchange processing enabled, if we submit our message once again, one of the two included body documents will be sent through the Send Port:

MessagingCarOut_{3EA23AD0-2D5C-4088-B349-564C9C55BF5B}.xml

The other will become suspended with an error information of:

An output message of the component "Unknown " in receive pipeline "Microsoft. BizTalk.DefaultPipelines.XMLReceive, Microsoft.BizTalk.DefaultPipelines, Version=3.0.1.0, Culture=neutral, PublicKeyToken=31bf3856ad364e35" is suspended due to the following error:

   The 'FuelConsumption' element has an invalid value according to its data type.
.

The sequence number of the suspended message is 2.

Referring back to our sample instance message, this is the second car that had the text ERROR in its FuelConsumption element.

This message does not need to be suspended. Instead, Failed Message Routing could be configured to route the failing messages for further processing as described previously in this chapter.

Validating and testing artifacts

This section will look at how you can validate and test Schemas and Maps using the Visual Studio user interface (UI), and make a brief introduction to unit testing.

Validating Schemas and Message Instances

In Visual Studio, when you develop Schema artifacts you have three options to test or validate this Schema through the UI. They are available through the context menu of a Schema in the Visual Studio Solution Explorer:

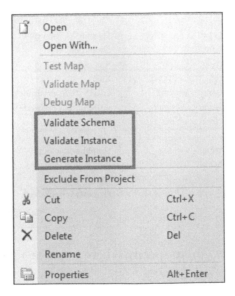

They are:

- **Validate Schema**
- **Validate Instance**
- **Generate Instance**

Validate Schema

Validate Schema can be useful for example if you receive a Schema from a third party or after you have completed work on a Schema that you built yourself. It will validate that the structure and implementation of the Schema is correct.

Validate Instance

Validate instance allows you to validate a sample input message against the Schema. This is a very useful option for example in situations where messages fail the disassemble stage in a production environment and it is not entirely clear why that is or where the error in the input is. More so for FlatFiles then XML files. Which input message to use is configured through the properties of the Schema:

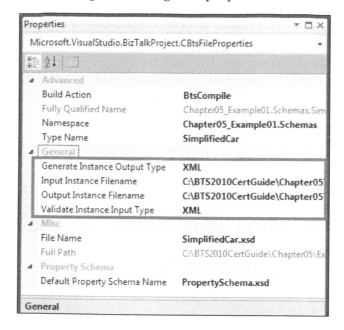

These properties also allow you to specify where to place a message that you generate from the Schema.

Generate Instance

When you generate an instance, if you do not specify a location to place the instance to generate in, it will be placed in the current user's `temp` folder. The instance generation procedure is not very advanced, so it may well produce outputs that will not validate, especially if you have put restrictions in the form of patterns on your fields. The data that it fills the instance with will be sample data that does not necessarily adhere to the rules of the field.

Validating, testing, and debugging Maps

When you develop Maps, you have three options to validate, test or debug this Map using the UI. These are available from the context menu of a Map in the Visual Studio Solution Explorer.

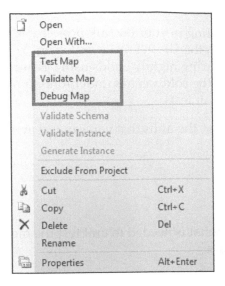

They are:

- **Test Map**
- **Validate Map**
- **Debug Map**

Test Map allows you to supply an input and let Visual Studio run the Map and produce an output. This allows you to test and validate that your mapping logic is doing what you expect. It is a good way to test common input files and edge cases while developing.

Validate Map, on top of validating the links and functoid configuration of the Map, also creates the resulting XSLT script and makes it available for viewing. Looking at the generated XSLT, it can teach you a thing or two about how the BizTalk Mapper works. It also helps you understand why your sequence of functoids is not resulting in the output you expect.

Debug Map gives you the possibility to debug the creation of the output by stepping through the XSLT script and viewing the input file getting processed and the output file getting built element by element. It's useful for more advanced troubleshooting scenarios.

Although all of these are highly useful and should be on your *To Learn* list, if you do not master them fully, it is outside of the scope of this book to go into any more detailed depth on any of these.

Unit testing

If you are serious about testing in your BizTalk projects, as you should be, then doing manual tests through the UI isn't really sufficient. You want automated tests and tests that can be run during nightly builds using Team Foundation Server or tests you can trigger when the solution has undergone some re-work. Such testing is done by implementing unit tests.

In the case of BizTalk Server, the units that you can test are:

* Schemas
* Maps
* Pipelines

This section will describe what is needed to unit test the most commonly tested artifacts; Schemas and Maps.

Unit testing Schemas

When you unit test a Schema, you use the **ValidateInstance** method and supply it with the path to an input XML (or FlatFile) document, and you specify which one of those you have supplied, as shown in the following example:

```
[TestMethod()]
public void ValidateSimplifiedCarInstanceTest()
{
    SimplifiedCar target = new SimplifiedCar();
    bool success = target.ValidateInstance(
        @"C:\BTS2010CertGuide\Chapter05\Example02-UnitTesting\
SimplifiedCar.xml",
        Microsoft.BizTalk.TestTools.Schema.OutputInstanceType.XML);
    Assert.IsTrue(success);
}
```

For the `ValidateInstance` method to be available, you must set **Enable Unit Testing** to `True` on the project that the Schema belongs to:

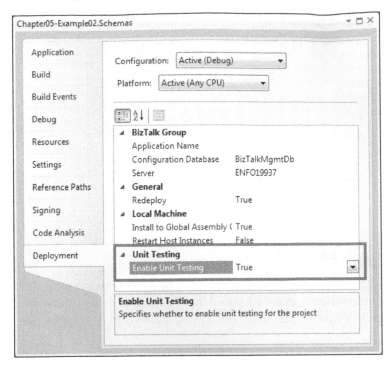

When you set this property to true another base class will be injected in the inheritance hierarchy of the Schema, the `TestableSchemaBase` class that holds the `ValidateInstance` method:

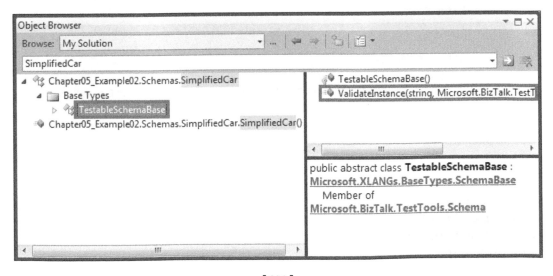

The references needed on the project level for unit testing to work are the **Microsoft. BizTalk.TestTools** and **Microsoft.XLANGs.BaseTypes** assemblies. However, these are added by default when you create a new empty project for BizTalk Server 2010 in Visual Studio 2010. If you are upgrading a project or have previously removed them, you may need to make sure they are there:

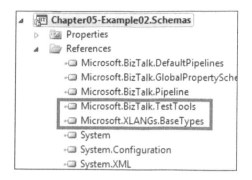

Unit testing Maps

Similarly, as when testing Schemas, testing Maps is done using a method that becomes available when you set **Enable Unit Testing** to `True` on the project that holds the Map. For Maps, this method is called **TestMap**. A sample usage is seen here:

```
[TestMethod()]
public void Map1OutputTest()
{
    Map1 target = new Map1();
    string input = @"C:\BTS2010CertGuide\Chapter05\Example02-
UnitTesting\SimplifiedCar.xml";
    string output = @"C:\BTS2010CertGuide\Chapter05\Example02-
UnitTesting\SimplifiedCar_MapOut.xml";
    target.TestMap(
        input,
        Microsoft.BizTalk.TestTools.Schema.InputInstanceType.Xml,
        output,
        Microsoft.BizTalk.TestTools.Schema.OutputInstanceType.XML);
    Assert.IsTrue(File.Exists(output));
}
```

Unlike the `ValidateSchema` method, the `TestMap` method has a void return. The way to validate that the Map executed successfully is to validate that the output was created. After that you will usually have a series of tests on the content of the output file to validate that the mapping logic did what we expected, given the input provided.

As with Schemas, enabling unit tests injects a new base class into the inheritance hierarchy of the Map, the `TestableMapBase` that contains the `TestMap` method:

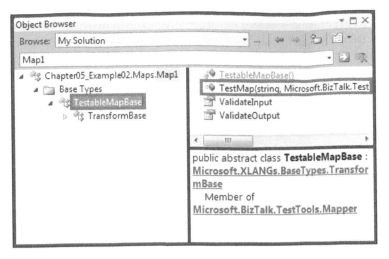

The same two references for testing Schemas are needed; Microsoft.BizTalk.TestTools and Microsoft.XLANGs.BaseTypes. No additional references are needed to test Maps.

Test your knowledge

1. HWLC Motors is having problems with a .NET component developed to calculate a car's fuel efficiency. Sometimes the component throws an exception. The class used from the component is marked as serializable. The Orchestration has no scopes configured. What two things must you do to be able to catch and handle the exception that occurs?

    a. Set the Orchestrations Compensation property to Custom.

    b. Add a scope shape to the orchestration and move the call to the .NET component within the scope. Set Transaction Type to None.

    c. Configure the orchestrations Transaction Type to Long Running.

    d. Add an exception block to the scope and handle the exception there.

    e. Add a scope shape to the Orchestration and move the call to the .NET component within the scope. Set Transaction Type to Atomic.

    f. Add a compensation block to the scope and add logic to compensate for exceptions that occur.

2. HWLC motors are developing a BizTalk Server 2010 solution to handle order fulfillment. As part of the Orchestration is a piece of logic that places an order to the factory to start construction on a new car. The logic is placed in an atomic scope. The orchestration has no other scopes. Later in the solution the customer is billed a down-payment for the car. HWLC has experienced problems with the customer having insufficient funds, which causes exceptions. What must you do to make sure that if that happens a cancellation is sent to the factory?

    a. Set the Compensation property to Custom for the scope and implement logic to send a cancellation.

    b. Add a new scope and place the existing scope inside the new scope. Add a compensation block to the new scope and implement logic to send a cancellation.

    c. Configure the Transaction Type of the Orchestration to be Long Running and implement logic to send a cancellation in the Orchestrations compensation block.

    d. Add a new scope and place the existing scope inside the new scope. Add an exception handling block to the new scope and implement logic to send a cancellation.

3. As part of a BizTalk Server 2010 solution for customer services, HWLC motors have implemented an Orchestration that submits a warranty claim to a subcontractor through a logical one-way port configured to use a Specify Later binding. The send is placed inside a Long Running scope. You need to make sure that the warranty claim has been successfully sent before the Orchestration continues processing. What must you do?

    a. Do nothing. As the logical port is configured with a binding of Specify Later, the physical port is synchronously called by the Orchestration and processing will not continue until port processing is done.

    b. Configure the physical port to use failed message routing.

    c. Configure the logical ports Delivery Notification property to Transmitted and implement add an exception handler to the scope to catch DeliveryFailureException.

    d. Set the scopes Synchronized property to True.

4. HWLC motors are monitoring insurance claims. As soon as a claim arrives that is above $10,000 it must immediately be sent to the claims department for priority assessment. The claims department uses a mainframe that receives files through a file share. If the Send Port fails to deliver the message to the primary file share, the port must immediately fail over to a secondary share. What should you do to enable this scenario?

    a. Configure the port with a backup transport. Set the Retry Count of the backup transport to 0.

    b. Configure the port with a backup transport. Set the Retry count of the Transport Advanced Options to 0.

    c. Configure the port with a backup transport. Set the Priority of the backup transport to 1.

    d. Configure the port for Ordered Delivery and to *stop sending subsequent messages on current message failure.*

5. HWLC motors has a BizTalk Server 2010 solution developed to route orders from a partner to an in house system based on a filter on the MessageType of the message. When the solution is deployed and messages start to arrive they get suspended with the error information "The published message could not be routed because no subscribers were found. This error occurs if the subscribing Orchestration or Send Port has not been enlisted, or if some of the message properties necessary for subscription evaluation have not been promoted. You should use the BizTalk Administration console to troubleshoot this failure. What must you do?

    a. Configure the Send Port to filter on ErrorReport.ReceivePortName.

    b. Configure the Send Port to use the XMLTransmit pipeline.

    c. Configure the Receive Location to use the XMLReceive pipeline.

    d. Use the BizTalk Server Administration console to edit the message context and then resume it.

Summary

In this chapter, we have looked at handling errors and exceptions, both in Orchestrations and in messaging solutions. We have also examined how we can compensate committed transactions in Orchestrations by adding compensation blocks. We have seen how compensation is triggered, either automatically or explicitly. We have also looked at utilizing Delivery Notifications. For messaging solutions, we have looked at common sources of errors, why they occur, and how we can handle them using failed message routing. Finally, we looked at recoverable interchange processing for recovering from errors in debatched messages and discussed what options are available to validate and test during development to mitigate errors occurring in runtime.

In the next chapter, we will cover administrative concepts and tasks such as installation and configuration, application state and deployment, message, port, and orchestration tracking, and other uses of the administration console.

6
Deploying, Tracking, and Administrating a BizTalk Server 2010 Solution

Managing and maintaining a BizTalk solution requires the same diligence that developing BizTalk applications requires. Administering these solutions can sometimes be a challenging endeavor, if the developer has not provided sufficient documentation or has implemented questionable design patterns.

BizTalk Server is often used to support mission-critical integration processes, which means there are often high pressure situations when things do not go as planned. These situations may include BizTalk entering a throttled state, or dependent systems being unavailable. Understanding the tools that BizTalk Administration Console provides, gives BizTalk Administrators an edge when these support issues occur. In some cases, using the BizTalk Administration Console correctly may prevent issues from even occurring in the first place.

The goal of this chapter is to review the features and tools that aid a BizTalk Administrator in ensuring their BizTalk environment is supportable, maintainable, and performs well.

The topics that are included in this chapter are as follows:

- Installing and configuring a multiserver BizTalk environment
- Deploying BizTalk applications
- BizTalk Application states (Started, Partially Started, Stopped)
- Configuring tracking

- Managing BizTalk solutions by using Administration Console
- BizTalk Settings Dashboard
- Test your knowledge

Installing and configuring a multiserver BizTalk environment

For BizTalk Administrators that are used to single server deployments, installing BizTalk in a multiserver environment can lead to some confusion. Many BizTalk resources are familiar with setting up a single node environment, such as a local desktop. Introducing multiple nodes may include complex infrastructure components, such as Clustering and Load Balancing. The following sections will reduce some of this confusion and give you some insight into some of the decisions that you need to make while building out a multiserver environment.

High Availability

Every BizTalk Server that you would like to participate in this BizTalk Group requires the BizTalk Runtime to be installed. Each of these BizTalk Servers will also require the Enterprise Single Sign-on Service to be installed and configured. As a result, we need to designate a Master Secret Server, preferably the one that provides redundancy through Microsoft Windows Clustering. It is generally recommended to have the Master Secret Server hosted on the same cluster that the SQL Server is running on when High Availability is required. The last major component we need to address is a common SQL Server backend that all BizTalk Servers will use as MessageBox, tracking and configuration databases.

The following diagram illustrates a typical two-node BizTalk environment with a Clustered SQL Server backend. In each of our BizTalk Servers, we are going to install BizTalk Runtime, the Administration Console, and Enterprise Single Sign-on. In the event we have requirements to host WCF or Web Services, we will also require Internet Information Services (IIS) to be installed. If one of our BizTalk Servers suffers a catastrophic failure, the remaining node(s) will pick up the work of the problematic server, provided the required Host Instances exist on the healthy server.

In order to have a redundant data store, we need to leverage Windows Clustering Services to Host a SQL Server instance, Enterprise Single Sign-on Service which will act as our Master Secret Server and Microsoft Distributed Transaction Coordinator (MSDTC). In the event of a catastrophic failure in our database tier, a passive node will be able to host these database services with little disruption to BizTalk.

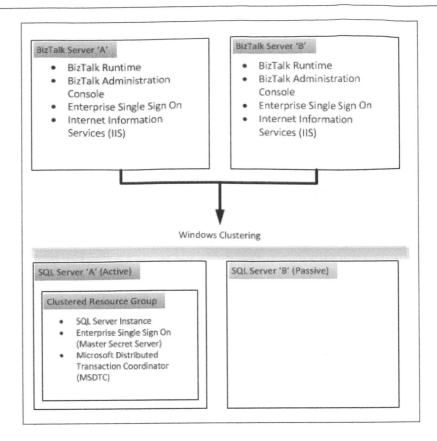

 An excellent post-configuration Database Optimization guide exists on MSDN, at the following URL:

`http://msdn.microsoft.com/en-us/library/`
`ee377048(v=bts.70).aspx`

This article provides advice on how to get better performance out of your SQL Server environment.

Installation setup

The order and method in which we install and configure our BizTalk Servers is very important. As with many server products by Microsoft, installing BizTalk is a two-step process, as follows:

1. Installation
2. Configuration

Installation

The first step that we need to take is to install BizTalk prerequisites, BizTalk Runtime and related components on the chosen BizTalk Server(s). This software can be installed even without the existence of an SQL Server. A detailed installation guide, that includes a list of prerequisite components, may be found at the following URL:

```
http://www.microsoft.com/download/en/details.aspx?id=11503
```

Configuration

Configuring a multinode BizTalk Group will involve making some decisions that we do not need to make in a single-node deployment. Some of these decisions include which server(s) will support our BizTalk Databases and Single Sign-On (SSO) System.

While configuring a multinode BizTalk Group, we need to select **Custom Configuration** in the BizTalk Server 2010 Configuration Wizard, as shown in the following screenshot:

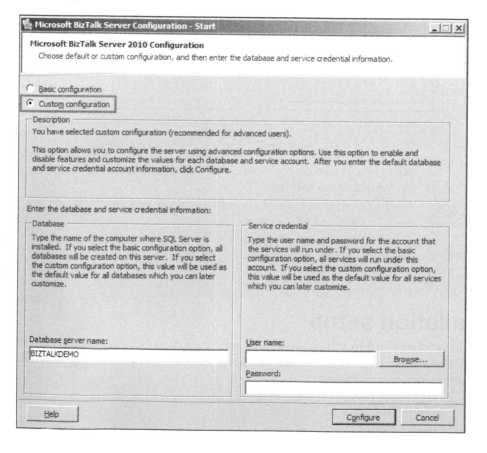

Configuring SSO

The configuration aspect of establishing a BizTalk environment requires a little more planning. Only one BizTalk node should be configured at a time. For the first node that is being configured, we want to select **Create a new SSO system**. Any subsequent nodes being configured should select **Join an existing SSO system**.

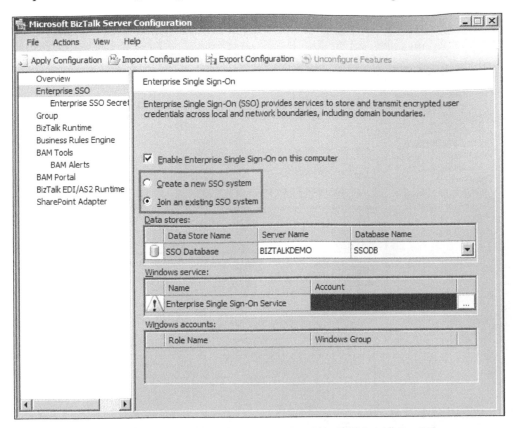

Setting up BizTalk Group

Configuring a BizTalk Group is very similar to configuring an SSO System. The reason for this is that the first node that is being configured will select **Create a new BizTalk Group**, whereas subsequent nodes will select **Join an existing BizTalk Group**.

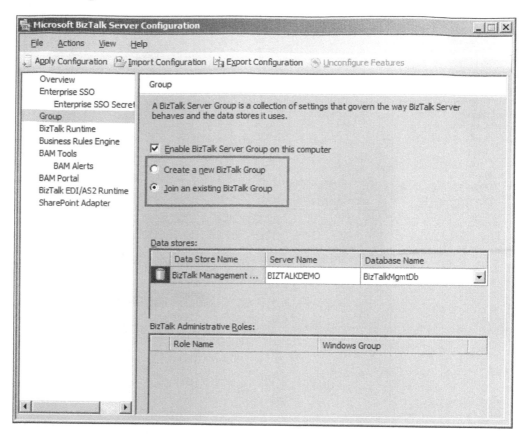

Configuring Runtime settings

When it comes to the **BizTalk Runtime** screen, we have the ability to create default In-process and Isolated Hosts and specify the accounts and groups that will support these Hosts. If we are installing BizTalk on a 64-bit system, we will have the opportunity to specify whether we want to create our default Hosts as 32-bit or 64-bit Hosts.

We also have the ability to specify whether or not to mark these Hosts as **Trusted**. **Trusted** Hosts are used to establish a trusted relationship between MessageBox and consuming services for authorization, and outbound party resolution purposes. For the purpose of this chapter, we will use the default settings and create Non-trusted Hosts.

If we would like to reuse this existing configuration in another environment or server, we have the ability to export our configuration by clicking on the **Export Configuration** button. If we decide to use this feature, then we will need to set our passwords in the new environment, as these details are not included in the exported XML file, as shown in the following screenshot:

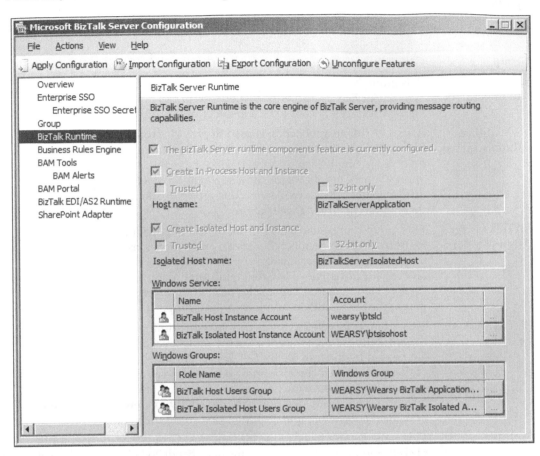

> The remaining screens in the configuration wizard pertain to non-core components and therefore are out of scope for this chapter. For more information pertaining to installing BizTalk in a multiserver environment, please refer to the Microsoft installation guide, which can be found at:
>
> http://www.microsoft.com/download/en/details. aspx?id=11503

Active Directory Groups and Users

When establishing a multiserver BizTalk environment, Active Directory Users and Groups must be used. The following table lists the necessary groups and a brief description of each group function. If you would like to see a more detailed explanation of these various roles, please refer to the following MSDN web page:

http://msdn.microsoft.com/en-us/library/aa577661.aspx

Group	Group Description
SSO Administrators	This group has sufficient permissions to administer the Enterprise Single Sign-on Service. The account we plan on running our Enterprise Single Sign-on Service(s) needs to be a member of this group.
SSO Affiliate Administrators	An SSO Affiliate application is used to provide credential mapping for Single Sign-on Services. Since we can have many different systems involved in Single Sign-on scenarios, we have the ability to create affiliate applications. This allows for some segregation of administration between different subsystems. We can use this group to add administrators for these different affiliate applications.
BizTalk Server Administrators	This group represents one of the more powerful groups in the BizTalk Platform. Having membership in this group provides us with the ability to install applications, manage applications, perform message inspection and resolution activities in Group Hub, and manipulate Send and Receive Handlers for adapters. Members of this group must also be a part of the SSO Affiliate Administrators Group.
BizTalk Server Operators	This group is targeted towards people with administration-like responsibilities that do not require the same level of permissions that are needed by those in the BizTalk Server Administrators Group. Some of these activities include stopping and starting applications, viewing service state and message flow, and terminating or resuming service instances. This group does not have the ability to view message context or content and to manipulate application configuration.
BizTalk Application Users	This is the default name of the BizTalk Host Group that the user for the BizTalk Server Application Host Instance needs to belong to. Microsoft recommends that for each Host that you create, you should also create a related Active Directory BizTalk Host Group.
BizTalk Isolated Host Users	Similar to BizTalk Application Users, this group is the default Host Group for accounts that run the BizTalk Server Isolated Host Instance(s). An example of using an Isolated Host would include a solution that has exposed a WCF Service through IIS. In our Receive Location for this WCF Service, we would specify an Isolated Host.
EDI Subsystem Users	Users within this group have access to the EDI database.

Group	Group Description
BAM Portal Users	Members of this group have access to the BAM Portal website. However, it is important to note that even though these users can access the BAM Portal website, it does not mean that these users have access to all views within the BAM Portal. Those permissions still need to be provided through the BAM "bm" command-line tool.
BizTalk SharePoint Adapter Enabled Hosts	Users within this group have access to the Windows SharePoint Services Adapter Web Service.
BizTalk B2B Operators Group	A new BizTalk role, that has been created in BizTalk 2010, that allows members to perform all party management operations.

Deploying BizTalk applications

In this section, we are going to discuss deploying BizTalk applications. There are several ways to deploy BizTalk applications including the following:

- Deploying from Visual Studio
- Building a Microsoft Installer (MSI) package that can be exported or imported between environments
- Using command line-based tools, such as MSBuild and BtsTask
- Leveraging community frameworks, such as BizTalk Deployment Framework and NANT

Using command line or third party-based deployment tools are out of scope for both the exam and this chapter, so we are not going to go into any detail in these areas. Instead, we will focus on deploying from Visual Studio and using MSI packages.

Sample deployment through Visual Studio

In order to walk properly through deployment scenarios, we need a sample solution. A sample solution may be found in the C:\BTS2010CertGuide\Chapter06\ Example01-Deployment folder called Example01-Deployment.sln. The business process behind this sample is that we have a business partner who has signed a contract to use some of our parts in the production of their vehicles. The name of this fictitious company is MBW Motors. When our company, HWLC Motors, discovers a recall, we require our partner companies, such as MBW Motors, to request replacement parts for the related recall.

Our simple solution will receive a recall request from MBW and transform it into a format that our recall system can support. We will then deliver this message to a file folder that our recall system can access.

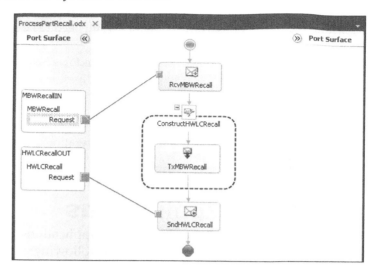

Preparing the solution

In order to deploy from Visual Studio, there are a few things that we need to take care of first:

1. Right-click on our **BizTalk Project**, and select **Properties**.
2. Click on the **Signing** label, and then select **<New...>**.

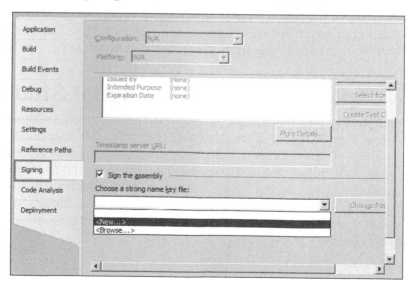

3. When prompted, provide the name **Example01-Deployment.snk** and clear the **Protect my key file with a password** checkbox.

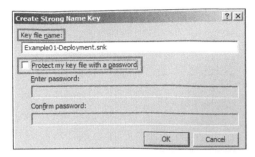

 All BizTalk assemblies and helper assemblies that may be called from BizTalk must be deployed to the Global Assembly Cache (GAC). In order to allow assemblies to be installed in the GAC, they must have Strong Name keys. Strong Name keys may be created from Visual Studio or through the sn–k<strongname>.snk command-line statement.

4. In BizTalk 2006, Microsoft introduced the concept of a BizTalk application. This is based around the idea that it would be nice to manage BizTalk interfaces that are logically related as one application. For instance, if we have an application for a specific department within a company, we could include the department name as a part of the BizTalk **Application Name**. We can then easily identify it when performing administrative tasks. With this in mind, we need to click on the **Deployment** label and then look for the **Application Name** textbox. For the purpose of this book, we are simply going to call our application **Chapter06-Example01**. Once this is complete, we can close this **Property** page, as shown in the following screenshot:

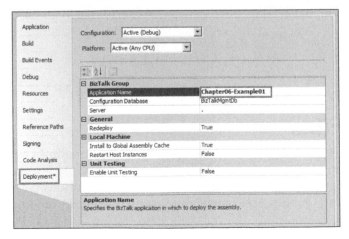

5. We are now ready to deploy our application, and can do so by right-clicking on our **Visual Studio Solution** and then clicking **Deploy Solution**.

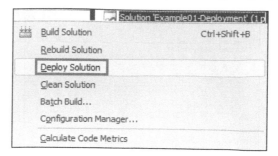

6. Provided our application has been deployed successfully, we can now launch BizTalk Administration Console and discover our application exists. Within the application, we will realize that it is pretty empty. We will discover our Orchestration in the **Orchestrations** folder but will not have any **Receive Ports**, **Receive Locations**, or **Send Ports**, as shown in the following screenshot:

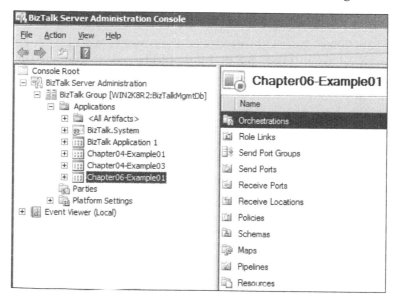

Binding Files

Binding Files are extremely important artifacts that can sometimes be difficult to manage. Binding Files provide BizTalk solutions with a lot of portability. It is Binding Files that allow us to move our BizTalk applications between the Development, Test, Quality Assurance, and Production environments.

There are many ways to manage Binding Files. In this section, we will discuss one of these methods. There are some Binding File Management Solutions, such as the BizTalk Deployment Framework, that aid in the management of Binding Files. Since third party tools are out of scope, in terms of the certification exam, we will not be discussing these methods. Instead, we will focus on a more manual approach.

To create a Binding File, we must first create our required Receive Location(s) and Send Port(s). Once we have completely configured our solution, we can export our configuration as a Binding File. Here are the steps that we need to perform:

1. Launch the BizTalk Administration Console and expand the **Chapter06-Example01** application.

2. On the **Receive Ports** label, right-click and select **New | One-way Receive Port...**, as shown in the following screenshot:

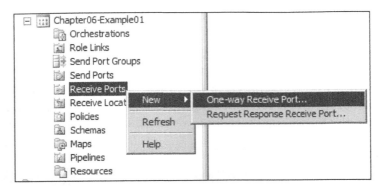

3. In the **Name:** textbox, enter **ReceiveRecall**, and then click on the **OK** button.

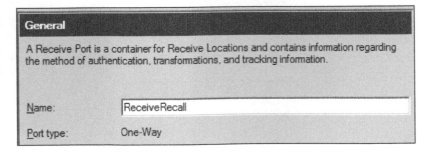

4. We now need to add a **Receive Location**, and can do so by right-clicking on the **Receive Locations** label and selecting **New** | **One-way Receive Location...**, as shown in the following screenshot:

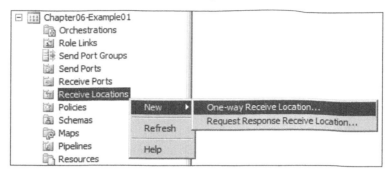

5. When prompted, click on **ReceiveRecall** Receive Port, and click on the **OK** button.

6. Provide a **Name:** of **ReceiveRecallMBWRecall**, a **Transport Type:** of FILE, a **URI:** of **C:\BTS2010CertGuide\Chapter06\FileDrop\DEV\MBW*. Copy.xml**, a **Receive handler:** of **BizTalkServerApplication** and a **Receive Pipeline:** of **XMLReceive**. Once this information has been populated, as shown in the following screenshot, we can click on the **OK** button:

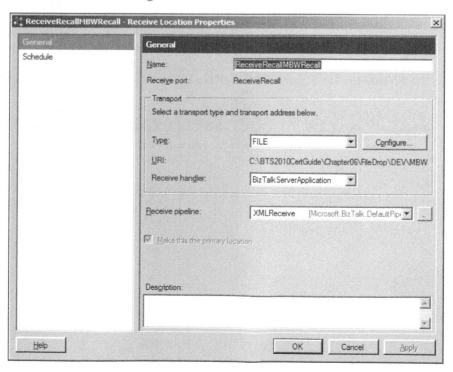

7. We now need to configure a Send Port. To do so, click on **Send Ports | New | Static One-way Send Port...**, as shown in the following screenshot:

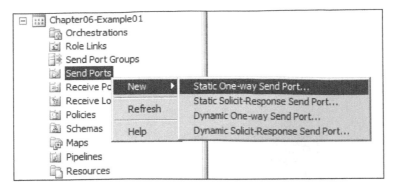

8. Provide a **Name:** of **SendRecallToHWLC**, a **Transport Type:** of **FILE**, a **URI:** of **C:\BTS2010CertGuide\Chapter06\FileDrop\ DEV\HWLCRecall%MessageID%.xml**, a **Send handler:** of **BizTalkServerApplication**, and a **Send Pipeline** of **PassThruTransmit**. Once this information has been populated, as shown in the following screenshot, we can click on the **OK** button:

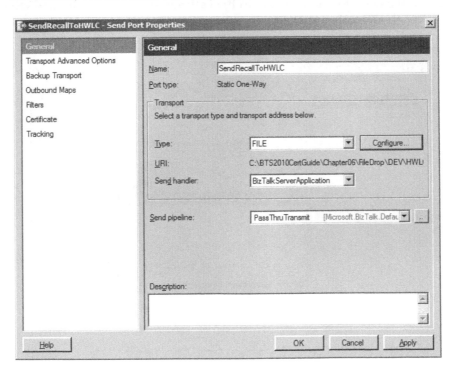

9. We now need to bind our Orchestration to our Receive and Send Ports. We can do so by double-clicking on **Orchestrations**, right-clicking on **Orchestrations**, and then clicking on **Properties...**, as shown in the following screenshot:

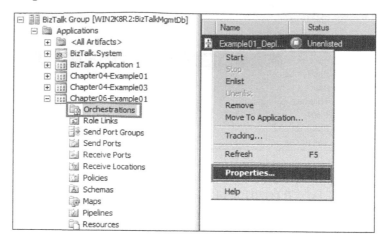

10. To finish binding our orchestration to our ports, click on the **Bindings** label. Next, we need to set our **Host:** to **BizTalkServerApplication**, **MBWRecallIn** to **ReceiveRecall**, and **HWLCRecallOUT** to **SendRecallToHWLC**, as shown in the following screenshot:

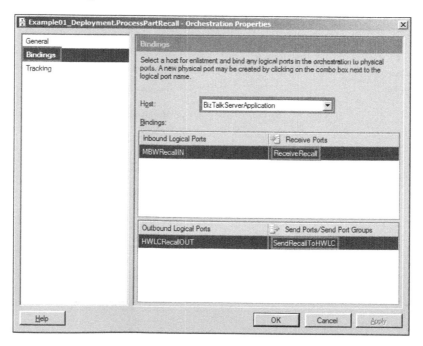

11. At this point, we have a configured application and are now in a position to export our configuration to a Binding File. To do so, we will simply right-click on the name of our BizTalk application, **Chapter06-Example01**, and select **Export | Bindings...**, as shown in the following screenshot:

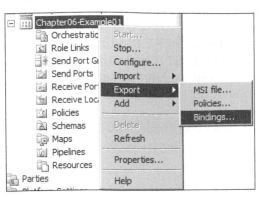

12. When prompted, we want to select **Export all bindings** from the current application and save our file as `C:\BTS2010CertGuide\Chapter06\Bindings\Chapter06-Example01.DEV.Binding.xml`.

13. The Binding File that we just created represents a Binding File that could be used in a Development environment. For convenience, Test Binding File has also been provided in the `C:\BTS2010CertGuide\Chapter06\Bindings\` folder, called `Chapter06-Example01.TEST.Binding.xml`. This new file represents a Binding File that we can use in a TEST environment. The only difference between the DEV and TEST file is that we use the appropriate subfolder in the `C:\BTS2010CertGuide\Chapter06\FileDrop` folder called `Test`.

14. Now that we have multiple Binding Files, we are going to add these files to our BizTalk application, as resources. We can do so by right-clicking on our BizTalk application, **Chapter06-Example01**, and then selecting **Add | Resources...**, as shown in the following screenshot:

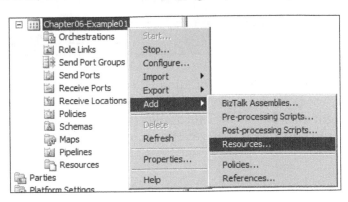

15. In the **Add Resources** dialog, we want to add both of our Binding Files that can be found in the `C:\BTS2010CertGuide\Chapter06\Bindings` folder of this chapter's sample code. We now want to specify which **Target Environment** each of these Binding Files belongs to. So, we can select the first file, **Chapter06-Example01.DEV.Binding.xml**, and then specify a **Target Environment:** of DEV. We want to perform this same action with our **Chapter06-Example01.TEST.Binding.xml** file, this time providing a **Target Environment** of TEST. Optionally, we can specify the **Overwrite all** checkbox, in the event we have added these resources to our BizTalk application previously, as shown in the following screenshot:

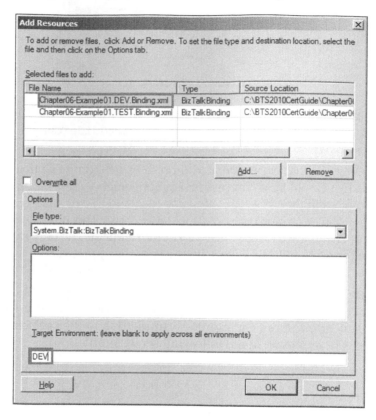

16. Now that we have added our Binding Files to our BizTalk application as resources, we can now export our application as an MSI file. To do so, we need to right-click on our BizTalk application, **Chapter06-Example01**, and then select **Export | MSI file...**, as shown in the following screenshot:

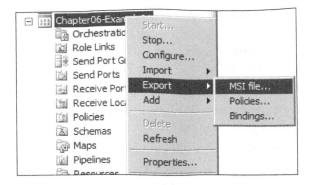

17. On the **Welcome** screen, click on **Next** to proceed to the next screen.

18. When prompted, we want to ensure that all of the artifacts we are interested in, including the ones in our MSI package, are checked. This includes our BizTalk assembly and Binding-related Files, as shown in the following screenshot:

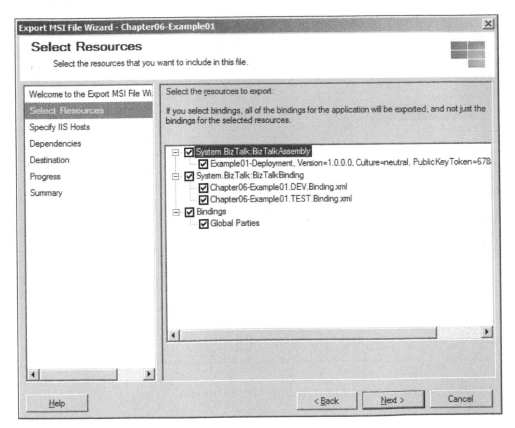

Our sample application does not use Trading Partner Management and Global Parties. If our application did, we could include Global Parties in our MSI package.

19. Since we are not hosting any Web or WCF Services, we can skip the **Specify IIS Hosts** screen, by clicking on **Next**.

20. On the **Dependencies** screen, click on **Next** to proceed.

21. In the **Destination** screen, provide a **Destination application name:** of **Chapter06-Example01**. In the **MSI file to generate:** textbox, enter **C:\BTS2010CertGuide\Chapter06\MSI\Chapter06-Example01.msi**. Finally, click on the **Export** button to write the MSI file to the disk, as shown in the following screenshot:

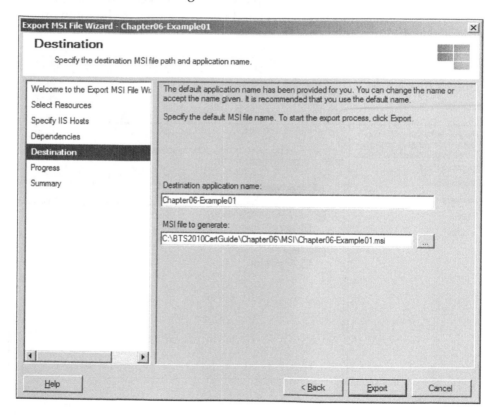

22. Click on the **Finish** button to close the **Summary** screen.

Sample deployment through MSI package

When the time comes to deploy our application to a different environment, we will have an MSI package that contains multiple Binding Files. For this purpose, in the next section, we are going to pretend that we are deploying our MSI package to a TEST environment and will therefore use the TEST Binding File when prompted. To keep things simple, we will just reuse our existing BizTalk environment and will delete our existing BizTalk application, as follows:

 The next section requires that the `C:\BTS2010CertGuide\Chapter06\FileDrop\TEST` folder exist. If you have extracted the sample source code that has been provided with this book, then this folder exists on your machine. If you have not extracted the source code, please create this folder to ensure this sample functions correctly.

1. We need to delete our existing BizTalk application for this chapter and can do so by right-clicking on **Chapter06-Example01**, and then clicking on **Delete**. Should the **Delete** option be disabled, it is probably because our application is currently started; it must be stopped before this command can be executed, as shown in the following screenshot:

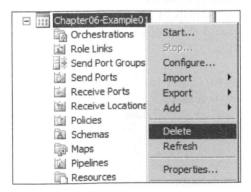

2. When asked whether you are sure you want to delete this application, click on the **Yes** button.

3. Deploying a BizTalk application, in most cases, is a two-step process. The first step is to run the MSI package from Windows, which will register the application with the Windows Operating System, and then load any related assemblies in the Global Assembly Cache (GAC). To do this, we want to find our MSI package in the `C:\BTS2010CertGuide\Chapter06\MSI` folder, right-click on it, and then select **Install**, as shown in the following screenshot:

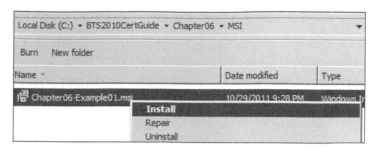

4. The installation wizard is straightforward, and we can simply accept the defaults.

5. Once we have completed the MSI package installation, we still need to import this MSI package in BizTalk Administration Console. At this point, the Windows Operating System is aware of our BizTalk application, but BizTalk itself is not. To import our MSI package, we can right-click on the **Applications** label and then select **Import | MSI file...**, as shown in the following screenshot:

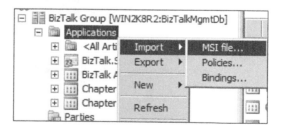

6. We now need to provide the location of our MSI package to the **Import MSI Wizard**. We can find our MSI package in the `C:\BTS2010CertGuide\Chapter06\MSI folder,` as shown in the following screenshot:

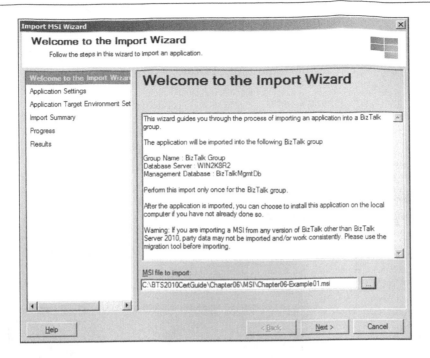

7. We now have the opportunity to provide an **Application name**. We will just accept the default value, which is **Chapter06-Example01**, as shown in the following screenshot:

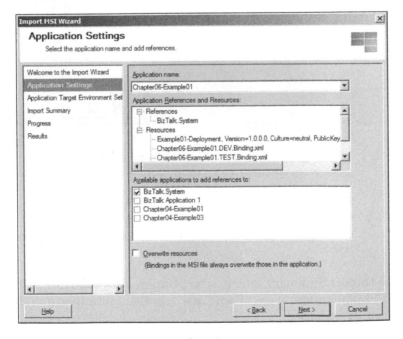

If we were redeploying an application, we would want to select **Overwrite resources**, but since we deleted our application prior to running the **Import MSI Wizard**, it is not required.

8. We now have the opportunity to specify our **Target Staging Environment**. Since this walkthrough is focusing on a deployment to our TEST environment, we will select **TEST** from the drop-down, as shown in the following screenshot:

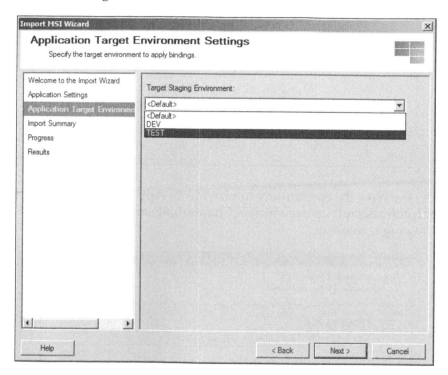

 When we added Binding Files as resources in the previous section, we specified a Target environment. If we did not provide a Target environment, then we would want to select **Default** in this previous screen. A Binding File that does not have a Target environment will be used when **Default** is selected as the **Target Staging Environment**, when importing an MSI.

9. On the **Import Summary** screen, select **Import** and, once finished, click on the **Finish** button. We will now discover that our application has been successfully imported.

Binding File dependencies

When importing Binding Files into a BizTalk environment, it is very important to ensure any assemblies and artifacts that the Binding File is referencing, exist. For instance, if we try to import a Binding File that references a particular Host, that Host must exist for the import to be successful.

Another area to be cautious about is specifying a Host within a Send Port configuration within our Binding File. A Host that is specified in a Send Port, or Receive Location for that matter, must also exist in the handler configuration of an adapter. The following screenshot illustrates how this configuration should be set up. Suppose we have a Send Port that is going to use the **FILE** adapter and will use a Host called **HWLCSend**. In order to configure this correctly, we need to navigate to the **Platform Settings** node, and then expand the **Adapters** node. We can now right-click on the **FILE** adapter and click on **New Send Handler**. We now have the ability to specify **HWLCSend** as a **Send Handler**. The next time we import a Binding File that is going to use the **HWLCSend** Host in a Send Port that uses the **FILE** adapter (as shown in the following screenshot), we will not receive any errors:

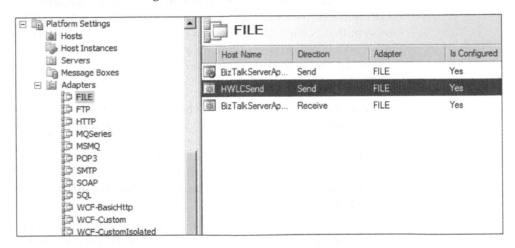

BizTalk Application states

BizTalk has many different application states. Understanding these states can be the difference between being a genius and a scapegoat. Modification of a BizTalk state is usually the result of an action that has taken place. In many cases, altering these states is due to an upcoming deployment, and we need to ensure that we allow messages that are currently being processed to complete without letting new messages into the BizTalk application. I am sure there are many horror stories out there about an inexperienced admin who accidently terminated some inflight messages because they did not understand these states.

Runtime Application states

There are three Runtime Application states. Setting these states is usually based upon explicit actions by an administrator, but can also occur if system resource(s), such as a source system, is not available. Do note that the following states do not account for Hosts being online or offline. We can have an application that is started, but if we have Host(s) that are offline, this application will not function properly.

The following table describes these Runtime states in more detail:

State	Description
Started	In this state, all BizTalk application artifacts are enabled and ready to perform processing.
Partially Started	When an application is **Partially Started**, it means that some of the application artifacts and resources are online. An application may be placed into this state either explicitly by an administrator or it may be the result of some dependent system resource(s) being offline. Consider a situation where we have a Receive Location that uses the FILE adapter to connect to a network file system that is currently offline. In this situation, we will have a Receive Location that automatically gets disabled, and therefore, the state of our application will flip from **Started** to **Partially Started**.
	We may have another situation where we have been asked to hold or queue messages because a destination system is either down or currently under maintenance. In this case, we want to stop the related Send Port, but leave the Send Port enlisted. This will allow BizTalk to queue these messages without sending them. It also results in the application state flipping to **Partially Started**.
Stopped	The final state is when an application is completely offline. This means we have no Receive Locations, Orchestrations, or Send Ports enlisted or capable of processing messages. An application enters this state through the actions of an administrator.

The following screenshot shows the working of these Runtime states:

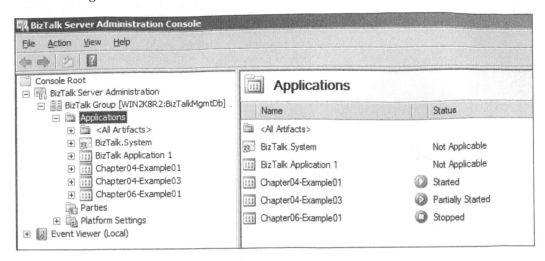

When stopping an application, BizTalk provides us with some options that allow us to control how the application will be stopped. Much like the Runtime states, stopping an application will affect the state of a Host.

The following table will further explain each option when shutting down an application:

State	Description
Partial Stop – Allow running instances to continue	This option is ideal when you have inflight messages that have a short duration. By stopping an application using this mode, we will have all of our Receive Locations disabled. Meanwhile, our Orchestration(s) and Send Port(s) will continue to function. This allows us to drain our application. No new messages can enter the application, but messages that are currently in-flight have the opportunity to complete.
Partial Stop – Suspend running instances	When we select Partial Stop – Suspend running instances, it is like pressing the pause button on the application. We cannot receive any new messages, and any Messages/Service instances that are currently being processed will be suspended. These messages/service instances may be resumed if we attempt to start our application. Using this option is ideal when we have some Long Running processes and it may not be feasible to wait for any active instances to complete.

State	Description
Full Stop – Terminate instances	The most destructive option of the three, when this method is used, any messages, or service instances, will be terminated. This means that if we are in the middle of processing a million-dollar purchase order, and we choose to stop an application using this mode, we will lose this purchase order. This method needs to be used selectively and by an administrator that clearly understands the impact of performing this action.

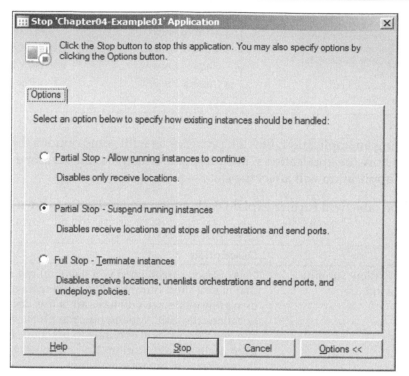

Tracking events in BizTalk Server

Tracking events in BizTalk Server can be an expensive but valuable endeavor. This activity is expensive as BizTalk will now need to look for specific properties, or message bodies, within Message or Orchestration instances and record this data. This activity can reduce the throughput of BizTalk Server, but can become extremely beneficial in support scenarios. If you have ever participated in a BizTalk Project that involved multiple teams, you will inevitably have been asked "What happened with message XYZ?" Using the tracking capabilities of BizTalk allows you to solve the mystery much more easily.

In this section, we are going to discuss some of the different ways in which a BizTalk Administrator can track events as they occur inside BizTalk.

Tracking Receive Ports

We can enable our tracking properties on a Receive Port by right-clicking on the **Receive Port** and then selecting **Properties**. Once in the **Property** screen of the **Receive Port**, we need to click on the **Tracking** label.

We will discover the following properties that we can set. The following table will elaborate on each of these properties and its purpose, as follows:

Property	Description
Track Message Bodies	These options are related to saving a copy of the message that has been received at two different stages.
Request message before port processing	When enabled, the content of the message will be saved before passing through any Pipeline.
Request message after port processing	Enable this option when you want to save the content of an inbound message after the message has passed through a Pipeline.
Track Message Properties	Use these options to track promoted properties at two different stages of receiving a message.
Request message before port processing	Setting this property allows us to track a promoted property when a message has been received, and before the message enters a Pipeline.
Request message after port processing	When enabled, promoted properties will be tracked after a message has been through a Pipeline. This option is very beneficial in situations where a custom Pipeline component has promoted a property inside a custom Pipeline.

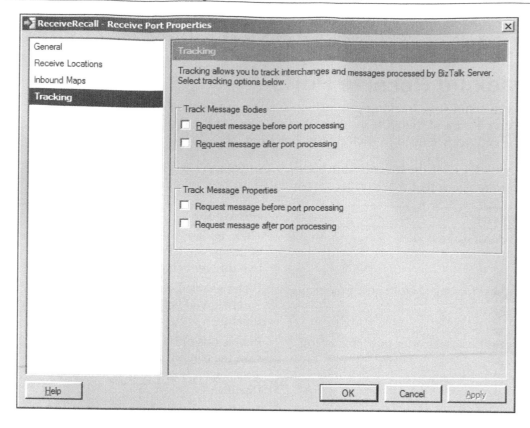

Tracking Orchestrations

Tracking an Orchestration is very similar to tracking a Receive Port. Much like a Receive Port, each Orchestration has its own tracking properties. To enable tracking on an Orchestration, right-click on it, and then select **Properties**. Once on this **Property** screen, click on the **Tracking** label.

However, we have a few more options that we can set; they are further discussed in the following table:

Property	Description
Track Events	These options are set by default and aid in identifying Orchestration events, so that we can query these events in the BizTalk Administration Console.
Orchestration start and end	Having this setting allows us to identify when an Orchestration started and finished inside of the BizTalk Administration Console.
Message send and receive	If we want to be able to record the time that a message was sent or received, then we need to enable this option.
Shape start and end	When enabled, this setting can help to troubleshoot performance bottlenecks. When we are debugging an Orchestration, we will be able to determine the amount of time that each shape took to execute.
Track Message Bodies	These properties are very similar to the properties that exist in a Receive or Send Port. It allows us to save a copy of the message content as messages are making their way through our Orchestration.
Before Orchestration processing	This property, and the remaining ones, are only enabled if **Message send and receive – Track Event** is enabled. When enabled, the message content will be saved prior to it, entering an Orchestration. This property becomes extremely useful in situations where we are using Direct Bound Ports and have not received a message through a traditional Receive Port.
After Orchestration processing	The content of a message, after it has been processed by an Orchestration, will be saved when this option is enabled. Once again, this property is very useful in Direct Bound Port situations. Otherwise, we would not have a Physical Send Port that we could enable message body tracking on.

Property	Description
Track Message Properties	Much like Receive Ports, we can track promoted properties for both incoming and outgoing messages. This time around, properties are tracked when a message enters or exits an Orchestration.
Incoming messages	When enabled, promoted properties will be tracked when a message enters an Orchestration.
Outgoing messages	After a message has left an orchestration, we are able to track promoted properties, when this option is enabled.

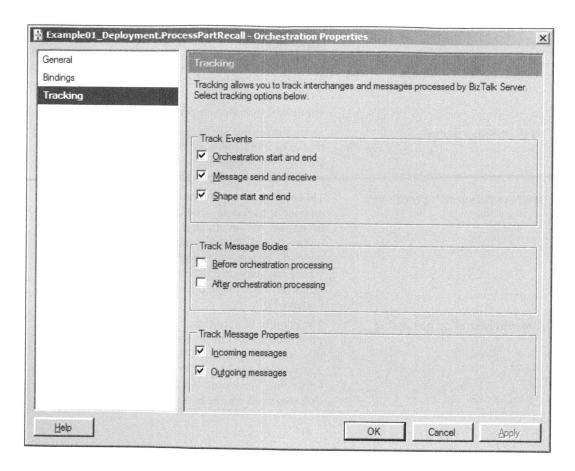

Provided we have promoted properties before deploying our application, we can enable and disable these tracking properties, as required. However, we cannot retroactively obtain details about an Orchestration or message if we do not have the tracking settings enabled. By setting these tracking options, any message or Orchestration processed, going forward, will be tracked.

Tracking Send Ports

Tracking Send Ports works the same way as Tracking Receive Ports, the difference being Tracking Send Ports will track messages entering and exiting a Send Port, as opposed to a Receive Port. The following table describes our tracking properties in more detail:

Property	Description
Track Message Bodies	These options are related to saving a copy of the message that is about to be sent at two different stages.
Request message before port processing	When enabled, the content of the message will be saved before passing through any Pipeline.
Request message after port processing	Enable this option when you want to save the content of an outbound message after the message has passed through a Pipeline.
Track Message Properties	Use these options to track promoted properties at two different stages of sending a message.
Request message before port processing	Setting this property allows us to track a promoted property when a message is about to be sent, but before the message enters a Pipeline.
Request message after port processing	When enabled, promoted properties will be tracked after a message has been through a Pipeline.

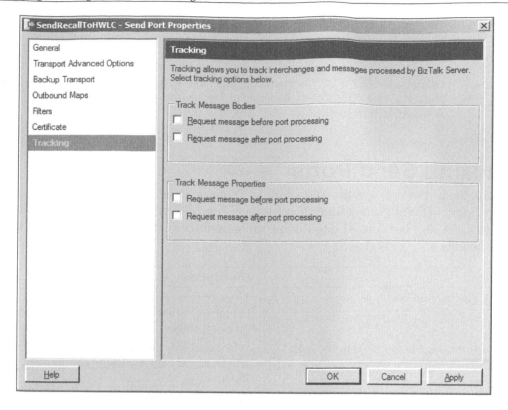

Managing BizTalk applications using BizTalk Administration Console

The BizTalk Administration Console is a very rich tool that allows us to manage all aspects of our BizTalk applications. We have already touched upon some of its capabilities, including managing Binding Files and MSI packages, in addition to managing Hosts and adapter Handlers. This section is going to focus more on the tools that allow us to determine the real-time health of our applications. This section has been broken down into the following six sections:

1. Configuration Overview
2. Work in Progress
3. Suspended Items
4. Grouped Service Instances
5. Tracked Service Instances
6. Tracked Message Events

Within the BizTalk Administration Console, each of these different sections provides links to queries that we can run against our `MessageBox` and `Tracking` databases. We also have the ability to create our own queries and save them, so that we can reuse them at a later time.

Configuration Overview

In this section of **Group Hub**, we will discover our **Group name**, the name of our **Server**, and the name of our Management **Database**. More importantly, we get a quick overview of the health of our BizTalk environment. We can see how many **Applications** have been installed and the summary of their health. There are three different states that are represented by icons. If all of our applications are stopped, this icon will be red. If we have some applications started and some partially started, or stopped, the icon will be blue. If all applications are started, the icon will be green.

The next area to dive into is the Host Instances state view. If all of our Host Instances are stopped, then this icon will be red. If we have some Host Instances started and some stopped, then we will see an icon with a red exclamation mark (!). Finally, if all Host Instances are online, the icon will be a green check mark, as shown in the following screenshot:

 In the event that your environment contains Clustered Host Instances, the BizTalk Administration Console is smart enough to detect this situation and will correctly display the state of our Host Instances, taking into account Active or Passive Host Instances.

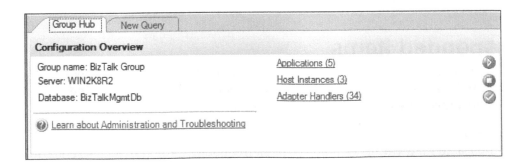

Work in Progress

This area deals with active processes that have not entered an exception or suspended state. The **Running service instances** link provides a query that will display the total amount of running instances.

Dehydrated orchestrations refer to Orchestrations that are currently sitting idle. These Orchestrations may have just sent out a message to a destination system and may now be waiting for a response back.

The messages that were not successfully sent to a downstream system, and have their Send Port configured to Retry, will show up in the **Retrying and idle ports** link.

A message that has been found by a subscription but cannot be sent out due to a Host Instance being offline will end up as **Ready service instances**. For instance, suppose we have a message that was received through a `ReceiveMessages` Host Instance. The Send Port that subscribes to this message uses a Host Instance called `SendMessages`, but this Host Instance is currently offline. This message will remain in this **Ready service instances** state until the `SendMessages` Host Instance comes back online.

The last state that we are going to discuss is called **Scheduled service instances**. In some situations, we may want to "save" our messages until a certain part of the day, and then release them. We can do so by setting a schedule on a Send Port. The number of messages that are currently in this state will be reflected here:

Work in Progress	
Running service instances	3
- Dehydrated orchestrations	0
- Retrying and idle ports	1
- Ready service instances	2
- Scheduled service instances	0

Suspended Items

At the top of this section, we will discover a summary of all of the different **Suspended service instances**. There are two different types of **Suspended service instances**; **Resumable** and **Non-resumable**.

Resumable instances can be restarted by a BizTalk Administrator. Messages may enter this state for a variety of reasons, but a frequent way that messages enter this state is when Retry Thresholds of a Send Port have been exceeded.

Message Instances that cannot be restarted will remain in a **Non-resumable** state. Messages may enter this state for many reasons, including whether a message is experiencing a routing failure or whether an Orchestration has encountered a catastrophic failure.

Suspended Items	
Suspended service instances	3
- Resumable	2
- Non-resumable	1

Group Suspended Service Instances

Within this section, we will discover four different links to queries. Each link will take us to a Query Results view, but the information will be grouped depending upon the link we clicked on.

The first link is called **Grouped by Application**. When selected, this link will take us to a Query Results page that will group all of the Suspended Instances, based upon the BizTalk application they belong to. This feature becomes very useful if we are only concerned with errors that belong to a specific application. It also declutters some unrelated Suspended Messages that you may not immediately be interested in.

The second Suspended Instance Group that we are interested in, is **Grouped by Error Code**. When this link is clicked, we will see all Suspended Instances grouped by their Error Code, regardless of which application they belong to. This type of query is good when trying to troubleshoot, whether or not an underlying shared component is causing an issue.

The **Grouped by Service Name** link, when clicked, will display all Suspended Instances that are grouped by their Service Name. A Service Name may include the name of a Receive Port, Orchestration, Send Port, or as in the following example, a Routing Failure.

The **Grouped by URI** link will take us to a Query Results screen that will group our exceptions by the URI that it is related to. This may be a Universal Naming Convention (UNC) path, Web Service URL, or even a Database Connection String, as follows:

Grouped Suspended Service Instances			
Grouped by Application		Grouped by Service Name	
Chapter06-Example01	3	ReceiveRecall	1
		Routing Failure Report for "Re...	1
		Click on header to see all results	
Grouped by Error Code		Grouped by URI	
0xc0c01680 (Routing Failure)	1	C:\BTS2010CertGuide\Chapt...	2
0xC0C01B4e (Routing Failure ...	1	C:\BTS2010CertGuide\Chapt...	1
Click on header to see all results			

Tracked Service Instances

Tracked Service Instances is a good way to search for particular service instances that may have been successful or terminated. By Service Instance, this includes messages that were received, sent, or Orchestrations. If we want to search for both these conditions, we can click on **Completed instances**, whereas if we want to only find Terminated Instances, we can click on the **Terminated instances** link.

> **Tracked Service Instances**
>
> Tracked service instances
>
> - Completed instances
>
> - Terminated instances

Tracked Message Events

If we are just interested in Message Events, we can click on the **Tracked Message Events** link. Message Events include Send and Receive Events. If we are only interested in **Transmission failure events**, we can click on this link. An example of a Transmission failure could include a Message Instance that has exceeded the threshold of a Send Port.

> **Tracked Message Events**
>
> Tracked message events
>
> - Transmission failure events

BizTalk Settings Dashboard

A common complaint with earlier versions of BizTalk included a lack of consistency when carrying out performance tuning. Tuning performance in these earlier versions of BizTalk usually involved tweaking registry settings, configuration files, and modifying settings in the BizTalk Administration Console.

Another common complaint was that modified settings often were applied to the entire BizTalk Group instead of more granular artifacts, such as Hosts. Microsoft made some significant enhancements to their performance tuning story in BizTalk 2010. No longer do we need to visit as many locations to tweak performance. Instead, we will find a BizTalk Settings Dashboard that will allow us to make performance tweaks to our BizTalk Group and Hosts, from a central location. Another beneficial feature is the ability to import and export our settings, which allows for better consistency and portability across our BizTalk environments.

Viewing and modifying performance tuning settings

In order to view and modify the BizTalk Settings Dashboard, we need to perform the following steps:

1. Within the BizTalk Administration Console, right-click on our **BizTalk Group**, and then select **Settings**, as shown in the following screenshot:

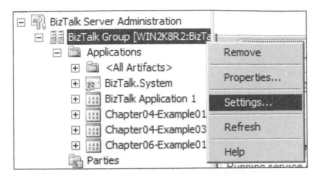

2. Within this BizTalk Settings Dashboard, we have settings related to our BizTalk Group, our Hosts, and our Host Instances. Going through each of these individual settings in detail is not within the scope of this chapter or the exam. We will concentrate on some of the more frequently used settings.

3. In the **Group** section of this dashboard, we will find global settings pertaining to our BizTalk Group. Some of the more important settings include:

Property	Description
Configuration refresh interval	Every time we make a change to our messaging configuration, there is always a delay before it takes effect. The default value is **60** seconds, which means if we make a change to a Receive Location, these changes will not take effect for these many seconds. Often, administrators get frustrated when they make a change to a configuration setting and become impatient. They then start performing unnecessary actions such as restarting Host Instances thinking these actions have resolved their issue. Instead, they just need to wait for the next Configuration refresh interval.
Large message size	In BizTalk 2006, Microsoft introduced a streaming approach to transforming large messages. This threshold will determine whether to try and transform complete messages versus breaking the message up into a series of batches.

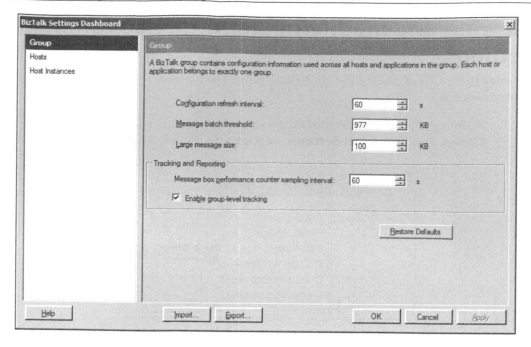

4. In the **Hosts** section of the Dashboard, we have the ability to isolate settings on a per-host basis. We have the ability to specify different configurations for each Host that we have configured in our BizTalk Group. We can isolate a Host by selecting our Host from the **Host:** drop-down, as shown in the following screenshot:

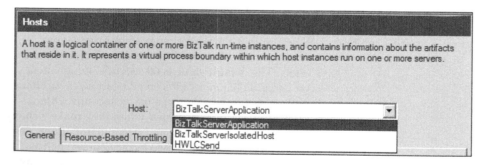

5. Once we have selected the Host that we want to manipulate, we have many different tabs where we can apply these settings, including:

   - General
   - Resource-based Throttling
   - Rate-based Throttling
   - Orchestration Throttling

6. The most compelling settings can be found on the **General** tab. On this tab, we will find the **Polling Intervals** section. One of the strengths of BizTalk is its ability to provide durable messaging. This means that while BizTalk is processing messages, they will be published to our BizTalk `MessageBox`. When this publishing occurs, BizTalk Subscriptions are evaluated. If a subscription is determined, the subscriber will pick up the Message Instance during its next Poll cycle. Both Orchestrations and Messaging, such as Send Ports, can pick up these messages from a Host Work Queue. While this type of architecture is very reliable, it does come at a cost. The default **Polling Intervals** are set for **500** milliseconds (**ms**) which means that, if we have a Send Port that wants to send out a message, a check will be made twice a second to see whether a message is available to be sent. For many organizations, checking a Host Work Queue twice a second more than satisfies their performance requirements. But for some, this just is not fast enough. For these organizations, we can tune these Hosts that have more demanding performance requirements, to check more often than the default settings permit. However, you do need to be careful in these situations, since polling more frequently can also put more stress on your SQL Servers.

7. The opposite scenario also applies. Consider we have a batch that runs infrequently, perhaps outside of core business hours. In this situation, there is no point in checking our Host Work Queue so often. So we can actually tune our BizTalk Host to check less frequently than the default setting, as shown in the following screenshot:

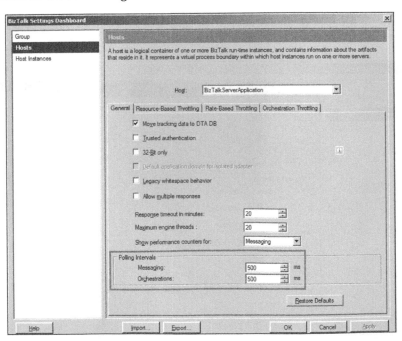

8. The final screen that we are going to discuss is the **Host Instances** screen. In the previous screen, we had the ability to specify Host-specific settings. We now have the opportunity to get even more granular by specifying a particular Host Instance setting. We can choose which Host Instance we want to manipulate, and on which server, by selecting it from the **Host Instance:** drop-down.

9. So why would we want to change settings at the Host Instance level? Perhaps we have different sets of hardware within our BizTalk Group. Consider having a Host called BizTalkServerApplication, that has Host Instances on two nodes: A and B. Node A has more memory than Node B, so we may want to tune Node B differently due to the differences in the memory foot print as shown in the following screenshot:

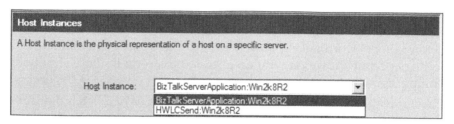

10. Once we have chosen our Host Instance, we now have the ability to modify settings related to the following:

- .NET CLR
- Orchestration Memory Throttling

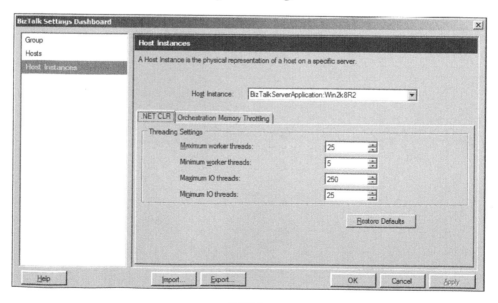

For more information related to performance tuning for BizTalk, please visit http://msdn.microsoft.com/en-us/library/ff629706.aspx.

Exporting and importing performance tuning settings

Now that Microsoft has made accessing Performance Tuning Settings from a single dashboard, they have also now provided a convenient way to import and export these settings. This is a really valuable feature. It allows us to make changes to our BizTalk Group in a Quality Assurance (QA) or TEST environment. Once we have tested our application and are happy, we can export these settings from this QA or TEST environment, and promote them to a Production environment.

To export our BizTalk Dashboard Settings, we need to perform the following steps:

1. While in the **BizTalk Settings Dashboard**, click on the **Export** button from the **Group**, **Host**, or **Host Instance** screen, and then click on the **OK** button, as shown in the following screenshot:

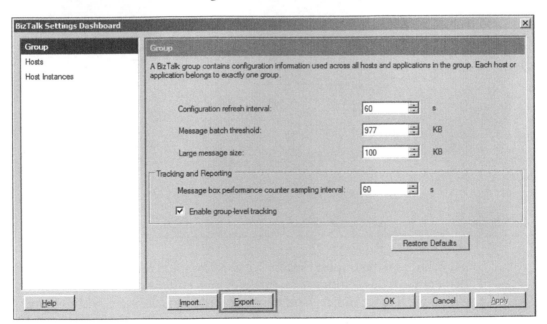

2. We are now prompted to provide a folder and a filename for our configuration to be stored in. Once we have provided this information, we should see a confirmation similar to the one in the following screenshot:

3. We now have an export of our settings from our current environment. If we want to import these settings to another environment, we can launch the **BizTalk Settings Dashboard**, and click on the **Import** button, as shown in the following screenshot:

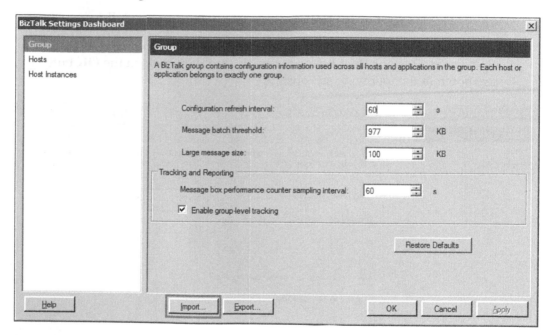

4. Upon clicking on the **Import** button, we are prompted for the location of our file that contains our settings from our previous environment. Once we have provided our file, we can click on the **Next** button to continue, as shown in the following screenshot:

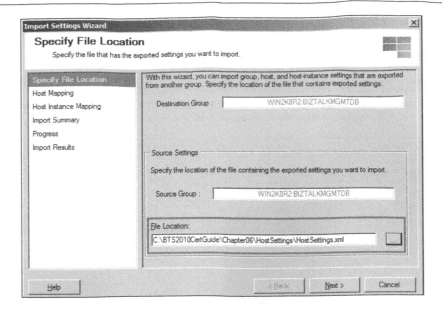

5. In the event that the environment where we generated our settings file is
    not an exact match to our Destination environment, BizTalk provides us
    with a **Host Mapping** tool. This tool will allow us to copy settings from
    any Host in our source file and map it to a **Destination Host**. We can find
    an example of this feature in the following screenshot. In this example, we
    set the HWLCSend settings to both the **BizTalkServerApplication** and
    HWLCSend Hosts in the Destination environment. Once we have completed
    our mapping, we can click on the **Next** button to continue, as shown in the
    following screenshot:

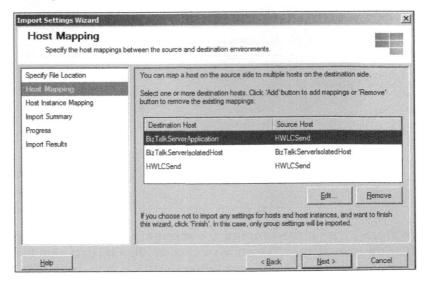

6. We also have the ability to perform **Host Instance Mapping** much like we have done with Hosts. Once we have completed this mapping, we can click on the **Next** button to continue, as shown in the following screenshot:

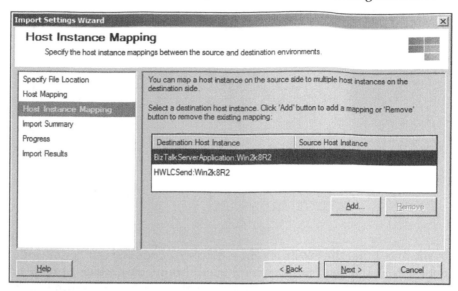

7. We now have an opportunity to review our settings. Once we are happy with them, we can click on the **Import** button to have these settings applied in our Destination environment, as shown in the following screenshot:

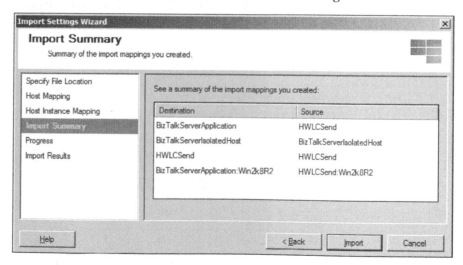

8. Once BizTalk has finished importing our settings, we will be prompted with a Summary Report. We can now click on the **Finish** button to close this wizard, as shown in the following screenshot:

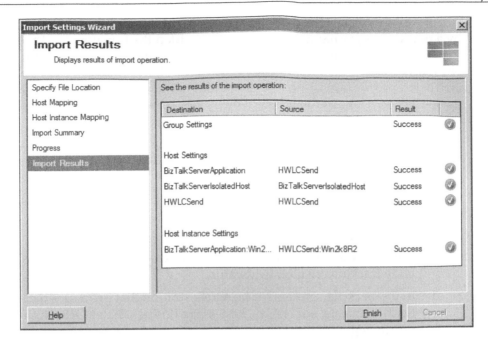

Test your knowledge

1. Yossi, a BizTalk Server Administrator at HWLC Motors, has been asked to shut down the Part Recall BizTalk application at 12 am. He is not supposed to allow any new Part Recall requests into the system after 12 am but needs to ensure any messages from the previous day are completed before completely turning off the application. Upon launching the BizTalk Administration Console, he discovers that there are five messages that are currently being processed that were received at 11:59 pm, from the previous day. What should Yossi do to prevent losing these five messages, while not allowing any new messages into the system?:

    a. Stop the BizTalkServer Application Host Instance(s).

    b. Stop the Part Recall Application with the option Partial Stop – Suspend running instances.

    c. Stop all Receive Locations, and then immediately stop the application with the option Full Stop – Terminate instances.

    d. Stop all Receive Locations, wait for the active instances to complete, and perform Full Stop – Terminate instances.

2. A new version of the HWLC Motors – Part Recall Application has been built by a new developer named Mick. Mick has added the functionality to receive Part Recall requests from another automobile manufacture named MGC. Since MGC will be sending in FlatFile versions of the requests, Mick has instructed Brooke, a BizTalk Administrator, to track only message bodies for the FlatFile versions of the inbound messages. How should Brooke configure tracking to support this scenario?:

    a. In the tracking settings for this Orchestration that processes these Recall requests, enable Track Message Bodies – Before Orchestration processing.

    b. In the Receive Port that supports receiving these Recall requests, enable Track Message Bodies – Request message before port processing.

    c. Brooke needs to perform no action. All Receive Ports have message body tracking enabled by default.

    d. In the tracking settings for the Orchestration that processes these Recall requests, enable Track Message Bodies – After Ochestration processing.

3. HWLC Motors has just successfully tested a new Credit Application System in their QA environment. Paige, a BizTalk Administrator with HWLC Motors, has updated a copy of the existing QA Binding File with the new URIs for both Receive Locations and Send Ports. BizTalk will communicate with all of these URIs using the FILE adapter. Within the QA Binding File, all Receive Locations and Send Ports were configured to use a Host called HWLCSendReceive. Paige has gone ahead and created these Host and Host Instance(s) in the Production environment. However, when she goes to import the updated Binding File, she gets an error and is unable to complete the operation. What could be wrong?:

    a. The user account that the HWLCSendReceive Host Instance(s) uses/use does not have appropriate access to the URIs that the Receive Locations and Send Port are trying to access.

    b. The FILE Adapter's Send and Receive Handlers have not been configured to use the HWLCSendReceive Host.

    c. When Paige imported the BizTalk Dashboard Settings from the QA environment, she must have made a mistake when performing the Host Mapping.

    d. The default Host, BizTalkServer Application, has not been added to the FILE adapter Send and Receive Handlers.

4. The Credit Application System that was recently deployed to production consumes a third-party web service. During some high volume periods, there are some warnings in the Event Viewer indicating that the web service is not currently available. Winson, a BizTalk Administrator at HWLC Motors, has determined that, during these situations, BizTalk is unable to submit all messages to this server on its first try. To ensure messages are not suspended, Winson has increased the Retry Count in the Send Port that communicates with this Web Service. Winson's boss, Steef-Jan, has asked him how many messages are currently being processed and were not successfully submitted on the first attempt. What steps should Winson take in order to provide his boss with the correct answer?:

    a. In the BizTalk Group Hub, Winson should click on the Suspended service instances – Non-resumable link.

    b. In the BizTalk Group Hub, Winson should click on the Running service instances – Ready service instances link.

    c. In the BizTalk Group Hub, Winson should click on the Running service instances – Retrying and idle ports link.

    d. In the BizTalk Group hub, Winson should click on the Running service instances – Scheduled service instances link.

5. Saravana, a BizTalk developer at HWLC Motors, needs to prepare an MSI package for the BizTalk Administration team so they can deploy the MSI package in production. Saravana needs to include a proper Binding File in this MSI package. When Saravana added his Binding File as a resource to his application, he forgot to include a Target environment. When the administrator installed the MSI package, there was not a Binding File that had a Target environment of production. The administrator just installed it using the `<Default>` Target Staging environment and default settings. What can Saravana expect his BizTalk application to look like after the administrator completes their activities?:

    a. Saravana's BizTalk application will be deployed, but will not have any Receive Locations, Send Ports, or bound Orchestrations.

    b. Saravana's application assemblies will be found in the Global Assembly Cache, but there will not be a BizTalk Application found in the BizTalk Administration Console.

    c. The default BizTalk application has been updated to include all of Saravana's Receive Locations and Send Ports that he specified in his Binding File.

    d. Saravana's BizTalk application will exist and will have been configured using the settings that he provided in his Binding File, which was added as a resource to his BizTalk application.

Summary

In this chapter, we discussed many topics related to administrating a BizTalk environment. Some of these concepts were new to BizTalk 2010, such as the BizTalk Settings Dashboard. For others, such as adding Hosts to Send and Receive Handlers for a particular adapter, go back to older versions.

On the exam, you can expect around 16% of the questions to pertain to BizTalk Server 2010 Administration. A thorough understanding of the content in this chapter should put you in a good position to do well on this section in the exam.

We are now going to switch gears and get into a more developer focused topic: *"Integrating Web Services and Windows Communication Foundation (WCF) Services"*. In this chapter we will learn how to expose and consume WCF Services.

7
Integrating Web Services and Windows Communication Foundation (WCF) Services

Service Oriented Architecture-based solutions (SOA) have been increasing in popularity over the past decade. In the Microsoft technology stack, WCF has played an important role in SOA solutions. With this in mind, an entire section has been included in the Microsoft BizTalk Server 2010 exam that deals specifically with WCF.

The WCF Framework is very rich and supports many different integration scenarios including synchronous and asynchronous messaging, encryption, reliability, interoperability with other Web Service platforms, transactions, message durability, and extensibility.

The extensibility features of WCF creates many opportunities for both BizTalk and non-BizTalk Applications that leverage WCF. As WCF continues to evolve, these new investments that Microsoft makes in the technology suddenly are made available to BizTalk without massive re-work or invasive software upgrades. An example of this is the ability to communicate with the Azure Service Bus. When Microsoft added capabilities to WCF in order to support this communication, BizTalk benefitted as well. Communicating with Azure is not in the scope of the exam, but this example illustrates just how extensible the Framework really is.

Starting with BizTalk Server 2006 R2, Microsoft shipped BizTalk with a set of WCF-based adapters for communicating with WCF-based applications and traditional Web Service-based applications.

Now that we have established some base information about WCF Adapters it is time to take a deeper dive into other WCF topics:

- Out of the box WCF Adapters
- Configuring a WCF Adapter
- Custom behaviors
- Exposing Schemas and Orchestrations by using publishing wizard
- Consuming WCF Services
- Handling web exceptions
- Test your knowledge

Out of the box WCF Adapters

In BizTalk 2010, Microsoft shipped five physical adapters that have pre-configured bindings including BasicHttpBinding, WsHttpBinding, NetTcpBinding, NetNamedPipeBinding, and NetMsmqBinding. Two Custom adapters are also included: one is called **WCF-Custom**, which is an in-process adapter and **WCF-CustomIsolated**, which is an out-of-process Adapter.

The following table includes a brief description of each of these adapters:

Adapter name	Adapter description
BasicHttpBinding	This adapter conforms to the WS-Interoperability (WS-I) basic profile. It is one of the more interoperable bindings allowing for communication with WCF and traditional Web Services.
WsHttpBinding	This adapter provides more security-related features than other adapters do. It conforms to the WS-Security and WS-Transaction specifications while supporting both text and Message Transmission Optimization Mechanism (MTOM) encoding.
NetTcpBinding	The NetTcpBinding adapter supports both WS-Security and WS-Transaction specifications such as WsHttpBinding. The difference being that NetTcpBinding does so over the TCP protocol and uses Binary message encoding.
NetNamedPipeBinding	This adapter provides cross-process communication in a secure and optimized manner. Transport security is used for the security model, named pipes for message delivery, and Binary for message encoding such as the NetTcpBinding.
NetMsmqBinding	This adapter provides the ability to connect to MSMQ queues from a BizTalk server so that we can build loosely coupled solutions and address disconnected client scenarios.

Adapter name	Adapter description
WCF-Custom	The WCF-Custom adapter takes advantage of WCF extensibility features by allowing us to plug in custom bindings. If you are familiar with the BizTalk Adapter Pack, this is how Microsoft has provided WCF-based adapters for connecting to Line of Business systems such as SAP, Oracle, and SQL Server.
WCF-CustomIsolated	This adapter allows us to use the extensibility features of WCF in an Isolated Host such as Internet Information Services (IIS).

 If you are interested in learning more about the WCF-Custom adapter and how you can leverage the BizTalk Adapter Pack to communicate with Line of Business Systems, please see http://www.packtpub. com/microsoft-biztalk-2010-line-of-business-systems- integration/book for more details.

Configuring a WCF Adapter

In this section, we are going to discuss how to configure the WCF-BasicHttp Adapter and then how to configure the WCF-Custom Adapter that will use the wsHttpBinding binding. When we configure the WCF-Custom adapter to use wsHttpBinding, we will discover some of the extensibility features that were discussed in the previous section.

Using out of the box WCF-BasicHttp Send Adapter

In this example, we are going to create a new Send Port that will use the WCF-BasicHttp Adapter and then we will explore the various configurations provided in the adapter. In order to do so there are a few steps that we need to follow:

1. Create a BizTalk Application and then add a Send Port by right-clicking on the **Send Ports | New | Static Solicit-Response Send Port**, as shown in the following screenshot:

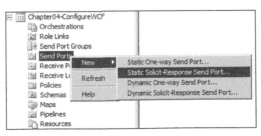

2. From the **Type** drop-down select **WCF-BasicHttp** and then click on the **Configure** button.

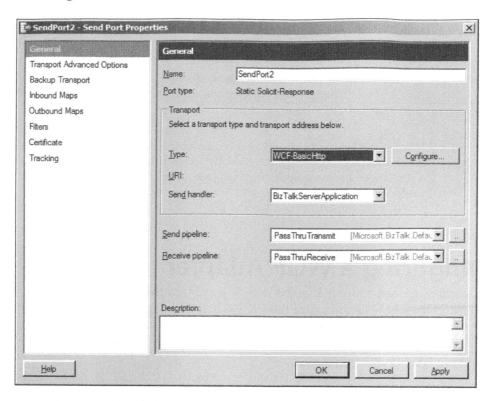

3. The first area that we want to configure an address is the **Address (URI)** textbox. In this textbox, we need to provide the location of the Web Service endpoint that we are going to be communicating with. The URI depicted in the following screenshot represents a fictitious Credit Check service.

4. The second area that we want to focus on is the **SOAP Action header**. The purpose of this text area is to provide a mapping between the name of the operation in our logical Send Port within an Orchestration and the **BTS. Operation** property so that we can submit the right message to the Web Method:

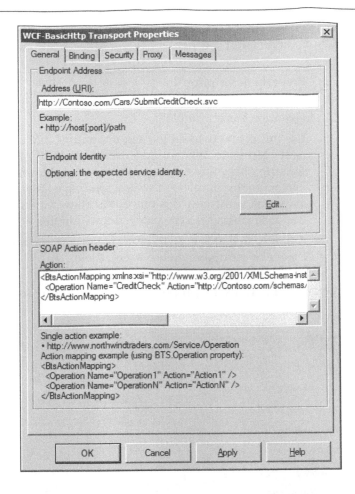

It is important to note that when we consume WCF Services and import the Binding Files, which are generated by the wizard, the SOAP Action header values in the Binding File match the value that exists in the logical port that was also generated for us. If we change the name of the operation in our logical Send Port, we will have a mismatch between our new value and the value that exists in the Binding File. If we make a change, to the operation name, in our Orchestration then we will also have to make a change to our Send Port to ensure we do not have unexpected run-time errors. If you are interested in reading more on this topic please refer to the following URL: `http://blogs.msdn.com/b/adapters/archive/2007/12/26/why-does-the-adapter-say-action-is-not-understood-even-though-i-am-using-the-binding-file-generated-by-the-consume-adapter-service-wizard.aspx`

5. The next tab that we want to explore is the **Binding** tab. Some properties of interest include the timeout settings.

Property name	Property description
Open timeout	This property represents the amount of time a channel open operation has to complete.
Send timeout	Use this property to set the amount of time that a send operation has to complete. When used as part of a solicit-response scenario, this value encompasses the total amount of time for the interaction to complete. If we are sending a large message, we may need to increase this timeout to allow for the request and response messages to be processed within this window.
Close timeout	A timespan that is used to indicate the amount of time that a channel close operation has to complete.

The following screenshot illustrates the properties that were discussed in the preceding table:

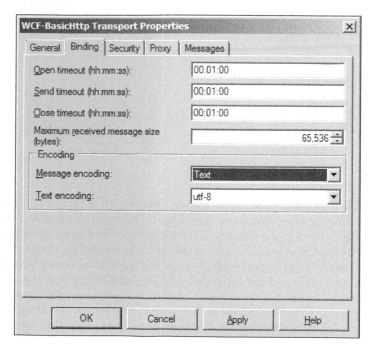

6. The next tab is the **Security** tab. Within this tab we have many different security modes that we can utilize.

Security Mode	Description
None	No credentials will be passed. This is the equivalent of providing anonymous credentials.
Transport	Secures the transport (communication) for mutual authentication and message protection. Messages will not be secure from an end to end perspective if there are any hops in between the source and destination systems.
Message	Uses the WS-Security specification to secure messages. Each message is self-contained to allow for the contents to be confidential while being able to be authenticated. Message level security allows for messages to remain secure across network hops that may exist between source and destination systems.
TransportWithMessageCredential	This mode is only available with some bindings including BasicHttpBinding, WSFederationHttpBinding, NetPeerTCPBinding, and WSHttpBinding. It provides the performance benefits of using the Transport Mode with the flexibility that the Message Security Mode provides. This allows for a message(s) to be secure including hops between the source and destination systems.
TransportCredentialsOnly	This Security Mode will provide credentials to a WCF Service, but does not provide protection when sending these credentials. In order to securely pass credentials across service calls, another means is required such as using Internet Protocol Security (IPsec).

The following screenshot illustrates the properties that were discussed in the preceding table:

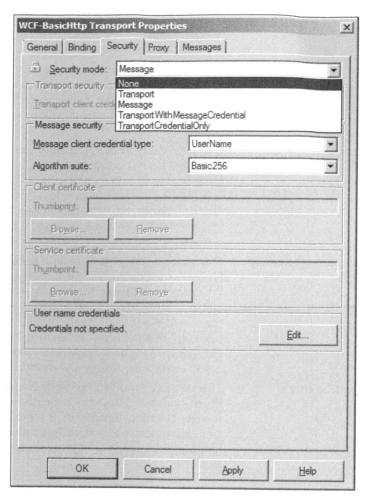

7. The **Proxy** tab is used to provide configuration information related to a Proxy Server. Some organizations implement Proxy Servers that filter out HTTP Requests based upon a URL. Chances are if you work for a large organization, your Web Browser is configured to use a Proxy Server. From my experience, this tab is not used very often, but is definitely beneficial should your organization implement proxy servers that filter outbound traffic.

Proxy settings	Setting description
Use send handler proxy settings	For a particular send handler, or Adapter, we have the ability to specify a global value that will be used for any Send Port that uses this default value. If the send handler does not have a value populated then no proxy server will be used.
Do not use proxy	In the event we have populated a send handler to include proxy server information and we do not want to use a proxy server for this particular interface we can override this global value by specifying **Do not use proxy**.
Use proxy	Use this option if you need to provide a proxy setting and want to override the value that exists in the send handler.

The following screenshot illustrates the properties that were discussed in the preceding table:

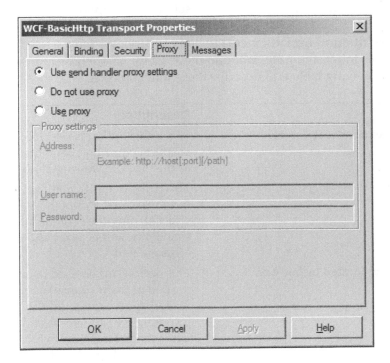

8. The last tab that we want to focus on is the **Messages** tab. In the **Outbound WCF message body** section we have two options with two different behaviors. The following table describes the differences between these two options.

Option	Description
Body — BizTalk request message body	This is the default option and is usually sufficient in most use cases. When this option is selected, BizTalk will use the message body that has been passed to the port as the message body of the outgoing SOAP message.
Template — content specified by template	This option can be used to add xml nodes that wrap around our BizTalk message. For instance if we needed to wrap our BizTalk message in a new root node or provide a namespace we can do so by selecting this option.

9. In the **Inbound BizTalk message body** section, we have a few options when it comes to receiving the inbound message for a Solicit Response Send Port. The following table will describe these three options.

Option	Description
Envelope — entire <soap:Envelope>	When this option is selected, the entire soap:Envelope and contents will be used as the BizTalk Message Body.
Body — contents of <soap:Body> element	This is the default value and satisfies most use cases. When this value is selected, only the contents of the soap:Body will be used as the BizTalk Message Body.
Path — content located by body path	This option can be used to extract a portion of the response message that BizTalk is receiving and use it as the incoming BizTalk message. What is interesting about this option is that you can have multiple Xpath statements separated by the '|' character.

10. The last section that we are going to explore is **Error Handling**. If we check
    the **Propagate fault message** checkbox, this fault message will be published
    to subscribing applications. If we do not enable this feature then any fault
    messages will end up being suspended and are available in the BizTalk
    Administration Console.

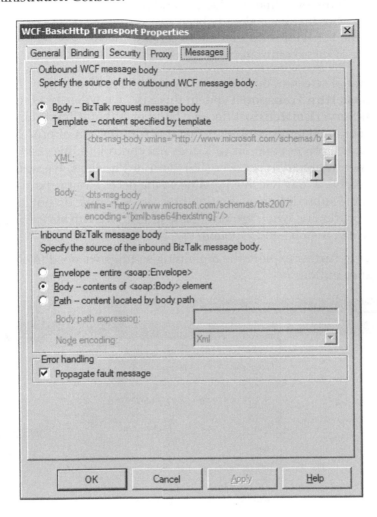

Using out of the box WCF-BasicHttp Receive Adapter

This chapter would not be complete if we only focused on the Send Port adapter. However, you will discover that the Receive and Send Adapters share some common properties. Properties that have already been covered in the Send Port have been omitted unless the behavior is different in Receive scenarios. We will further investigate some of these common properties:

1. In the initial screen of our Receive Location we will select the **WCF-BasicHttp Transport Type**. In this case, we will select the default **BizTalkServerIsolatedHost** Receive handler. What is important to understand about this handler is that it is running out of process, which means it is a process that BizTalk does not control. In this case, the Host is Internet Information Services (IIS). For our Pipelines, we want to select **XMLReceive** as our Receive Pipeline so the necessary properties can be used in the subscription evaluation process. Since we do not have any special processing when providing a response, we will stick with the **PassThruTransmit** Send Pipeline.

2. In order to further explore the remaining settings we need to click on the **Configure** button:

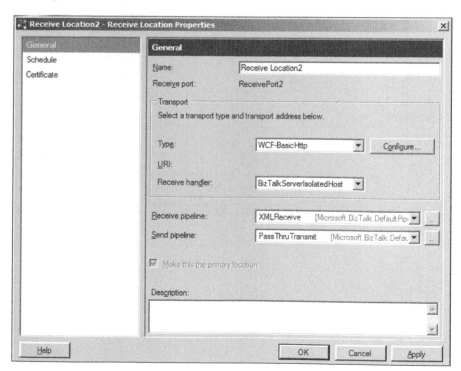

3. Once we have clicked on the **Configure** button, we will discover that a new dialog appears with four tabs. The first tab that we are going to discuss is the **General** tab. The primary configuration that needs to be made on this tab is providing the local address of the web service in the **Address (URI):** textbox. In this case we do not need to provide the name of the server or protocol (`http://`). The address is relative to the default website that exists in Internet Information Services (IIS):

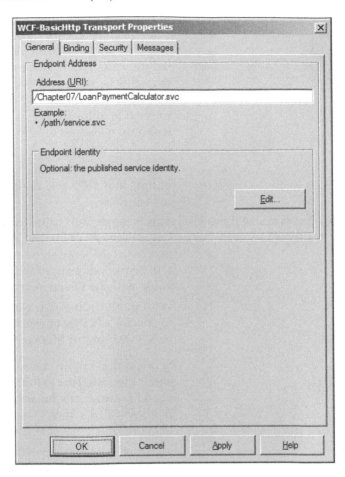

4. On the **Binding** tab we have the ability to specify the following properties.

Property	Description
Open timeout	This property represents the amount of time that a channel open operation has to complete.
Send timeout	Use this property to set the amount of time that a send operation has to complete. When used as part of a solicit-response scenario, this value encompasses the total amount of time for the interaction to complete. If we are sending a large message, we may need to increase this timeout to allow for the request and response messages to be processed within this window.
Close timeout	A timespan is used to indicate the amount of time that a channel close operation has to complete.
Maximum received message size (bytes)	This is the default value for the maximum size a message can be in order to be processed. In some scenarios, where you will be receiving larger messages, this value will need to be increased.
Message encoding	Within this drop-down we have the ability to specify whether or not we will use **Text** or **MTOM** for our **Message encoding**. Services that involve receiving XML should use the **Text** value where as if we need to receive any binary data, such as images or PDFs, then you will want to use **MTOM**.
Text encoding	Provided we have chosen **Text** as our Message encoding type, we have the ability to specify how that text should be encoded. Our options include utf-8, utf-16, or utf-16BE.
Maximum concurrent calls	Indicates the maximum amount of service calls being processed across a Service Host object.

The following screenshot illustrates the properties that were discussed in the preceding table:

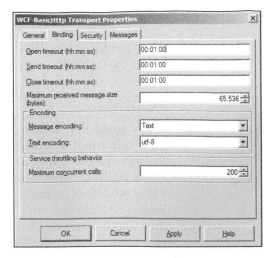

1. In the **Security** tab we will discover options that are very similar to those exposed in the WCF Send Ports. As we have already discussed many of those options, we will focus on an option that is not included in the Send Port configuration.

2. When a Security mode, other than **None** is selected, the **Use Single Sign-On** checkbox will become visible/enabled. By enabling this checkbox, the WCF Adapter can now issue an SSO ticket. The WCF Adapter requires credentials that will be associated with the ticket. Using this feature allows for user context to be passed from source applications to destination. This then allows BizTalk to execute operations on other systems on behalf of this user:

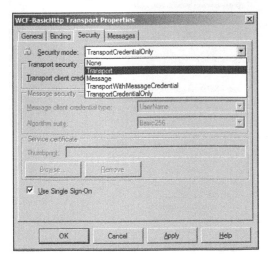

3. The final tab that we will discuss is the **Messages** tab. Once again this tab is very similar to the **Messages** tab that exists on WCF Send Ports. We will once again focus on the properties that have not already been covered in this chapter.

4. The area we are going to focus on is the **Error handling** section. Within this section we have the ability to enable the following options:

Property	Description
Suspend request message on failure	When enabled, if there is a Receive Pipeline error or routing failure, BizTalk will suspend the incoming message and it will be available in the BizTalk Administration Console. The client will consider the transmission of this message to be successful, but will not receive an exception message back by default.
Include exception detail in faults	If the client does require exception information to be passed back then this property needs to be checked. The end result is a SOAP fault will be returned back to the caller.

The following screenshot illustrates the properties that were discussed in the preceding table:

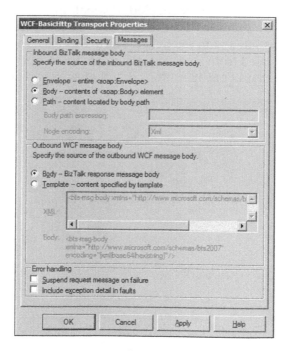

Custom behaviors

One of the benefits of using the WCF-Custom or WCF-CustomIsolated adapters is the ability to specify a **custom behavior**. A custom behavior acts as an interceptor and can be used in both receiving and sending scenarios. If you are not familiar with custom behaviors, you are probably wondering why they exist since we have BizTalk Pipelines. Remember, WCF is not a technology that is exclusively used by BizTalk. WCF can be used outside of BizTalk and therefore custom behaviors benefit non-BizTalk solutions as well. The ability to intercept messages as they are being received or sent is something that other Web Service technologies do not provide. So having this capability is one reason to use WCF adapters over the classic SOAP adapter.

Once you have compiled a custom behavior and placed it in the Global Assembly Cache (GAC), it now needs to be registered. In WCF applications that do not involve BizTalk, custom behaviors need to be registered inside the server's `machine.config` file. You can, generally, find the `machine.config` file here: `c:\<windows>\Microsoft.NET\Framework\<version>\config\machine.config`. Another option that we have when registering custom behaviors is to do so in the adapter's handler configuration.

To register a custom behavior in a handler's configuration:

1. Navigate to **Adapters** and then select **WCF-Custom**, as shown in the following screenshot:

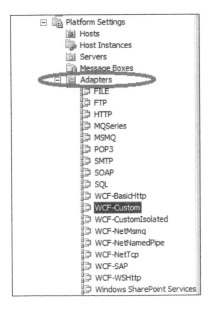

2. In the center pane, you should see all of the available handlers available for this adapter. Double-click on **BizTalkServerApplication Send** or **Receive** handler:

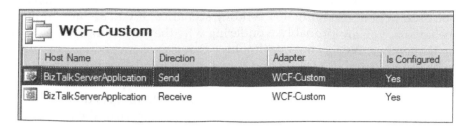

3. Now click on the **Properties** button:

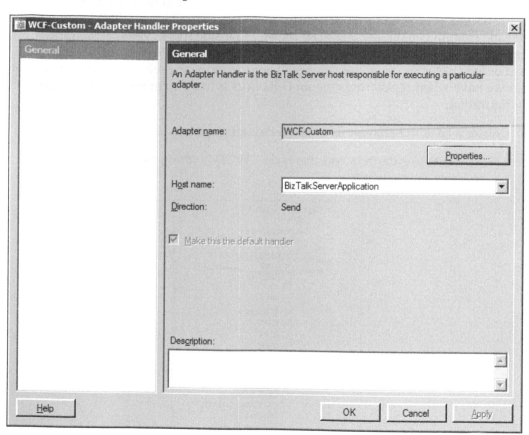

4. We now have the ability to import a file that contains our registration information for our custom behavior assembly. We can do so by clicking on the **Import** button and then select our configuration file:

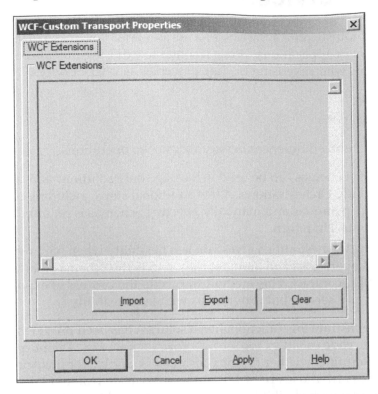

So which location is a better place to store custom behavior registrations? In many situations it is personal preference, but it is important to understand that you can have the configuration of a custom behavior in one location only.

If you have a mixture of Custom WCF and BizTalk then perhaps using the `machine.config` is a better place to store this configuration, as it will all be in one place. If you do not have a mixture of Custom WCF and BizTalk then perhaps you want to store your Custom behavior configuration in BizTalk. In the event that you have multiple BizTalk Servers, storing this information inside your BizTalk configuration may also reduce maintenance complexity.

 Some organizations have restrictions on editing files that exist underneath the `C:\Windows` folder. In these situations, you can leverage the adapter's handler configuration instead.

Exposing Schemas and Orchestrations as WCF Services

In this section, we are going to move away from some of the theoretical aspects of WCF and actually expose a BizTalk process as a WCF Service so that it can be consumed by client applications. When it comes to exposing BizTalk Services we have two options when exposing BizTalk processes as WCF Services:

- Schemas
- Orchestrations

There are a few subtle differences between these two operations:

- Exposing Schemas can be used in message only solutions and processes that include Orchestrations. A few additional steps, including naming Web Method operations and manually selecting Schemas is required, but you get more control in return.

- Exposing Orchestrations gives you less flexibility when naming your Web Method operations and automatically selects the Schemas that will be used in our WSDL contract. This method speeds up the process of exposing a BizTalk process as a service but provides us with less flexibility.

In order to demonstrate this functionality, a solution has been provided in this chapter's sample code called `Example01-ExposeWCFService`. The purpose of this sample is to determine whether or not a customer is eligible for financing from our car dealership. In order to keep things simple, we will keep all our business logic that will determine their eligibility in BizTalk as opposed to a database or business rules engine.

The focus of this example is discussing how to expose a WCF Service, so we will not go into extensive details around other aspects of the BizTalk solution.

Within our solution, we will find three different BizTalk projects: one that will be used to include our Maps, another for our Orchestration, and finally one for our Schemas. Here are some additional details about the artifacts that make up our solution.

Artifact Name	Artifact Description
`FinanceRequest_to_DealerFinanceApprovedResponse.btm`	This map will perform the transformation when a customer's credit rating has been approved.
`FinanceRequest_to_DealerFinanceRejectedResponse.btm`	This map will perform the transformation when a customer's credit rating has been rejected.

Artifact Name	Artifact Description
`processCustomerFinanceRequests.odx`	The BizTalk Orchestration that will manage our business process.
`CustomerFinanceRequest.xsd`	The Schema for the message that we are expecting from a client application.
`CustomerFinanceResponse.xsd`	The Schema for the message we will be providing back to our client once we have determined whether or not our client has been approved for financing.

The following screenshot illustrates the BizTalk solution that was discussed in the preceding table:

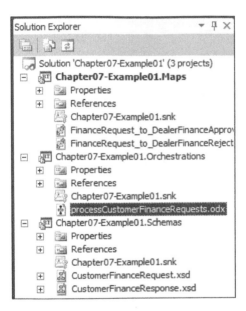

If we further examine our BizTalk Orchestration, we will discover the following logic:

1. Receiving an instance of our `CustomerFinanceRequest.xsd` message through a Logical Port that has been configured to receive a request and send a response.

2. A Decide shape will determine whether or not this customer's finance request will be approved or not. The business rule is if the customer has a **Credit Score** that is greater than **5** and had a greater income than the loan amount, they will be approved. In order to easily facilitate this logic some of the elements included in the `CustomerFinanceRequest.xsd` have been marked as distinguished fields.

3. If the customer has acceptable credit then we will call the
`FinanceRequest_to_DealerFinanceApprovedResponse.btm` map.

4. Should the customer not have acceptable credit then we need to call the
`FinanceRequest_to_DealerFinanceRejectedResponse.btm` map.

5. Finally, we need to send an instance of our `CustomerFinanceResponse.xsd`
back to the calling client.

The following screenshot illustrates the steps that were previously described:

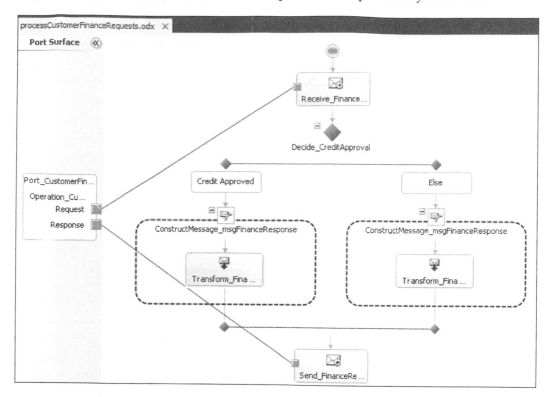

At this point, we can deploy our application into an application called `Chapter07-Example01`. Once our deployment is complete, we can focus on our second activity, which is exposing our two Schemas as WCF Services. Choosing to expose our Schemas, as opposed to Orchestrations, gives us more flexibility into how our artifacts are named and also gives us more flexibility should we need to modify our Schemas in the future.

In order to expose our Schemas as a WCF Service we need to perform the following steps:

1. From the **Tools** menu in Visual Studio, click on **BizTalk WCF Service Publishing Wizard**, as shown in the following screenshot:

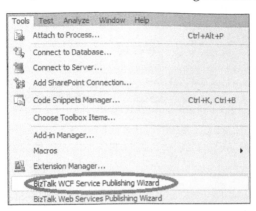

2. Within this step of the wizard, we have a few options that we need to consider:

Feature	Description
Service Endpoint	Select this value if you are interested in exposing a service. When you do so, it will enable the three following additional properties that we can manipulate.
Adapter name (Transport type):	By setting this property we have the ability to specify which adapter we want to use when exposing this service. The options include WCF-BasicHttp, WCF-WSHttp, and WCF-CustomIsolated.
Enable metadata endpoint	If we want to expose metadata, so that client code can be generated through tools such as ServiceUtil.exe, then we need to enable this property.
Create BizTalk receive locations in the following application	By enabling this feature and specifying a BizTalk Application, this wizard will automatically create a Receive Port and Receive Location in the application that we specify. This is part of the reason why we previously deployed our BizTalk Application so that we would have an application available during this part of the wizard.
Metadata only endpoint (MEX)	If we were only interested in exposing metadata then we would select this property.

The following screenshot illustrates the properties that were discussed in the preceding table:

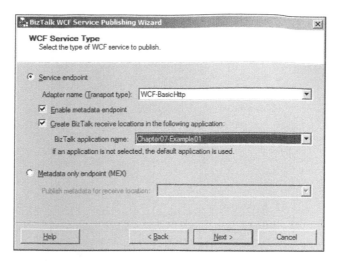

 If we decide that we want to change the adapter for this service after we have published our WCF Service, the only way to do so is to run this wizard again and re-publish our service using the adapter that we would like to use.

1. In our scenario, we are going to select **Publish schemas as WCF Service** and then click on the **Next** button:

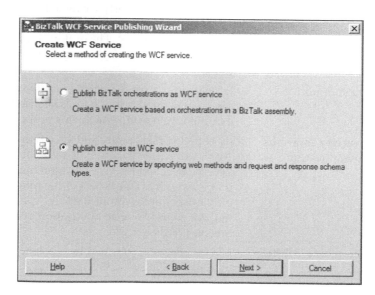

2. We now have the ability to specify the name of our virtual directory that will be created inside of IIS, the name of our Service, the name of our Web Method and provide both request and response Schemas. After we have provided this information, we can then click on the **Next** button:

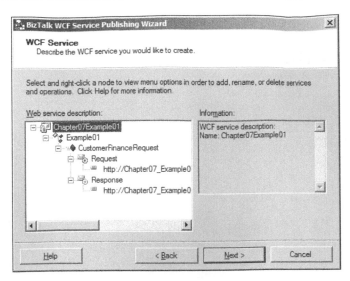

3. The next property that we have the ability to manipulate is the **Target namespace of the WCF Service**. In our solution, we will provide **http://Chapter07.Example01/** and then click on the **Next** button:

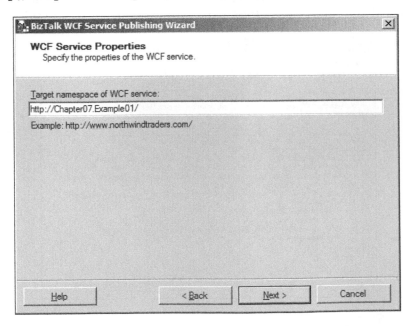

4. We now need to provide the location, or URL, for our service that will be deployed to the local machine. What we will discover later on is that a virtual directory called **Chapter07Example01** will be added to our default website in IIS. The other property we can manipulate is called **Allow anonymous access to WCF Service**. For the purpose of this demonstration we will enable this property and click the **Next** button:

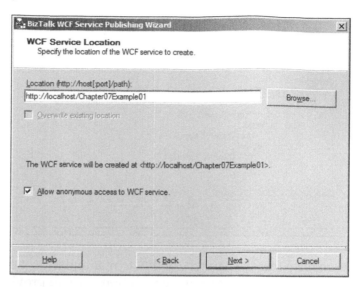

5. Our last step to complete is to review our metadata that is about to be exposed and then click on the **Create** button provided we are satisfied.

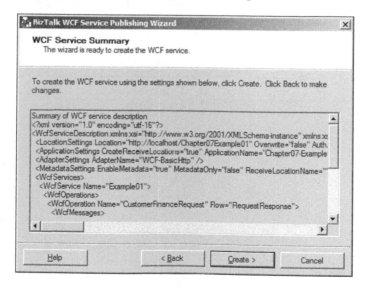

6. Provided everything executes correctly, we should see the confirmation message indicating that our service has been created successfully:

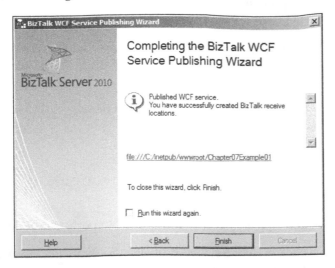

7. If we launch IIS now, we will discover that our WCF Service has been created and we now have our **Example01.svc** file and our **Web.config** file, as shown in the following screenshot:

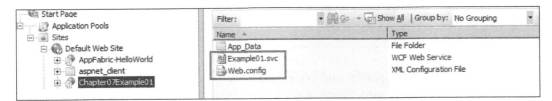

 By default, when this virtual directory is created, it will use the Default Application Pool identity to run this web application. By default, this Application Pool identity will not have access to BizTalk resources and therefore you will get an error when you try to browse to this service via a web browser. In order to fix this issue, create an Application Pool that has an identity of the BizTalk Isolated Host Instance user and then configure this Web Application to use this newly created Application Pool.

Testing our WCF Service

Before we can test our application we need to ensure that we have our application fully configured, started, and we have a Host Instance enabled for our Orchestration.

In order to simplify our test we are going to leverage a tool called **WCFTestClient**, which is available as part of our Visual Studio installation. For 64-bit systems we can find the application here:

```
C:\Program Files (x86)\Microsoft Visual Studio 10.0\Common7\IDE\
WcfTestClient.exe
```

For 32-bit systems we can find it here:

```
C:\Program Files\Microsoft Visual Studio 10.0\Common7\IDE\
WcfTestClient.exe
```

With our WCFTestClient application open, we need to perform the following steps:

1. Right mouse click on **My Service Projects** and then click on **Add Service...** as shown in the following screenshot:

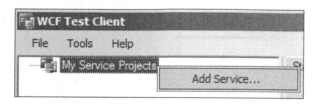

2. Now we need to specify our WCF Service URI, which in this case happens to be `http://localhost/Chapter07Example01/Example01.svc` and click the **OK** button:

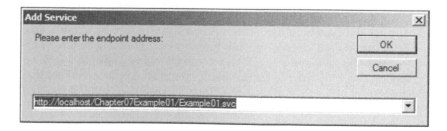

3. Our **Request** message needs to be populated and then we can click on the **Invoke** button. After a few seconds, we should receive a reply and have it displayed in our **Response** section.

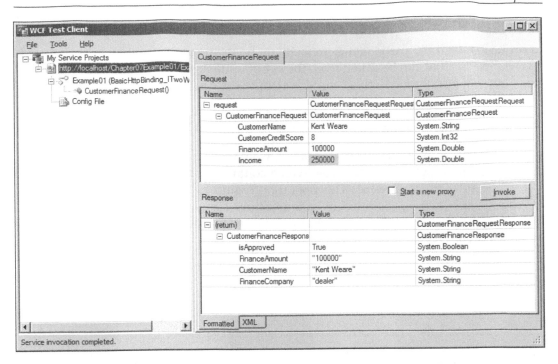

Consuming WCF Services from BizTalk Server 2010

In the previous section, we discussed how BizTalk can expose WCF Services that can be consumed by client applications. In this section, we are going to turn our previous scenario around and have BizTalk be the client and consume a WCF Service.

Our business process in our previous example was a finance service that a car manufacturer provides to its customers. This car manufacturer has some strict financing rules that require the customer to have a Credit Score that is greater than 5 and their income must be greater than the loan amount. As the car manufacturer wants to sell more cars but does not want to take on additional financing risks, they have established an agreement with a third party financing agency. So, if a customer does not fit the financing criteria of the car manufacturer then they can try to get credit from this third party agency. The third party agency has looser requirements than the car manufacturer but in turn charges more interest.

Sample WCF Service

In order for the third party agency to facilitate financing requests, they have exposed a WCF Service that can be called from the car manufacturer's BizTalk Server. This WCF Service is included in this chapter's sample code in the following folder:

```
C:\BTS2010CertGuide\Chapter07\Example02-ConsumeWCFService\Example02-
ThirdPartyFinanceService
```

In the `ThirdPartyFinanceService.cs` file, we will discover our interface called `IThirdPartyFinanceService`, which contains one operation called `ThirdPartyFinanceApproval`. This operation requires that a business object of type `FinanceRequest` is provided and in return a business object of type `FinanceResponse` will be returned. Both of these business objects are defined in the following code:

```
namespace Example02_ThirdPartyFinanceService
{

    [ServiceContract]
    public interface IThirdPartyFinanceService
    {
        [OperationContract]
        FinanceResponse ThirdPartyFinanceApproval
            (FinanceRequest fRequest);
    }


    [DataContract]
    public class FinanceRequest
    {
        string customerName ="";
        int   customerCreditScore = 0;
        double financeAmount = 0;
        double income = 0;

        [DataMember]
        public string CustomerName
        {
            get { return customerName; }
            set { customerName = value; }
        }

        [DataMember]
        public int CustomerCreditScore
```

```
{
    get { return customerCreditScore; }
    set { customerCreditScore = value; }
}

[DataMember]
public double FinanceAmount
{
    get { return financeAmount; }
    set { financeAmount = value; }
}

[DataMember]
public double Income
{
    get { return income; }
    set { income = value; }
}
}

[DataContract]
public class FinanceResponse
{
    bool isApproved = false;
    double financeAmount = 0;
    string customerName = "";
    string financeCompany = "";

    [DataMember]
    public bool IsApproved
    {
        get { return isApproved; }
        set { isApproved = value; }
    }

    [DataMember]
    public double FinanceAmount
    {
        get { return financeAmount; }
        set { financeAmount = value; }
    }

    [DataMember]
    public string CustomerName
```

```
        {
            get { return customerName; }
            set { customerName = value; }
        }

        [DataMember]
        public string FinanceCompany
        {
            get { return financeCompany; }
            set { financeCompany = value; }
        }

    }
}
```

In the `ThirdPartyFinanceService.svc.cs` file, we will find the implementation of the `ThirdPartyFinanceApproval` operation that was declared in the previous code listing. This operation may be found inside the `ThirdPartyFinanceService` class, which implements our interface called `IThirdPartyFinanceService`.

The `ThirdPartyFinanceService` has less restrictive financing requirements than the car manufacturer's BizTalk solution. In this service, a customer's financing will be approved if their Credit Score is greater than 2 and they have an income that is greater than $10,000:

```
namespace Example02_ThirdPartyFinanceService
{

    public class ThirdPartyFinanceService : IThirdPartyFinanceService
    {


        public FinanceResponse ThirdPartyFinanceApproval(FinanceReque
st fRequest)
        {
            FinanceResponse fResponse = new FinanceResponse();

            fResponse.CustomerName = fRequest.CustomerName;
            fResponse.FinanceCompany = "Wearsy Inc.";
            fResponse.FinanceAmount = fRequest.FinanceAmount;

            if (fRequest.CustomerCreditScore > 2 && fRequest.Income >
10000)
            {
                fResponse.IsApproved = true;
```

```
        }
        else
        {
            fResponse.IsApproved = false;
        }

        return fResponse;
    }
  }
}
```

Consuming our WCF Service from BizTalk

We need a published endpoint that we can consume from our BizTalk solution inside of Visual Studio in order to generate our required Schemas and logical port. The following steps will allow us to consume the **Third Party Finance** WCF Service that is available in this chapter's source code:

1. One way to publish this WCF Service is to simply start the debugger in our **C# - WCF Service Project**. In order to do this, we simply press *F5* or click on the green arrow, as shown in the following screenshot:

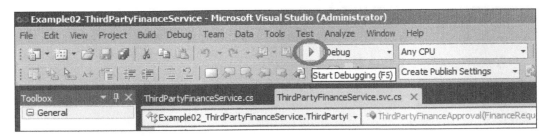

2. Once we have pressed the *F5* button or clicked the green arrow, we will discover that a local development server instance has been initialized. We now need to double-click on the yellow icon as shown in the following screenshot:

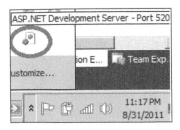

3. After we have clicked on this icon the following dialog will be displayed. Click on the following hyperlink to display the contents of this directory:

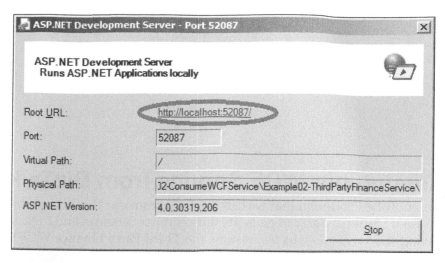

4. In this directory listing, we will discover our service called **ThirdPartyFinanceService.svc**. If we click on this link we will launch the landing page for our service:

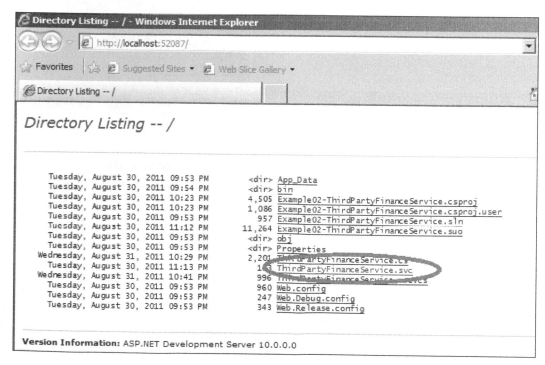

5. We now have a URL that we can use from within our BizTalk solution.

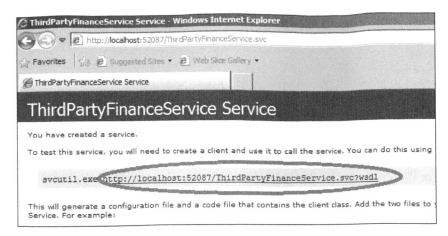

 As we are going to be building upon the solution that we built in the previous example, a copy of that solution has been made available in the following folder: `C:\BTS2010CertGuide\Chapter07\Example02-ConsumeWCFService\Example02-ConsumeWCFService`. This will allow us to simply re-deploy our application that will contain the changes we are about to make without forcing us to re-publish our WCF Service that we built in the previous example.

6. From our BizTalk solution, we now need to generate Schemas that are based upon our WCF Service's request and response message types that we just built. In order to do this, we need to right-click on our **Chapter07-Example01. Schemas** project, then select **Add,** and then select **Add Generated Items**:

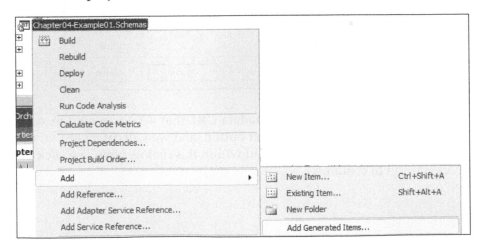

7. We now want to select the **Consume WCF Service** label, and then click on the **Consume WCF Service** label and click on the **Add** button:

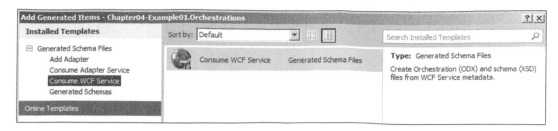

8. The **Welcome to the BizTalk WCF Service Consuming Wizard** dialog should now appear. Click the **Next** button to proceed.

9. We now want to select **Metadata Exchange (MEX)** endpoint and click the **Next** button. This will allow us to provide the URL of the third party financing service that we just launched:

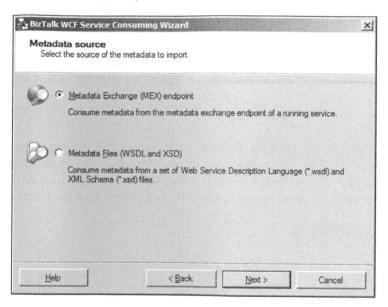

10. We now want to provide the **Metadata URL** that we discovered in step 5. Next, we will need to click the **Get** button, and we will discover that our **Service Description** page will load within this dialog. Now, we click on the **Next** button to continue:

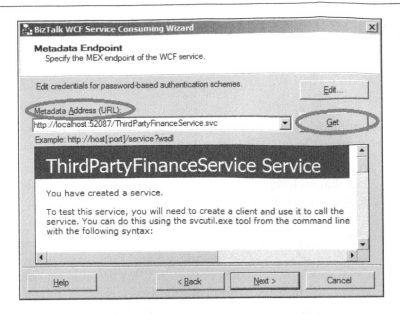

11. We now have the opportunity to modify the target namespace, but we will just leave it as is. In order to import the Schemas of our service, we need to click on the **Import** button:

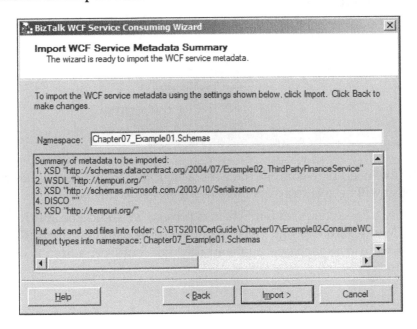

12. We can now click on the **Finish** button to complete the wizard.

Configuring generated WCF Service artifacts

In the previous section, we consumed a WCF Service. The result of this action is we now have several artifacts in our BizTalk solution including an Orchestration, Schemas, and Binding Files. We now need to configure these artifacts by performing the following steps:

1. If we examine our Schemas project we will discover several new artifacts have been added to our solution including:

   ° A Binding File, called `ThirdPartyFinanceService.BindingInfo.xml` that includes a Send Port based upon the WCF-BasicHttp adapter. We can import this Binding File into our Application within the BizTalk Administration Console.

   ° A Binding File, called `ThirdPartyFinanceService_Custom.BindingInfo.xml` that includes a Send Port based upon the WCF-Custom adapter. We can import this Binding File into our application within the BizTalk Administration Console.

   ° An Orchestration that contains a logical port and multi-part messages that we can leverage to call this third party service.

   ° Schemas that represent the structures we can expect to send and receive.

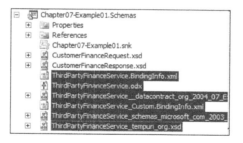

2. We now need to re-compile our Schemas project so that the Orchestrations project will be able to access these newly added artifacts.

3. Once we have compiled our Schemas project, we should be able to create a new **Multi-part Message Type**, in our **processCustomerFinanceRequests. odx** Orchestration, based upon our Schemas that were added to our Schemas project.

4. With our multi-part messages created, we now need to create a request and response message based upon these new multi-part types.

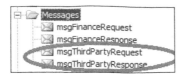

5. Next, we need to add a map called `FinanceRequest_to_ThirdPartyFinanceRequest.btm`, which will transform our incoming **CustomerFinanceRequest** into a **ThirdPartyFinanceApproval** request that we can send to our third party agency:

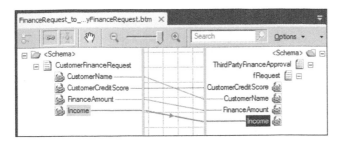

6. We also want to add a map that will deal with the responses generated from the third party financing company called `ThirdPartyFinanceResponse_to_FinanceResponse.btm`:

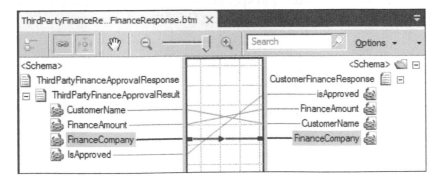

7. In order for our Orchestration project to access these new maps we need to re-compile our Maps project.

8. Since we are going to leverage a third party finance service for customers who do not qualify for dealer financing, we can remove the **ConstructMessage_msgFinanceResponse** shape:

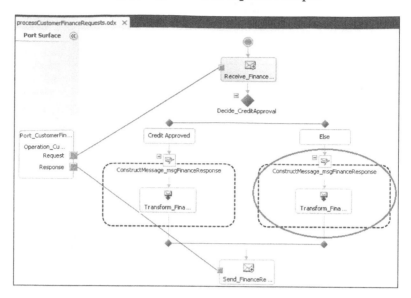

9. We now want to insert the **FinanceRequest_to_ThirdPartyFinanceRequest. btm** map, that we created in step 5 of this section, in the **Else** branch.

10. After inserting this map, we need to add both **Send** and **Receive** shapes. In the **Send** shape we want to specify **msgThirdPartyRequest** and in the **Receive** shape we want to specify **msgThirdPartyResponse**:

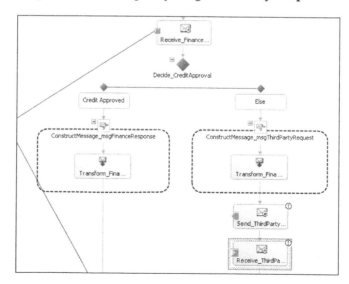

11. The next item that we need to address is adding a logical port that will support sending and receiving messages to and from the WCF Service. In this case, we want to leverage the logical Port type that was created for us when we used the wizard to consume our third party service. However, since we specified our Schemas project when we ran this wizard, we now have an Orchestration in our Schemas project. Even though we have a reference from our Orchestration project to our Schemas project, we cannot access this logical Port Type by default. By default the **Type Modifier** is set to **Internal**. If we want to use this logical Port Type in our Orchestration project then we need to set our **Type Modifier** to be **Public**:

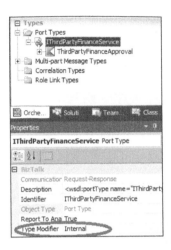

12. We also need to modify our **Multi-part Message Types** so that they also have a **Type Modifer** of **Public**:

> Another option that we have is to exclude this Orchestration that was generated by the Consume WCF Service wizard and add it to our Orchestration project. Once we have added it to our Orchestration project, we would need to modify our .NET Namespace so that it is conformed to the rest of the project.

13. Once we have modified our logical port type so that it can be accessed from other projects, we now want to re-compile our Schemas project so that we can access this logical Port Type by dragging a Port shape onto our **processCustomerFinanceRequests.odx** Orchestration. When we do this, a **Port Configuration Wizard** will launch. In the **Port Configuration Wizard** dialog, provide a name for this port such as **Port_ThirdPartyService** and then click on the **Next** button:

14. When prompted to select a Port Type, choose **Use an existing Port Type**, and then select our **ThirdPartyFinanceService** Port Type:

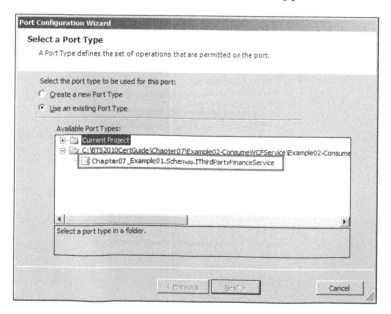

15. When prompted to select a **Port direction of communication,** choose **I'll be sending a request and receiving a response.** The type of **Port binding** that we need to choose is **Specify later:**

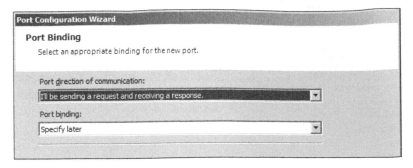

16. Click on **Finish** to complete the wizard and then drag lines from our newly added Send and Receive shapes to this new logical port.

17. We now need to add our `ThirdPartyFinanceResponse_to_ FinanceResponse.btm` map that we created in step 6 of this section so that we can transform our response from our third party service into the response type that we return back to our calling client.

18. The end result is that our **Else** branch will look similar to the following screenshot:

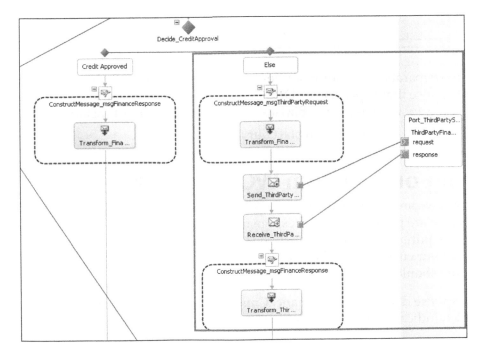

19. We can now deploy our application and then import the
    `ThirdPartyFinanceService.BindingInfo.xml` Binding File that was
    generated by the Consume WCF Service Wizard. Once we have imported
    this Binding File we will discover that the following Send Port has
    been created:

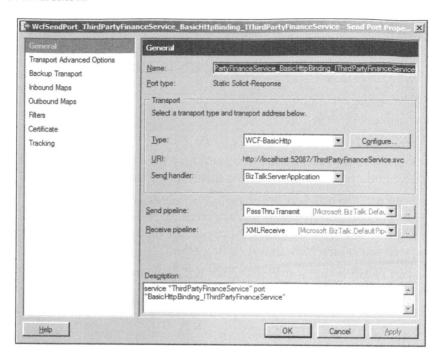

20. In preparation of testing our new application, we need to restart the Host
    Instance that supports our Orchestration and messaging processes. In this
    scenario, we will use the BizTalkServerApplication Host Instance.

21. We also need to bind and start our application.

Testing our Custom WCF Service

Once again we are going to leverage the WCF Test tool as our client application.
This time we are going to send a message into BizTalk that will not satisfy the dealer
financing requirements but will satisfy our third party financing requirements. This
means that our customer Credit Score should be less than **5**, but greater than **2** and
our income should be greater than $10,000.

In our response document, the **FinanceCompany** being returned should be **Wearsy
Inc.**, which indicates that it was our third party service responding:

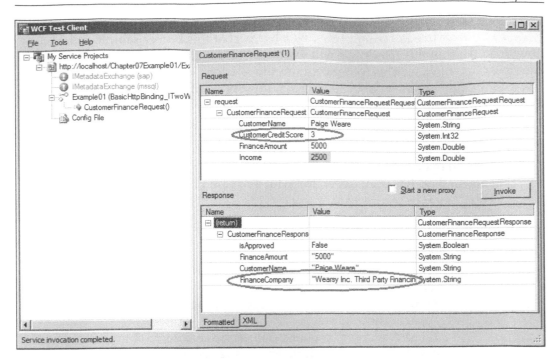

Handling web exceptions

When BizTalk consumes WCF Services, the opportunity exists for exceptions to be thrown. When this event occurs, we need to catch these exceptions and deal with them gracefully. If we do not handle them properly, we can expect suspended service instances inside the BizTalk Administration Console.

The scenario that we are about to walk through will demonstrate how BizTalk can handle Typed Exceptions that have been thrown from a Custom WCF Service. The business scenario is some customers at our car dealership may want to have custom paint applied to their new or used car. The car dealership will leverage an external **Autobody** shop to perform this work. However, some cars and colors are not valid to have this work done. This service will validate whether or not the car can have custom paint applied to it. In situations where a desired color has not been passed in, the WCF Service will throw a typed exception called `PaintServiceException`.

The source code for this demonstration can be found in the C:\BTS2010CertGuide\ Chapter07\Example03-Exceptions, which is part of this book's sample code download. Within this folder, we will discover a folder called Example03- CustomPaintService. This folder contains our Custom WCF Service project called Example03-CustomPaintService.csproj. If we open this project we will discover the following:

1. We are storing our operation and data contracts in a file called ICustomPaintService.cs. Within this file, we will discover that we have an operation contract called CheckCustomPaintAvailability. This method has been decorated with a FaultContract that is of type PaintServiceException:

```
namespace Example03_CustomPaintService
{
    [ServiceContract(Namespace="http://Chapter07-Example03")]
    public interface ICustomPaintService
    {
        //Our Web Method that contains a Fault Contract attribute
        [OperationContract]
        [FaultContract(typeof(PaintServiceException))]
        CarResponse CheckCustomPaintAvailability(Car car);
    }
```

2. Our first data contract represents our request object, which happens to be a car. Within this object, we have three properties including a car model, car year, and a desired color:

```
    [DataContract]
    public class Car
    {
        string carModel = "";
        int carYear = 0;
        string desiredColor = "";

        [DataMember]
        public string CarModel
        {
            get { return carModel; }
            set { carModel = value; }
        }
        [DataMember]
        public string DesiredColor
        {
            get { return desiredColor; }
            set { desiredColor = value; }
```

```
    }
    [DataMember]
    public int CarYear
    {
        get { return carYear; }
        set { carYear = value; }
    }
}
```

3. Our response object is called `CarResponse` and has two properties including whether the service request is valid, from a business perspective, and the desired color being returned:

```
[DataContract]
public class CarResponse
{
    bool isValid = false;
    string desiredColor = "";

    [DataMember]
    public bool IsValid
    {
        get { return isValid; }
        set { isValid = value; }
    }


    [DataMember]
    public string DesiredColor
    {
        get { return desiredColor; }
        set { desiredColor = value; }
    }
}
```

4. The last data contract that we need to deal with is the one that represents our Typed Exception. We are calling this typed exception `PaintServiceException` and it has three properties including an error code, error message, and details:

```
[DataContract]
public class PaintServiceException
{

    int errorcode=0;
    string errormessage="";
```

```
string details="";

public PaintServiceException()
{

}

[DataMember]
public int ErrorCode
{
    get { return errorcode; }
    set { errorcode = value; }
}

[DataMember]
public string ErrorMessage
{
    get { return errormessage; }
    set { errormessage = value; }
}

[DataMember]
public string Details
{
    get { return details; }
    set { details = value; }
}

}

}
```

5. The next file that we want to look at is called `CustomPaintService.svc.cs`. Within this file, we will discover our Web Method that we declared in the previous steps. An area that we want to focus on is where we determine the following code line is: `car.DesiredColor == null || car.DesiredColor==""`. If either of these situations exists, we want to populate our Typed Fault Exception object called `pse` and then throw a new `FaultException`, passing in our `pse` object. Otherwise, if all information has been processed, we will construct a `CarResponse` object and indicate whether this is a valid scenario:

```
namespace Example03_CustomPaintService
{
```

```
public class CustomPaintService : ICustomPaintService
{

    public CarResponse CheckCustomPaintAvailability(Car car)
    {
        try
        {
            CarResponse carResponse = new CarResponse();

            if (car.DesiredColor == null
                || car.DesiredColor =="")
            {
                PaintServiceException pse =
                    new PaintServiceException();
                pse.ErrorCode = 123;
                pse.ErrorMessage = "A Desired Color
                    must be provided";
                pse.Details = "CheckCustomPaintAvailability
                    Method is missing a required parameter";
                throw new FaultException
                    <PaintServiceException>
                    (pse,new FaultReason
                    ("CheckCustomPaintAvailability
                     Method raised an Exception"));
            }

            if (car.CarYear > 2010 && car.DesiredColor
                != "Hot Pink")
            {
                carResponse.DesiredColor =
                    car.DesiredColor;
                carResponse.IsValid = true;
            }
            else
            {
                carResponse.DesiredColor = car.DesiredColor;
                carResponse.IsValid = false;

            }

            return carResponse;
        }
        catch (Exception ex)
        {
```

```
            throw ex;
        }




            }
        }
    }
```

6. Once we have built our Custom WCF Service, we will need to consume it from BizTalk much like we did earlier in this chapter. You can find a BizTalk Solution called Chapter07-Example03.sln in the C:\BTS2010CertGuide\ Chapter07\Example03-Exceptions folder that has this step already completed.

7. When we consume our WCF Service this time, we will discover a difference. This time around we will add a Configured Port to our Orchestration that will include a PaintServiceExceptionFault operation:

8. We will not connect this operation to a Send or Receive shape. Instead, we need to wrap our Send/Receive shapes that communicate with our WCF Service around a Scope so that we can add an Exception Handler. For the purpose of our scenario this Scope shape can have its **Transaction Type** set to **None**:

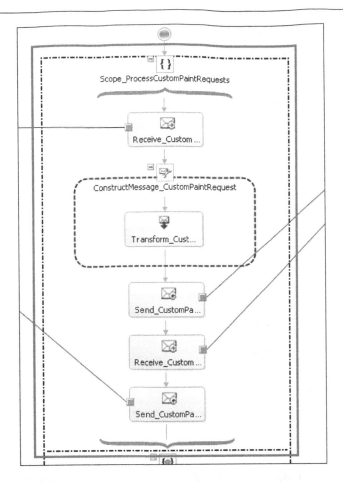

9. When we go to configure our exception handler, we can actually use this `PaintServiceExceptionFault` operation as our Exception type:

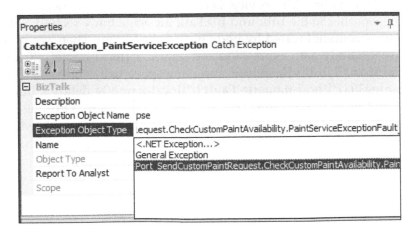

10. If an exception is raised, the Exception Handler will catch it and process it. In this case, we want to simply write out the result to a File Drop. It is important to note that when a typed exception is caught, we will have an instance of the Exception Object that we configured in our Exception handler. If we want to actually send that message, we need to assign this object to an instance of our PaintServiceExceptionFault message:

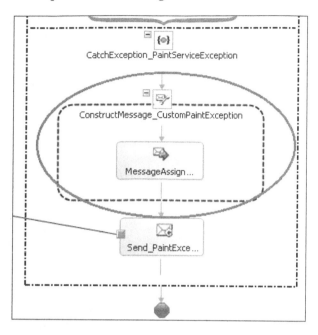

11. Once we have made these changes, we need to deploy our application. Once our application has been deployed, we need to make a modification to our WCF Send Port so that we can handle our Typed Exception message being returned from our WCF Service. On the **Messages** tab, we need to modify some properties in the **Inbound BizTalk message body** section. Select the **Path – content located by body path** radio button. Then, we need to modify the **Body path expression** and set it to **/*[local-name()='CheckCus tomPaintAvailabilityResponse' and namespace-uri()='http://Chapter07-Example03'] | /*[local-name()='Fault']/*[local-name()='detail']/*[local-nam e()='PaintServiceException']**. We also need to ensure that **Propagate fault message** remains enabled so that our application will be aware when faults have been raised:

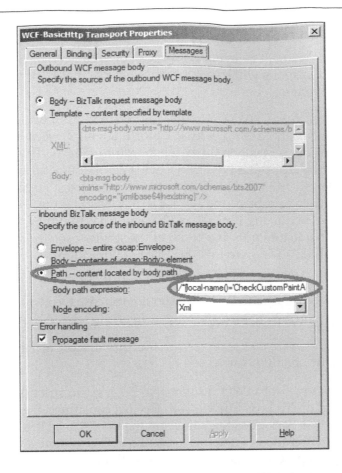

By specifying an Xpath expression, we have the ability to
receive either a valid response or typed exception from
the WCF Service. While somewhat discrete, BizTalk does
support the ability to provide multiple Xpath statements
by separating them by using a delimiter.

12. Sample files exist in the `C:\BTS2010CertGuide\Chapter07\Example03-`
`Exceptions\FileDrop` folder that allows us to test both successful and
unsuccessful scenarios. In the case of our unsuccessful scenario, BizTalk
will catch a typed exception and write the results to disk.

Test your knowledge

The following questions will test your knowledge of Web Services and WCF Services Integration. These questions will re-enforce the concepts that were previously discussed in this chapter:

1. A car manufacturer, HWLC Motors, has outfitted its Sport Utility Vehicle (SUV) lineup with FireBridge tires. Unfortunately, this line of FireBridge tires had a factory recall on them due to factory defects. The FireBridge Company has exposed a WCF Service that car manufacturers can use to order replacement tires. Due to the popularity of these FireBridge tires their WCF Service is very busy and service requests are taking longer to complete. HWLC Motors is using BizTalk and have noticed that they are receiving some client-side timeouts as a result of the service execution times increasing. What should HWLC do to their BizTalk configuration?

    a. In the WCF Send Port, they should increase the Open timeout property

    b. In the WCF Send Port, they should decrease the Send timeout property

    c. In the WCF Send Port, they should increase the Send timeout property

    d. In the `BTSNTSvc.exe.config` file, the ServiceCallTimeOut property value should be increased

2. Tom, a developer for HWLC Motors, has been given strict BizTalk naming conventions by his boss Mikael. Tom has just consumed the third party financing WCF Service in BizTalk using the WCF-BasicHttp binding. In order to comply with Mikael's naming convention, Tom renames the operation, on the logical port used to communicate with the WCF Service, from ThirdPartyFinanceApproval to `External_ ThirdPartyFinanceApproval`. Tom then compiles/deploys his application and then imports the Binding File that was generated during the Consume WCF Service Wizard. Upon running the service for the first time, Tom discovers a runtime error and attributes it to the mismatch between his logical port naming and the SOAP Action header that is configured in his WCF Send Port. What must he do to resolve the problem?

    a. Re-run the Consume WCF Service wizard and specify an operation name of External_ ThirdPartyFinanceApproval.

    b. Ask the makers of the third party financing service to add the UseCustomOperation property to the services' `web.config`.

c. In the WCF Send Port, remove the SOAP Action header entirely. BizTalk will then rely upon its Pub/Sub architecture to route the message.

d. Update the WCF Send Port's SOAP Action header and change the operation name to External_ ThirdPartyFinanceApproval.

3. Richard, another developer at HWLC Motors has consumed the Custom Paint Service from his BizTalk Orchestration using the WCF-BasicHttp binding. He has configured this application to catch Typed Exceptions from the Paint Service. However, when a Paint service exception is thrown, it ends up getting suspended inside of the BizTalk Administration Console and never makes it back into his BizTalk Application. How should he fix it?

a. In the WCF Send Port he should enable the Propagate fault message property.

b. He should change his WCF Send Port to use the WCF-Custom Adapter instead due to its additional exception handling capabilities.

c. In his WCF Send Port, he should modify the Outbound WCF message body to use a template. In this template, he will provide the name of the Paint Service Exception he expects to receive back from the service.

d. He needs to run the Consume WCF Adapter wizard again this time enabling the Use Custom Exceptions feature.

4. Tom has exposed an Orchestration as a WCF Service and has chosen to use the WCF-BasicHttp adapter when running the BizTalk WCF Service Publishing wizard. He has successfully deployed and configured his application. Mikael, his boss, has decided he would like to use the WCF-WSHttp adapter instead due to the additional security features that are available. What must Tom do in order to successfully use the WCF-WSHttp adapter?

a. In the BizTalk Administration Console, Tom needs to modify his WCF Receive Location to use the WCF-WSHttp adapter instead.

b. Run the BizTalk WCF Service Publishing wizard again, this time selecting the WCF-WSHttp Adapter.

c. In the BizTalk Administration Console, Tom needs to modify his WCF Receive Location to use the WCF-Custom adapter. Inside the Receive Location's configuration he must set the binding to wsHttpBinding.

d. No change is required. The WCF-BasicHttp adapter can also leverage the WCF-WSHttp security features.

5. HWLC has changed its policy around processing orders from individual dealerships. Dealerships used to be able to submit order requests throughout the day. Now dealerships are being asked to submit orders once per day. It is expected that some busy dealerships may be sending messages that are more than 1048576 bytes (1 mb). What setting(s) need to be changed inside of HWLC's WCF two-way Receive Location?

    a. WCF two-way Receive Locations cannot accept messages that large. Instead, a one-way Receive Location and a one-way Send Port should be used instead.

    b. The Open timeout needs to be increased to satisfy these new requirements.

    c. The Maximum received message size needs to be increased to satisfy these new requirements.

    d. All dealerships must increase the Send timeout in their client applications in order to satisfy these new requirements.

Summary

In this chapter, we were introduced to some of the concepts involved with WCF and WCF adapters. We then covered Exposing and Consuming WCF and Web Services. As you have probably noticed, WCF is an extremely large and complicated topic. Luckily for BizTalk developers, Microsoft has provided wizards and the BizTalk Administration Console to reduce the complexities involved in building and consuming these types of services.

On the exam, you can expect around 14% of the questions to be centered around WCF and Web Services. A thorough understanding of this chapter will put you in a good position to do well in the examination.

In the next chapter, we will investigate a set of diverse technologies including Business Activity Monitoring (BAM), Business Rules Engine (BRE), Radio Frequency Identification (RFID), and Electronic Data Interchange. These technologies make up *Chapter 8, Implementing Extended Capabilities*, which aligns to the same set of competencies that will be tested in the exam.

8
Implementing Extended Capabilities

In this chapter, we will look at additional features that come with the BizTalk product and also other products that ship with the BizTalk license.

Along with BizTalk Server, several other features are available with the BizTalk Server license. The rules engine helps with implementing and maintaining complex Business Rules in both BizTalk and other applications. Also, a Radio Frequency Identification (RFID) Server enables receiving information from warehouses and so on, using the RFID technology.

In this chapter, we will discuss the following topics:

- Business Rules Engine (BRE)
- Electronic Data Interchange (EDI)
- Radio Frequency Identification (RFID)
- Business Activity Monitoring (BAM)
- Test your knowledge

Business Rules Engine (BRE)

Business Rules Engine, known as **BRE**, is an engine used for controlling and maintaining rules for both BizTalk and other applications.

Key Concepts

Rule

Business Rules are statements that govern the conduct of business processes. Business Rules consist of a condition and one or more consequent actions. Conditions are `true` or `false`, otherwise known as Boolean expressions, that consist of one or more predicates applied to facts. Multiple conditions can be combined to provide for complex computations. Complex conditions can be constructed by joining multiple simple conditions using AND, OR, and NOT modifiers, for example, when evaluating a customer order, you could have a rule, such as *If customer exists AND total order amount > 1000, OR if customer exists AND customer rating = excellent, THEN set discount amount = 10%*.

Policy

Policies are logical rule sets. You compose a version of a policy, save it, test it by applying it to facts, and when you are satisfied with the results, publish it and deploy it to a production environment. Policies are versioned and deployed, so if a rule changes, you simply create a new version of the policy, test the policy, and then deploy it. You do not have to recompile or modify Orchestrations or other business processes that are using a particular business policy.

When called from an Orchestration, Business Rule Engine will always execute the latest version of a policy. Changes made to a Business Rule policy will be immediate. The next time the policy is called from an Orchestration, the most recently deployed version will be used. After it is published, a Business Rule policy is immutable and can be changed only by creating a new version.

Vocabulary

Vocabularies are user-defined names for the facts used in rule conditions and actions. Vocabulary definitions render rules easier to read, understand, and share for the various workers within a particular business domain, for example, the source location for a particular fact might be a field in a particular record within a database, represented as a SQL Query. Instead of employing the SQL Query (an abstract procedural statement, difficult for most people to memorize or recognize) in the rule, a name meaningful to all the relevant parties in the development and deployment process can be associated with the query by creating a vocabulary definition. When you create a new vocabulary definition, you can choose from one of the following:

- Constant Value, Range of Values, or Set of Values
- .NET Class or Class Member
- XML Document Element or Attribute
- Database Table or Column

Creating the necessary vocabulary for Business Rules makes reading, comprehending, and updating the Business Rules much easier. In addition to the vocabularies you can create, Business Rule Composer uses predefined vocabularies for the predicates and functions used in rule evaluations and actions.

Rule store

The **rule store** is a repository for business policies and vocabularies. Policies and vocabularies are deployed to the rule store. The rule store is, by default, the Business Rule Database (BizTalkRuleEngineDb). This database is created while configuring Business Rules for the BizTalk Group. Additionally, policies and vocabularies can be exported to an XML file to simplify modification and deployment between test and production environments.

Creating a BizTalk Solution with rules

In the following example, we will create a small BizTalk solution and have it call rules inside the Rule Engine, and based on the rules and content of messages, either approve or deny a loan application.

The first step will be to add a policy determining whether a loan application is approved.

We will need a Schema that represents the loan application entering BizTalk and the BRE.

Create a Schema

To create a Schema, you will need to complete the following steps:

1. Create a solution called **Chapter08.Example01**.
2. Create a project called **Chapter08.Example01** and a Schema called **LoanApp.xsd**.
3. Have the Schema look somewhat similar to the following screenshot, and make the **Status** element distinguished:

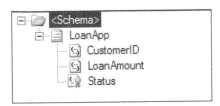

4. Build the project.

Now we need to set up a policy for when an order is approved. We want to look at **LoanAmount** and set the **Status** to **Approved**, if the loan is approved.

Creating a Policy

To create a policy, you will need to complete the following steps:

1. Open **Microsoft Business Rule Composer**, found in the **Start** Menu, under **Programs | Microsoft BizTalk Server 2010.**

2. In **Policy Explorer,** right-click on **Policies,** and choose **Add New Policy.**

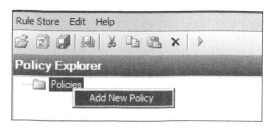

3. Name the policy **Chapter08.Example01.ApproveLoan.**

4. Right-click on **Version 1.0 (not saved)**, and select **Add New Rule.**

5. Name the rule **ApprovedByAmount.**

6. On the right-hand side, right-click on **Conditions,** and select **Predicates->LessThan.**

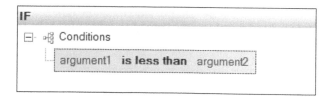

7. We now need to make a condition saying that if the **LoanAmount** on the **Loan Application** is less than 100, then we will automatically approve the loan. Click on **argument2**, and type **100.**

8. To insert **argument1**, we need the composer to be familiar with the **LoanApp** Schema.

Importing a Schema into Rule Composer

To import a Schema into Rule Composer, you will need to complete the following steps:

1. In **Facts Explorer**, choose the **XML Schemas** tab.

2. Right-click on **Schemas**, and choose **Browse**.

3. Locate the **LoanApp.xsd** file created previously in Visual Studio.

4. Choose the Schema, and click on **Open**.

5. Expand the **LoanApp** Schema.

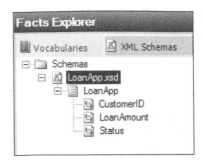

6. Drag the **LoanAmount** element into **argument1**.

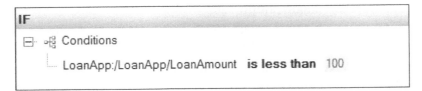

As we can see, this statement is not very readable, since the **LoanAmount** element contains a long XPath expression. Since the Rule Composer is supposed to be used by individuals other than just developers, we will later look at how to make it appear with more readable names and terms.

For now, let us keep the condition as it is and tell the engine what to do with the **Status**, if the condition is met.

Adding an Action

Now that we have specified a condition, we need to add an Action that will take place when the condition is met, as follows:

1. Drag the **Status** field from the Schema to **Actions**, under **THEN**.

2. Click on **<enter a value>** and type **Approved**. Again, this does not look very readable and contains XPath expressions, but we will deal with that later.

3. Save the policy by right-clicking on **Version 1.0 (not saved)** and selecting **Save**.

Testing the policy

Now, we will test the policy we have created with both an XML instance in which the condition is met (should be approved) and another in which the condition is not met (should not be approved), as follows:

1. Generated from the Schema, create two XML instances of the **LoanApp** Schema. Give both of them **Status: New**, and give one of them **LoanAmount: 200** and the other **LoanAmount: 20**.

2. Place them in an easily accessible folder, and test that they are both valid XML instances, by opening them in Internet Explorer.

3. Right-click on **ApproveLoan | Version 1.0**, inside the composer, and select **Test Policy**.

4. Under **XML Documents**, select the Schema and choose **Add Instance**.

5. Locate the document with **Amount = 20** and select it.

6. Click on **Test**. A large trace will now be shown in the composer. This has to do with the Rule Engine using the **Rete algorithm**, where everything is analyzed in a sort of network. This book will not dig deeper into this behavior.

7. Open the XML file tested, and verify that **Status** was changed to **Approved**. Change it back to **New**.

8. Test the other XML document with **Amount = 200**, by selecting the other document. Remove the old instance before clicking on **Test**.

9. Verify that, this time, the **Status** did not change since the condition was not met.

10. Publish the policy by right-clicking on **Version 1.0** and selecting **Publish**.

Publishing the policy will allow us to work with it, and from here, it will be immutable, meaning that after it has been published, it cannot be altered. In case we need to change it, we will be required to make a new version.

The Rule Composer does not hold any ELSE logic that allows us to set **Status** to **Denied** if the condition is not met. If we were to do that, we would need to create a new rule and negate the first one (in this case, greater than or equal to 100). This is because of the way the Rete algorithm is executed.

So, with the policy working, we will now build a small orchestration (inside BizTalk) that can test it.

Creating an Orchestration

We will not go into details about how to create Orchestrations. Please refer to *Chapter 4, Developing BizTalk Artifacts – Creating Orchestrations*, for a more detailed Orchestration description. The steps are as follows:

1. Create an Orchestration that resembles the following diagram:

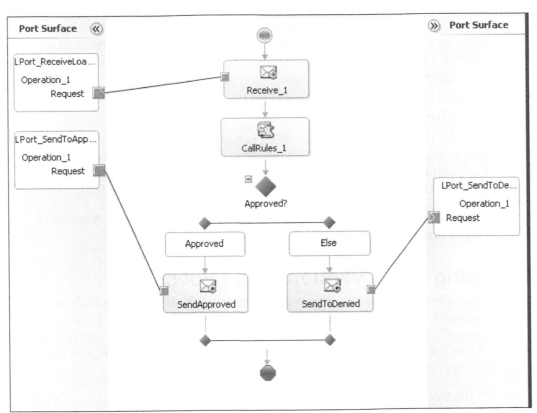

2. The Orchestration must have the following features:
    - Receives a LoanApp instance
    - The **Approved** decide shape uses the Boolean expression: **LoanAppMessage.Status == "Approved"**.

3. Double-click on the **CallRules_1** shape, and select the policy **ApproveLoan**.

4. In **Parameter Name**, select the **LoanApp** message received in the **Receive_1** receive shape.

5. Deploy the Orchestration, and create and bind all the required ports.

Deploying the policy and testing

We now need to deploy the policy in order to test whether the Orchestration can use the policy.

1. Test the solution by submitting one of the XML documents previously created to the Orchestration.

2. Check the **Event Viewer**. The error **No versions of rule set ApproveLoan are deployed** should appear. This is because a rule called from an Orchestration must be deployed. The error message also shows that the Orchestrations do not call a specific version of the rule set but rather the deployed version with the highest version number.

3. In the composer, deploy the **Version 1.0**; note that the status changes from **Published** to **Deployed**.

4. Test the flow again. Note that when changing the state of policies and so on, inside the composer, it might be necessary to restart both the Host Instance(s) and the RuleEngineUpdateService.exe file, since both of them cache information.

The flow should now result in one of the documents being sent to the Approved Send Port and another one being sent to the Denied.

Deploying a new version of the Policy

We are now asked to change the approved limit from 100 to 1000 (in which case both XML documents will be approved). As we discussed earlier, we cannot change an existing policy Version, so we must create a new Version of the policy. If we create Version 1.1 of the policy and deploy it, the Orchestration will automatically start using the newer and higher version.

1. In the Composer, right-click on the **ApproveLoan** policy and choose **Add New Version**.

2. A red **Version 1.1** should now appear, as shown in the following screenshot:

3. Right-click on **Version 1.0 | ApprovedByAmount** and select **Copy**.

4. Right-click on **Version 1.1** and select **Paste**.

5. In the new **ApprovedByAmount** field, change **100** to **1000**.

6. Publish and deploy **Version 1.1**.

7. Restart Hosts and the rule service.

8. Test the documents.

Now both of the test documents should be **Approved**.

Adding Vocabulary

As we discussed previously, we can make the conditions and actions appear more human-readable in the Composer, so that it becomes easier for non-IT personnel to create and change rules.

To do this, we use **Vocabulary**. In this exercise, we will create a better name for the **LoanAmount** and **Status** fields, as follows:

1. Under **Vocabularies**, right-click on **Vocabularies** and select **Add New Vocabulary**.

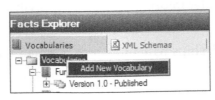

2. Name the new Vocabulary **Loan**.

3. Right-click on **Version 1.0**, and choose **Add new definition**.

4. Choose **XML document Element or Attribute**.

5. Click on **Next**.

6. Click on **Browse**.

7. Locate the LoanApp Schema, and click on **Open**.

8. Expand the Schema and select **LoanAmount**, and click on **OK**.

9. Name the definition **Total Loan Amount**.

10. Choose **Perform "Get" operation**, and name the **Display name Total Loan Amount**.

11. Click on **Finish**.

12. Make a new version of the **ApproveLoan** policy, and copy and paste the old **ApprovedByAmount** field to the new version.

13. Delete the left-hand side of the condition by selecting it and pressing *Delete*, so that **argument1** appears again.

14. Publish **Version 1.0** of the **Loan** Vocabulary. (Note: Vocabularies do not need to be deployed, but must be published before they can be used in a Policy.)

15. Drag **Total Loan Amount** to **argument1**.

Now we have a better appearance of the condition, and it will be easier for a non-programmer to make rule changes in the Composer, especially if the rules become more complex.

Electronic Data Interchange (EDI)

Since BizTalk Server 2006 R2, Microsoft has introduced out-of-the-box EDI capabilities in BizTalk.

EDI documents are like Flat files, which we discussed in an earlier chapter. There are, however, two major differences:

- EDI is standardized, the Schemas are already created
- EDI deals with header information not found in the actual message (Schema), but which must be configured using parties

The out-of-the-box BizTalk ships with numerous Schemas for the following EDI standards:

- X12
- EDIFACT
- HIPAA
- EANCOM

In this chapter, we will use EDIFACT as an example, but most of the mechanisms surrounding the BizTalk EDI capabilities will be the same, whether the standard used is X12, EDIFACT, and so on. As an example of EDIFACT, we will try and process an EDIFACT order Version D96A.

The order looks similar to the following screenshot:

```
Chapter08Order.txt - Notepad                                   _|□|x|
File  Edit  Format  View  Help
UNA:+,? '
UNB+UNOB:2+57000000001232:14+57000000001230:14+100909:0920+B12345++++0++0'
UNH+H12345+ORDERS:D:96A:UN'
BGM+220+12345+9+NA'
DTM+137:20110517:102'
DTM+2:20110923:102'
NAD+SU+5790000702954::9'
NAD+BY+5790000050017::9'
LIN+1++11111:EN'
QTY+21:132'
PRI+AAA:1388,9::TU'
UNS+S'
CNT+2:1'
UNT+12+H12345'
UNZ+1+B12345'
```

What we will do is receive the document in a Receive Location that uses the EdiReceive Pipeline, and by using the out-of-the-box Schema for EDIFACT Order D96A, the Pipeline should be able to create an EDI XML.message.

Finding and deploying the EDIFACT Schema

When starting an EDI project, the first thing we need to do is get the Schemas needed for the documents we will receive and/or send, as follows:

1. With developer tools installed on the BizTalk environment, go to the folder `%Program Files%\Microsoft BizTalk Server 2010\XSD_Schema\EDI` and locate the self-extracting file named `MicrosoftEdiXSDTemplates.exe`.

2. Extract the file by double-clicking on it. This only has to be done once.

3. A new folder, named `MicrosoftEdiXSDTemplates`, is created. In this folder, locate the following `EDIFACT\D96A\EFACT_D96A_ORDERS.xsd` file.

4. Create a BizTalk Visual Studio Project and name it **Chapter08.Example03**.

5. Add an existing item, and add the `EFACT_D96A_ORDERS.xsd` file located earlier.

6. Sign the assembly, and deploy it to a BizTalk Application named **BTS2010CertGuide-Ch08**.

Adding a reference to BizTalk EDI application

With the EDIFACT Schema deployed, we now need to set up a Receive Port, with a Receive Location that uses the EdiReceive Pipeline. The Pipeline is located in the BizTalk EDI application, and therefore our **BTS2010CertGuide-Ch08** Application needs a reference to **BizTalk EDI Application**, as follows:

1. Right-click on the **BTS2010CertGuide-Ch08** application, and select **Properties**.

2. Select **References** and click on **Add**, and then select the **BizTalk EDI Application** and click on **OK**.

3. Refresh the Application. The list of applications is shown in the following screenshot:

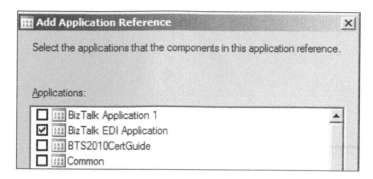

Setting up a Receive Port, Location, and a Send Port

For the next step, we will need to set up both Receive and Send Ports, so that we can monitor messages going through BizTalk and see how the EDI functionality works.

1. Set up a new Receive Port, **CG0802_Receive**, and a Receive Location, using the FILE adapter that points to a new file folder, and select the EdiReceive Pipeline.

2. Set up a Send Port that subscribes to all messages from the Receive Port (**BTS.ReceivePortName == CG0102_Receive**), use a FILE Adapter, and point to an output folder.

3. Start your application. (When the BizTalk EDI Application is referenced, starting the application will suggest starting the EDI Application as well; this is not needed right now and should be unchecked.)

4. Run the sample order through the application. The result should be a file sent through the Send Port.

5. Examine the XML sent from the Send Port, as shown in the following screenshot:

```xml
<?xml version="1.0"?>
<ns0:EFACT_D96A_ORDERS xmlns:ns0="http://schemas.microsoft.com/BizTalk/EDI/EDIFACT/2006">
  <UNH>
      <UNH1>H12345</UNH1>
    <UNH2>
        <UNH2.1>ORDERS</UNH2.1>
        <UNH2.2>D</UNH2.2>
        <UNH2.3>96A</UNH2.3>
        <UNH2.4>UN</UNH2.4>
    </UNH2>
  </UNH>
  <ns0:BGM>
    <ns0:C002>
        <C00201>220</C00201>
    </ns0:C002>
    <BGM02>12345</BGM02>
    <BGM03>9</BGM03>
    <BGM04>NA</BGM04>
  </ns0:BGM>
  <ns0:DTM>
    <ns0:C507>
        <C50701>137</C50701>
        <C50702>20110517</C50702>
        <C50703>102</C50703>
    </ns0:C507>
  </ns0:DTM>
```

The top of the XML output should look similar to the preceding screenshot. Notice the namespace and the root element, and how they match the root element and the namespace of the order Schema we deployed earlier from Visual Studio (shown in the following screenshot).

Setting up the Parties

As of now, BizTalk can process an incoming EDIFACT message and convert it to XML. The EDIFACT document is being accepted by the EdiReceive Pipeline, and is transformed to XML, so further processing can take place.

At some point (especially when sending EDI documents), we might, however, need to set up Parties so that the EdiReceive and EdiSend Pipelines know which trading partners the message came from or is being sent to.

Examine an unrecognized message

To set up parties for receiving EDIFACT, we must tell the EdiReceive Pipeline how to identify from whom the document originated.

To do this, we use the **UNB segment**, where information about the sender and receiver is stored as shown in the following screenshot:

In the order example, the UNB segment reads:

- Sender: 57000000001232 (EAN number code 14) (MyPartner)
- Receiver: 57000000001230 (EAN number code 14) (Myself)

So what we need to do now is set up two Parties, that is, sender and the receiver.

The first thing we will do is to examine how the context of an EDI message appears when parties are not recognized:

1. Stop the Send Port (not `Unenlist`, just `Stop`).
2. Send an order through the application.
3. Go to the **Group Hub** in the **Administration Console**, and click on **Suspended Items | Resumable.**
4. Examine the **Context Properties** of the message most recently suspended.

AgreementPartIDOnReceive	0	Not Promoted	http://schemas.microsoft.com/Edi/PropertySchema
UNB2_2	14	Promoted	http://schemas.microsoft.com/Edi/PropertySchema
UNB3_1	57000000001230	Promoted	http://schemas.microsoft.com/Edi/PropertySchema
AgreementID	0	Not Promoted	http://schemas.microsoft.com/Edi/PropertySchema
AgreementName	BTSGuestParty	Not Promoted	http://schemas.microsoft.com/Edi/PropertySchema
UNB3_2	14	Promoted	http://schemas.microsoft.com/Edi/PropertySchema
UNH2_1	ORDERS	Promoted	http://schemas.microsoft.com/Edi/PropertySchema
ReceiverPartyName	RECEIVE-PARTNER	Not Promoted	http://schemas.microsoft.com/Edi/PropertySchema
ReuseEnvelope	False	Promoted	http://schemas.microsoft.com/Edi/PropertySchema
SenderPartyName	BTS-SENDER	Not Promoted	http://schemas.microsoft.com/Edi/PropertySchema
UNA_Segment	UNA:+,? '	Not Promoted	http://schemas.microsoft.com/Edi/PropertySchema
UNH2_2	D	Promoted	http://schemas.microsoft.com/Edi/PropertySchema
UNB11	0	Promoted	http://schemas.microsoft.com/Edi/PropertySchema
UNB2_1	57000000001232	Promoted	http://schemas.microsoft.com/Edi/PropertySchema
UNB_Segment	UNB+UNOB:2+57000000001232:14+57000000001230.14+100909:0...	Not Promoted	http://schemas.microsoft.com/Edi/PropertySchema
UNH2_3	96A	Promoted	http://schemas.microsoft.com/Edi/PropertySchema

Notice that **ReceivePartyName** and **SenderPartyName** do not have any meaningful values. This indicates that the **Edidisassembler** Pipeline Component did not find any matching Agreement between the two Parties in the UNB segment, so we need to set up such an Agreement.

Set up the Parties and the Agreement for receiving

For BizTalk to know what partner-specific properties should be applied for the incoming and outgoing EDI messages, we need to set up Parties and Agreements, as follows:

1. In the **BizTalk Administration Console**, go to **Parties**.

2. Right-click on **Parties** and choose **New | Party**

3. Name the Party **MySelf**, and click on **OK**

4. Expand the **MySelf** Party, and find the profile **MySelf_Profile**.

5. Double-click on the profile.

6. Under **Identities**, in the **Name** drop-down list, choose **EAN (European Article Numbering Association)**. Note that **Qualifier 14** is automatically selected.

7. In **Value**, type **57000000001230**.

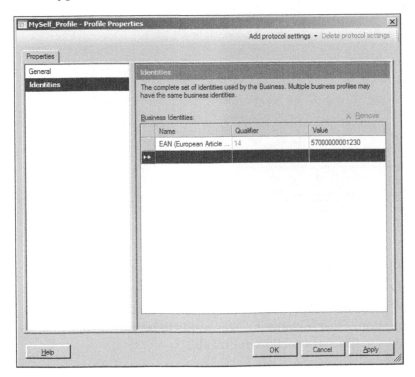

8. Click on **OK**, and do the same for the **MyPartner** Party with EAN number **57000000001232**. We now need to set up an Agreement between the two Parties.

9. Right-click on **MyPartner_Profile**, and choose **New | Agreement**.

10. Name the Agreement **AgreementWithMyPartner**.

11. Choose **EDIFACT** as **Protocol**.

12. Choose **MySelf** as **Second Party**.

13. Two new tabs should now appear, **MyPartner->MySelf** and **MySelf->MyPartner**, as shown in the following screenshot:

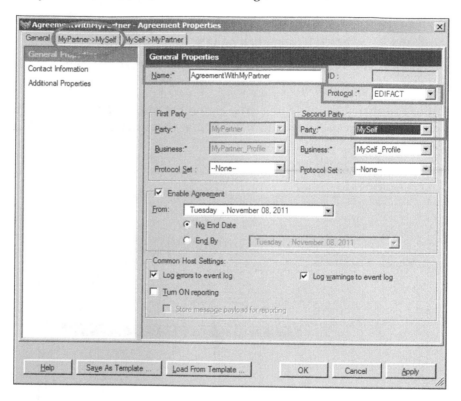

14. Click on the **MyPartner->Myself** tab.

15. Click on **Interchange Settings-Identifiers**.

16. Verify that **UNB2.1** is the EAN number of the sender and **UNB3.1** is the EAN number of the receiver, and click on **OK**.

17. Restart your Host Instance(s). This needs to be done every time something changes in the Party section in BizTalk.

18. Send an order through BizTalk, making sure that the Send Port is still in a stopped state.

19. Examine the **Context**, the **AgreementName**, **SenderPartyName**, and **ReceiverPartyName** should now be populated with correct data.

20. Start the Send Port again. This indicates that the Parties are now recognized on reception of the message.

Changing the Schema

Often, when working with EDI, trading partners are going to send invalid EDI, which is EDI not conforming 100% to the standard.

All the Schemas available in BizTalk will, by default, only allow EDI documents to pass through the EdiDisassembler Pipeline Component and be transformed to XML that complies with the standard.

For example, we receive orders as shown before, but in the **DTM** (DateTime) segment, instead of **code 137** (Document Date), the sender sends **70** as the code.

This is not allowed according to the UN specification available at the following URL:

`http://www.unece.org/trade/untdid/d96a/uncl/uncl2005.htm`

1. Make a copy of the order, and change **DTM+137** to **DTM+70**.

2. Run it through BizTalk, and check **EventLog**.

An error message similar to the following screenshot should now be present in the Event Viewer:

```
Error encountered during parsing. The Edifact transaction set with id 'H12345' contained in
interchange (without group) with id 'B12345', with sender id '57000000001232', receiver id
'57000000001230' is being suspended with following errors:
Error: 1 (Field level error)
        SegmentID: DTM
        Position in TS: 3
        Data Element ID: C50701
        Position in Segment: 2
        Position in Field: 1
        Data Value: 70
        12: Invalid value in data element
```

This is because 70 is not allowed in this field. If we are to allow MyPartner to send **DTM+70** in the documents (even though the preferred approach would be to ask the partner to send valid EDI, this is not always possible), we need to give the partner its own Schema representation of **EFACT_D96A_ORDERS**.

Now, since we cannot change the root element name of the Schema as that has to comply with certain patterns, the only way to create a new Schema is to change the targetNamespace.

Fortunately, this can be set up in Agreements as well.

Set up an alternate namespace for the Agreement

We now need to set up a new namespace to be used for the MyPartner->MySelf Agreement, so that messages being received with this Agreement will be given another namespace and will therefore be validated using an alternative Schema, as follows:

1. Under **Parties**, click on **MyPartner**, and double-click on **AgreementWithMyPartner**.

2. Go to the **MyPartner->MySelf** tab.

3. Under **Transaction Set Settings | Local Host Settings**, scroll to the right and locate targetNamespace.

4. Change targetNamespace from http://schemas.microsoft.com/ BizTalk/EDI/EDIFACT/2006 to http://schemas.microsoft.com/ BizTalk/EDI/EDIFACT/2006/MyPartner. (Note: The namespace drop-down list suggests http://schemas.microsoft.com/BizTalk/EDI/Edifact without a capitalized EDIFACT; this will NOT work, so make sure EDIFACT is capitalized.)

5. Click on **OK**, and restart the Host Instance(s).

6. Run the **DTM+70** document through the application, and again check the **EventLog**.

There is now an error indicating that the EdiReceive Pipeline is searching for a Schema specification with the namespace we just added in the Agreement and root element named EFACT_D96A_ORDERS.

So now we need to deploy such a Schema, and allow the value 70 in the DTM segments.

Deploy an alternate Schema

Now we need to create an alternate Schema with the new namespace and where DTM+70 is allowed in the DTM segment, as follows:

1. Go to the Visual Studio Project created earlier that holds the original order Schema.

2. Change the targetNamespace of the Schema to the new namespace specified in the Agreement.

3. Go to the **DTM** record, and expand it.

4. Expand **C507**.

5. Select the **C50701** element, and choose **Enumeration** under **Properties**.

6. Add **70** to the list.

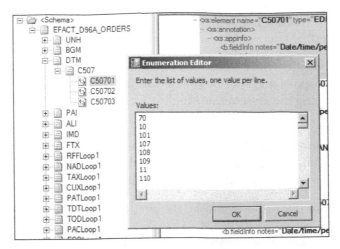

7. Rebuild the solution, click on **OK** to any information that might appear about cleanup.

8. Deploy the solution, and restart the Host Instance(s).

9. Submit the new order with **DTM+70**.

10. Verify that the XML file was outputted without any problems. Examine the XML, as shown in the following screenshot:

```
<?xml version="1.0"?>
- <ns0:EFACT_D96A_ORDERS xmlns:ns0="http://schemas.microsoft.com/BizTalk/EDI/EDIFACT/2006/MyPartner">
  - <UNH>
      <UNH1>H12345</UNH1>
    - <UNH2>
        <UNH2.1>ORDERS</UNH2.1>
        <UNH2.2>D</UNH2.2>
        <UNH2.3>96A</UNH2.3>
        <UNH2.4>UN</UNH2.4>
      </UNH2>
  </UNH>
  - <ns0:BGM>
    - <ns0:C002>
        <C00201>220</C00201>
      </ns0:C002>
      <BGM02>12345</BGM02>
      <BGM03>9</BGM03>
      <BGM04>NA</BGM04>
  </ns0:BGM>
  - <ns0:DTM>
    - <ns0:C507>
        <C50701>70</C50701>
        <C50702>20110517</C50702>
        <C50703>102</C50703>
      </ns0:C507>
  </ns0:DTM>
```

As shown, the XML now outputted has a custom namespace (.../MyPartner), and we have allowed DTM to hold the qualifying value of **70**.

Setting up a Party and Agreement for sending

When sending EDIFACT, more information must be provided to BizTalk through the Parties in order for BizTalk to know how the partner expects the EDI to be structured.

The way EDI really differs here from XML, Flat file, and so on, is that the metadata structure and envelope of an EDI document cannot be determined, neither from the XML message entering the Assembler Pipeline Component (EdiAssembler) nor from the Schema.

If we take our previous example where we received an EDIFACT order and transformed it to XML, we can now try and take the same XML, send it through the EdiSend Pipeline, and configure it to yet another party (MyPartner2).

Again, have a look at our order example, shown in the following screenshot:

```
Chapter08Order.txt - Notepad
File  Edit  Format  View  Help
UNA:+.?
UNB+UNOB:2+57000000001232:14+57000000000001230:14+100909:0920+B12345++++0++0'
UNH+H12345+ORDERS:D:96A:UN'
BGM+220+12345+9+NA'
DTM+137/:20110517:102'
DTM+2:20110923:102'
NAD+SU+5790000702954::9'
NAD+BY+5790000050017::9'
LIN+1++11111:EN'
QTY+21:132'
PRI+AAA:1388,9::TU'
UNS+S'
CNT+2:1'
UNT+12+H12345'
UNZ+1+B12345'
```

The UNA segment is metadata about how the document is delimited, how decimal numbers are presented, and how to escape a reserved character.

The UNB segment tells the encoding of the document, the sender and the receiver, and several other document metadata.

None of these metadata can be created from the EDI Schema or the XML being sent to the Send Port, since they will be partner-specific.

So what must be done is that these properties must be set up in a Partner Agreement, and then the Send Port must be connected to that agreement (as opposed to when receiving EDI, the Send Pipeline will have no way of knowing which party to use without being explicitly told).

Setting up a new Party for sending

We will now make yet another Party for sending, so that the differences in EDI properties can be examined:

1. Make a new file Send Port named **CG0802_SendToPartner2**. Make a subscription identical to the first Send Port (**BTS.ReceivePortName == CG0802_Receive**), and select the **EdiSend** Pipeline. Make the file extension **%MessageID%.txt** instead of **%MessageID%.xml**.

2. Make a new Party called **MyPartner2**.

3. Specify **57000000001233** as the **Party profile EAN number**, like it was done in the previous exercise.

4. Right-click on **MyPartner2_Profile**, and select **New | Agreement**.

5. Name it **AgreementWithMyPartner2**, choose **EDIFACT**, and select **Myself** as **Second Party**.

6. Select the **MySelf->MyPartner2** tab.

7. Check the **Identifiers**; both **UNB2** and **UNB3** should be filled out with EAN numbers, and **Code Qualifiers** with **14**.

8. In **Envelopes**, check the **Apply UNB Segment**

9. Under **Character set and separators**, select the following:

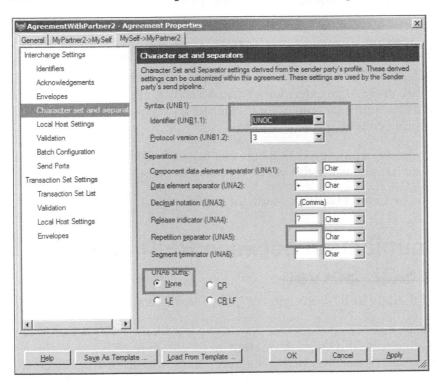

10. Most of the values are left as default, but choosing **UNOC** for **Identifier** will encode the document with the Western European character set (ISO-8859-1). Most EDIFACT users use a space in UNA5 so as to make sure to put a space instead of *, and also we will leave the **Suffix** at **None**, which will make the EDIFACT appear as one line. If we want Carriage Returns after each segment, which will make the EDIFACT more readable, select **CR LF**.

11. Go to **Send Ports**, and choose **CG0802_SendToPartner2**.

12. Click on **OK**, and restart the Host Instance(s).

13. Submit a new message in the application. Examine the output from the **SendToPartner2** Send Port as follows:

```
File  Edit  Format  View  Help
UNA:+,? 'UNB+UNOC:3+57000000001230:14+570000000001233:14+111108:1544+1++++0++0'UNH+1+ORDERS:D:96A:UN'BGM+220+12
+5790000050017::9'LIN+1++11111:EN'QTY+21:132'PRI+AAA:1388,9::TU'UNS+S'CNT+2:1'UNT+12+1'UNZ+1+1'
```

Notice that the UNA segment has a comma (,), which indicates that decimal numbers should be presented with commas. Also notice that **PRI+AAA:1388,9** is a decimal number with commas. If we change the Agreement UNA3 from comma to decimal, this will change.

Also, notice that the UNB segment is using the correct sender and receiver EANs, and that the whole document is just one line, as specified in the agreement.

Radio Frequency Identification (RFID)

The BizTalk RFID Server is a separate server product that ships with the BizTalk Server license. It is not an extension or adapter to BizTalk Server, but rather a server used for communicating with various RFID and sensor services, which then communicate with the actual devices.

The out-of-the-box communication between the RFID Server and the BizTalk Server will typically happen using the MSMQ Protocol or an SQL Server.

This is done by Event Handlers inside the RFID Server.

Communication between RFID and BizTalk using SQL Server

The out-of-the-box RFID ships with an Event Handler called `SqlServerSink`.

As soon as the `SqlServerSink` component is enabled, the RFID Server will automatically write RFID tag information into a database called `RFIDsink`. If there is no such database present, the component will automatically create it.

Once this is set up, a WCF SQL Receive adapter can set up polling from an already installed stored procedure called `GetAndDeleteEventsForBizTalk`.

When using the SqlServerSink Handler, the `EventTypes` property can be used to specify which RFID tags should be logged. This property should be set to `GenericEvents`, if the handler should only log custom tag events. The available `EventTypes` are as follows:

- TagReadEvent
- TagListReadEvent
- GenericEvent

More information about configuring `SqlServerSink` can be found at `http://msdn.microsoft.com/en-us/library/dd352322(v=bts.10).aspx`.

Business Activity Monitoring (BAM)

BAM is typically used for "bringing BizTalk to the world", in the sense that it is often somewhat transparent to the outside world what goes on inside BizTalk. If errors occur in BizTalk, these will be handled both by BizTalk and the operators, but what about all the stuff that did not fail? BAM is used to show just that.

Here are some examples of questions that BAM could give the answer to:

- How many orders did we receive last month?
- Was the order with ID 1005 ever received, and when did BizTalk ship it to the ERP system?

Out of the box, there is no easy way of supplying these answers to the business, outside of BizTalk. By using the built-in tracking, we could give the answers, but that would both be very tedious and would require fields such as `OrderID` to be promoted (see *Chapter 2, Developing BizTalk Artifacts – Creating Schemas and Pipelines*, for promotions and so on).

BAM, on the other hand, can do all this easily without requiring certain features, such as Promotion, to be present in the BizTalk Solution.

BAM is non-intrusive, which means we can apply it to an existing BizTalk application, without BAM making any changes or performance impact to that solution. This means that BAM can easily be applied after a solution is already deployed and running in production, totally independent. Also, even if BAM was failing, as it had been developed with errors or the BAM databases was unavailable and so on, the BAM Solution would not cause the actual BizTalk Solution to fail.

The typical use of BAM with BizTalk will enable us to receive information from the following points in the BizTalk flow:

- Receive Pipelines
- Orchestration shapes
- Send Pipelines

Each time a message enters one of the preceding items inside BizTalk, BAM is able to collect data from this event. The examples of data from such events could be:

- Time of event
- Data from the actual message
- Data from the context of the message
- Various message properties, such as `MessageID`, `InstanceID`, and so on

The information collected will be stored in SQL tables (when working with BAM known as Activities).

Creating Activities

A BAM Activity is somewhat similar to a SQL table. Examples of Activities inside BAM could be:

- Order Processed
- Invoice Processed
- Order Sent
- Invoice Sent

If we have a BizTalk setup where orders are received and processed and maybe sent to multiple applications or systems, we could have a one-to-many relationship between processing an order and sending it, since processing it could result in sending it to three systems, and we want to track all the three events. In that case, we would need two activities (two tables): an **Order Processed** Activity and an **Order Sent** Activity.

As mentioned before, each Activity will be represented by SQL tables. If an activity named `TestBAM` is created, five Activity tables will be created in the primary BAM database named **BAMPrimaryImport**, as follows:

- **bam_TestBAM_Active**
- **bam_TestBAM_ActiveRelationships**
- **bam_TestBAM_Completed**

- **bam_TestBAM_CompletedRelationships**
- **bam_TestBAM_Continuations**

Along with the tables, each Activity also implements a package in Integration Services, called BAM_DM_TestBAM. This package should be scheduled to run frequently to maintain and archive the Activity data. When this package is run, the **_Completed** and **_CompletedRelationships** tables will be split into subtables with internal unique names, so as time goes by, more and more tables will appear, but the applications reading the BAM Activity data will not notice this, since they should only access the data through views, and the views are updated each time a new subtable is created using the SQL Union statement.

Here is an example of how a BAM Activity would be represented in the **BAMPrimaryImport** database, after the maintenance package has run for the first time:

```
⊞  ▦  dbo.bam_TestBAM_A88BA880_2B85_4C7C_8AAB_061A0B3D579E
⊞  ▦  dbo.bam_TestBAM_A88BA880_2B85_4C7C_8AAB_061A0B3D579E_Relationships
⊞  ▦  dbo.bam_TestBAM_Active
⊞  ▦  dbo.bam_TestBAM_ActiveRelationships
⊞  ▦  dbo.bam_TestBAM_Completed
⊞  ▦  dbo.bam_TestBAM_CompletedRelationships
⊞  ▦  dbo.bam_TestBAM_Continuations
```

The tables we shall pay the closest attention to are **_Active** and **_Completed**. The _Active table is where Activity instances reside before the Activity profile has completed, after which they will be moved to the **_Completed** table.

Activities are created by using Microsoft Excel 2010 or 2007.

Setting up the BAM add-in inside Microsoft Excel

Microsoft Excel needs to be installed on the BizTalk Development environments where Activities need to be created. It is only necessary to have Excel installed on development servers, and it should not be installed on the production or test environments.

Also **BAM Client**, found under **Additional Software** when installing BizTalk, should be installed on the developing environment. This will result in an add-in being installed in Excel, and this add-in can now be activated, as shown in the following screenshot, by selecting **File | Options | Add-Ins | Go**.

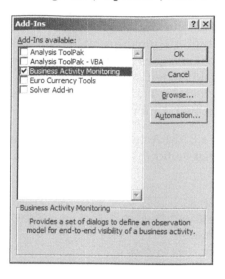

Make sure that **Business Activity Monitoring** is selected.

Now BAM should be visible under the menu **Add-Ins**.

Creating an activity inside Excel

We are going to make an Activity that extracts both internal BizTalk metadata and data from the actual XML message sent through BizTalk. For that, we will need to deploy a Schema and set up a Receive Port receiving the messages and a Send Port that subscribes to all the messages coming from the Receive Port.

The Schema should look as shown in the following screenshot (notice that no promotion of any kind is needed):

The Schema and XML documents used do not have to be identical with this example. The two elements we will be working with are **OrderID** and **OrderTotal**, both of which we want to collate to the BAM Activity we create.

Deploy the Schema, and generate an instance of an XML document that matches the Schema. Set up a Receive Port and Send Port flow in BizTalk, use the **XMLReceive** Pipeline on the Receive side, and verify that the flow is working.

Now we will make an Activity called **ReceiveOrder**, as follows:

1. Start up Excel, and create a new Activity by clicking on **Add-Ins | BAM | BAM Activity**, as shown in the following screenshot:

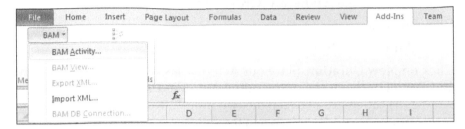

2. Click on **New Activity**.
3. In **Activity name**, type **ReceiveOrder**.
4. Click on **New Item**, and create **OrderID**, as shown in the following screenshot:

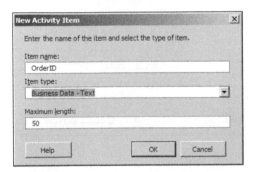

5. Create three more items, as shown in the following screenshot:

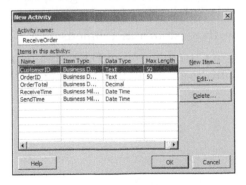

6. Click on **OK**.

7. A welcome screen for creating views is now shown. If no views are needed, we can click on **Cancel** at this time, but often at least one view per Activity is needed, if the data is to be used in the **BAM Portal**.

8. Click on **Next**.

9. Click on **Next** again (**Create a new view** should be selected).

10. Enter a view name (**vwReceiveOrder**), and select the **ReceiveOrder** Activity.

11. Click on **Next**.

12. Select **All Items** to be present in the view.

13. Click on **New Duration**. Since our Activity has two milestones (**ReceiveTime** and **SendTime**), we can create a duration called **TimeInBizTalk**, which will be the difference between the two milestones. Make sure that **Time resolution** is **Second**, as shown in the following screenshot:

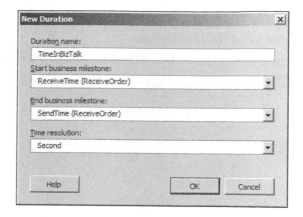

14. Click on **Next**.

15. In the **Aggregation Dimensions and Measures**, we will create a pivot table that shows the number of orders received, grouped by the **CustomerID** and also the average order total per customer.

16. First, we will create the customer as a dimension. Click on **New Dimension**.

17. Name the dimension **Customer**, select **Data dimension**, add **CustomerID**, and then click on **OK**, as shown in the following screenshot:

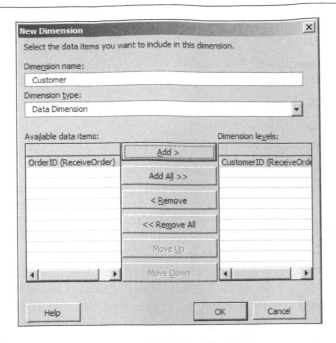

18. We now need two measures: total number of orders received, and the average order total.

19. Click on **New Measure**.

20. In Measure name, type **TotalReceived**, select **Count**, and set **Base activity** to **ReceiveOrder**, as shown in the following screenshot:

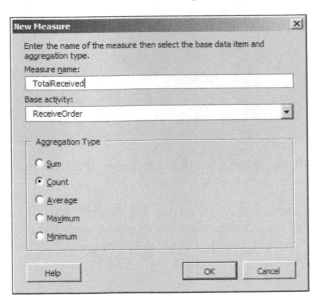

21. Now create another measure for the order total average. Click on **New Measure**.

22. Name the measure as **AverageTotal**. Choose **Aggregation Type: Average** and **Base data item: OrderTotal (ReceiveOrder)**.

23. Click on **OK**.

24. Click on **Next, Next,** and **Finish**.

25. The pivot table now needs to be dimensioned.

26. On the right-hand side, under **PivotTable Field List**, check **Customer, TotalReceived,** and then **AverageTotal**. We have now created an Activity and a view with an aggregation inside our Excel spreadsheet. If we click on the created table on the spreadsheet and then go to the **BAM Add-In**, there now appears a Toolbar command called **Mark the selected pivot table as Real Time Aggregation**. This feature is disabled by default and should only be enabled in situations where real time is absolutely necessary for the viewers of the aggregation. The performance impact of enabling this can be severe, and usually, having the aggregation populated on a scheduled basis (twice a day, once every hour, and so on) will be sufficient. It is also worth noting that real-time aggregation will have certain limitations on the aggregations created, and not all functionalities can be used when using it.

27. Leave the real-time aggregation disabled. Select **BAM | Export XML**, as shown in the following screenshot:

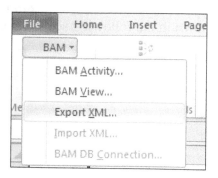

28. Save the XML file in an appropriate location, and name it `Chapter08.Example02.OrderActivity_v10.xml`.

It is good practice to never overwrite an existing Activity file but rather give it a new version number every time changes have been made, since the original file might be needed to remove Activities and views (see the Remove-all option described in the next part of the chapter).

Deploy the Activity and view

When the Activities and views are saved as XML, they can be deployed in the BAM databases by using the bm.exe command-line tool.

If the BAM client tools are installed, the bm.exe tool can be located in the %Program Files%\Microsoft BizTalk Server 2010\Tracking folder

- If we need to work with the tool a lot, it is recommended that the path be made into a system path, so that it can be accessed by the command line, no matter where we are located.

When working with the Activity files, bm.exe has three main options:

- Deploy-all (deploys all Activities and views from scratch)
- Update-all (only deploys new Activities and/or views; updating existing Activities and views are only allowed if no existing items are updated or deleted)
- Remove-all (removes all Activities and views previously deployed; the XML file used must match the Activities and views in the database)

1. To deploy the Activity and view created earlier, locate the XML file that was exported from Excel, and run the following command (remember that the Tracking folder needs to be in the system path for easy access):

```
E:\BAM>bm.exe deploy-all -definitionFile:Chapter08.Example02.OrderActivity_v10.x
ml
Microsoft (R) Business Activity Monitoring Utility version 3.7.467.0
Copyright (C) Microsoft Corporation. All rights reserved.

Using 'BAMPrimaryImport' BAM Primary Import database on server 'ALASKA'...

Deploying Activity... Done.
Deploying View... Done.
Deploying Security... Done.

E:\BAM>
```

2. Once the Activity and view has been created, go to the **BAMPrimaryImport** database, and verify whether five tables were created with the names **bam_ReceiveOrder***, and whether those five views exist with the name **bam_vwReceiveOrder***.

3. With the Activity created, we now need to Map the Activity to the events and data inside our BizTalk flow, so that BAM will pick up data and write it to our tables, at certain points inside BizTalk.

Creating a Tracking Profile

To map the Activity to the events inside BizTalk, we use the Tracking Profile Editor tool that ships with BizTalk, located under **Programs | Microsoft BizTalk Server 2010**, as follows:

1. Open the Tracking Profile Editor.
2. Click on **Click here to import a BAM Activity Definition**.
3. Find the **ReceiveOrder** Activity in the list; use **Filter** if needed, as shown in the following screenshot:

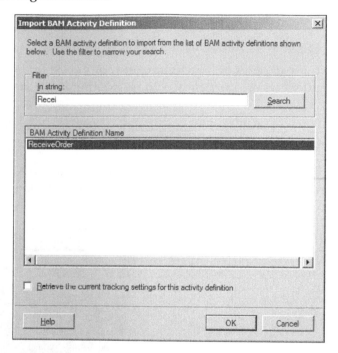

4. Select **ReceiveOrder**, and click on **OK**. We are now back to the Tracking Profile Editor main page, and the left-hand side should now contain our **ReceiveOrder** Activity with the items that need to be mapped. (Note: The **ActivityID** item is not required for what we are doing right now. It is primarily used for doing BAM relationships which are out of the scope of this book.) For now, we will map the following four items (all of them from the Receive Port):

    ◦ CustomerID (taken from the message)
    ◦ OrderID (taken from the message)
    ◦ OrderTotal (taken from the message)
    ◦ ReceiveTime (taken from the Receive port)

We will not map the SendTime milestone for now. The first step will be to map the three items that are taken from the message.

1. Click on **Select Event Source**, and select **Select Messaging Payload**.

2. A list of all deployed BizTalk assemblies that contain Schemas and Pipelines is now shown. Find the assembly previously deployed with the Order Schema, and click on **Next**.

3. Now a list of Schemas inside the assembly is shown. In this case, there should be only one Schema; select the Schema and click on **OK**.

4. The Tracking Profile Editor should now look somewhat similar to the following screenshot:

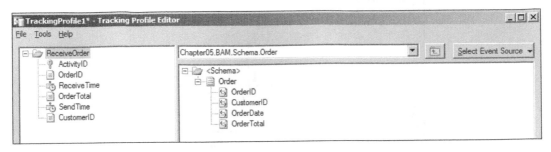

5. Now the three items **OrderID**, **OrderTotal** and **CustomerID**, need to be mapped to the correct elements in the Schema. Do the following for all three items:

    ○ Drag **OrderID** from the right-hand side (the Schema) to **OrderID** on the left-hand side (the Activity).

    ○ Right-click on **OrderID** in the Activity, and select **Set Port Mappings**, as shown in the following screenshot:

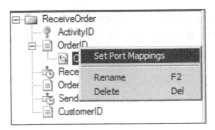

○ In the **Select Ports** window, find the Receive Port created earlier and add it to the right-hand side, as shown in the following screenshot:

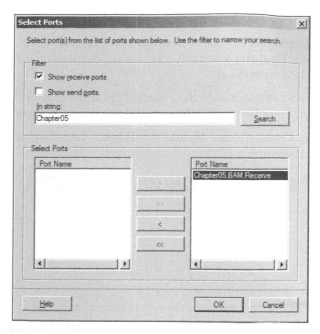

○ Click on **OK**. Do the same for **OrderTotal** and **CustomerID**.

6. Now we need to map **ReceiveTime** from the Port. This information is not found in the Order Schema, but on the messaging properties in BizTalk.

7. Click on **Select Event Source**, and select **Select Messaging Property**.

8. Expand **MessageProperties**, and drag **PortStartTime** to **ReceiveTime** on the Activity.

9. Map the port like we did with **OrderID**, and so on. The Tracking Profile should now look similar to the following screenshot; check whether all four mappings have the Receive Port mapped:

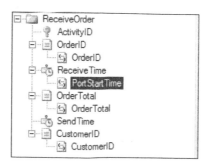

10. Save the Tracking Profile in the same folder that the Activity was exported to from Excel; name it `ReceiveOrder_Tracking_v10.btt`.

11. Go to the command line, and execute the following statement in the folder that the `.btt` file was saved to:

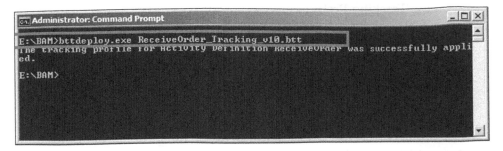

12. We are now ready to test the solution. Before sending messages through our BizTalk application, verify that all Activity tables are empty, by opening the SQL Server Management Studio, and select the following in the BAMPrimaryImport database:

```
select * from
dbo.bam_ReceiveOrder_AllInstances
```

13. The `select` statement should return zero rows. Before starting this test, please ensure that at least one Host Instance of a Host with **Allow Host Tracking** enabled is running, since a Tracking Host Instance is required to move data to the tracking tables.

14. Submit a message through the Receive Port, and verify that the flow is completed as expected. Run the select again, and verify that we now have one row in our Activity table. Now we need to map the last item in our Activity: SendTime. Start by undeploying the Tracking Profile, so that we can edit it and redeploy it. When undeploying a Tracking Profile in a production environment, all Receive Locations running in the affected applications should be disabled, so that no data is lost.

15. Undeploy the Tracking Profile by typing the following in the Command Prompt:

16. Now that the Tracking Profile is undeployed, we can change all we want in the existing profile. If we wanted to keep the profile alive while we were editing it, we could save the edited profile as v20, and then when ready to deploy, we could remove v10 and deploy v20 afterwards.

17. Open the **Tracking Profile Editor** again, and open the tracking file (.btt).

18. Open the **Messaging Properties**, and drag **PortEndTime** to **SendTime**, on the Activity.

19. Map **PortEndTime** to the Send Port of our application.

20. Save the profile, and deploy it using bttdeploy.

Now test the solution again by submitting another message through the solution. Note that this time two entries were made, one when the message went through the Receive Port, which also holds the data from the actual message, and also an entry from the Send Port, which only holds SendTime and some internal data.

This is not what we wanted. The purpose of the Activity was to create one row every time an order entered our system, and have some data written from the Receive Port and other data from the Send Port.

The reason this is happening is because the Receive and the Send Port are different instances inside BizTalk, and BAM will see a new instance as a new row, unless we tell it otherwise. What we need to do is to set up a Continuation.

Creating Continuations

What we will do now is tell BAM that the two instances (Receive and Send Port) should be considered as one Activity entry, by using OrderID for correlating between the two instances, as follows:

1. Undeploy the Tracking Profile created earlier.

2. Clear the Activity table by executing the following SQL statement in the **BAMPrimaryImport** database:

   ```
   delete from dbo.bam_ReceiveOrder_Completed
   ```

3. Open the Tracking Profile Editor.

4. Right-click on the **ReceiveOrder** folder in the top-left, and add a new **Continuation** and a new **ContinuationID**.

5. Rename both, and give them exactly the same name as shown in the following screenshot:

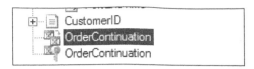

6. On the right-hand side, select Order Schema, if not already chosen. Select the **OrderID** element.

7. Right-click on the Continuation, and select **Associate Selected Data**. The **OrderID** should now appear as a child.

8. Do the same for the **ContinuationID**, as shown in the following screenshot:

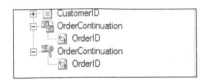

9. Map the **Continuation** (icon with no key) to the Receive Port.

10. Map the **ContinuationID** (icon with key) to the Send Port.

11. Deploy the Tracking Profile.

When testing the solution now, we should get a result with only one row being written to the Activity table with all five items populated.

We can also check the view created earlier to see the duration (TimeInBizTalk).

Run the following `select` statement in the **BAMPrimaryImport** database:

```
select * from dbo.bam_vwReceiveOrder_ViewReceiveOrder_View
```

There should now be a new column **TimeInBizTalk**, which should hold a very small number in seconds.

BAM Portal

Once the data starts being populated in the Activity tables, the BAM Portal can be used to track the data and view aggregations.

The BAM Portal ships with the BizTalk installation, and when set up correctly, should be accessible from a web browser by typing the following URL:

```
http://BizTalkServerName/BAM/default.aspx
```

The URL may vary, since the default website could be configured to a port other than 80.

In the portal, only created views (with or without aggregations) will be shown. The BAM Activities are not intended to have their data utilized directly, but only through the views created in Excel.

The main reason for creating and using views is so that people from different business backgrounds can view the data relevant to them and also be given aliases for item names and so on.

It is also possible to restrict the view of views to certain windows groups and so on, which we shall look at later in this chapter.

When opening the portal, the user should be presented with a list of the views that the user currently has access to.

The views are located on the left-hand side, under **My Views**, as shown in the following screenshot:

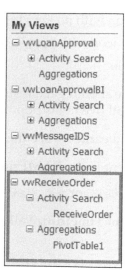

We should now be able to see the view called **vwReceiveOrder** with one aggregation called **PivotTable1**.

Submit a couple of documents into BizTalk, try to use different CustomerIDs, and change the total amount, so that data will be more realistic to analyze. Make sure to submit different OrderIDs each time, and remember at least one of the OrderIDs submitted.

Searching for an order

We will now use the Portal to search for a specific order:

1. In the BAM portal under **vwReceiveOrder**, click on **Activity Search | ReceiveOrder**.

2. Select all columns and add them to **Items to show**.

3. Enter a valid orderID in the **Value** section.

4. Click on **Execute Query**; the order should now appear at the bottom of the page as shown in the following screenshot:

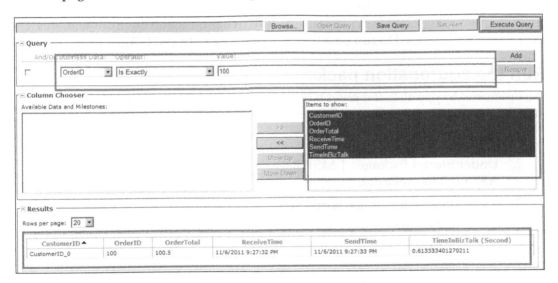

When using the Activity search, activities from both _Active and _Completed tables are searched.

Populating the aggregation

Click on the **PivotTable1** link under **My views**, and click on **OK** on the warning. We are now presented with a Pivot Table View, but with no data in it. Click on the red exclamation mark (refresh) to confirm this, as shown in the following screenshot:

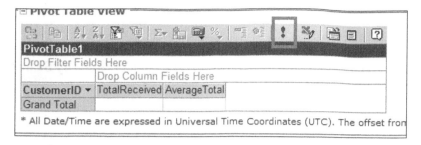

The reason that the aggregation is empty is because real-time aggregation was not selected while creating it inside Excel. To populate the aggregation, a view package created under Integration Services must be run (in a production environment, this job should be scheduled to run on a frequent basis using the SQL Agent).

Run the aggregation package

We now need to populate the pivot table by running the aggregation package located in SQL Server Integration Services, as follows:

1. Open Integration Services.
2. Under **Stored Packages | MSDB**, there should be a package named **BAM_AN_vwReceiveOrder**.
3. Right-click on the package, and select **Run Package**.
4. Click on **Execute**.
5. Click on **Close** when the button is enabled.
6. Go back to the BAM Portal, view the aggregation again, and refresh.
7. Data should now appear in the pivot table.

With population aggregations, only data from the _Completed tables is used.

Creating view permissions

We will now look at how to set up permissions for viewing the BAM views.

Roles and permissions

The various views created can be limited for certain departments in the company. We can control the level of access per view by granting certain users or groups access to the views.

This is again done by using the bm.exe tool.

To grant the local windows group named **ALASKA\BAMViewviewers** access to the view named **vwReceiveOrder**, type the following in a command prompt:

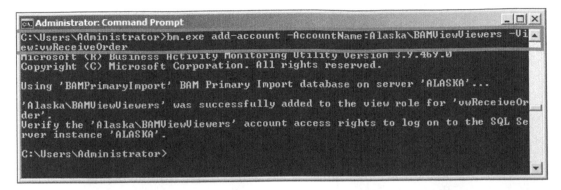

Test your knowledge

1. You have two customers, Customer1 and Customer2, who both receive EDI invoices. Both of them have agreed to receive invoices in a format decided by your company, so the same Map can be applied to each of their Send Ports. They do, however, have different requirements concerning the structure and envelope of the documents. What should you do?

   a. Make a new Schema and a new Map for Customer2. Deploy the Schema and Map, and use it on the Customer2 Send Port.

   b. Set up Agreements for Customer1 and Customer2 under BizTalk Parties, and link the Agreements to each Send Port.

   c. Create a Pipeline component that can change the structure of the messages on the fly, and deploy it in a Pipeline before the EdiAssembler has executed.

   d. Set up a Send Port Group, and add both Send Ports to the Group.

2. You have deployed a policy in the Business Rule Composer that is being used by several BizTalk applications. You now need to change the policy, and use some different values and boundaries. What should you do?

   a. In the BRE Composer, undeploy, then unpublish the policy, change it to the new values and boundaries, and republish and redeploy it.

   b. Make a new version of the policy, and publish it.

   c. Make a new version of the policy, and deploy it.

   d. Make a new version of the policy, and publish it. Change all Orchestrations that call the policy to use the new version.

3. You need to create a BAM Activity for receiving invoices. The Business Managers have given you a list of required fields from the invoice messages they would like to extract. How should you create the Activity?

   a. In Excel, use the BAM Add-in to create an Activity file. Deploy the Activity by using the `bm.exe` command line tool.

   b. In Excel, use the BAM Add-in to create an Activity file. Deploy the Activity by using the `bttdeploy.exe` command line tool.

   c. In the Tracking Profile Editor, select an Activity and deploy it, using the `bttdeploy.exe` command line tool.

   d. In the Tracking Profile Editor, select an Activity and deploy it, using the `bm.exe` command line tool.

4. You have created and deployed a BAM Activity, but no data is being sent to it when messages run through BizTalk. What should you do?

   a. In Excel, use the BAM Add-in to create a new Activity and deploy it using the `bm.exe` command line tool.

   b. In the Tracking Profile Editor, link the Activity to the events and messages in BizTalk, and deploy the profile by using the `bm.exe` command line tool.

   c. In Excel, use the BAM Add-in to create a new Activity and deploy it using the `bttdeploy.exe` command line tool.

   d. In the Tracking Profile Editor, link the Activity to the events and messages in BizTalk, and deploy the profile by using the `bttdeploy.exe` command line tool.

5. One of your customers is sending X12 EDI documents. You want BizTalk to process the documents. How should you approach this?

    a. Use the EDISend Pipeline, EDI Schemas, and the Party setup.

    b. Create a Flat File Schema for processing the X12 documents. Create a Flat File Pipeline, and deploy both.

    c. Use the EDIReceive Pipeline, EDI Schemas, and the Party setup.

    d. Create a Custom X12 Assembler Pipeline component.

Summary

This chapter has dealt with some of the extended capabilities of BizTalk, looking at Business Activity Monitoring (BAM), Business Rules Engine (BRE), Microsoft BizTalk Server RFID, and the EDI capabilities in BizTalk Server. This chapter should prepare the reader for the questions that might be asked regarding these topics.

Certification Test-taking— Tips and Tricks

9

In addition to providing content that educates you, the reader, on important technical information, concepts and techniques, we want to provide you with a better understanding of what the process of taking a certification is like, starting with preparation, what to expect through the actual exam itself, and the follow-up once done. Due to this, while the other chapters of the book are to the point and technical, this chapter is less so. The following areas are discussed:

- Exam preparation
- At the test center
- Exam structure
- Time management
- Answering questions

Exam preparation

We all learn in different ways. The preparation that works best for one of us does not necessarily work for someone else. You need to find the way that you learn the best, and learn the way you learn. At the same time, it is a proven fact that, while we are different, we all learn best when we get information through more than one channel and more than one experience. Reading, hearing, seeing, trying, perhaps even showing or teaching, all adds to your understanding of a topic. There is simply nothing that measures up to the experience built up by different kinds of exposure over time, but being prepared and knowing what will happen and being aware of the process as well as the technology might just be the thing that tips the scale in your favor.

Preparation sources

The following are examples of different kinds of material you can use to prepare:

- Literature
- Classes
- Webcasts
- Labs
- Training kits
- Sample code
- Practice tests
- Colleagues and peers
- Forums, blogs, and other online sources

We will go through these and try to highlight what and when each of these is good to use.

Literature

If reading is your thing, read this book from cover to cover. Being written specifically to help you pass the certification, it covers the topics needed to get you up-to-date on the certification objectives. However, it is not written for the BizTalk beginner. Should you crave for more basic and introductory content, as well as simply more, there are a lot of good BizTalk books out there.

You can of course also read the BizTalk documentation, although it is not meant to be read cover to cover as a book. It serves as a good reference, but is little like a book. You can turn to the documentation, once you have closely narrowed down the topics on which you lack knowledge or need improvement.

For most of us, having read something does not lend expertise, but it does help to strengthen the knowledge that is already there, store new knowledge to be recollected, and tickle the senses at the right time.

Classes

Although Microsoft has not released a Microsoft Official Curriculum (MOC) course for BizTalk Server since BizTalk was in its 2006 version, there are many training providers that have kept up-to-date with BizTalk Server versions. You should be able to find at least one training provider in your area that has training for BizTalk Server 2010. If you cannot, then there are BizTalk Server 2010 trainings available online from companies such as Pluralsight and Quicklearn.

Classes will give you different kinds of exposure to BizTalk. You will hear the trainer talk about it, you will see him demonstrate it, and you will get a chance to try it on your own, under controlled and well-prepared circumstances during labs. You will probably not get as effective and well-rounded training elsewhere as the hours spent in class while doing it on your own.

Classes tend to be most effective for beginners or less-experienced BizTalk developers. Experienced developers will most likely find classes to contain things they already know well, mixed with new and previously forgotten knowledge. For experienced developers, other sources to prepare for certification are often more effective.

Webcasts

Webcasts often have a shorter format and are made to cover a specific topic. Some webcasts are very general in nature and do not provide much value as certification preparation, but there are also webcasts that are made specifically to cover a part of BizTalk in more detail. Those webcasts are great, if they cover an area you need improvement in. Many BizTalk developers are not closely accustomed to all parts of BizTalk; most often, the extended capabilities such as Business Activity Monitoring, the Business Rules Engine, EDI, and RFID, are areas where there are gaps in exposure. For those specific areas, getting up-to-date with a targeted webcast is very useful. The places that contain or link to BizTalk Server webcasts and videos include:

- BizTalk Server Developer Center webcasts: `http://msdn.microsoft.com/en-us/biztalk/aa937645`
- BizTalk Server Developer Center videos: `http://msdn.microsoft.com/en-us/biztalk/dd849956.aspx`
- Cloudcasts BizTalk community webcasts: `http://www.cloudcasts.net/Default.aspx?category=BizTalk`
- Cloudcasts BizTalk community webcasts, the Light and Easy series: `http://www.cloudcasts.net/Default.aspx?category=BizTalk+Light+and+Easy`
- Cloudcasts BizTalk community webcasts, ESB Toolkit: `http://www.cloudcasts.net/Default.aspx?category=BizTalk+ESB+Toolkit`
- BizTalk247 BizTalk Server webcasts: `http://www.biztalk247.com/webcasts.aspx`
- BizTalk247 BizTalk Server videos: `http://www.biztalk247.com/videos.aspx`

Although many new features have been added and much improvement has been made, much of the BizTalk Server still remains relatively unchanged since BizTalk Server 2004. This means that any content that covers earlier versions of BizTalk may very well still be valid. However, some specifics such as EDI have changed dramatically, so be alert when viewing webcasts made for previous versions.

The ESB Toolkit is not one of the objectives for the exam.

Labs

Labs or hands-on training exercises are great ways to acquire new knowledge by doing it yourself. There are many different ways you can get this: classes, online training, or downloadable material.

If you are not attending a class and do not have an environment setup where you can experiment, then one option is to run BizTalk Server Virtual Labs (http://www.microsoft.com/biztalk/en/us/virtual-labs.aspx). These are preconfigured, online-hosted virtual machines for you to do labs on.

Training kits

If you have a machine and want more time to play around with the topics than you are given in the virtual lab, and if you want to be able to come back to the content more than once and not lose your progress, you might be better off downloading and installing one of the available training kits. Most of these do not come as a bunch of word documents alone, but include a complete virtual machine for you to use. Some of them are as follows:

- What's new in BizTalk Server 2010 Training Kit: http://www.microsoft.com/download/en/details.aspx?id=17956

- BizTalk Server 2010 VHD (with the What's new in BizTalk Server 2010 Training Kit preinstalled): http://www.microsoft.com/download/en/details.aspx?id=13624

- BizTalk Server 2010 Developer Training Kit (including VHD): http://www.microsoft.com/download/en/details.aspx?id=14865

- BizTalk Server 2010 Administrator Training Kit (including VHD): http://www.microsoft.com/download/en/details.aspx?id=27148

- BizTalk Server 2010 ESB Training Kit (including. VHD):
  `http://www.microsoft.com/download/en/details.aspx?id=27151`

 The ESB Toolkit is not one of the objectives for the exam.

You could also download the required software and build a virtual machine yourself. You will gain additional insight into the BizTalk Server by going through the installation and configuration required. If you have access to the Microsoft Developer Network (MSDN) or TechNet, then you can download and install a full, non-expiring version of the software. If you don't have any of these subscriptions, you can still download trial versions that usually have a limited amount of time that you are allowed to use them for.

 The BizTalk Server 2010 Developer Edition itself is free, but its pre-requisites are not.

Sample code

If you don't want a full training kit but just want to get your hands on code that shows some specific feature, there are a lot of samples available for download:

- BizTalk Server SDK samples (also available in your BizTalk install folder):
  `http://msdn.microsoft.com/en-us/library/aa560186.aspx`

- BizTalk Server code samples: `http://msdn.microsoft.com/en-us/biztalk/aa937647`

- BizTalk Server 2010 Adapter Pack samples: `http://msdn.microsoft.com/en-us/biztalk/gg491395`

 The BizTalk Server 2010 Adapter Pack is not one of the objectives for the exam.

Blogs are also a great resource for samples, but there are too many of them to point out, and since the content varies greatly in quality and is not something that has been verified as part of the process of this book, no links will be added to point to blogs.

Besides sample code that is limited to showing specific features, there are also tutorials and scenarios that show complete architectures, as follows:

- BizTalk Server Tutorials: `http://msdn.microsoft.com/en-us/library/aa560270.aspx`

- BizTalk Server Scenarios for Business Solutions: `http://msdn.microsoft.com/en-us/library/aa561965.aspx`

Again, there are more places than this. A simple search on any search engine using words such as "BizTalk Server Tutorials" will turn up a number of hits.

Practice tests

Practice tests are useful as they make you comfortable with the functionality and working of the test engine. Recommended practice test providers are those that have a good spread of questions that are not copies of the exam itself, but cover similar topics. They also have explanations of which answers are correct and which are incorrect, and why, similar to the *Test your knowledge* section in this book. At the time of writing this book, no practice tests are currently available for the BizTalk Server 2010 Exam. However, there are practice tests available for previous versions of BizTalk and the exams that cover those versions, for example, the BizTalk Server 2006 Exam. Those tests will serve the purpose of making you comfortable with the format to a large extent, and at the same time the content they cover is mostly viable for BizTalk Server 2010 as well. They will, however, not cover all the topics.

This book is also a very good source of practice with the type and style of the questions, although you will not get them framed in a test engine similar to the live one.

Colleagues and peers

If you know someone who is experienced in BizTalk, take the opportunity to pick their brain on the topics that you feel hesitant about. Even if they have taken the exam themselves, they would not be able to give you direct insight into the questions or the topics covered, since they will have committed themselves to an NDA when taking the exam. However, they will be able to give you general directions and help.

Forums, blogs and other online sources

BizTalk Server, in its current core architecture, has been around for many years and has a large user base. As such, there is a large community out there that writes articles and blogs, and staffs many forums. You are almost guaranteed to find someone out there who has had the same or similar problem or questions. One place that allows the community to contribute to the documentation provided by Microsoft is the TechNet Wiki; the page at `http://social.technet.microsoft.com/wiki/contents/articles/2240.biztalk-server-resources-on-the-technet-wiki.aspx` summarizes the articles that focus on BizTalk Server.

If you do not find what you are looking for, there are places you can ask your questions and get them answered, for example, the MSDN BizTalk Server forums: `http://social.msdn.microsoft.com/Forums/en-US/category/biztalkserver`.

Getting familiar with the certification objectives

One of the main things about studying for the exam is ofcourse to know what the exam covers. If the exam is your objective, do not overstudy. Learning is fun, and the risk of learning too much is virtually non-existent. However, the possibility that you will end up learning more than you need to pass the exam is equally large. Often, if you study towards a goal, you can be more focused, get a learning path, and be more selective in what you need to learn right now. You should study the exam objectives that you find here: `http://www.microsoft.com/learning/en/us/exam.aspx?ID=70-595#tab2`.

Study time

Set aside time to study. Many of us are lucky enough to be able to work and study at once, since what we do all day is architecting, developing, or administrating BizTalk Server solutions. Usually though, even in those situations, our daily routines and what we do does not touch each and every part of BizTalk Server. Since feeling confident about ourselves when taking the exam helps, even though it might not be altogether necessary to get a passing score, try to find time to at least briefly look at the topics that you are not that familiar with, to build that confidence.

Depending on the way that you study best, here are a few suggestions on how you can sneak that study time into your daily routines:

- **Commute**: If reading is your choice, then the time that you are commuting—using public transportation (not while driving!)—is prime time. Many of us can easily find an hour or more each day, in which we would not be doing much anyway. Some, even more.

- **As part of your work role**: If you can find time at work, then you will easily get many hours of study done daily during paid work time. Perhaps you can enforce concepts or incorporate techniques from this book or ideas brought forward in the exam objectives as part of your solutions. Hands-on is a good way to learn!

- **Expanding your horizons at work**: If it does not fit your daily routine, then perhaps by volunteering to take part of an EDI prestudy, or a PoC, on how to allow business users to best interact with your BizTalk Server solutions by defining rules in the Business Rules Composer, or how you should configure your solution using the new settings dashboard to best handle your combination of integrations. This combines research with hands-on learning!

- **Before or after work**: Take the first 20 minutes when you get to work to look at something new, or re-enforce a lesser-known topic. Getting to work 20 minutes early can usually be worked into a new routine, and if you are there 20 minutes before the others, it is also usually a very quiet and focused time of the day.

- **At home**: Instead of channel zapping or viewing that useless TV show that neither educates nor enriches you, do a lab!

- **Before bed**: Although you should not do this if you are tired, if you spend the last 30 minutes before going to bed with BizTalk topics, then not only will you be able to wind down, you will also think BizTalk when you go to sleep.

As you learn how you can best fit time to study into your schedule and your routines, set goals. Decide what you need to learn before going to take the exam, and plan that across the days leading up to the exam. Leave enough room in the schedule to make sure you have time for everything that you feel you need to. Better to look at some things twice rather than finding that the day of the exam is upon you and that you have not had time to finish your studies. Remember, build confidence.

Incentives

Many of us work better with a good incentive—find yours. It could be anything. Here are a few common ones:

Knowledge

- To know more
- To become a better (more knowledgeable) developer or architect or consultant or employee

Money

- To earn more—to be able to bill more or get a better salary
- An employer-supplied gratification or gift

Opportunities

- To get a new job, a more fun job, or more challenging work
- To be more sought after and have more choices
- To get new opportunities or new roles

If you cannot find a goal, or one does not really fit your situation, give yourself an incentive, perhaps something along the lines of "When I pass the exam, I will…

- …go out to a really nice dinner at restaurant X."
- …go to see X play the Y at the Z."
- …go to the city of AABC over the weekend."
- …visit that spa I pass when I drive to work for a new treatment."

Vouchers and offers

Take advantage of offers and vouchers for test takers. Microsoft and Prometric (the exam provider) will often have valid offers for you to take advantage of, for example:

- Second chance free
- Discounted exam costs
- Two-for-one

Current offers are listed at `http://www.microsoft.com/learning/en/us/special-offers.aspx`.

There are also Microsoft Partner Network partner discounts; learn more at `https://partner.microsoft.com/40143914?msp_id=examoffers`.

Finally, you can also turn to your Microsoft Certified Trainer (MCT) and ask them for a voucher that will get you a discount on the certification.

Learn more

Microsoft maintains a Certification Preparation and Test Taking FAQ section at `http://www.microsoft.com/learning/en/us/certification/exam-prep.aspx`.

At the test center

Prometric is the current exam provider for Microsoft certifications, at the time of writing this book. Usually, your Certified Provider of Learning Solutions (CPLS) or Learning Partner will be a Prometric test center where you take the exam. You can usually contact either the test center or Prometric. The test center can add a handling fee on top of the certification fee, but on the other hand, will often be able to bill your company or employer directly, while you will have to supply a credit card when registering directly with Prometric.

On the day of the certification, these are the most important points that you should keep in mind when arriving at and taking the exam at the test center:

- Be on time. However, if you are not, most of the time this will not be an issue; you are still allowed to take the exam, should you arrive late.

- Bring photo ID. You will need to be able to prove who you are. You should bring two pieces of ID (though they need not be two pieces of photo ID).

- You will not be allowed to bring anything into the test room. No phones, no books, no notes.

- You will be supplied a scratch pad on which you can make notes on anything you want during the exam. This will have to be turned in once you are done.

- You will be monitored during the exam through video surveillance.

- The computer on which you do the exam has very limited functionality — you will only have access to the test itself, no internet, no help files, no development environment.

- You are allowed to take breaks.

Prometric maintains an FAQ section at `http://www.prometric.com/TestTakers/FAQs/default.htm`.

Exam structure

The exam itself has a simple structure that is divided into three parts.

Before the exam

Before starting the exam, you will go through a series of informational screens, including information on how much time you have, in all, to complete the exam and information on the Non-disclosure Agreement (NDA) that you must agree to, to be allowed to take the exam. This agreement prohibits you from discussing the content of the exam or the questions. Reviewing the agreement is not included in the time you have to complete the exam.

Questions

A Microsoft exam will have somewhere between 35 and 80 questions. The norm is 40 to 50, but part of the NDA is the exact number of questions for this particular exam, so this book will not disclose it.

A question screen of the exam will have the following general appearance:

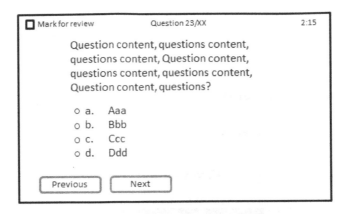

Questions are single- or multiple-choice questions.

You will always be able to keep track of the time you have left, and which question you are on, out of the total number of questions. You will also be able to mark the question for review and navigate between questions, either by going to the next or previous questions.

After the last question, you will come to a review screen where you will see which questions you have marked for review and will be able to return to them, or any other question you choose, in an easy manner.

After the exam

Whenever you decide you are done with answering and reviewing questions, you can choose to end the exam. At this point, you will get a chance to give comments on the certification material or any of the questions. You will also get your score immediately, once done, and learn whether you passed or not.

With it, you will get a report on how you did on the different areas. You will get it printed and can take it home regardless, whether you passed or failed. This will help you understand which areas you were strong in and which need development. If you passed, you passed; there is no coming back to take the exam again to improve your score. But, if you did not pass, take careful note of this report. The certification report will generally look something like this:

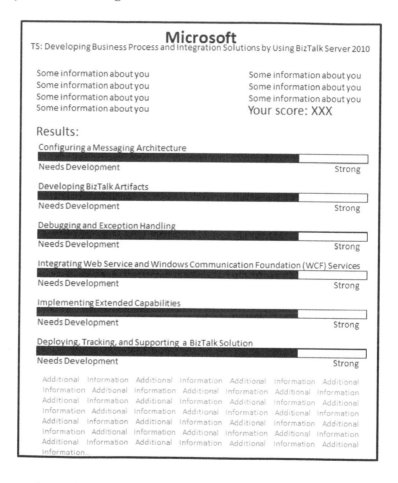

Once done, you leave the exam room and need to hand in the scratch pad and sign out.

Time management

For most certification test takers, time never becomes an issue. The total time is around three hours. However, if the exam is not available in your native language, you will get additional time added to your exam time to compensate for that fact.

Even so, managing your time during the certification can help you reduce the feeling that time is running away from you.

Do not spend too much time on any one question. If you feel you cannot answer a question after reading the questions and the suggested answers, mark it for review. Do not overthink it. Do not turn it every other way, and do not feel bad. Very few will ace them all.

For example, say that we have 50 questions and three hours. That means an average of 3.6 minutes per question. You will, without a doubt, find some questions easy. Those will be answered quickly, leaving time for the ones where you need to think more.

Do not spend too little time on any question. Do not speed through. Be thorough. There will be no bonus points given out if you complete in record time.

Take advantage of the fact that you are allowed to take breaks. If you feel your concentration is failing you or you are feeling tired, take a break. Many test centers provide free drinks and snacks.

 Interviewing experienced BizTalk developers that have taken the exam shows that they typically need between about 45 and 90 minutes.

However, you should not benchmark yourself against others.

If your colleague who has taken the exam did it in 60 minutes and you are in your 70th minute and are only on question 32, do not worry. You will probably score better than they did.

If the other eight people who were in the room doing exams at the same time as you are all done and have left and you are in your 140th minute and on question 40, do not worry. They are probably not even taking the same exam that you are.

Answering questions

There are a few cardinal rules to answering exam questions. The foremost one is *answer the question*. You will get no reduction in score for incorrect answers, but you will absolutely get no points if you do not answer. Always answer.

Besides that, consider these points as you address questions:

- Always make sure you have read the question thoroughly
- Do not assume that you know the question before you have read it all through
- Do not assume you know the answer before you have read the question
- Make sure that you have read and understood all requirements
- There is no trickery
- There are no hidden requirements
- Only take into account what is stated
- Take into account all that is stated
- Do not read other things into the question than stated
- Do not make assumptions about circumstances not stated
- Do not try to put your own requirements or preferences into the question

There is also a set of rules that applies to the answers in the exam that is good to keep in mind:

- Only one answer is correct
- Only one answer can solve all the requirements
- No second answer can fulfill the requirements or solve the problem even if it presents a really silly and stupid way to do it
- You will not be asked what the quickest or most direct answer is (since only one answer is allowed to solve the problem)
- You will not be asked which answer is the best answer (since only one answer is allowed to solve the problem)
- All answers are real and possible to perform
- No answer is impossible or illegal
- No answer may present a series of steps, properties, settings, concepts, or otherwise, that cannot be found or done in BizTalk Server
- No answer may present an illegal combination or faulty context (goes back to "no answer is impossible or illegal")

Keeping in mind time management, if you feel that after having read the question as stated and looking at the answers, that you do not know the answer, mark the question for review and move on.

If, on the other hand, you think that two answers are equally possible, read the question and review the answers again, perhaps there is a requirement in an aspect of the answer that you missed. If you still feel that two questions are equally plausible, choose the one that makes the most sense, based on what you know of BizTalk Server best practices, technology, and services.

Not all questions have the same style. A team of experts have been involved in making sure that the questions cover topics that are important and have the right combination of answers. However, they are written by different people, and different people have slightly different styles. So there are some guidelines that apply to most questions.

Most questions will have four alternative answers. Out of those four, two can often be discounted without deep knowledge and using common sense, for example:

1. Mooremountain Motors is a big dealership that offers many different kinds of brands. As a result, they are receiving invoices from many different car manufacturers. Jill, a developer at Mooremountain Motors, has developed an Orchestration that handles a canonical version of an invoice. She has also developed Maps from each of the manufacturers' Invoice Schemas to the Canonical Schema. What must she do to ensure that the Orchestration receives the canonical message and not the manufacturers' formats?:

    a. In the Orchestration, after the initiating Receive shape, configure a Transform shape with the Maps.

    b. Create a Send Port Group and a Send Port for each of the manufacturers. Configure the Send Ports with the Maps.

    c. Create a Receive Port and Receive Location. Configure the Receive Port with the Maps.

    d. Configure a Receive Port and Receive Location. Configure the Receive Pipeline to be the XML Receive Pipeline and set the `Validate document` structure property to `true`.

In the preceding question, based on very basic knowledge about how the BizTalk Server works, you will be able to rule out configuring Send Port Group and Send Ports, since the requirement is that the Orchestration should get the canonical formatted invoices. Also, for that same reason, the transformation cannot occur in the Orchestration, since that is too late. The two remaining options both talk about the receive side. Configuring a Pipeline and the `Xml Disassemblers Validate document structure` property has very little to do with canonical formats and transformations. So, you can rule that out. Finally then, you are down to receiving and Maps, which is the only option that fits.

However, sometimes it might not be that easy, and sometimes you might not have the knowledge necessary to decide which of the last two is correct. When you are down to two options, it is a matter of knowing or having had enough exposure to BizTalk to have a feeling or hunch about the correct answer.

Knowing which answers are incorrect is often as useful in these situations as knowing which is correct.

You can also find help in unexpected places. One question can contain the answer to a previous question.

2. HWLC Motors is receiving XML documents in a Receive Port. The Port is configured with a Map to transform the incoming documents to a canonical format before triggering the correct Orchestration, based on the content of the document. Once in a while, a document arrives that cannot be routed to a subscribing Orchestration. Roger, an administrator, is tasked to set up a Send Port that outputs the incoming documents from this port in their original format. If that happens, what must he do?:

    a. Enable Failed Message Routing on the Receive Port. Create a second Receive Port to receive the failed messages.

    b. Enable Failed Message Routing on the Receive Port. Create a Send Port to receive the failed messages.

    c. Enable Failed Message Routing on the Receive Port. Create a Send Port to receive the failed messages, and configure it to Map from the canonical format to the original format.

    d. Create a Send Port to subscribe to all messages, so that a subscriber can always be found to get rid of the routing errors.

Now, obviously, if you read this question once you have read the previous one, had you been ever so slightly hesitant on whether having Maps on the Receive Port was the correct choice, you will now know and can return to the previous question and easily supply the correct answer.

Test makers do their best to avoid this from happening, but subtle references can still be found, and even though they might not always contain the answer, they might jog your memory enough to make a difference.

Once you are done, you will reach the review screen and can make a pass over the questions again, perhaps even all questions, and not just the questions marked for review. This can help finding cross-references between questions that will help you solve those final questions.

10
Sample Certification Test Questions

This chapter holds additional sample exam questions. They are categorized to align to their exam skill area. This allows you to measure your skill in the areas most relevant to you so that you can pinpoint where you need improvement.

Answers to the questions in this chapter are made available in *Appendix B, Sample Certification Test Questions – Answers*.

Configuring a Messaging Architecture

1. You have two Send Ports that both wish to subscribe to all Order messages from the ERP system. What should you do?

    a. Create two Receive Locations in one Receive Port; make both Receive Locations receive orders from the ERP system. Create one Send Port, make the Send Port subscribe to all orders.

    b. Create two Receive Ports with one Receive Location in each; make both Receive Locations receive orders from the ERP system. Create one Send Port, make the Send Port subscribe to all orders.

    c. Create one Send Port. Configure transport options for one of the destinations and backup transport for the other destination. Set the filter to `BTS.MessageType == Order`.

    d. Create one Receive Port with one Receive Location in it; make the location receive orders from the ERP system. Create a Send Port Group. Make the Group subscribe to orders. Create two Send Ports and add the Send Ports to the Group.

2. You need to send invoices to a partner using the FTP Adapter. The partner has requested a special XML format that differs in structure from the canonical invoice format that you use in your Application. What should you do (choose all that apply)?

   a. Use the PassThruReceive Pipeline on the Receive Port

   b. Use the PassThruTransmit Pipeline on the Send Port

   c. Create a Map from the partner format to the Canonical invoice

   d. Create a Map from the Canonical invoice format to the desired partner format

   e. Apply a Map on the Send Port

3. HWLC Motors uses two BizTalk Servers, but only one Host (HostA) and one Host Instance per Server. High availability is a requirement, and this is the reason that two BizTalk Servers were set up. We want to ensure that FTP Receive only happens on one of the servers. What should you do (choose all that apply)?

   a. Turn off the Host Instance for HostA on one of the servers

   b. Create a new Host (HostB)

   c. Cluster HostB

   d. Create a Receive Handler for the FTP Adapter for HostB, and delete the Receive Handler for HostA

   e. Make all Receive Locations using the FTP Handler run under HostB

4. You have several Pipelines; both Receive and Send, deployed in a BizTalk Application **Common**. The Pipelines will be needed in several Applications. You create a new Application **ApplicationA** and start to create Receive Ports and Receive Locations. When choosing a Pipeline for your Receive Location, you notice that the Pipelines deployed in the **Common** Application, do not appear in the drop-down list of available Receive Pipelines. What should you do?

   a. Make a reference in **ApplicationA** to the default BizTalk Application

   b. Redeploy all the Pipelines in the **ApplicationA** Application

   c. Make a reference in **ApplicationA** to the **Common** Application

   d. Make a reference in **Common** to **ApplicationA**

5. You want to make sure that all Receive Locations in the entire BizTalk Group are disabled. What should you do?

   a. Stop all running Host Instances.

   b. In the BizTalk Administration Console, open the Group Hub and choose **New Query**. Query **Running Service Instances** and make sure that the query doesn't return any rows.

   c. In the BizTalk Administration Console, open the **Group Hub** and select **Applications**. Check that all Applications are in a stopped state.

   d. In the BizTalk Administration Console, choose the **All Artifacts Application** and open **Receive Locations**. Check that all locations are disabled.

Developing BizTalk Artifacts

1. HWLC Motors is receiving shipment content details from their suppliers. They receive many each day. They need to manually audit some of them. You need to make sure that they can separate out all shipments that have a TotalSum of $1 million or more. You set up a Send Port to receive shipments. What must you do before you can subscribe to orders equal to or greater than a TotalSum of $1 million?

   a. Make the TotalSum a distinguished field

   b. Promote the TotalSum field

   c. On the root node of the Schema, configure Body XPath to point to the TotalSum field

   d. On the file properties of the Schema, set the **Default Property Schema Name** value to **GreaterThanOrEqualTo**

2. As part of the integration with a major investment bank, HWLC Motors needs to exchange data with an old legacy system. Unfortunately the system creates incorrect XML that would cause disassemble and validation exceptions. A component has been developed to correct the XML on arrival to mitigate errors in later processing. In what Pipeline stage must the component be placed?

   a. The Pre-assemble stage

   b. The Assemble stage

   c. The Disassemble stage

   d. The Decode stage

3. Mooremountain Motors is a big dealership that offers different kinds of brands. As a result they are receiving invoices from many different car manufacturers. Jill, a developer at Mooremountain Motors, has developed an Orchestration that handles a Canonical version of an invoice. She has also developed Maps from each of the manufacturers' invoice Schemas to the Canonical Schema. What must she do to ensure that the Orchestration receives the Canonical message?

    a. Create a Receive Port and Receive Location. Configure the Receive Port with Maps that transform from the Canonical format to the manufacturer formats.

    b. Create a Send Port for each of the manufacturers. Configure the Send Ports with Maps that transforms from the Canonical format to each of the manufacturer formats.

    c. Create a Receive Port and Receive Location. Configure the Receive Port with Maps that transform from the manufacturer formats to the Canonical formats.

    d. Configure a Receive Port and receive location. Configure the receive Pipeline to be the XMLReceive Pipeline and set the **Validate document structure** property to **True**.

4. HWLC Motors is having problems with an Orchestration in production. The Orchestration has plenty of trace statements that can be turned on or off to output meaningful information that would help the troubleshooting process. The server processes must remain active at all times; Host Instances cannot be restarted. What would be a suitable location to store the state of the trace output flag?

    a. Create an external .NET component to store the value. Update the .NET component in the GAC to change the value when needed.

    b. Create a configuration value in BizTalk's configuration file to store the value. Update the value in the `config` file when needed.

    c. Create an Orchestration variable to hold the value. Re-deploy the Orchestration to change the value when needed.

    d. Create an SSO Application to hold the value. Update the value in the SSO application to change the value when needed.

5. Bo, a developer for HWLC Motors, is developing an integration that will exchange purchase order messages in an asynchronous request response pattern over MSMQ. The request is sent out on one queue and the response arrives at another queue. The OrderId is unique and included in both the request and response messages. Requirements dictate that the response must be handled by the same Orchestration that sent the request. What must you do in the Orchestration to enable this scenario?

   a. Create a Correlation Set. Configure the Send shape to initialize the Correlation Set and the Receive shape to follow the Correlation Set.

   b. Set **Ordered Delivery** to **True** on the Orchestrations Receive Port.

   c. Create a Correlation Set. Configure the Receive shape to initialize the Correlation Set and the Send shape to follow the Correlation Set.

   d. Place the Receive and Send shapes in a scope. Make sure that the scope's **Synchronized** property is set to **True**.

Debugging and exception handling

1. Elisa is an administrator for HWLC's BizTalk Server 2010 platform. She is receiving messages through the ReceiveNewCustomer Receive Port. She wants to route any message that fails processing to the SendFailureNotification Send Port that is configured to use SMTP to send the failed messages by mail to her. How must she configure the SendFailureNotification Send Port to receive failures that occurred on the ReceiveNewCustomer Receive Port?

   a. Enable Failed Message Routing for the ReceiveNewCustomer port. Configure the SendFailureNotification Send Port to have a filter on BTS.ReceivePortName = ReceiveNewCustomer.

   b. Enable Failed Message Routing for the SendFailureNotification port. Configure the SendFailureNotification port to filter on BTS. ReceivePortName = ReceiveNewCustomer.

   c. Enable Failed Message Routing for the SendFailureNotification port. Configure the SendFailureNotification Send Port to have a filter on ErrorReport.ReceivePortName = ReceiveNewCustomer.

   d. Enable Failed Message Routing for the ReceiveNewCustomer port. Configure the SendFailureNotification Send Port to have a filter on ErrorReport.ReceivePortName = ReceiveNewCustomer.

2. HWLC have nightly batch loads of customer information from a legacy system into a new RDMS system. The new system has very strict rules set up and do not allow null values for vital fields or strings in integer fields. The Schema used to receive data from the legacy system in BizTalk Server 2010 has implemented those rules. The legacy system has not implemented these rules and HWLC are experiencing that customers arrive with incorrect data. The customer batch is de-batched in the receive Pipelines XMLDisassembler component and entered into the new system one by one. HWLC wants all correctly formatted customers to be entered into the new system and wants only incorrectly formatted customers to be suspended, not the whole batch. What must be done to allow the correct messages to proceed?

   a. On the Receive Port from the legacy system, enable Ordered Delivery and make sure that Stop sending subsequent messages on current message failure is not enabled.

   b. On the Send Port to the RDMS system, enable Ordered Delivery and make sure that Stop sending subsequent messages on current message failure is not enabled.

   c. On the Receive Port from the legacy system, set `RecoverableInterchangeProcessing` to `True` on the XMLDisassembler component.

   d. On the Send Port to the RDMS system, set `ProcessingInstructionsOptions` to `1` on the XMLAssembler component.

3. Carly, a developer at HWLC, has been tasked with creating unit tests for a BizTalk Server 2010 solution. A senior developer has told her to use the `ValidateInstance` method to unit test Schemas. She instantiates the Schema class, but can find no such method. What must she do to be able to use the `ValidateInstance` method?

   a. Manually add references to Microsoft.BizTalk.TestTools and Microsoft.XLANGs.BaseTypes.

   b. Set the projects **Enable Unit Testing** option to **True**.

   c. Cast the Schema class to a `TestableSchemaBase` class.

   d. Configure the `Input Instance Filename` property of the Schema file to point to the instance to validate.

4. HWLC has implemented an Orchestration that processes sensor data. The sensor data is delivered once every second. The next message to arrive makes the previous message obsolete. Suspending the instance in case of failure is not meaningful. The requirement is that a warning needs to be logged to the EventLog and then the Orchestration should end without leaving any suspended instances. What must be done to the Orchestration to allow this behavior?

   a. Implement the Orchestration without using any scopes. Ensure that the **Report to Analyst** property of the Orchestration is set to **True**.

   b. Implement the Orchestration using a scope to encapsulate all logic. Ensure that the **Report to Analyst** property of the scope is set to **True**.

   c. Implement the Orchestration using a scope to encapsulate all logic. Add an exception block to catch the exception. Use the EventLog class to write to the eventlog. Use the Throw Exception shape to re-throw the exception and end the Orchestration.

   d. On the Receive Port where the sensor data message is first received by BizTalk, select **Enable routing** for failed messages.

5. HWLC has implemented a process that receives sensor data from an engine performance test bench system. The data is sent to a downstream service for further processing through a solicit-response port. On occasion the service is unavailable. The Orchestration has encapsulated all its logic inside a scope and has implemented an exception block to catch the exception and use a Terminate shape to end gracefully without suspending the Orchestration instance. When the Orchestration terminates, there are still suspended messages left on the Send Port. What must you do so there are no messages suspended on the port when errors occur?

   a. Enable Failed Message Routing on the Send port. Configure an Orchestration to filter on the ErrorReport.SendPortName property.

   b. Enable Failed Message Routing on the Send port. Configure an Orchestration to Filter on BTS.AckType = NACK and BTS.AckSendPortName.

   c. Configure an Orchestration to Filter on BTS.AckType = NACK and BTS.AckSendPortName.

   d. Configure the logical port in the Orchestration with Delivery Notification so that the Orchestration waits for the port processing to complete and throws a DeliveryFailureException if there are failures.

Deploying, tracking, and supporting a BizTalk solution

1. Nicki has just optimized HWLC's QA environment, by setting Messaging and Orchestration polling settings that will improve performance of the environment. She now needs to get these settings into a Production environment. What should she do?

    a. Request a database backup of the BizTalkMgmtDB and have it restored in the Production environment.

    b. Copy the `BTSNTSVC.exe.config` from the QA server and place it in the correct folder on the Production server.

    c. Launch the BizTalk settings dashboard and export settings from the QA environment. Import these settings into the Production environment using the BizTalk settings dashboard.

    d. Export the `SSOConfig` database from the QA environment and restore this database in Production.

2. HWLC has just built a two-node BizTalk farm. Juan, who is new to the company, is ready to deploy his first application. What steps must he take to ensure that his application can run on both BizTalk nodes?

    a. He must first create a Clustered Host Instance and then import his MSI package on both nodes.

    b. He must run the installation program of his application on the first node so his assemblies are installed in the GAC. On the second node he only needs to import his MSI package using the BizTalk Administration Console on the second node.

    c. He must run the installation program of his application on both nodes so his assemblies are installed in the GAC. He must then import his MSI package on either node.

    d. He must run the installation program of his application on the first node. He must then import his MSI package using the BizTalk Administration Console on the first node.

3. HWLC's Human Resources department has asked that no messages be sent to their Payroll system until 10 pm tonight due to system maintenance. At 10 pm, any outstanding messages need to be sent. Jose is planning on attending the big game tonight. What steps can Jose perform to solve this problem?

    a. Jose can stop the Send Port that is used to communicate with the Payroll system before he leaves work. When he arrives in the morning he can start the Send Port.

    b. In the Send Port, that is used to communicate with the Payroll system, Jose can enable a Service window that won't send any messages until 10 pm.

    c. Jose can do nothing and let BizTalk's retry mechanism take care of resubmitting any messages that need to be sent. The Send Port that is used to communicate with the Payroll system currently is using the default Retry count and Retry interval settings.

    d. Jose should stop his application using the **Partial Stop - Allow running instances to continue** option. The next morning, he can just start his application up.

4. Nick is working in his local development environment. He has a bug that has resulted in 10 suspended messages. Nick has addressed the bug and now wants to re-deploy his application but can't. What step must he take before he can re-deploy it successfully?

    a. Stop his application with the **Partial Stop - Suspend running instances** option

    b. Restart his Host Instances

    c. Stop his application with the **Full Stop - Terminate instances** option

    d. Stop his Host Instances

5. HWLC has an Orchestration that has been deployed that uses a Direct bound port for receiving messages. Erin would like to track message bodies for these incoming messages. Where should she enable tracking message bodies for these messages?

    a. In the Direct Bound Receive Port, she should enable **Track Message bodies Request before Port Processing**

    b. In the **Orchestration's Tracking** options, she should enable **Track Message Bodies – Before Orchestration processing**

    c. In the **Orchestration's Tracking** options, she should enable **Track Message Bodies – After Orchestration processing**

    d. In the Direct Bound Receive Port, she should enable **Track Message bodies Request after Port Processing**

Integrating Web Services and Windows Communication Foundation (WCF) Services

1. Stephen has just deployed a new application in HWLC's Production environment. This particular application uses a Custom Behavior to authenticate service requests from a third party Customer Relationship System (CRM). He needs to specify this endpoint behavior for this service but is unable to modify the server's `machine.config` file. Where else can he register this endpoint behavior?

   a. Registry

   b. `BTSNTSvc.exe.config`

   c. WCF Send Handler

   d. `Web.config`

2. Kim, a HWLC BizTalk developer, has been asked to consume a third party Web Service, over the Internet that is written in Java hosted on the Unix platform. Which WCF binding do you suggest she use?

   a. BasicHttpBinding

   b. NetTcpBinding

   c. NetNamedPipeBinding

   d. NetPeerTcpBinding

3. Alan has just developed a BizTalk Application that will communicate with a third party finance WCF Service. At the last minute, the third party financing company added a new root node to their existing Request Schema. Alan's application has just gone live and he is receiving errors due to a mismatch between the message he is sending and the message the third party financing application is expecting. What should Alan do to solve this problem without deploying any application(s)?

   a. Re-consume the WCF Service from Visual Studio, recompile and deploy the application

   b. In his Send Port, specify an Outbound WCF Message Body Template and include this new root node

   c. Change the existing Send Port to use the PassThruTransmit Pipeline

   d. Build another WCF Service to intercept the BizTalk request and then pass through a request that conforms to the third party financing application's specification

4. You have just exposed a BizTalk Orchestration as a WCF Service to IIS and have enabled anonymous access to the service. You have started the application in the BizTalk Administration Console and all required Host Instances have been started. When you browse to your WCF Service's URL in a Web Browser you are presented with an error. What could the problem be based upon the following options?

    a. You have not restarted IIS.

    b. You need to add your user name to the authorization section of the service's `Web.config`.

    c. The Default Application Pool's identity does not have sufficient permissions. You need to create and use an Application Pool that uses the same identity as the BizTalk Isolated Host Instance.

    d. WCF Services cannot have anonymous access enabled.

5. Javid has just finished exposing his BizTalk Orchestration as a WCF Service using the BizTalk WCF Service Publishing Wizard. He has also deployed his application to his BizTalk server and ensured all related assemblies have been added to the Global Assembly Cache. Calvin, a business analyst with HWLC, has just informed Javid that he needs to add another field to his Web Service Request Schema called DateRequiredBy. Javid has added this field to his Web Service Request Schema, compiled his BizTalk solution and then has re-run the BizTalk WCF Service Publishing Wizard. When prompted, he selects the updated BizTalk assembly that includes his Web Service Request Schema and new DateRequiredBy field. In Javid's test application, he consumes his updated Web Service to discover that his DateRequiredBy field has not been published. What must he do in order to have the DateRequiredBy field published?

    a. Before re-running the BizTalk WCF Service Publishing Wizard, he needs to restart his Host Instance that he has configured his Orchestration to use

    b. He must restart Internet Information Services (IIS) after re-publishing his WCF Service

    c. Before re-running the BizTalk WCF Service Publishing Wizard, Javid must add his updated assembly that contains his Schema, to the GAC

    d. In order to update a WCF Service that has been exposed by the BizTalk WCF Service Publishing Wizard, he must delete the original Virtual Directory from IIS

Implementing extended capabilities

1. You want to remove a BAM Activity `act1`, which is already deployed. What should you do?

   a. Go to the `BAMPrimaryImport` database and delete all tables and view that contains the name `act1`

   b. Use the command line tool `bm.exe` with the **Remove all** option

   c. Use the command line tool `bttdeploy.exe` with the **Remove** option

   d. Create an empty Activity in Excel with the name **act1**. Export the Activity to XML. Use the bm.exe tool with the update all option, and use the newly created XML file to delete the Activity.

2. You have set up a BizTalk RFID Server that receives RFID tags from your warehouse. The BizTalk Server team already has an existing BizTalk Application where File, FTP, WCF-SQL, and HTTP Adapters are used. You would like to have the tag information submitted to BizTalk. What should you do?

   a. Write an RFID WCF binding and use the WCF-Custom Receive Adapter in BizTalk to receive the tags.

   b. Write a custom processing Pipeline that writes files to a shared folder, and deploy it to the RFID server. Make the BizTalk Server poll the files by using a File Receive Adapter.

   c. Set up the SqlServerSink Event Handler in RFID. Create a WCF-SQL Receive Location in BizTalk and poll from the `rfidsink` database created by the Event Handler.

   d. Set up the SqlServerSink Event Handler in RFID. Create a trigger on the relevant `rfidsink` tables that pushes data from the tables to a file share. Use the FILE Adapter in BizTalk to pick up the messages.

3. The managers want to know what is happening in BizTalk on a weekly basis. How many orders we received, what the average order size was, and so on. How should you implement this capability?

   a. Set up an additional Send Port that subscribes to all messages, use the SMTP Adapter, and mail the messages to the managers

   b. Use BAM Activities and tracking profiles to populate BAM Activities, extract the needed information from the orders, and build reports on top of the Activities

   c. Use the Rules Engine to set up RuleSets, where a condition is met every time an order is received

   d. Enable Tracking on the Receive Ports and have the managers use the Group Hub to query **Tracked Service Instances**

4. You have set up several rules for your BizTalk Application inside the Rules Engine Composer. Several times a year these rules needs to be altered, and this process should be handled by non-IT staff. What should you do to make the rules appear more human-readable when the users update the Rules?

    a. Create new Schemas inside BizTalk that uses non-IT terms

    b. Create a vocabulary inside the Rules Engine Composer using non-technical phrases

    c. Create a new rule and apply synonyms for each rule terms

    d. Create a new version of the existing rules and apply synonyms for all technical phrases

5. You receive EDIFACT orders from several partners through the same FTP Receive Location. When receiving an order 96A EDIFACT message from a partner, you realize that the message does not conform to the EDIFACT standard, and a segment that allows only numbers 1 to 5, contains number 6. You talk to the business and you agree that the partner should continue to send a 6 in that segment, as you don't use the value for anything. You agree that only this partner and only this particular extra rule will be allowed. How should you make BizTalk accept the particular field to allow 1 to 6 instead of 1 to 5?

    a. In the Party Agreement for the partner, deselect **Perform EDI Data Type Validation**.

    b. On the Receive Locations **EDIReceive** Pipeline, set **Validate document** to **False**.

    c. Alter the order 96A Schema and extend the Enumeration for the segment with a 6.

    d. Create a new Order 96A Schema and extend the Enumeration for the Segment with a 6. Give the Schema a new Namespace, and set up the Namespace on the specific partners Agreement.

    e. Write a custom Pipeline Component that replaces the 6 with a 5.

Test Your Knowledge— Answers

In order to allow the reader to consider the answers to the questions in the *Test your knowledge* section of the previous chapters, the answers are separated from the questions. This appendix holds the answers. A second appendix holds the answers to the additional *Chapter 10, Sample Certification Test Questions*.

In order to help with a better understanding of the answers, a very brief explanation is given as to why the answer is correct, and in cases where it's relevant why the other options are not.

Chapter 1, Configuring a Messaging Architecture

1. Answer: c

   When signing a message, the trading partner will use his/her own private certificate. When the receiver (us) needs to verify the validity of the signature, a public key instance of the certificate must be used and stored in local machine/other people.

2. Answer: b, c

   In this case, routing for failed messages need to be set up on the Receive Port (there will be no Send Port activity when a message fails on the receive side). When failed message routing is enabled, all normal Context properties such as BTS.ReceivePortName are unpromoted, and only Context properties in the ErrorReport namespace can be used for routing.

3. Answer: b

    Receive Locations should still be enabled and the BizTalk service(s) should still be running, so that other subscribers will still get their messages. Setting a Send Port state to *Unenlisted* state will cause the Send Port to stop subscribing to messages, and will therefore never receive the messages received in BizTalk while the state was *Unenlisted*. Setting the port to a stopped state will allow the port to receive all messages intended for the port and not send them, until the port is started again.

4. Answer: c

    If a message is published to the MessageBox without a message type Context Property, no disassembler has been executed in the Receive Port, and out of the box only the PassThruReceive pipeline has that lack of disassemblers. Therefore, we must assume that it has been used, and as we are receiving XML messages, using the XMLReceive pipeline should solve the problem.

5. Answer: c

    POP3 is the only out of the box adapter that has the capabilities of receiving e-mails from an exchange server. Also, the body part index should be 0, because the actual body part is required.

Chapter 2, Developing BizTalk Artifacts— Creating Schemas and Pipelines

1. Answer: a

    Rob needs to import the Customer schema to Supplier schema as it has a different namespace and the Customer schema holds the type that he wants to use in the Supplier schema. Include should be used if it is the same namespace. Defining a new schema will not help us reuse the existing type.

2. Answer: d

    In a Public Key Infrastructure (PKI), the partner will distribute his public key to allow the signature created using the private key to be validated. The MIME/SMIME Decoder component is used to validate signed messages in a Receive Pipeline.

Chapter 3, Developing BizTalk Artifacts—Creating Maps

1.   Answer: c

     The Scripting functoid should be used to call a .NET component from within a Map. It should be configured to call an external assembly. Although, inline C# can technically be used to call a method in an external assembly that violates the statement that no additional code should be written. The Expression shape cannot be used in Maps as it is an Orchestration shape. Activities are Windows Workflow artifact, not BizTalk.

2.   Answer: b

     The Greater Than functoid should be used because you want to output nodes with a value greater than 70,000 not equal to or less than. Conditional mapping using logical functoids can be used to control output of a node. Although, a Value mapping functoid is also capable of that because it takes a Boolean as its first input and the value as its second input.

Chapter 4, Developing BizTalk Artifacts—Creating Orchestrations

1.   Answer: c

     The Microsoft.XLANGs.BaseTypes.Address is a property that must be set on the port for a port with Dynamic binding. It cannot be set on the message. Whether you do it in a Message Assignment shape or an Expression shape is not important. There is no BTS.ReceivedFileName property.

2.   Answer: b

     In order to configure a block of logic so that either everything commits or nothing commits, you should place the logic within an Atomic scope. In order to be able to use an Atomic scope, the Orchestration must be configured to have a Long Running transaction type. Although, configuring the Orchestration as Atomic will treat the logic as a unit. It will also treat the entire Orchestration as a unit, which was not the goal and might not be possible.

Chapter 5, Debugging and Exception Handling

1. Answer: b, d

    A scope is needed to handle an exception within an Orchestration. In order to be able to catch an exception, the scope does not have to be transactional, but it must have an exception block. Transactional scopes cause additional persistence points and should be avoided if they are not needed.

2. Answer: a

    If no exception handler is implemented, the default exception handler will trigger. The default exception handler will trigger the compensation block of any nested scopes, if they have one, therefore a compensation block must be added to the scope to allow compensation to be made. Compensation for what happened inside the scope should be done in that Scopes Compensation block, not in a Parent scope or an Orchestrations Compensation block. Also, compensating logic should be placed in the compensation block, not an exception block.

3. Answer: c

    Port processing halts while delivering to the MessageBox only. What happens after that when a physical Send Port processes messages matching its subscription is by default nothing the Orchestration is aware of. Delivery Notification can be configured to Transmitted on a logical Send Ports in the Orchestration to halt processing until the physical Send Ports processing is successful before completing a Scope. If the physical Port fails, a DeliveryFailureException will be raised. Failed message routing routes the message in case of port failure, but does nothing to affect Orchestration processing. The Synchronized property has nothing to do with this behavior.

4. Answer: b

    For a port to fail processing on its first attempt (immediately), the **Retry count** on the **Transport Advanced Options** pane must be set to **0**. It will then try to use the backup transport. Configuring the **Retry count** or **Priority** of the backup transport does not affect the primary transport behavior. This scenario has nothing to do with Ordered Delivery.

5. Answer: c

   Although there are several things that could potentially be wrong. Of the possible answers only option c will affect how the message is interpreted or how it is routed and potentially solve the problem. Messages cannot be edited in the Administration Console and re-configuring Send Port does not affect how the message is processed by the Receive Port and Pipeline.

Chapter 6, Deploying, Tracking, and Administrating a BizTalk Server 2010 Solution

1. Answer: d

   We need to let our application drain by not allowing any new message instances to be received while any existing messages can complete. By stopping all Receive Locations, we cannot receive any new messages. By waiting for any active instances to complete, we can safely perform a Full stop once we know there are no messages currently being processed.

2. Answer: b

   As we are interested in tracking just the flat file that BizTalk received, we want to enable Track Message Bodies – Request message before port processing. By doing so, we are capturing a copy of the message before our flat file reaches our custom pipeline that will include our flat file disassembler.

3. Answer: b

   Whenever we configure a new Host in an environment, we need to be sensitive to the Adapters that will be using this new Host. When this occurs, we need to add this Host as a Send and/or Receive Handler depending upon whether we will use our Host in a Send Port or Receive Location.

4. Answer: c

   In this scenario, we want to see how many message instances are currently retrying. In order to discover this, we need to run the Running service instances – Retrying and idle ports query from BizTalk Group Hub.

5. Answer: d

When we need to export an MSI file from a BizTalk application, we have the ability to add binding files as resources. We can tag these Binding Files with a Target Environment that will allow us to distinguish one Binding File from another. If we do not provide a Binding File with a Target Environment then this Binding File will be treated as the default Binding File. So when we go to use this MSI package in another environment, we will only see the default Binding File.

Chapter 7, Integrating Web Services and Windows Communication Foundation (WCF) Services

1. Answer: c

When a service is taking a longer time than we expect to complete, we need to increase the Send timeout property, which will allow our Send Port to wait longer before throwing a timeout exception.

2. Answer: d

As we changed our logical port's Operation name inside of our Orchestration and deployed it, our only option is to update the Physical Send Port's SOAP Action header so that it matches the value that we specified inside our Orchestration.

3. Answer: a

We need to configure our Send Port to pass on the exception that we received from the Custom Paint service. In order to do this, we need to enable the Propagate fault message inside our Send Port's configuration.

4. Answer: b

Our only option in this case is to actually re-run the BizTalk WCF Service Publishing wizard. The reason for this is when this wizard generates our WCF Service and related folder in the c:\inetpub folder, references to the Adapter we selected in the wizard exist.

5. Answer: c

The default message size that a WCF Receive Location can handle is 65,536 bytes. If we are planning on receiving a message that is larger than this value then we need to increase the Maximum received message size value.

Chapter 8, Implementing Extended Capabilities

1. Answer: b

   Agreements is what is used to set up various customer specific EDI properties.

2. Answer: c

   We cannot unpublish an existing rule, and for a new rule to take effect in BizTalk, it needs to be deployed. Changes in the Orchestrations are not needed, because they will always use the highest version deployed.

3. Answer: a

   Excel and bm.exe are the tools used for creating Activities. Bttdeploy.exe is the tool used for deploying Tracking Profiles.

4. Answer: d

   After deploying an activity, a tracking profile needs to be set up, so that BAM can Map the activity items to items/events in BizTalk. Bttdeploy.exe is the tool used to deploy the tracking profile created in the tracking profile editor.

5. Answer: c

   It is on the Receive side (Disassemble) that BizTalk needs to process incoming EDI messages.

B

Sample Certification Test Questions—Answers

In order to allow the reader to consider the answers to the questions in *Chapter 10, Sample Certification Test Questions*, the answers are separated from the questions. This appendix holds the answers. A previous appendix holds the answers to the additional *Test your knowledge* section of the chapters.

In order to help with a better understanding of the answers, a very brief explanation is given as to why the answer is correct and in cases where it's relevant why the other options are not.

Configuring a messaging architecture

1. Answer: d

   If multiple ports need to implement the same subscription, Send Port Groups should be used, so that the subscription only needs to be implemented once, and any changes to the subscription can be maintained in one place.

2. Answer: b, d, e

   PassThruReceive on the receive side will cause BizTalk to not recognize the MessageType and therefore we will not be able to Map on the Send Port. The Map should be from the canonical format to the partner format.

3. Answer: b, c, d, e

   We need a new Host, so that HostA will still do all the work except receiving FTP. The new Host needs to be clustered so that if one server fails, a Host Instance will start on the other Server.

4. Answer: c

This should be done using references, and it is in the Application that needs to access artifacts from another Application, the reference needs to be made. The same Pipelines cannot be redeployed in another Application in BizTalk, when already residing in another Application.

5. Answer: d

By choosing **All artifacts** we can get an overview of everything inside BizTalk, not limited to a certain Application. The other answers either stops too much or otherwise doesn't fulfill the requirement of disabling all locations.

Developing BizTalk Artifacts

1. Answer: b

A distinguished field is used only to create an alias for xpath statements for expressions in Orchestrations. The Body xpath property of the root node is used with envelope Schemas to point out the node that contains the body of the document. Changing the Default Property Schema Name property on the schema file only affects what the filename of the created property schema will be when you do a Quick Promotion.

2. Answer: c

The Pre-assemble and Assemble stage are stages in a send Pipeline and would do nothing to affect the XML in a receive. Therefore the Decode stage, the Receive Pipeline stage before the Disassemble stage (that throws the exception), is correct.

3. Answer: c

Maps are configured on Receive Ports. As the Orchestration needs the canonical format you need a Map that transforms *to* the canonical format. As the files are received into BizTalk, configuring a Send Port is pointless. Pipelines in general, the XMLReceive Pipeline or the Validate document structure property of the XML Disassembler has nothing to do with Maps.

4. Answer: d

As both the external component and the Orchestration are .NET components, they will load into the Host Instances memory. When they are updated on disk or in the GAC they will not be refreshed unless the Host Instances are restarted (or a sufficient amount of time passes for the assemblies to unload). Storing the value in BizTalk's configuration file also requires a Host Instance restart for the BizTalk Server to retrieve the new value as the config file is read only when the service starts.

5. Answer: a

    Scope and their **Synchronized** property ensure that data being read is not simultaneously written to by other branches of a Parallel shape. It has nothing to do with this scenario. As we are sending a message out and receiving a response we need to initialize the correlation set on the Receive shape and follow it on the Send shape. The `Ordered Delivery` property makes sure that messages are delivered to the Orchestration in the same order that they were written to the `MessageBox`.

Debugging and exception handling

1. Answer: d

    You must enable Failed Message Routing on the Receive Port where processing fails, and you must add a filter on ErrorReport.ReceivePortName to the SendFailureNotification Port. The BTS.ReceivePortName property is available, but will not be promoted in a failed message and cannot be used for routing.

2. Answer: c

    RecoverableInterchangeProcessing is a property on the XMLDisassembler component. Configured to `True` it allows successfully processed messages from a batch through while suspending only the incorrect ones. By default the property is `False`, which means that one incorrectly formatted message fails the entire batch. Ordered Delivery does not help with this, nor does processing instructions.

3. Answer: b

    You need to set Enable Unit Testing to `True`. References to Microsoft.BizTalk. TestTools and Microsoft.XLANGs.BaseTypes are needed, but you do not need to add them manually. Also, when setting Enable Unit Testing to `True`, the Schema will get the `TestableSchemaBase` as its base class, which surfaces the `ValidateInstance` method on the Schema class. You cannot cast a Schema that does not inherit from the `TestableSchemaBase` class to that class and use the `ValidateInstance` method.

4. Answer: d

    You need to use a scope with an exception block to be able to catch the exception. Once caught, the Orchestration will terminate without suspending. The Throw Exception shape will re-throw the exception and cause the Orchestration to become suspended. The Report to Analyst option is connected to the Orchestration Designer for Business Analysts (ODBA), and has nothing to do with exception handling.

5. Answer: a

In order to get rid of suspended messages on a Send Port that fails processing, you must enable Failed Message Routing and create a subscription that matches any of the ErrorReport properties, for example SendPortName. Subscribing to BTS.AckType and BTS.AckSendPortName will get you the NACK message (the exception) but you will not avoid the suspended message. Also, Delivery Notification does not help you avoid suspended messages either.

Deploying, tracking, and supporting a BizTalk solution

1. Answer: c

The BizTalk Settings Dashboard provides us with the ability to import and export our settings allowing for a very portable solution between BizTalk environments.

2. Answer: c

When dealing with multiple BizTalk nodes, all related assemblies must be installed in the Global Assembly Cache. Our MSI package only needs to be imported on one node.

3. Answer: b

The best solution is to take advantage of the Service Window of the Send Port. This way we will have our messages queued and in a Scheduled service instances state. When the clock strikes 10 pm, our messages will automatically be delivered. We also will not be actively communicating with the Payroll system, as this was one of the requirements of the solution.

4. Answer: c

If we have suspended instances, we cannot redeploy an Application. As this is just a development environment, it is safe just to terminate them. Of the options listed, the only way to terminate these messages is through stopping the Application using the **Terminate instances** option.

5. Answer: b

As Direct Bound Ports do not show up as physical ports in the BizTalk Administration Console, we must rely upon using Orchestration tracking. As we want to track the message body as it is received, then we need to use the **Track Message Bodies - Before Orchestration** processing.

Integrating Web Services and Windows Communication Foundation (WCF) Services

1. Answer: c

   The WCF Send Handler provides the ability to import a WCF Extension/ Custom Behavior. We can access this function by clicking on the **Properties** button inside the WCF Custom Send Handler.

2. Answer: a

   Of the answers available for this question, the BasicHttpBinding is the most interoperable binding.

3. Answer: b

   WCF-based Send Ports provide the ability to alter an outbound message by specifying an XML template. By using this template we can wrap our message with additional XML tags that will conform to the third party financing company's specification.

4. Answer: c

   When the BizTalk WCF Service Publishing Wizard runs, it will create a Web Application inside IIS. The problem is that the Web Application will use the Default Application pool. Unless this Default Application pool has been modified to use the identity of the BizTalk Isolated Host Instance account, the Application Pool will not have sufficient BizTalk rights to launch our Web Service in a browser.

5. Answer: c

   The BizTalk WCF Service Publishing Wizard will use the latest version of our Schema's assembly that is in the GAC. It is not enough to just recompile our Application and then select the most recent assembly.

Implementing extended capabilities

1. Answer: b

   Bm.exe is the tool used for deploying, updating, and removing activities. The commands are:
   - Deploy-all
   - Update-all
   - Remove-all

2. Answer: c

   Out of the box, RFID server ships with a SQL Server Event Handler, which will automatically create a Database and polling Stored Procedures and submit data to the tables.

3. Answer: b

   For exposing business data to the rest of the business, BAM is used. The Rules Engine will not work for this, and tracking and sending mail will not give the ability to view averages, and so on.

4. Answer: b

   Vocabularies inside the Rules Engine Composer are used for giving the rules a more human-readable language.

5. Answer: d

   We should not disable validation all together, because there could be other problems with the documents received, that we do not want to allow. Writing a custom Pipeline component will work, but it will work for all partners, so will changing the original Order 96A Schema.

Index

Symbols

10^n, scientific functoids 126
32-bit only parameter, host 16
.NET assemblies
  integrating with 162, 163
.NET helper component 161
.NET identity, schema identity
  namespace 75
  Typename 75

A

absolute value, mathematical functoids 126
ACID rule 155
action, BizTalk Solution
  adding 348
activating receive shape 153
activity, BAM
  creating 366, 367
  creating, inside Excel 368-372
  deploying 373
adapter
  about 8
  examples 9
  handler, managing 19, 20
  on receive side 8
  on send side 12
Add >> button 77
add days, date/time functoids 124
add-in, BAM
  creating, inside Excel 367, 368
addition, mathematical functoids 125
advanced functoids
  about 127
  assert functoid 136

conditional mapping 134, 135
copy-based mapping 136
looping 128
maps 142
orchestrations 143, 144
scripting functoid 137
After orchestration processing property 267
agreement
  alternate namespace, setting up 360
Allow anonymous access to WCF Service
      property 312
allow host tracking parameter, host 15
any node, records 80
append mode 51
application IDs, cross reference functoids
  Get Application ID 122
  Get Common ID 122
  Remove Application ID 123
  Set Common ID 122
  working with 121
Application Programming Interfaces (APIs)
      161
applications
  about 20
  another application, referencing 21
  creating, steps 20
application values, cross reference functoids
  about 123
  Get Application Value 123
  Set Common Value 123
ApproveLoan Policy 350
arc tangent functoid, scientific functoids 126
artificats
  CustomerFinanceRequest.xsd 307
  CustomerFinanceResponse.xsd 307

FinanceRequest_to_DealerFinanceApprove-
dResponse.btm 306
FinanceRequest_to_DealerFinanceReject-
edResponse.btm 306
processCustomerFinanceRequests.odx 307
ASCII to Character, conversion functoids
119
assemble stage, send pipeline 94
assert functoid, advanced functoids 136
Assign_CarOut shape 194
Atomicity, Consistency, Isolation, and
Durability. *See* **ACID rule**
atomic transactions 155
atomic transaction type
isolation levels 157
properties 157
At the Test Center, certification test-takers
396
attribute groups, records 80
authenticating
ports 23, 24
authentication trusted parameter, host 15
average, cumulative functoids 119

B

BAM
about 365
activity, creating 366, 367
activity, creating inside Excel 368-372
activity, deploying 373
add-in, setting up inside Excel 367, 368
continuations, creating 378, 379
portal 379, 380
tracking profile, creating 374-378
uses 366
view, deploying 373
view permissions, creating 382
BAM Portal
about 379, 380
aggregation package, running 382
aggregation, populating 382
order, searching for 381
BAM Portal Users 245
Base-specified Logarithm, scientific
functoids 126
BasicHttpBinding adapter 288

Before orchestration processing property
267
binding files
about 248
creating 249-256
dependencies 261
managing, ways 249
binding tab, Out of box WCF-BasicHttp
Receive Adapter
CloseTimeout property 300
maximum concurrent calls property 300
Maximum received message size (bytes)
property 300
Message encoding property 300
OpenTimeout property 300
SendTimeout property 300
text encoding property 300
binding tab, Out of box WCF-BasicHttp
Send Adapter 292
CloseTimeout property 292
OpenTimeout property 292
SendTimeout property 292
BizTalk247 BizTalk Server webcasts
URL 389
BizTalk
and RFID communicating, SQL Server used
364, 365
BizTalk Administration Console
about 12
Group Hub 12
The Group Hub 13
BizTalk applications, deploying
binding file, dependencies 261
binding files 248-256
through MSI package 257-260
through Visual Studio 245-248
BizTalk applications management, BizTalk
Administration Console
about 270
configuration overview 271
group suspended service instances 273
suspended items 272
tracked message events 274
tracked service instances 274
work in progress 271
BizTalk Application, states
about 261

runtime application states 262
BizTalk Application Users 244
BizTalk Artifacts
  answers 420, 421, 428, 429
  questions 407, 408, 409
BizTalk B2B Operators Group 245
BizTalk Framework Assembler component
  97
BizTalk Framework Disassembler
  component 96
BizTalk Group
  setting up 242
BizTalk Isolated Host Users 244
BizTalk platform settings and Applications
  about 12
  adapter handlers, managing 19, 20
  applications 20
  BizTalk Administration Console 12
  group hub 13
  Group Hub 12
  hosts 13
BizTalk Runtime screen 242
BizTalk Server
  about 237, 238
  Active Directory Groups 244, 245
  Active Directory Users 244, 245
  BizTalk Group, setting up 242
  configuring 240
  high availability 238, 239
  installation, setting up 239, 240
  runtime settings, configuring 242, 243
  SSO, configuring 241
BizTalk Server 2010
  WCF Services, consuming 315
BizTalk Server 2010 Adapter Pack samples,
  URL 391
BizTalk Server 2010 Administrator Training
  Kit (including VHD)
  URL 390
BizTalk Server 2010 Developer Training Kit
  (including VHD)
  URL 390
BizTalk Server 2010 ESB Training Kit
  (including. VHD)
  URL 391
BizTalk Server 2010 Training Kit
  URL 390

BizTalk Server 2010 VHD
  URL 390
BizTalk Server Administrators 244
BizTalk Server code samples, URL 391
BizTalk Server Developer Center videos
  URL 389
BizTalk Server Developer Center webcasts
  URL 389
BizTalkServerIsolatedHost Receive handler
  298
BizTalk Server Operators 244
BizTalk Server Scenarios for Business Solu-
  tions
  URL 392
BizTalk Server SDK Samples, URL 391
BizTalk Server Tutorials
  URL 392
BizTalk Settings Dashboard
  about 274
  performance tuning settings, exporting
    279, 280
  performance tuning settings, importing
    280-282
  performance tuning settings, modifying
    275-279
  performance tuning settings, viewing
    275-279
BizTalk SharePoint Adapter Enabled Hosts
  245
BizTalk Solution
  answers 423, 424, 430
  questions 412, 413
BizTalk Solution, creating with rules
  action, adding 348
  new version policy, deploying 350
  orchestration, creating 349, 350
  policy, creating 346
  policy, deploying 350
  policy, testing 348-350
  schema, creating 345
  schema, importing into rule composer 347
  vocabulary, adding 351, 352
BlobSign (2) option 111
blogs, certification test-takers
  about 393
  BizTalk Server Scenarios for Business
    Solutions, URL 392

BizTalk Server Tutorials, URL 392
bm.exe, activity file
  options 373
body option 296
Body XPath property 83, 223
BRE
  about 343
  BizTalk Solution, creating with rules 345
  Business Rules 344
  policies 344
  rule store 345
  vocabulary 344
BTS2010CertGuide-Ch01 application 54
BTSNTSvc.exe.config
  configuration information, storing in 159
BTS.Operation property 290
Business Activity Monitoring. *See* BAM
business rules, BRE 344
Business Rules Engine. *See* BRE

C

call 153
call orchestration shape 151, 153
call rules shape 152
canonical messages
  about 64
  advantages 64, 65
CarRegistry Schema 134
certification test-takers
  answering questions 400-402
  At the Test Center 396
  exam, preparing for 387
  exam structure 396
  incentives 394
  objectives 393
  sources, for exam preparation 388-392
  time management 399
  tips 387
  tricks 387
  vouchers and offers 395
Character to ASCII, conversion functoids 119
classes, certification test-takers 388, 389
CloseTimeout property 292, 300
Cloudcasts BizTalk community webcasts, URL 389

CodeHelper class 138
colleagues and peers, certification test-takers 392
Common Logarithm, scientific functoids 126
compensate shape 151
CompensateShipNotice block 198
compensation block, exceptions
  about 191, 192
  default compensation 192
  default exception handler 192
Completed table 367
complex types, records
  about 80
  used, for creating reusable types 89, 90
component element 82
concatenate, cumulative functoids 119
conditional mapping
  Value Mapping (Flattening) Functoid 134
  Value Mapping Functoid 134
configuration information storage, orchestration
  .NET helper component used 161
  about 159
  business rules 161
  in BTSNTSvc.exe.config 159
  in machine.config 160
  in web.config, for isolated hosts 160
  on host handlers 160
  orchestration variables 159
  Single Sign-On (SSO) 161
  through message 160
  through message context 161
Configuration refresh interval property 275
Configure Pipeline dialog 100
construct message shape 149
containers shape
  group shape 150
  scope shape 150
content-based routing
  applications, creating 53, 54
  configuring 52
  folders, creating 53, 54
  messages, debugging 58-61
  receive locations, creating 54-57
  receive port, creating 54-57
  send port, setting up 61, 62

send port, setting up for send port group 62, 63

send port, setting up for system II 62, 63

context properties
  about 11
  not promoted 11
  promoted 11

continuations, BAM
  creating 378, 379

conversion functoids
  about 119
  ASCII to Character 119
  Character to ASCII 119
  Hexadecimal 119
  Octal 119

convoys
  about 183
  parallel convoys 184
  sequential convoys 184

copy-based mapping, advanced functoids
  mass copy functoid 136

core adapters, configuring
  about 40
  file adapter 49
  FTP adapter 46
  HTTP send adapter 40
  POP3 adapter 43
  SMTP adapter 44, 45

correlation, configuration
  about 180
  convoys 183
  types, working with 180-182

correlation type
  about 180
  enabling 181-183
  instantiating 180

Cosine, scientific functoids 126

Create button 312

create new (default) mode 51

cross reference functoids
  about 120
  application IDs, working with 121
  application values, working with 123
  Get Application ID 122
  Get Application Value 123
  Get Common ID 122
  Remove Application ID 123

Set Common ID 122
Set Common Value 123

cumulative functoids
  about 119
  average 119
  concatenate 119
  maximum 119
  minimum 119
  sum 119

custom behavior
  about 303
  registering, in handlers configuration 303-305

CustomerFinanceRequest.xsd, artificats 307

CustomerFinanceResponse.xsd, artificats 307

Customer Relationship Management (CRM) 131

Custom XSLT property 117

D

database functoids
  about 119
  table query functoids 120

database lookup, table query functoids 120

date and time, date/time functoids 124

date, date/time functoids 124

date formats, schemas
  controlling 86, 87

date/time functoids
  about 124
  add days 124
  date 124
  date and time 124
  time 124

de-batching 65

debug map 229, 230

debug orchestration 208-213

decide shape 150

decode stage, receive pipeline 93

default exception handler 192

Default Property Schemas property 78

dehydrated orchestrations 272

dehydration persistence orchestration 154, 155

delay shape 150

DeliveryFailureException 206
Derived By property 85
description property 221
design-time-determined filter criteria 153
direct option, port binding option 165
  about 170
  dynamic send port 178
  MessageBox (filter-based) 170, 171
  partner orchestration option 175, 176
  self correlating direct binding 171-175
disabled state, receive locations 26
disassemble stage, receive pipeline 93
distinguished field
  node, promoting as 78, 79
Distributed Transaction Coordinator (DTC)
  157
division, mathematical functoids 126
document schemas, XML Validator 104
DTM (DateTime) segment 359
dynamic send port, port binding option 165
  about 178
  using, in orchestration 178-180

E

EANCOM, EDI 352
EDI
  about 352
  and flatfiles, differences 352
  EDIFACT Schema, finding 353
  location, setting up 354, 355
  parties, setting up 355
  receive port, setting up 354, 355
  reference, adding 354
  send port, setting up 354, 355
  standards 352
EDIFACT, EDI 352
EDIFACT Schema
  deploying 353
EdiReceive Pipeline 355
EdiSend Pipeline 355
EDI Subsystem Users 244
Electronic Data Interchange. *See* EDI
enabled state, receive locations 26
Enable routing for failed messages option
  219
encode stage, send pipeline 95

envelope option 296
envelope property 223
envelope schemas
  about 72
  creating 83, 84
envelopes, pipeline
  working with 105-107
ErrorReport namespace, properties
  description property 221
  ErrorType property 220
  FailureAdapter property 221
  FailureCategory property 220
  FailureCode property 220
  FailureInstanceID property 221
  FailureMessageID property 221
  FailureTime property 221
  InboundTransportLocation property 220
  MessageType property 220
  OutboundTransportLocation property 220
  ProcessingServer property 220
  ReceivePortName property 220
  RoutingFailureReportID property 221
  SendPortName property 220
error return, table query functoids 120
error threshold state, receive locations
  27, 28
ErrorType property 220
events tracking, BizTalk Server
  about 264
  orchestrations, tracking 266-269
  Receive Ports, tracking 265
  send ports, tracking 269
EventTypes property 365
exam preparation
  about 387
  certification, objectives 393
  sources 388
  study time 393, 394
exam preparation, sources
  blogs 393
  classes 388, 389
  colleagues and peers 392
  forums 393
  hands-on training exercise 390
  labs 390
  literature 388
  online resources 393

practice tests 392
sample code 391
training kits 390, 391
webcasts 389, 390
exam structure, certification test-takers
about 396
after exam 398
before exam 397
questions 397
Excel
activity, creating 368-372
BAM add-in, creating 367, 368
exception handling
answers 422, 429, 430
questions 409-411
exceptions
catching 190, 191
compensation 191, 192
default compensation 192
default exception handler 192
delivery notification 203-208
exception handling scenario, sample
193-203
handling 188
scopes 188
throwing 189
throwing, steps 189
Export Configuration button 243
expression shape 152
extended capabilities
answers 425, 432
questions 416
Extensible Stylesheet Language
Transformations. *See* XSLT
external assemblies, scripting functoid
using 137-139

F

Failed Message Routing option 37, 217, 218
FailureAdapter property 221
FailureCategory property 220
FailureCode property 220
FailureInstanceID property 221
FailureMessageID property 221
FailureTime property 221

FILE adapter
about 18
append mode 51
create new (default) mode 51
credentials 52
files, receiving 49, 50
files, sending 50, 51
overwrite mode 51
FinanceRequest_to_DealerFinanceApprove-
dResponse.btm, artificats 306
FinanceRequest_to_DealerFinanceReject-
edResponse.btm, artificats 306
fire-and-forget style asynchronous
instantiation 153
Flat File Assembler component 97
Flat File Disassembler component 97
flat file schemas 73
flow control shape
compensate shape 151
decide shape 150
delay shape 150
listen shape 150
loop shape 150
parallel actions shape 150
suspend shape 151
terminate shape 151
throw exception shape 151
Following Correlation Sets property 182
forums, certification test-takers 393
forward partner orchestration 176
FTP adapter
about 46
receive FTP 47, 48
send FTP 48, 49
FuelConsumption element 227
Full Stop - Terminate instances 264
functoid configuration 229
functoids
about 118
categories 118
functoids, categories
advanced functoids 127
conversion functoids 119
cross reference functoids 120
cumulative functoids 119
database functoids 119

date/time functoids 124
logical functoids 124, 125
mathematical functoids 125, 126
scientific functoids 126, 127
string functoids 127
table query functoids 120

G

generate instance 228
Get Application ID, application IDs 122
Get Application Value, application values
  123
Get Common ID, application IDs 122
Global Assembly Cache (GAC) 139
Grouped by Application 273
Grouped by Error Code 273
Grouped by Service Name link 273
Grouped by URI link 273
Group Hub 12
group shape 150
group suspended service instances, BizTalk
  applications management
  Grouped by Application 273
  Grouped by Error Code 273
  Grouped by Service Name link 273
  Grouped by URI link 273

H

Hexadecimal, conversion functoids 119
HIPAA, EDI 352
host
  32-bit only parameter 16
  about 13
  allow host tracking parameter 15
  authentication trusted parameter 15
  creating, steps 14, 15
  guidelines 16, 17
  in-Process host 14
  instance, creating 17, 18
  isolated host 14, 16
  Make this the default host in the group
    parameter 16
  multiple host instances, example 17
  name parameter 15
  processing host 16
  receive host 16

send host 16
tracking host 16
type parameter 15
Windows group parameter 16
host handlers
  configuration information, storing in 160
hosts section 276
HTTP send adapter
  about 40
  receiving 41-43
  sending 40

I

IIS 289
import 90
Import button 280
Inbound BizTalk message body section, Out
  of box WCF-BasicHttp Send Adapter
  Body - contents of <soap
    Body> element option 296
  Envelope - entire <soap
    Envelope> option 296
  Path - content located by body path option
    296
InboundTransportLocation property 220
incentives
  about 394
  knowledge 395
  money 395
  opportunities 395
include 90, 91
include exception detail in faults property
  302
incoming messages property 268
index functoid, looping 128
Initializing Correlation Sets property 182
inline code, scripting functoid
  using 139, 140
inline XSLT, scripting functoid
  using 141, 142
in-process Adapter
  WCF-Custom 288
in-Process host 14
instance
  generating 228
  validating 228

integer formats
    restricting 87, 88
integer, mathematical functoids 126
Internet Information Services. *See* IIS
inverse partner orchestration 177
IsNil functoid 125
isolated host
    about 14, 16
    limitations 14
isolation levels, atomic transaction type
    read committed 157
    repeatable read 157
    serializable 157
iteration functoid, looping 129
IThirdPartyFinanceService interface 318

L

labs, certification test-takers 390
Large message size property 275
listen shape 150
literature, certification test-takers 388
LoanAmount element 347
location
    setting up 354, 355
logical AND functoid 125
logical date functoid 125
logical existence functoid 125
logical functoids
    about 124
    IsNil functoid 125
    logical AND functoid 125
    logical date functoid 125
    logical existence functoid 125
    logical NOT functoid 125
    logical numeric functoid 125
    logical OR functoid 125
    logical string functoid 125
logical NOT functoid 125
logical numeric functoid 125
logical OR functoid 125
logical ports
    versus physical ports 164, 165
logical string functoid 125
LongRunningScope shape 198
long running transaction type 155, 156

looping, advanced functoids
    about 128
    index functoid 128
    iteration functoid 129
    looping functoid 130
    Nil value functoid 129
    record count functoid 129
    table looping functoid 131-134
looping functoid 130
loop shape 150

M

machine.config
    configuration information, storing in 160
Make this the default host in the group
        parameter, host 16
maps
    creating 115, 116
    debugging 229
    on receive side 10
    on send side 11
    testing 229
    validating 229
maps, advanced functoids 142
mass copy functoid 136
Master Secret Server and Microsoft
        Distributed Transaction Coordinator.
        See MSDTC
mathematical functoids
    about 125
    absolute value 126
    addition 125
    division 126
    integer 126
    modulo 126
    multiplication 126
    round 126
    square root 126
    subtraction 125
maximum concurrent calls property 300
maximum, cumulative functoids 119
Maximum received message size (bytes)
        property 300
maxOccurs property 82
message and data handling shape
    about 148

construct message shape 149
message assignment shape 149
receive shape 148
send shape 149
transform shape 149
message assignment shape 149
MessageBox
    about 10
    purpose 10
**MessageBox (filter-based), direct port
        binding option 170, 171**
message context
    configuration information, storing via 161
message encoding property 300
message, receiving
    about 8
    adapter 8
    maps 10
    pipeline 9
messages
    configuration information, storing via 160
    debugging 58-61
message, security mode 293
message send and receive property 267
message, sending
    adapter 12
    maps 11
    pipeline 12
**messages tab, Out of box WCF-BasicHttp
        Receive Adapter 302**
**messages tab, Out of box WCF-BasicHttp
        Send Adapter 296**
    Body - BizTalk request message body 296
    Template - content specified by template
        296
MessageType property 220
MessageType, XML identity 74
messaging architecture
    answers 419, 420, 427, 428
    questions 405-407
messaging errors
    route errors 217-222
    subscription errors 213-215
    transmission errors 215-217
messaging patterns
    adapter independence 66
    canonical messages 64, 65
    de-batching 65
    flows using, ways 66
    implementing 64
Metadata Exchange. *See* **MEX**
Metadata only endpoint. *See* **MEX**
Metadata URL 322
MEX 309, 322
Microsoft.BizTalk.TestTools assembly 232
Microsoft Installer. *See* **MSI**
Microsoft Official Curriculum (MOC) 388
**Microsoft.XLANGs.BaseTypes assembly
        232**
MIME/SMIME Decoder component 97, 112
MIME/SMIME Encoder component 98, 108
minimum, cumulative functoids 119
modulo, mathematical functoids 126
MSDN
    Post-configuration Database Optimization
        guide, URL 239
MSDTC 238
MSI 245
MSI package
    used, for deploying BizTalk applications
        257-260
multiplication, mathematical functoids 126

N

name parameter, host 15
namespace, .NET identity 75
**Natural Exponential Function, scientific
        functoids 126**
Natural Logarithm, scientific functoids 126
nesting transaction type 158
NetMsmqBinding adapter 288
NetNamedPipeBinding adapter 288
NetTcpBinding adapter 288
Next button 280
Nil value functoid, looping 129
node
    promoting, as distinguished field 78, 79
    promoting, to property field 75-78
none, security mode 293
non-resumable instances 272
not promoted, context properties 11

O

Octal, conversion functoids 119
OK button 78
one-way flow 66
online resources, certification test-takers
    393
OpenTimeout property 292, 300
orchestration
    about 11, 147
    activating 152
    activating receive shape 153
    call or start orchestration 153
    debugging 208-212
    developing 147, 148
    dynamic send port, using 178-180
    exposing, as WCF Services 306-313
    logical ports versus physical ports 164, 165
    persistence 153, 154
    ports versus port types 164
    shapes 148
    transactions 155
orchestration, activating
    activating receive shape 153
    call or start orchestration 153
orchestration bindings, configuration
    logical ports versus physical ports 164, 165
    port binding, options 165
    ports versus port types 164
orchestration, BizTalk Solution
    creating 349, 350
orchestration nesting
    call orchestration shape 151
    start orchestration shape 152
orchestrations, advanced functoids 143, 144
orchestration start and end property 267
orchestrations tracking
    after orchestration processing property 267
    before orchestration processing property
        267
    incoming messages property 268
    message send and receive property 267
    orchestration start and end property 267
    outgoing messages property 268
    shape start and end property 267
    track events property 267
    track mesage properties property 268

track message bodies property 267
orchestration variables
    configuration information, storing in 159
ordered delivery
    about 37, 38
    receive locations 38
    send ports 38, 39
OrderNo property 181, 183
Order Processed Activity 366
Order Sent Activity 366
other shapes
    call rules shape 152
    expression shape 152
OutboundTransportLocation property 220
outgoing messages property 268
Out of box WCF Adapters
    BasicHttpBinding 288
    NetMsmqBinding 288
    NetNamedPipeBinding 288
    NetTcpBinding 288
    WCF-Custom 289
    WCF-CustomIsolated 289
    WsHttpBinding 288
Out of box WCF-BasicHttp Receive Adapter
    binding tab 300
    messages tab 302
    security tab 301
    used, for configuring WCF Adapter
        298-302
Out of box WCF-BasicHttp Send Adapter
    binding tab 292
    messages tab 296
    used, for configuring WCF Adapter
        289-296
Out-of-process Adapter
    WCF-CustomIsolated adapter 288
overwrite mode 51

P

PaintServiceException 331
PaintServiceExceptionFault operation 337
parallel actions shape 150
parallel convoys 184
partially started, runtime application state
    262

Partial Stop - Allow running instances to continue, runtime application state 263
Partial Stop - Suspend running instances, runtime application state 263
parties, EDI
  agreement, setting up 362
  alternate message, setting up for agreement 360
  and agreements 357-359
  new party, setting up for sending 363, 364
  schema, changing 359
  setting up 355-362
  unrecognized message, examining 356, 357
partner orchestration, direct port binding option
  about 175
  forward partner orchestration 176
  inverse partner orchestration 177
Party Resolution component 98
PassThruReceive Pipeline 9, 28, 95
PassThruTransmit pipeline 95, 101
path option 296
pattern property 86
performance tuning settings, BizTalk Settings Dashboard
  exporting 279, 280
  importing 280-282
  modifying 275-279
PersistenceExceptions 157
persistence, orchestration
  about 153
  dehydration 154, 155
  occurrences 154
  rehydration 154, 155
physical ports
  versus logical ports 164, 165
pipeline, custom
  BizTalk Framework Assembler component 97
  BizTalk Framework Disassembler component 96
  Flat File Assembler component 97
  Flat File Disassembler component 97
  MIME/SMIME Decoder component 97
  MIME/SMIME Encoder component 98
  Party Resolution component 98

XML Assembler component 97
XML Disassembler component 97
XML Validator component 98
pipeline, default
  about 95
  PassThruReceive pipeline 95
  PassThruTransmit pipeline 95
  XMLReceive pipeline 95
  XMLTransmit pipeline 96
pipelines
  about 9, 91, 92
  configuring 99, 100
  custom pipelines 96, 98
  default pipelines 95
  envelopes, working with 105, 106
  on receive side 9
  on send side 12
  receive pipelines 92
  secure data, working with 107
  send pipelines 94
  stages 92
  XML message 101
policies, BRE 344
policy, BizTalk Solution
  creating 346
  deploying 350
  new version, deploying 350
  testing 348-350
Polling Intervals section 277
POP3 adapter 43
port binding, options
  about 165
  direct option 165, 170
  dynamic send port 165
  specify later option 165-169
  specify now option 165-168
Port Configuration Wizard 166
ports
  about 22
  authenticating 23, 24
  backups transport 33
  binding options 165
  failed message routing 37
  filters, configuring 34
  maps, receiving 28, 29
  ordered delivery 37
  receive locations 24-26

receive ports 22, 23
sending 30, 31
send port groups 36
send port maps 33
send ports, dynamic 35
send port, states 34, 35
Transport Advanced Options 31, 32
versus port types 164
port types
type modifier property 164
versus port 164
practice tests, certification test-takers 392
pre-assemble stage, send pipeline 94
priority parameter, Transport Advanced
Options 31
processCustomerFinanceRequests.odx,
artificats 307
processCustomerFinanceRequests.odx
Orchestration 324
processing host 16
ProcessingServer property 220
promoted, context properties 11
promoted property
about 75
node, promoting as distinguished field
78, 79
quick promotion option 78
steps 76-78
propagate fault message checkbox 297
property field
node, promoting 75-78
Property Fields tab 77
property schemas 73
proxy tab, Out of box WCF-BasicHttp Send
Adapter 294
do not use proxy 295
use proxy 295
use send handler proxy settings 295
publish/subscribe mechanism
about 7
adapter 8, 12
adapter, examples 8
context properties 11
maps 10, 11
MessageBox 10
message, receiving 8
message, sending 11

orchestrations 7, 11
pipeline 9, 12
pipeline, examples 9
request-response receive ports 7
send ports 7
subscription 10, 11
working 8

Q

QA 279
Quality Assurance. *See* **QA**
quick promote property 78
quick promotion option 78

R

Radio Frequency Identification. *See* **RFID**
RcvFF pipeline 101
read committed, isolation levels 157
ready service instances 272
receive host 16
receive locations
about 24-26
creating 54-57
disabled state 26
enabled state 26
error threshold state 27, 28
testing 57
receive pipeline
about 92, 166
decode stage 93
disassemble stage 93
resolve party stage 94
stages 92
validate stage 94
ReceivePortID property 183
ReceivePortName property 220
receive ports
about 22, 23
creating 54-57
port authentication 23, 24
port maps, receiving 28-30
receive locations 24-26
service windows 26
setting up 354, 355

receive ports tracking
Request message after port processing property 265
Request message before port processing property 265
Track Message Bodies property 265
Track Message Properties property 265
receive shape 148
record count functoid, looping 129
records, schema structure
any node 80
attribute groups 80
attributes 80
complex types 80
simple types 80
recoverable interchange processing, XML Validator 104
redefine 91
reference
adding, to BizTalk EDI application 354
rehydration persistence orchestration 154, 155
Remove Application ID, application IDs 123
reoccurring parts, schemas
creating 81-83
repeatable read, isolation levels 157
Request message after port processing property 265, 269
Request message before port processing property 265, 269
request-response flow 66
resolve party stage, receive pipeline 94
resumable instances 272
retry count parameter, Transport Advanced Options 31
retrying and idle ports link 272
retry interval parameter, Transport Advanced Options 31
RetryTransactionExceptions 157
reusable type
creating, complex types used 89, 90
creating, simple types used 88, 89
Reverse method 138
RFID
about 364

and BizTalk communicating, SQL Server used 364, 365
round, mathematical functoids 126
route errors
about 217
Enable routing for failed messages option 219
ErrorReport namespace, properties 220
Failed Message Routing option 218
interchange processing, recoverable 222-227
RoutingFailureReportID property 221
rule composer
schema, importing in 347
rule store, BRE 345
Running service instances link 271
runtime application states
about 262
Full Stop - Terminate instances, runtime application state 264
partially started 262
Partial Stop - Allow running instances to continue 263
Partial Stop - Suspend running instances 263
started 262
stopped 262
runtime settings
configuring 242

S

sample certification test
answers 427
questions 405
sample code, certification test-takers
BizTalk Server 2010 Adapter Pack samples, URL 391
BizTalk Server code samples, URL 391
BizTalk Server SDK Samples, URL 391
scheduled service instances 272
schema, BizTalk Solution
creating 345
importing, into rule composer 347
schema, EDI
alternate schema, deploying 360, 361

schema hierarchies
  import 90
  include 90, 91
  redefine 91
schema identity
  .NET identity 74
  about 73
  XML identity 74
schemas
  about 72
  creating 72
  custom formatting restrictions, specifying
    85
  datatypes 85
  date formats, controlling 86, 87
  envelope schemas, creating 83, 84
  evelope schemas 72
  exposing, as WCF Services 306-313
  flat file schemas 73
  formatting 85
  hierarchies, creating 90
  identity 73
  integer formats, restricting 87, 88
  property schemas 73
  reoccurring parts, creating 81-83
  reusable type, creating 88
  string values, restricting 85, 86
  structure, creating 79, 80
  types 72
  validating 227, 228
  XML Schema Document (XSD) 72
schemas, structure
  attributes 79
  elements 79
  record 79, 80
scientific functoids
  10^n 126
  about 126
  arc tangent functoid 126
  Base-specified Logarithm 126
  Common Logarithm 126
  Cosine 126
  Natural Exponential Function 126
  Natural Logarithm 126
  Sine 126
  Tangent 126
  X^Y 126

scopes
  about 156
  properties 156
  synchronized scope 156
  transaction type scope 156
scopes, exceptions
  about 188
  compensation blocks, adding 188
  configured as atomic 188
  configured as long running 188
  configured as transaction type 188
  exception handling, adding 188
scope shape 150
scripting functoid, advanced functoids
  about 137
  external assemblies, using 137-139
  inline code, using 139, 140
  inline XSLT, using 141, 142
secure data, pipeline
  decryption, verifying 112, 113
  MIME/SMIME Encoder component, using
    108-111
  signature, verifying 112, 113
  working with 107
security tab, Out of box WCF-BasicHttp
    Receive Adapter 301
security tab, Out of box WCF-BasicHttp
    Send Adapter 293
  message mode 293
  none mode 293
  TransportCredentialsOnly mode 293
  transport mode 293
  TransportWithMessageCredential mode
    293
self correlating, direct port binding option
  about 171
  using, steps for 172-175
send host 16
send pipeline
  about 94
  assemble stage 94
  encode stage 95
  pre-assemble stage 94
  stages 92, 94
send port
  about 30
  backup transport 33

dynamic 35, 36
filters (subscriptions), configuring 34
groups 36
maps 33
setting up 61, 62, 354, 355
setting up, for send port group 62, 63
setting up, for System II 62, 63
started, state 34
states 34
stopped, state 34
Transport Advanced Options 31, 32
unenlisted, state 35
send port group
send port, setting up 62, 63
SendPortName property 220
send ports tracking
Request message after port processing
property 269
Request message before port processing
property 269
track message bodies property 269
track message properties property 269
send shape 149
SendShipNotice operation 197
SendShipNotice send shape 195
SendTimeout property 292, 300
sequential convoys 184
serializable, isolation levels 157
serialization 154
Service Oriented Architecture. *See* **SOA**
Set Common ID, application IDs 122
Set Common Value, application values 123
shapes, orchestrations
about 148
containers 150
flow control 150, 151
message and data handling 148, 149
orchestration nesting 151
others 152
shape start and end property 267
simple types
used, for creating reusable types 88, 89
simple types, records 80
SimplifiedCar message 194
SimplifiedCar schema 193
Sine, scientific functoids 126

SMTP adapter 44, 45
SndSecureMessage Pipeline 109
SOA 287
specify later option, port binding option
165-169
specify now option, port binding option
165-168
SQL Server
used, for RFID and BizTalk communication
364, 365
SqlServerSink component 364
square root, mathematical functoids 126
SSO
configuring 241
SSO Administrators 244
SSO Affiliate Administrators 244
started, runtime application state 262
started state, send port 34
start orchestration
fire-and-forget style asynchronous
instantiation 153
start orchestration shape 152
stopped, runtime application state 262
stopped state, send port 34
string functoids 127
string values, schemas
restricting 85, 86
study time, certification test-takers
improving, tips for 394
subscription 10, 11
subscription errors
about 213-215
reasons, for failure 213-215
subtraction, mathematical functoids 125
sum, cumulative functoids 119
suspended items, BizTalk applications
management
non-resumable instances 272
resumable instances 272
suspend request message on failure
property 302
suspend shape 151
synchronized scope 156
System II
send port, setting up 62, 63

T

table looping functoid 131-134
table query functoids
  about 120
  database lookup 120
  error return 120
  value extractor 120
Tangent, scientific functoids 126
Target File Name property 66
targetNamespace, XML identity 74
template option 296
Terminated instances link 274
terminate shape 151
test
  answers 427
  questions 405
TestableSchemaBase class 231
test map 229
TestMap method 232, 233
text encoding property 300
ThirdPartyFinanceService.BindingInfo.xml
    binding file 324, 330
ThirdPartyFinanceService class 318
ThirdPartyFinanceService_Custom.Binding-
    Info.xml binding file 324
throw exceptions
  steps 189
throw exception shape 151
time, date/time functoids 124
time management, certification test-takers
    399
Timeout property 156
tracked message events, BizTalk
    applications management 274
tracked service instances, BizTalk
    applications management
  about 274
  Completed instances 274
  Terminated instances link 274
track events property 267
tracking host 16
tracking profile, BAM
  creating 374-378
track mesage properties property
    265, 268, 269
track message bodies property 265, 267, 269

training kits, certification test-takers 390
  BizTalk Server 2010 Administrator Training
    Kit (including VHD), URL 390
  BizTalk Server 2010 Developer Training Kit
    (including VHD), URL 390
  BizTalk Server 2010 ESB Training Kit (in-
    cluding. VHD), URL 391
  BizTalk Server 2010 Training Kit, URL 390
  BizTalk Server 2010 VHD, URL 390
transactions, orchestration
  about 155
  atomic transactions 155
  atomic transaction type 157
  long running transactions 155
  long running transaction type 156
  nesting 158
  reach 158, 159
  scopes 156
Transaction Type property 156
transaction type scope 156
transform shape 149
transmission errors 215-217
Transport Advanced Options
  priority parameter 31
  retry count parameter 31
  retry interval parameter 31
TransportCredentialsOnly, security mode
    293
transport, security mode 293
TransportWithMessageCredential, security
    mode 293
troubleshooting, advanced functoids 136
Trusted Hosts 242
type modifier property, port types
  about 164
  internal 164
  private 164
  public 164
Typename, .NET identity 75
type parameter, host 15

U

UNB segment 356
unenlisted state, send port 35
unit testing
  about 230

maps 232, 233
schemas 230-232
use send handler proxy settings 295
Use Single Sign-On checkbox 301

V

ValidateDocument property 225
ValidateInstance method 228, 230, 231
validate map 229, 230
ValidateSchema method 227, 228, 232
validate stage, receive pipeline 94
value extractor, table query functoids 120
Value Mapping (Flattening) Functoid,
  conditional mapping 134
Value Mapping Functoid, conditional
  mapping 134
view, BAM
  deploying 373
view permissions, BAM
  creating 382
  roles 383
Visual Studio
  used, for deploying BizTalk applications
    245-248
vocabulary, BizTalk Solution
  adding 351, 352
vocabulary, BRE 344
vouchers and offers, certification test-takers
  395

W

WCF Adapter, configuring
  Out of box WCF-BasicHttp Receive Adapter
    used 298-302
  Out of box WCF-BasicHttp Send Adapter
    used 289-296
WCF Adapters. See **Out of box WCF**
  Adapters
WCF-BasicHttp Receive Adapter. See **Out of**
  box WCF-BasicHttp Send Adapter
WCF-BasicHttp Send Adapter. See **Out of**
  box WCF-BasicHttp Send Adapter
WCF-Custom adapter 288, 289
WCF-CustomIsolated adapter 288, 289
WCF Framework 287

WCF Services
  and Web services, integrating 414, 415
  answers 424, 431
  consuming, from BizTalk 319-323
  consuming, from BizTalk Server 2010 315
  custom WCF service, testing 330
  generated WCF artifacts, configuring
    324-330
  orchestrations, exposing as 306-313
  sample 318
  schemas, exposing as 306-313
  testing 314
WCF Services, consuming from BizTalk
  Server 2010
  custom WCF service, testing 330
  generated WCF Service Artifacts,
    configuring 324-330
  steps 319-323
  WCF service, sample 316, 318
WCFTestClient 314
webcasts, certification test-takers
  BizTalk247 BizTalk Server webcasts, URL
    389
  BizTalk Server Developer Center videos,
    URL 389
  BizTalk Server Developer Center webcasts,
    URL 389
  Cloudcasts BizTalk community webcasts,
    URL 389
web.config
  for isolated hosts, configuration information
    storing in 160
web exceptions
  handling 331-338
Web Services
  and WCF services, integrating 414, 415
  answers 424
Windows Communication Foundation
  Services. See **WCF Services**
Windows group parameter, host 16
Work in Progress 13
work in progress, BizTalk applications
  management
  about 271
  dehydrated orchestrations 272
  ready service instances 272

retrying and idle ports link 272
Running service instances link 271
scheduled service instances 272
written. *See* **not promoted, context properties**
WsHttpBinding adapter 288
WS-I 288
WS-Interoperability. *See* **WS-I**

X

X12, EDI 352
XLANG expression 194
XML Assembler
  about 103
  document schemas 104
  envelope schemas 104
  preserve byte order 103
  processing instructions, adding 103
  processing instructions scope, adding 103
  processing instructions text, adding 103
  target charset 103
  XML declaration, adding 103
XML Assembler component 97
XML Disassembler
  about 101
  document schemas 102
  document structure, validating 103
  envelope schemas 102
  recoverable interchange processing 102
  unrecognized messages, allowing 102
XML disassembler component 225
XML Disassembler component 97
XML identity, schema identity
  about 74
  MessageType 74
  targetNamespace 74

XML messages, pipeline
  Byte Order, preserving 103
  disassesmbling 101
  document schemas 102, 104
  document structure, validating 103
  envelope schemas 102-104
  instructions, processing 103
  interchange processing, recoverable 102
  parsing 101
  preserve byte order 103
  processing instructions, adding 103
  processing instructions text, adding 103
  target charset 103
  unrecognized messages, allowing 102
  validating data 104
  working with 101
  XML Assembler, properties 103
  XML declaration, adding 103
XMLReceive pipeline 9, 95, 101
XML Schema Document. *See* **XSD**
XMLTransmit pipeline 96
XML Validator
  about 104
  properties 104
XML Validator component 98
XML Validator, properties
  document schemas 104
  recoverable interchange processing 104
XSD 72
XSD import 90
XSD include 90, 91
XSD redefine 91
XSLT
  about 117
  URL 118
X^Y, scientific functoids 126

About Packt Publishing

Packt, pronounced 'packed', published its first book "Mastering phpMyAdmin for Effective MySQL Management" in April 2004 and subsequently continued to specialize in publishing highly focused books on specific technologies and solutions.

Our books and publications share the experiences of your fellow IT professionals in adapting and customizing today's systems, applications, and frameworks. Our solution based books give you the knowledge and power to customize the software and technologies you're using to get the job done. Packt books are more specific and less general than the IT books you have seen in the past. Our unique business model allows us to bring you more focused information, giving you more of what you need to know, and less of what you don't.

Packt is a modern, yet unique publishing company, which focuses on producing quality, cutting-edge books for communities of developers, administrators, and newbies alike. For more information, please visit our website: www.packtpub.com.

About Packt Enterprise

In 2010, Packt launched two new brands, Packt Enterprise and Packt Open Source, in order to continue its focus on specialization. This book is part of the Packt Enterprise brand, home to books published on enterprise software – software created by major vendors, including (but not limited to) IBM, Microsoft and Oracle, often for use in other corporations. Its titles will offer information relevant to a range of users of this software, including administrators, developers, architects, and end users.

Writing for Packt

We welcome all inquiries from people who are interested in authoring. Book proposals should be sent to author@packtpub.com. If your book idea is still at an early stage and you would like to discuss it first before writing a formal book proposal, contact us; one of our commissioning editors will get in touch with you.

We're not just looking for published authors; if you have strong technical skills but no writing experience, our experienced editors can help you develop a writing career, or simply get some additional reward for your expertise.

(MCTS): Microsoft Windows
Small Business Server 2011 Standard,
Configuring (70-169) Certification Guide

A compact certification guide to help you prepare for and
pass the Microsoft Windows Small Business Server 2011
Standard, Configuring (70-169) exam

(MCTS): Microsoft Windows Small Business Server 2011 Standard, Configuring (70-169) Certification Guide

ISBN: 978-1-84968-516-0   Paperback: 221 pages

A compact certification guide to help you prepare for and pass the Microsoft Windows Small Business Server 2011 Standard, Configuring (70-169) exam

1. This book and e-book will provide all that you need to know to pass the Microsoft Small Business Server 2011 Standard, Configuring (70-169) exam

2. Includes a comprehensive set of test questions and answers that will prepare you for the actual exam

3. The layout and content of the book closely matches that of the skills measured by the exam, which makes it easy to focus your learning and maximize your study time in areas where you need improvement

IBM Cognos TM1 Developer's
Certification Guide

Fast track your way to COG-310 certification!

James D. Miller

IBM Cognos TM1 Developer's Certification guide

ISBN: 978-1-84968-490-3   Paperback: 240 pages

Fast track your way to COG-310 certification!

1. Successfully clear COG-310 certification

2. Master the major components that make up Cognos TM1 and learn the function of each

3. Understand the advantages of using Rules versus Turbo Integrator

Please check **www.PacktPub.com** for information on our titles

Force.com Developer Certification Handbook (DEV401)

A comprehensive handbook to guide Force.com developers through important fundamentals and prepare them for the DEV401 exam

Siddhesh Kabe

Force.com Developer Certification Handbook (DEV401)

ISBN: 978-1-84968-348-7   Paperback: 280 pages

A comprehensive handbook to guide Force.com developers through important fundamentals and prepared them for the DEV401 exam

1. Simple and to-the-point examples that can be tried out in your developer org

2. A practical book for professionals who want to take the DEV 401 Certification exam

3. Sample questions for every topic in an exam pattern to help you prepare better, and tips to get things started

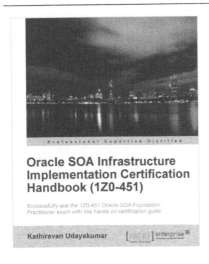

Oracle SOA Infrastructure Implementation Certification Handbook (1Z0-451)

Successfully ace the 1Z0-451 Oracle SOA Foundation Practitioner exam with this hands on certification guide

Kathiravan Udayakumar

Oracle SOA Infrastructure Implementation Certification Handbook (1Z0-451)

ISBN: 978-1-84968-340-1   Paperback: 372 pages

Successfully ace the 1Z0-451 Oracle SOA Foundation Practitioner exam

1. Successfully clear the first stepping stone towards becoming an Oracle Service Oriented Architecture Infrastructure Implementation Certified Expert

2. The only book available to guide you through the prescribed syllabus for the 1Z0-451 Oracle SOA Foundation Practitioner exam

3. Learn from a range of self-test questions to fully equip you with the knowledge to pass this exam

Please check **www.PacktPub.com** for information on our titles